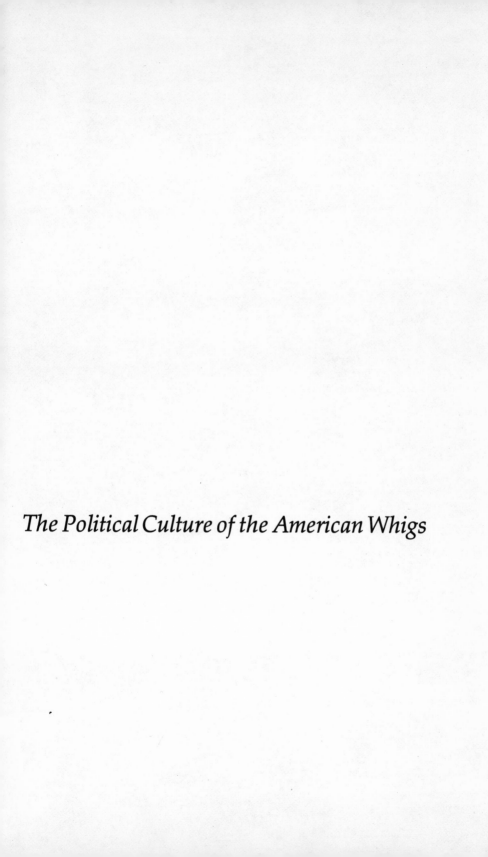

The Political Culture of the American Whigs

Daniel Walker Howe

The Political Culture of the American Whigs

The University of Chicago Press · Chicago and London

The University of Chicago Press, Chicago 60637
The University of Chicago Press, Ltd., London
©1979 by The University of Chicago
All rights reserved. Published 1979
Printed in the United States of America
85 84 83 82 81 80 79   5 4 3 2 1

Daniel Walker Howe is Professor of History at
the University of California, Los Angeles. His
other publications include *The Unitarian Conscience* and *The American Whigs: An Anthology*.

Library of Congress Cataloging in Publication Data

Howe, Daniel Walker.
  The political culture of the American Whigs.

  Includes bibliographical references and index.
  1. Whig Party.   2. United States—Politics and
government—1783–1865.   I. Title.
JK2331.H68   329'.4   79–12576
ISBN 0–226–35478–4

To the Shumways of Algona, Iowa

Contents

Contents

Acknowledgments

To acknowledge help is both a duty and a pleasure, as a Whig moral precept might have put it. Much of the work on this book has been made possible by grants from the Charles Warren Center of Harvard University, the National Endowment for the Humanities, and the University of California at Los Angeles. I also wish to thank the libraries whose facilities I used: the Harvard College Library, the Yale University Library, the Research Library at UCLA, the Huntington Library in San Marino, California, and the Rhodes House Library in Oxford. Many kind friends have given me the benefit of their criticisms and counsel, including Ruth Bloch, Harold Brackman, Frank Otto Gatell, David D. Hall, James Henretta, Bruce Kuklick, Peter Loewenberg, James McPherson, Robert Middlekauff, Jeffrey Nelson, and Kathryn Kish Sklar. Martin Ridge of the Huntington Library generously hosted a discussion of the manuscript, and I thank all those who participated. A series of unusually capable research assistants at UCLA included Jesse Battan, Geraldine Moyle, Robert Rydell, Peter Singer, and Patricia Wilson. From time to time I have imposed on my wife, Sandra Shumway Howe, to read chapters and criticize them. I am grateful to her for doing so, but, much more, for what she has taught me about living and loving.

Sherman Oaks, California, 1978

Introduction

We usually refer to the second quarter of the nineteenth century in America as "the age of Jackson" or "the age of Jacksonian Democracy." Even though there were two major parties, one of them so dominates our image of the period that it requires some effort to recall that the Jacksonian Democrats had an opposition. This volume attempts to redress that imbalance. If it is successful, it will do for the Whigs something like what Marvin Meyers' *Jacksonian Persuasion* did for their Democratic rivals or what Eric Foner's *Free Soil, Free Labor, Free Men* did for the early Republicans, though I have taken neither of those works as a pattern.[1] Here in the introduction I try to explain the assumptions and methods that underlie the book. Readers who find this discussion rather theoretical may prefer to pass over it and begin with chapter one.

When this project first took shape in my mind, I expected to call the book that resulted "The Political Thought of the American Whigs." After living with the sources for a while and discussing the work with others, I realized the inadequacy of the term "political thought" to describe what I was studying. Not only the explicit analyses and proposals of the Whigs, but also the mood, metaphors, values,

1

and style of Whig political attitudes mattered. Nor could these be altogether divorced from actions. "Political thought" would have suggested a history of theory alone, but what I needed was an expression that would subsume thought and feeling, word and deed. So I selected the more inclusive term "political culture."

I use the word "culture" to mean an evolving system of beliefs, attitudes, and techniques for solving problems, transmitted from generation to generation and finding expression in the innumerable activities that people learn: religion, child-rearing customs, the arts and professions, and, of course, politics. It will be clear that I am indebted to the cultural anthropologists for this definition.[2] Literary scholars have generally employed a more restricted definition of "culture," yet I have also profited from their insights, particularly the insight that language is a mode of action. On the subject of "political culture" and its use of language I have benefited especially from the work of J. G. A. Pocock.[3]

To understand the Whigs, one must understand how they used language to exhort, persuade, and conciliate; one must also understand how their responses to the problems they faced were affected by their distinctive culture. This is not to say that the problems themselves were imaginary. One occasion will serve to illustrate all these points. On September 10, 1840, fifty thousand Whigs (they claimed) rallied on Bunker Hill. They adopted a declaration condemning "party spirit" and "irregular ambition"—terms that mean little unless one understands Whig political language and its cultural referents. Their resolution's defense of "liberty of speech and of the press" responded to real threats, it should be acknowledged: Democratic administrations had been censoring the mails. It is also important to realize why the Bunker Hill Whigs added: "We believe, especially, in the benign influence of religious feeling and moral instruction on the social, as well as on the individual, happiness of man."[4] My hope is that this book will unpack the load of meanings carried by the language of the American Whigs and relate that language to an identifiable political culture.

The anthropologist Clifford Geertz has described "ideology" as a consciously formulated, integrated belief system, typically arising during a time of social strain. The ideology becomes the basis of programs of action and provides the believers with a sense of identity.[5] In the hands of its most articulate systematizers, Whiggery attained a level of coherence and prescriptiveness that entitles one to speak of it as an ideology in these terms. Henry Clay's American System and the New School Calvinism of Nathaniel William Taylor and

Lyman Beecher were economic and religious ideologies, respectively, each expressing important aspects of Whiggery. For most purposes, however, I have preferred the broader expression "culture." All Whigs did not share all aspects of the party's consciousness, and Whigs could disagree over the application of their principles, especially when it came to the slavery issue. Whiggery blended its programmatic innovations with long-standing tradition and its explicit programs with implicit values. By emphasizing that culture is a set of problem-solving techniques, I hope to retain something of the sense of purposefulness and connection with social structure that the word ideology conveys so well.[6]

There is a special appropriateness in treating Whiggery as a culture rather than merely as a party, because the culture was more powerful than the party. Sometimes the Whigs were more successful in implementing their policies than at winning elections. When one looks at their broader social objectives (such as public education or the development of didactic domestic literature), there is a striking contrast between the brief life of their party and the lasting influence of their culture. The Whigs themselves claimed to attach more importance to their principles than to their party, since they tended to disparage political parties. Here, as in so many other matters, I am inclined to credit their protestations. The Whigs considered electoral politics to be only one of many modes through which society could be influenced, as their activities in business, religion, the law, and extrapolitical reforms bear witness. While the Jacksonians won more presidential elections, the Whigs probably contributed more to shaping the new industrial society of Victorian America.[7]

Much of what follows is structured around biographies of individual Whigs. The approach offers advantages of accuracy and subtlety that too often are lost in collective portraits of an age or movement. "Ideas do not exist of themselves," a historian has recently reminded us. "They have to be thought; they are the creation of human minds." One could press the point even further and say that ideas are the creation of entire human personalities—"breathing, excreting, hating, mocking. . . ."[8] I attempt here to show how the political ideas of the Whigs derived from their whole experience of life: the attitudes they grew up with, the problems they confronted, the purposes they conceived. Focusing upon a series of individuals gives concreteness and specificity to this approach. The analysis can move from a political text to the life of the person who composed it and then outward to the social group of which he was a member.

Anthropology has alerted us to the connection between culture and personality. For all the inevitable differences among the men who became Whigs, there was an ideal personality type that influenced them, whether by striking a responsive chord or by compelling them to resort to self-discipline or even subterfuge in an effort to conform to it. This ideal personality type was an artifact of the culture, as I hope to explain. After my book was substantially finished, Philip Greven's *The Protestant Temperament* became available, with its thesis that "an understanding of temperament is indispensable for our understanding of the past." This is a point of view I heartily endorse and to which I hope I have added some support. David Brion Davis has defined my objective aptly: "By showing how cultural tensions and contradictions may be internalized, struggled with, and resolved within actual individuals, biography offers the most promising key to the synthesis of culture and history."[9]

The Whigs' responses to social problems often mirrored their responses to personal problems. Their devotion to productivity, equanimity, discipline, and improvement can be traced on a psychic as well as a social or political level. There was a personal, as there was a social, ideal toward which Whigs strove, and these two were broadly congruent. Looking back on their striving, we become conscious of a great irony: dedicated as they were to the ideal that an individual could and should reshape himself and the world around him through the exercise of willpower, the Whigs themselves were, in fact, profoundly conditioned by the situation into which they were born.

No individual perfectly embodies the culture in which he participates; each person carries his own version of it, so to speak. By examining a series of such versions, however, an inquirer can gradually synthesize them into a model of the culture of the group. This is what an anthropologist in the field would do by talking with a series of informants, and this is what I have tried to do as a historian of Whig culture. My selection of "informants"—that is, of individuals through whom to study Whiggery—was governed by two broad considerations. I wanted people who were influential in defining the activities and scope of the Whig party; I also wanted to pick those who would offer the most insight into Whig culture. The first criterion restricted me to men, though there were women, like Sara Josepha Hale and Catharine Beecher, who developed what might be called feminine versions of Whiggery. The second criterion manifested my conviction that articulate, self-conscious spokesmen, while not always "typical" of most Whig voters, would reveal the fullest development and elaboration of Whig culture. Certain prominent party leaders were obvious choices; in other cases a measure of subjective judgment was required. I looked for variety in background and vocation, in an effort to track the implications of Whiggery in different aspects of the culture. I included both reformers and conservatives as well as the archetypal Centrist, Henry Clay. Since they represented about half the voters in the country, the Whigs were necessarily a diverse lot. By its very conception, this book focuses on what they had in common rather than what set them apart from each other. However, some were more attractive people than others, and it will not be too difficult to notice that I find John Quincy Adams and Horace Greeley, for example, more congenial than Rufus Choate.

Two southerners, Henry Clay and Alexander Stephens, and two westerners, Joshua Giddings and Abraham Lincoln, figure prominently in this book, but a majority of those treated come from the Northeast. This is not something for which I apologize; it is an intrinsic feature of Whiggery. When Arthur M. Schlesinger, Jr., investigated the Jacksonians, he concluded that the Democratic party got most of its ideas and early impetus from its northeastern members.[10] This was even more true for the Whig party. New England gave majorities to Adams and Clay in 1824, '28, and '32, when few states outside the region did, and it always remained the homeland of Whig culture. Western Whigs, after all, were often migrants from the East, inasmuch as few of them were European immigrants. Since so many of the issues dividing Democrats and Whigs concerned economic development, it was logical that the parties should polarize most where economic development had advanced farthest. Scalogram analysis of congressional voting behavior shows a sharp divergence between parties, but it is widest in the Northeast; the southern parties differed more moderately. (After about 1843 the pattern changes: the southerners become the most committed of Democrats, but the most committed Whig congressmen are still from the Northeast.)[11]

Several problems bedevil writers on intellectual history. One has to do with the relationship between "thought" and "action," another with the relationship between "high" and "popular" culture, and a third with the relationship between "rational" and "emotional" appeals. I should like to address each briefly, for, in dealing with the American Whigs, I have found each to imply a false dichotomy.

Much of the difficulty in relating thought to action stems from a quasi-Cartesian dualism frequently implicit in scholarly writing: a separation between two realms of reality, the "ideal" and the "material." A more satisfactory metaphysic for students of culture to employ might be explained this way: "To speak of a person's mind is to speak of certain ways in which some of the incidents of his life are ordered, to talk of his abilities, liabilities, and inclinations to do and undergo certain sorts of things."[12] The biographical sketches that follow try to exemplify this approach. We observe individuals employing culture, that is, learned behavior patterns, as a set of strategies for coping with problems. Speaking and writing are forms of action and often, in a political context, important ones; I have found the language of the Whigs particularly revealing of their "abilities, liabilities, and inclinations."

The relationship of thought to action described here is an immediate one. Most of the sources examined were *pièces de circonstance*. They show what ideas occurred most readily when American Whigs were confronted by specific problems. The Whigs did not begin with a philosophy and then try to implement it; they built up their world view and put it to work, as people generally do, by interacting with the world. To learn about their political culture is to learn something of how they looked at life and what it would have been like to live in their situation. Quentin Skinner offers a useful analysis; he argues that political culture affects behavior more often in negative than in positive ways. Instead of supplying motives for doing things (which probably stem from basic material or psychological drives), culture channels behavior, at once facilitating certain courses and limiting the alternatives considered.[13] If we apply this analysis to the Whigs, we can see that, whatever selfish motives Henry Clay and Nicholas Biddle may have had in their "Bank War" with Andrew Jackson, their course of action was influenced by the tradition of "country-party" opposition to a strong executive, because it was available and potent. Even if they exploited it cynically, their actions were still conditioned by it. The political culture of the Whigs, then, did not entirely "cause" their behavior and certainly did not make them all altruistic idealists, but it did restrict the options they would consider.

Much has been made in recent years of the difference between the ideas or culture of intellectuals and those of other (sometimes called "real") people. This can be a useful distinction in our time, when an alienated or at least critical intelligentsia has become a well-recognized feature of the social landscape. In a study of antebellum Whig political culture, it creates confusion. No alienated intelligentsia then existed in America except for the Concord Transcendentalists, who did not commit themselves as a group to either political party. The gap between the level of sophistication in "high-brow" scholarship and "middle-brow" journalism or political discourse (to adapt Van Wyck Brooks' catchy twentieth-century terms) was much narrower, if indeed there was a gap at all.[14] Scholarship in America was nothing like so specialized or professionalized as it has since become. It was an age when partisan politics and organized religion dominated the culture far more than they do today, and when political and religious loyalties were fierce. The press was largely the creature of political parties and religious denominations, owned and operated for their partisan ends. The political press transmitted the views of party leaders to the electorate. Whig organs like the *National Intelligencer* of Washington, D.C., the *American Review* of New York (renamed the *American Whig Review* after the Whigs reconciled themselves to avowing partisanship), and the *North American Review* of Boston trusted in a basic groundwork of opinions and attitudes held in common by their readers. They published as much to affirm as to persuade, appealing to Whigs everywhere, confident that they were addressing a like-minded constituency.

When examining political rhetoric, we do well to remember that the presence of emotion does not preclude rationality. Too often intellectual historians discuss the symbolic, emotive aspects of politics in ways that suggest, however subtly, a condescension toward their subjects. If people employed evocative symbols or otherwise invoked emotional response, it is implied that they must have been abandoning rationality. The symbol, one must insist, is not less than the thing itself but more; it is the thing plus an emotive connotation that enhances but does not necessarily misrepresent its meaning. The Bank of the United States, for example, served as an emotionally charged symbol of big business and special privilege during the controversies between Democrats and Whigs, but it was a symbol that participated in the reality of that which it symbolized, in the same way that a powerful monarch serves to symbolize his nation.[15]

The possibility that a kernel of rationality is contained within even the largest husk of emotionalism should never be overlooked. The Whig campaign of 1840 is generally supposed to have been all hullabaloo, devoid of serious issues. Surprisingly enough, it was not. William Henry Harrison was well known to the electorate from his presidential race in 1836. He combined his emotional appeal as a folk hero with an attack on abuses of executive power, which he promised to correct. Harrison delivered campaign speeches in Ohio, but a national speaking tour was not customary in his time. The addresses made by his supporters were consequently all the more important, and both Clay and Webster made major policy statements on economic issues.[16] Checking through Whig mass-circulation campaign literature for 1840, one finds not only songs and doggerel rhymes but also Richard Hildreth's *The Contrast: William Henry Harrison versus Martin Van Buren*, Calvin Colton's *The Crisis of the Country*, and Henry C. Carey's *Answers to the Questions*, all of which are intellectually serious, if polemical, confrontations with the issues. Ephemeral Whig periodicals appearing during the campaign, such as *The Log Cabin* and *Letters to the People of the United States*, demonstrate the same combination of reason with emotion. William Ellery Channing's reflective essay "On the Elevation of the Laboring Classes" was not written as party propaganda, but the Whigs used it as such. As for the Democrats, their campaign literature showed no lower level of discourse—and, of course, Democratic statements of 1840 included that pioneering masterpiece of class-conflict analysis, Orestes Brownson's *The Laboring Classes*.[17]

When the election of 1840 was over, the response of the new administration to victory indicated that something substantial had been decided. Harrison summoned a special session of Congress to enact the Whig economic program. In partial fulfillment of his campaign promise of executive restraint, he announced that he would not run for reelection. A month after his inauguration, President Harrison died, and the Whig triumph turned to ashes. His last words, apparently addressed to Vice President Tyler, were these: "Sir—I wish you to understand the true principles of Government. I wish them carried out. I ask nothing more."[18]

One other set of polarities within Whiggery demands preliminary comment. This is the interplay between "old" and "new." At first, Whig political culture startled me by its old-fashioned quality. The continuities with colonial times were numerous: the emphasis on English Old Whig ideas, associated with the eighteenth-century "country party" and the Puritan-Dissenting tradition; the dislike of big cities, which Whigs shared with Democrats; the importance the Whigs attached to reinvigorating Protestantism and recapitulating the Reformation; their admiration for Cicero and Burke; their desire to limit sovereignty in the name of "mixed government"; and their suspicions of "faction" and "corruption." The mere fact that such attitudes were old, however, does not mean that they were without vitality or utility during the first half of the nineteenth century. The people who held them were not fools, and they should not be patronized when we write about them. For this reason, among others, I argue against labeling their fear of conspiracy "paranoid."

As I explored the political culture of the Whigs more fully, I became aware of the innovations in it; less immediately conspicuous than the continuities with the past, they were in the long run more important. In the first place, the Whigs believed that industrialization and improved technology held out great hope for the betterment of mankind, and they offered them as a substitute for the transformation of social institutions. Here they were departing from the attitudes of the eighteenth century, when people had placed more faith in social and political changes than in material changes as instruments of progress. By increasing total wealth, the Whigs hoped to avoid having to equalize its distribution. Repeatedly they warned that the Jacksonians would "level downwards" and stifle economic growth. The Whigs bade farewell to the distrust of wealth and commerce that had so long characterized the "country party." But the Whigs did not abandon their colonial cultural inheritance when they espoused economic development; they continued to employ and adapt traditional ideas. Both the northern Whig entrepreneur Appleton and the southern Whig planter Clay combined economic capitalism with social paternalism, while the Pennsylvanian Henry C. Carey subsumed his economic arguments within an implicit framework of eighteenth-century Scottish moral philosophy.

Another impulse toward innovation within Whiggery was originally religious. Whig political culture was profoundly influenced by the Second Great Awakening, an outburst of evangelical activity which, even more than the First Great Awakening in the eighteenth century, sought to transform society along moral lines. For the religious crusaders who led the temperance, peace, antislavery, missionary, and other benevolent societies, it was not enough to win individual souls to Christ; society as a whole must respond to His call. American Whigs, many of them members of the evangelical sects, typically believed in the collective redemption of society—"believed in" it, that is, in the triple sense of thinking it possible, thinking it desirable, and expecting it to occur. This religious impulse fused in the minds of many Whigs with their desire for economic development to create a vision of national progress that would be both moral and material. Society would become more prosperous and at the same time cleansed of its sins. The drive toward the redemption of society sometimes became secularized, and to illustrate this I have chosen Horace Greeley and William H. Seward. For them, efficiency, education, rationality, and uniformity were ends in themselves rather than means to economic security or divine grace. Years ago Max Weber coined the expression "the spirit of capitalism" to describe such an outlook; more recently, some social scientists have tried to understand it as part of a process of "modernization."[19]

My object in writing this book has been synthetic in several ways. In relating culture to politics, I have sought to connect ideas with action, spokesmen with constituencies, and reason with emotion. The book is synthetic in another way, too: it draws upon both socioeconomic and ethnoreligious interpretations of politics in the early national period. The threads are knit together in the studies of individual lives. "The real, central theme of history is not what happened, but what people felt about it when it was happening," G. M. Young has written.[20] I would modify that dictum slightly: what people felt is an important part of what happened to them, and unless we understand how they felt, we will not understand what happened.

Forty years ago, Perry Miller's great works on the Puritans showed us that respect for a body of thought is not the same thing as believing in it. More recently, Eugene D. Genovese's studies of the slaveholding planters have brought home the same point. I am not a latter-day Whig in the sense of being an apologist for a protective tariff or for Nicholas Biddle's banking policies. However, through writing this book I have come to realize just how deeply I still share some of the values of Whig culture. Although I sometimes employ Marxian and Freudian terminology in describing the Whigs, I do not intend thereby to disparage them. Indeed, I have been surprised to discover how much I admire their "bourgeois" virtues and "compulsive" energies.

The challenge for intellectual history, as I conceive the enterprise, is to mediate between the history of ideas per se and the history of politics and society. This necessitates judicious application of tools borrowed from psychology, anthropology, and language studies as well as modern social theory. By meeting the challenge successfully, intellectual history can demonstrate that it is not the rival, much less the adversary, of political and social history but their complement.

One

The Whigs and Their Age

"Of all the parties that have existed in the United States, the famous Whig party was the most feeble in ideas." So wrote Henry Adams in 1879, and his dismissive assessment proved to be remarkably durable. The judgment seems to have originated with antislavery ex-Whigs like George W. Julian and Joshua R. Giddings. It expressed the bitterness of disillusionment; these men had invested much of themselves in the party but had been unable, in the end, to carry its leadership with them on the slavery question. Because the Whig party had failed them on a matter of principle, they charged it with having had no principles.[1] During the twentieth century, this view of the Whigs persisted. "While the shifting of parties on alleged principles is a common phenomenon of politics, yet possibly no party was ever so thoroughly committed to it as was the Whig," declared Henry Mueller in 1922. The opinion that the Whigs were unprincipled opportunists has been widely shared by the two most prominent schools of American historiography: the progressive historians, who have accused the Whigs of insincerity, and the consensus historians, who have insisted on the nonideological nature of all American politics.[2] To look at the writings of the Whigs themselves, however, is to find a

11

different statement of the case. They claimed that the two major parties of their day embodied "two great conflicting ideas, which go to the root" of American life, and they repeatedly formulated cohesive presentations of their own philosophy.[3]

The Whigs and the Democrats were the two major rivals of what historians term the second American party system. The Federalists and Jeffersonian Republicans composed the first, the Republicans and Democrats, the third and present system. There were political factions of various kinds in colonial America as well; but since they were local and usually informal in organization, they are not counted in enumerating the nationwide systems. The second party system took shape out of the factionalism of the late 1820s and early 1830s. It lasted until the mid-1850s, when the Whig party disintegrated and the modern Republican party was born.

There are, of course, reasons why the Whigs have been less well remembered than the Democrats. The most important is that the Whigs were less successful in competing for national office, and in history, as in life, nothing succeeds like success. Another is that the Democratic party still survives as an institution (it is the oldest political party in the world), while the Whig party does not. The Whigs were also the victims of sheer bad luck. American history is usually written from the vantage point of the White House; but the two presidents whom the Whigs elected, William Henry Harrison in 1840 and Zachary Taylor in 1848, both died in office after serving, respectively, only one month and sixteen months. The great Whig senators, Daniel Webster and Henry Clay, of course have permanent places in the American memory, but no purely congressional leader has ever been able to capture the public imagination as successfully as have our most dynamic chief executives.

Nevertheless, the Whigs should not be ignored by anyone seeking to understand America and its past. In fact, the Whig party was more powerful than a quick look at the presidential elections of the period would indicate. (The Democrats won five to the Whigs' two.) The actual strength of the two major parties in the days of the Whigs and Jacksonians was almost equal. In most parts of the country only a few percentage points separated winners from losers at the polls. Indeed, the fairly even distribution of partisan strength is one of the distinctive characteristics of the second American party system. In the time of the first and third party systems there have been cities, states, and whole regions that have been virtually one-party monopolies; under the second system it was rare for either party to enjoy such overwhelming dominance over an extensive area. The relative weakness of the Whig party in presidential politics gives little sign of its strength in congressional, state, and local politics.

As one of the two major parties in a constitutional democracy, the Whigs counted approximately half the voting population as at least occasional supporters. So large a constituency was naturally very heterogeneous. There were Whigs in all occupational groups, economic classes, social strata, geographic regions, and religious denominations. Despite this diversity, one can hazard some gener- alizations about the kinds of people who became Whigs, just as politi- cal scientists today (aided by far more complete data) can distinguish Republicans from Democrats in the population. Business and profes- sional men tended to be Whigs. Industrial workers did not necessar- ily vote against their employers; frequently, wage earners and others who felt they had a stake in the growth of manufacturing were also Whigs. With regard to people engaged in agriculture it is harder to judge, but there is reason to believe that farmers who produced for a commercial market were more likely to be Whigs than were those engaged in self-sustaining, or subsistence, agriculture. The Whig party was especially strong in southern New England and in parts of the country (such as eastern Tennessee) that hoped for government- aided economic-development projects—"internal improvements," as they were then called. People of New England extraction and mem- bers of the sects of New England Protestantism (Congregationalists, Unitarians, "New School" Presbyterians) also seem to have voted Whig in disproportionate numbers. Statistical evidence is spotty, but observers at the time usually assumed that people with greater in- come, education, and respectability were more likely to be Whig. "The active, enterprizing, intelligent, well-meaning & wealthy part of the people," Ralph Waldo Emerson called them.[4] Yet those at the very bottom of the social ladder also generally supported the Whigs: the blacks, insofar as they were permitted political participation, found the Whigs decidedly the lesser of white evils.

The lifetime of the Whig party (roughly, 1834–54) was an era of intense political excitement. The nation faced momentous choices regarding war and peace, imperialism, ethnic diversity, the educa- tional system (or lack thereof), and the expropriation of the American Indians. The very nature of the federal Constitution and the su- premacy of the national government lay open to question; many state constitutions were also being written or rewritten and their legisla- tures reapportioned. At these constitutional conventions and on other occasions, fundamental issues of political obligation were raised. Over economic matters, politicians diverged sharply, debat-

ing the financial structure of the country and the money people
handled every day; the sources of federal revenue and the possibility
of sharing it with the states; government aid to business and business aid to government; the right of individuals, corporations, and
governments to go bankrupt; and the right of labor—and of
capital—to organize. Slavery and race relations constituted the prime
moral issue of the day, but there were many others, among them the
punishment of criminals, relationships between the sexes, federal
funding for insane asylums, and laws regulating or prohibiting alcohol, which many people were coming to regard for the first time as
a dangerous drug. All this took place in an atmosphere of violence,
both individual and collective. Dueling, lynching, rioting, slave in-
surrections and plots, rebellions in Rhode Island and New York,
warfare in Florida, Texas, and Mexico and along the frontier—these
too became political issues.

"The spirit of the age," Frances Wright observed, was "to be a little
fanatical."[5] She spoke truly (if half in jest), for the questions being
argued were important ones and they stirred deep passions. Mass
politics was new, political parties were new, and the electorate was
not yet jaded. The base of political participation, as measured by
the voting qualifications, was wider in Jacksonian America (notwithstanding the exclusion of women and most nonwhites) than in
any previous time or contemporary other place. What is more, this
potential for widespread participation was realized, for the percentage of white men going to the polls soared from 27 in 1824 to 78 in
1840. Because the two major parties were fairly evenly matched,
competition between them was keen. Elections were frequent because there were many annual and biennial terms of office, and the
voting days in different states were staggered throughout the year.
Results of national elections trickled in slowly for weeks. United
States senators were chosen by state legislatures that sometimes
spent months reaching a decision. Thus, political agitation was more
or less constant.

The parties' energetic campaigning produced not only high voter
participation but also a high degree of party regularity. Neither the
participation nor the regularity has been equaled in America since.[6]
Straight party voting was facilitated by ballots printed by the parties
themselves, often listing only their own candidates; to vote for
someone else, it was then necessary literally to "scratch the ticket"
and write in a different name. But high voter participation and
polarization between the parties also reflected diverging programs
on matters of deep concern. When the second American party system

emerged from a confusion of personal and factional rivalries within the Jeffersonian Republican party in the 1820s, voters sorted themselves out into two parties with recognizably differing approaches to government: the Democrats and the Whigs.

Party politics was our first national sport, and the public played and watched the great game with enthusiasm. Torchlight parades, electioneering songs and slogans, debates, and speeches were popular entertainment. But there was a serious side to all this "politicking" that is sometimes overlooked. If the press was intensely partisan (on both sides) and many voters were fervently committed, it was not simply out of longing for diversion. The fact is that the politicians were talking about important matters. The politics of the 1830s and the 1840s centered on issues to a far greater extent than did the politics of, say, the post-Reconstruction era.

Some historians have felt that the intensive political campaigning and frequent elections of the mid-nineteenth century "exaggerated" the amount of social conflict that actually existed.[7] It is certainly true that party feeling ran high. In 1835 an attempt was made on the life of Andrew Jackson by a man now thought to have been insane. The president suspected that his political opposition was behind the attack. And a young Whig politician, who was really a very decent person, commented that, although it was good that Jackson had survived, it was appropriate that "the chief who violated the Constitution, proscribed public virtue, and introduced high-handed corruption into public affairs and debauchery into private circles" (a reference to the wife of Secretary of War Eaton) should have been the object of the first assassination attempt on an American president.[8] Typically, however, Whig-Jacksonian political conflicts expressed broad social divisions rather than incidents involving pathological individuals or imaginary dangers. What is more, even technical issues like the tariff were often debated with considerable sophistication and accurate perception of where one's interests lay.[9] On balance, the intense involvement of multitudes in politics probably manifested "the worth, not the evils," of democracy.[10]

In recent years an impressive body of scholarship has demonstrated the importance of the differences between the Democratic and Whig parties. Detailed analyses of voting patterns in Congress and the state legislatures have revealed both the sharpness of partisanship and its substance.[11] Investigators who have looked at individual states have been finding that the voters as well as the politicians were concerned about issues and were purposeful in making political choices. As a result, political historians are now more willing to acknowledge that Whiggery had a coherence and a program.[12]

The chief reason for remembering the Whig party today is that it advanced a particular program of national development. The Whig economic platform called for purposeful intervention by the federal government in the form of tariffs to protect domestic industry, subsidies for internal improvements, and a national bank to regulate the currency and make tax revenues available for private investment. Taken together, the various facets of this program disclose a vision of America as an economically diversified country in which commerce and industry would take their place alongside agriculture. Practically all Americans expected and wanted their nation to grow and prosper, but they disagreed as to how progress might best be achieved. The Democrats inclined toward free trade and laissez-faire; when government action was required, they preferred to leave it to the states and local communities. The Whigs were more concerned with providing centralized direction to social policy.

Yet the meaning of Whig ideas and how they differed from those of the Democrats have frequently been masked from later observers. The conventions of heroic oratory, moral philosophy, and "country-party" fear of conspiracy, when not recognized as such, can make Whig statements seem platitudinous, obfuscating, or hysterical. Moreover, Democrats and Whigs could arrive at similar policy conclusions from entirely different premises; their common support for public education, general laws of incorporation, and the introduction of bankruptcy proceedings are examples of a consensus on means obscuring differences with respect to ends. Sometimes party issues had more intellectual significance than is immediately apparent; the award of legislative printing contracts, for example, not only bestowed material favors on one's friends but influenced how fully and accurately one's speeches would be reported. Records printed by enemies had a way of being unsympathetic abridgments of remarks. Even issues that seem like mere gossip today, such as the accusation of adultery against President Jackson and his wife Rachel, can reveal something about the attitudes of a party's constituency. This issue, like the charges against Secretary Eaton and Peggy O'Neale, cast the Whigs in their accustomed role as defenders of middle-class morality.

The most important single issue dividing the parties, and the source of the most acute disappointment to the Whigs after President Harrison had been succeeded by Tyler, concerned the banking system.[13] Jackson's veto of the recharter of the Second Bank of the

United States in 1832 became the point of departure for a generation of political partisanship. The banking-currency issue (that is, the right of banks to issue their own paper money) mattered at the state as well as the federal level. Many states redrafted their constitutions during the Jacksonian period and had to decide whether they would authorize state banking monopolies (usually mixed public-private corporations), specially chartered banks, "free banking," or no banks of issue at all. As time went by, the parties tended to polarize with respect not only to rechartering a national bank but to the function of banking in general. The Democrats gradually became more committed to "hard money" (specie or government-issued currency), while the Whigs became defenders of "the credit system" (in which banks were the issuers of currency).[14]

Besides their alternative economic programs, the parties also possessed different ethnic constituencies. The Whigs were predominantly the party of Yankee Protestants and British-American immigrants. The Democrats were stronger among folk of Dutch and German descent and among Catholics.[15] These ethnic identities coexisted with the parties' economic identities in ways historians have not altogether sorted out, but it would be a mistake to assume that the ethnic and economic interpretations of the second party system are mutually exclusive. Very likely the affluent were attracted to Whiggery by the party's economic program, poor men more often by its ethnic identification.[16] In many situations, of course, the ethnic and economic appeals would have reinforced each other. The parties' ethnic appeals were no less real than their economic ones; the act of voting can express "a blend of ethnic, class, or status resentments in quite rational fashion, given available perceptions of 'friends' and 'enemies.'"[17]

An ethnic partisanship that was quite rational is evident in the support that black voters gave to the Whig party in reaction to the strident white supremacy that was the stock-in-trade of so many Democratic spokesmen. Only four states in the far Northeast allowed black men to vote on the same basis as white men; elsewhere blacks either had to meet higher qualifications than whites or were disfranchised altogether. In New York state, some 3,000 black men could meet the $250 property test imposed on them to vote; had they been exempted from it, as white men were, there would have been 10,000 black voters and Henry Clay would have been elected president in 1844. Black suffrage was a partisan issue that the Democrats strenuously opposed and the Whigs, somewhat less strenuously, supported. The Democrats succeeded in disfranchising blacks altogether in New Jersey, Connecticut, and Pennsylvania during the Jacksonian period; only in Rhode Island did the blacks gain suffrage through the Whigs. Eventually, blacks became disillusioned with the slender returns Whiggery won for them; when the Whig party was disintegrating, they were among those who were drifting away from it.[18]

Much scholarship during the past two decades has demonstrated the usefulness of treating political parties as "reference groups" possessing distinctive "value systems."[19] Not the least of the advantages of reference-group theory is its applicability to both economic-class and ethnoreligious segments of the population, offering the hope of transcending the debate over which of these factors separated Democrats from Whigs. Whigs thought of themselves as the "sober, industrious, thriving people"—a self-image that included moral as well as economic virtues.[20] The party battles of the Whig-Jacksonian era can be seen as conflicts over values that included but went beyond politics, strictly defined. Whiggery was as much a cultural or moral posture as an economic or political program.

The value context of Whiggery was established by the Second Great Awakening, a series of religious revivals that reached its highest peaks of fervor during the lifetime of the Whig party. The Awakening has been well described as "a comprehensive program designed to Christianize every aspect of American life."[21] Leaders of the Awakening like Charles G. Finney considered politics "an indispensable part of religion." For their part, Whig political leaders like Henry Clay and Daniel Webster cultivated good public and private relations with clerical opinion-shapers. Clay, for example, introduced a congressional resolution for a day of national "humiliation and prayer" in response to a cholera epidemic (Jacksonians blocked it as violating the separation of church and state). Webster unsuccessfully contested the will of Stephen Girard, a wealthy Philadelphian who had left a bequest for an orphanage in which no clergyman could set foot.[22] If the Church of England was the Tory party at prayer, the Whig party in the United States was in many ways the evangelical united front at the polling place.

An important feature of the Whig program was its coherence. Whig positions on banking, the tariff, internal improvements, the sale of public lands, and the distribution of federal revenue to the states were interlocking facets of one economic program. But the broader consistency of Whiggery went beyond the specific provisions of Henry Clay's "American System." The moral issues the party espoused sometimes had direct relevance to its economic program. For example, the repudiation of bonds by several Democratic state legislatures after the Panic of 1839 was generally denounced by Whigs throughout the country as defaulting upon a moral obligation as well as hindering economic development.[23] At other times the relationship was indirect; Whig moral opposition to the dispossession of the American Indians, for example, was not unrelated to Whig land policy. Often, of course, the economic issues themselves were argued in moral and broadly symbolic terms. The banking-currency debate has recently been interpreted as a conflict between two political cultures in the western states.[24]

In their own eyes, the Whigs had a more coherent, rational, and constructive program than their antagonists, whom they accused of relying on patronage, passion, and sheer negativism. They may not have been wrong to think this. Despite the frequent assertions by historians that the Whig party was held together merely by desire for office, there is reason to believe that it was, if anything, more issue-oriented or program-oriented, and less concerned with office as such, than the Democrats.[25] That Whiggery was more constructive, in a literal sense, than Democracy is clear. Each of the two times the Whigs elected a president, he called a special session of Congress to act on a legislative program. The antebellum Democratic presidents, by contrast, are known for their vetoes: Jackson's of the Bank and the Maysville Road, Polk's of river and harbor improvements, Pierce's of aid to insane asylums, Buchanan's of a homestead act.[26] When Martin Van Buren complained, during the Panic of 1837, that people "looked to the government for too much," Henry Clay retorted that the people were "entitled to the protecting care of a paternal government." And a less directly interested contemporary confided these observations to his journal: "Since I have been in N.Y. I have grown less diffident of my political opinions. I supposed once the Democracy might be right. I see that they are aimless. Whigs have the best men, Democrats the best cause. But the last are destructive, not constructive. What hope, what end have they?"[27]

Historians have generally treated aspects of the Whig program in the course of trying to define Jacksonian Democracy. Arthur M. Schlesinger, Jr.'s, seminal description of "the Age of Jackson" includes an excellent chapter on the Whigs, though it concludes that "the widening chasm between private belief and public profession took all seriousness out of Whiggery as a social philosophy." Marvin Meyers' fascinating study of "the Jacksonian persuasion" proposes that the Whigs appealed to Americans' hopes; the Democrats, to Americans' fears. This distinction works well for economic policy, though in other realms the Whigs, too, had their apprehensions. On

cultural and moral issues, such as immigration, temperance, or slavery, it was more often the Whigs who were anxious and the Democrats who were optimistic or complacent.[28]

One of the most useful characterizations of Whig policy that has
been offered is that it supported "the positive liberal state." This
ideal implied the belief that the state should actively seek "to promote the general welfare, raise the level of opportunity for all men,
and aid all individuals to develop their full potentialities." The
Democrats, by contrast, believed in a "negative liberal state," which
left men free to pursue their own definition of happiness.[29] A great
advantage of this distinction between the parties is that it implies a
connection between the economic and moral aspects of Whiggery. In
both cases, the Whigs believed in asserting active control. They
wanted "improvements" both economic and moral, and they did not
believe in leaving others alone.

For all its helpfulness, however, there is danger in calling the
Whigs champions of "the positive liberal state." It makes them
sound too much like twentieth-century liberals. Actually, the differences between the Whigs and twentieth-century liberals are more
important than the similarities. Whig policies did not have the object
of redistributing wealth or diminishing the influence of the
privileged. Furthermore, the Whigs distrusted executives in both
state and federal government (they had been traumatized by the
conduct of Jackson), whereas twentieth-century liberals have endorsed strong executives more often than not. For all their innovations in economic policy, the Whigs usually thought of themselves as
conservatives, as custodians of an identifiable political and cultural
heritage. Most deeply separating the Whigs from twentieth-century
liberals were their moral absolutism, their paternalism, and their
concern with imposing discipline.

The terms "positive liberal" and "negative liberal" have another
disadvantage: they suggest that the Whigs and Democrats differed
only as to means, that they were agreed upon ends. But the specific
disagreements over policy between the parties were rooted in the
larger differences between them regarding the nature and destiny of
American society. Whigs and Democrats presented the electorate
with rival images of national purpose. To put things very broadly,
the Whigs proposed a society that would be economically diverse but
culturally uniform; the Democrats preferred the economic uniformity
of a society of small farmers and artisans but were more tolerant of
cultural and moral diversity.

One historian has proposed that the Democrats were primarily interested in the quantitative expansion of American society through *space*, while the Whigs were concerned with its qualitative development through *time*.[30] This is a perceptive distinction. For the Democrats, "manifest destiny" was the logical consequence of their preoccupation with a uniform agricultural empire. For the Whigs, on the other hand, "internal improvement," or economic (and moral) development, was more important than external expansion. As Horace Greeley noted in 1851:

> Opposed to the instinct of boundless acquisition stands that of Internal Improvement. A nation cannot simultaneously devote its energies to the absorption of others' territories and the improvement of its own. In a state of war, not law only is silent, but the pioneer's axe, the canal-digger's mattock, and the housebuilder's trowel also.[31]

In the pages that follow, the exponents of Whiggery will be found to share certain preoccupations. Though the Whigs were a diverse lot, the number of thematic reverberations in their political and social expression is remarkable. Three in particular seem to stand out. First, because of their commitment to "improvement," Whigs were much more concerned than Democrats with providing conscious direction to the forces of change. For them, real progress was not likely to occur automatically; it required careful, purposeful planning. Social progress took place much as the education of the individual did, through careful cultivation of that which was valued and rigorous suppression of that which was not. Second, while Jacksonian rhetoric emphasized "equality" (restricted in practice to equality of opportunity for white males), Whig rhetoric emphasized "morality"—or "duties" rather than "rights." Whig morality was corporate as well as individual; the community, like its members, was expected to set an example of virtue and to enforce it when possible. A third recurring theme in Whig rhetoric was the organic unity of society. Whereas the Jacksonians often spoke of the conflicting interests of "producers" and "nonproducers," the "house of have" and the "house of want," the Whigs were usually concerned with muting social conflict. In their determined assertion of the interdependence of different classes, regions, and interest groups, one recognizes the same analogy between the individual and society that also characterized the other two main principles of Whig social thought.

In the long run, the Whigs' contribution to American society proved at least as great as that of their Democratic contemporaries.

The economic and technological changes going on in the nineteenth century ultimately produced an economy more like that envisioned by the Whigs than like the arcadia the Jeffersonians and Jacksonians idealized. Most of the Whigs' economic platform was enacted by their successors: the Republican party firmly established a protective tariff and subsidized business enterprise, and the Democrats under Wilson finally organized a nationwide banking system, though it operated on different principles from those the Whigs had envisioned. The political evolution of the country has consistently increased the power of the federal government; "states' rights" retains less power as a political rallying cry than ever. Some of the social reforms the Whigs supported have passed into history so completely that by now we are more conscious of their shortcomings than of their achievements (free public education, for example). Other Whig objectives were never attained (such as respect for the rights of the Indians) or proved disastrous when finally implemented (like prohibition of liquor). As for the Jacksonians, the individualism and egalitarianism they preached have firmly taken root in the American character; the imposition of that cultural uniformity sought by the Whigs has long since become a lost cause. But as long as there are still people who strive to awaken a sense of public responsibility in politics and the arts, the spirit of the Whig reformers will not be altogether dead. Since America has become diversified both economically and culturally, perhaps one could say that the Whigs and Jacksonians have each had half their vision fulfilled.[32]

Two

The Language and Values of the Whigs

Every debate is controlled by certain conventions of discourse. The spirited debate between Whigs and Jacksonian Democrats had its own conventions, the most striking of which was probably "constitutionalism." Even a contemporary marveled in later years how "everything was reduced to a Constitutional question, in those days."[1] All participants in American politics accepted the Constitution of 1787 as authoritative in defining political possibilities. Political dialogue proceeded by reference to the meaning of the Constitution, just as contemporary theologians debated the meaning of the Bible because they acknowledged its authority. In this sense, the American historians who have spoken of political "consensus" are right. Universal recognition of the Constitution served to structure political debate and ensure that participants did not talk past each other. But the tendency to debate the constitutionality of issues rather than their expediency did little to temper the discussion; if anything, it exacerbated differences. If one calls an opponent's proposals unconstitutional, it makes them seem more dangerous and illegitimate than if they were simply unwise. People are quite capable of coming to blows over the interpretation of

23

mutually acknowledged authoritative documents, as the American Civil War and unnumbered wars of religion attest.

The habit of appealing to legal texts extended beyond the Constitution itself. When the government deposits were removed from the Bank of the United States, the Whigs cast their protest largely in terms of an accusation that Jackson's secretary of the treasury had exceeded his statutory authority. When the Democrats were advocating the annexation of Texas, they claimed that the area had originally been included in the treaty ceding Louisiana and thus called for its "reannexation." Whigs and Democrats alike frequently carried on the process of legislation in the spirit of litigation. No doubt this was partly because so many politicians were lawyers; in a larger sense, it reflected a culture in which legal and theological disputations were the principal modes of intellectual exercise and training.

Constitutional exegesis seems in retrospect an unfortunate turn for political discussion to have taken. Debate frequently degenerated into a low level of special pleading, with participants adopting such hopelessly contrived positions as the denial of plenary congressional power over the territories or the denial of the president's pocket-veto power. It is hard to escape concluding that the country would have been better served if political leaders could have directly confronted the substance of such issues as what kind of banking system the country ought to have or what should be done about slavery, instead of wrangling interminably over what approach the wording of the Constitution authorized. American statesmen of the time remind one of carpenters who spend so much time worrying over their tools that they neglect their woodworking. Yet it would be a mistake to dismiss the constitutional concerns of the Whig-Jacksonian era as unreal. Contemporaries were not yet sure what meaning the Constitution would take on; they did not feel as comfortable with it as Americans have since become. And though they sometimes cried wolf, we must remember that often their fears for the Constitution were justified. Calhoun's assertion of the right of nullification and Jackson's claim that he was not obliged to defer to the Supreme Court as arbiter of the Constitution did indeed threaten the foundations of American polity. Blatant violations of the Constitution actually occurred, such as Georgia's dispossession of the Cherokee Indians and the annexation of Texas by joint resolution of Congress instead of by treaty. In such circumstances, constitutional procedures became political issues because their operation could not be taken for granted.

Perhaps the most important feature of any debate consists in the questions the participants ignore. The constitutional controversies of the middle period are no exception; they reveal remarkable blind spots. Why didn't they use the commerce clause to prohibit the interstate slave trade or even ban the products of slave labor from interstate commerce? Few people dared mention the first, and, as far as we can tell, no one at all thought of the second. The options were foreclosed not by lack of ingenuity in textual interpretation but by unreflective racial prejudice and unquestioning devotion to property rights. In such ways the politics of the age was determined by its culture. Antebellum constitutionalism well illustrates the power of culturally transmitted attitudes to constrict the range of political choice.[2]

Another great characteristic of American political discourse in the antebellum period, one that has been less studied, was its oratorical rhetoric. Although American legislative bodies today rely on their committees to do most of their work, debate on the floor was far more prominent then. However, the word "debate" must be taken in a special sense. Few statesmen of the time excelled in quick repartée; what was more typical of them was the long, prepared set piece. If constitutional logic was designed to appeal to the head, this oratorical rhetoric was designed to supplement it with an appeal to the heart, to persuade or condemn. The rhetoric of denunciation was particularly rich, making the political expression of recent times seem tame by comparison. Even the congressional critics of Lyndon Johnson and Richard Nixon had but an impoverished vocabulary of opposition compared with the critics of Jackson and Polk.

Political orations of the Whig-Jacksonian period are best understood as a species of oral literature.[3] Oral literature was extremely important in nineteenth-century America, for it included not only political oratory and ministers' sermons but also lyceum addresses, public dialogues or "conversations," lawyers' oral arguments (a form of entertainment in the courthouse-centered county seats), and commemorative orations, such as those marking college commencements or Washington's Birthday. Oratory played a prominent part in the educational process of the time. Whereas children today, in the interest of speed, are taught to read without incipient vocalization, expressive reading aloud was emphasized then, together with oral/aural drills now neglected. Manuals of elocution illustrated the appropriate gestures by which various moods should be conveyed. Americans had an appetite for eloquence comparable only to the eagerness of the early Protestant Reformers to hear sermons. In large part this was because speech-making provided occasions for the affirmation of group identity. Orations weighed down the long public ceremonies to which Americans attached a seriousness that could be literally deadly. Both of the presidents whom the Whig party elected died in office as the result of exposure during such ceremonies: Zachary Taylor after the dedication of the Washington Monument and William Henry Harrison after his own inauguration.

To recover an appreciation for the vanished sensibility that attached such importance to oral performance is demonstrably essential if we are to understand American literature in the time of Emerson, Bronson Alcott, and Margaret Fuller.[4] But this appreciation is also vital for comprehending the political spirit of the age. Many of the characteristics that strike us in Whig-Jacksonian political dialogue—pomposity, sentimentality, self-righteousness—were conventions of the oratory of the day. Scholars sometimes undervalue oral communication. Our assumption is that important statements are written down; what is spoken is not taken with full seriousness. But antebellum Americans felt differently. When Joshua Giddings (for example) delivered his philippics against slavery in the House of Representatives, even his enemies flocked to the chamber to hear him; it occurred to no one to dismiss his words as mere talk. An important address was a "media event," covered by the newspapers and national magazines, typically reprinted in pamphlet form. At this point in our history, the medium of print, far from displacing the spoken word, was called in to reinforce it. But the printed version seldom did justice to the drama of the setting and the manner of delivery. There were textbooks on eloquence without number, but they invariably conceded that they could not capture the elusive quality of the rapport between speaker and audience, and contemporary accounts of the great oral performances made the same concession.[5]

The prominence of oratory in antebellum life has been explained in terms of America's escape from the past, her people's preoccupation with "the concrete, the relevant, the here-and-now."[6] A more persuasive case can be made that oratory in America reflected just the opposite: the continued vitality of the past. The oratorical tradition had antecedents in the Puritan emphasis on the sermon in church. But what kept it alive more than anything else was the perpetuation of classical learning. In earlier centuries, of course, formal orations had been entirely in Latin, and, even in mid-nineteenth-century America, political orators sprinkled their discourse with Latin quotations as a way of authenticating their message. More important than such citations, however, was the influence of the classics in providing role models for orators. The image of the republican patriot was one men of that generation coveted, and the image included prowess as an orator. Sometimes their models came from modern history, like the Irish orators Henry Grattan, Daniel O'Connell, and Edmund Burke. More often they came directly from antiquity; Webster was likened to Demosthenes, Clay to Themistocles, and Edward Everett to Cicero.[7] Later, when classics and the elocution idealized by the classics ceased to provide the basis for education, American oratory as a literary genre withered and eventually died.

Intimately connected with oratory was rhetoric. To us, the term "rhetorical" connotes something ornamental. To antebellum Americans, however, rhetoric was a *practical* art: the study of persuasion. Used in this sense, "rhetoric" did not necessarily refer to oral presentations, though it customarily did. While philosophers might pursue wisdom per se, persuasive rhetoric provided men of affairs with an indispensable tool for applying wisdom to everyday life. Rhetoric thus mediated between thought and action. Our loss of this meaning for rhetoric results from our bifurcation of thought from action, a split that would have been incomprehensible to earlier generations. The concept of persuasive rhetoric prevalent in Whig-Jacksonian America took as its point of departure the ideals of Renaissance humanists and their classical models. During the eighteenth and nineteenth centuries, this Renaissance rhetoric had been supplemented by ideas derived from Locke and François Fénelon, which placed the study of persuasion in the context of a new science of communication.[8]

Rhetorical ability, everyone agreed, was crucial in a republic, for free men who could not be coerced had to be persuaded. (George Santayana would later observe, "Eloquence is a republican art, as conversation is an aristocratic one.")[9] From the Whig point of view, this lent a particular importance to oratory as a means of social control. Jacksonians were less concerned that statesmen should play a didactic role and tell people what was good for them; Democrats saw the orator as the people's spokesman. But for the Whigs, the orator performed a double service: he must not only defend the people's true interests but show the people themselves where those interests lay. This extra importance of oratory for the Whigs perhaps helps explain why, of the three most celebrated legislative orators of the generation—Webster, Clay, and Calhoun—two were Whigs and none was a Jacksonian.

The study of persuasive rhetoric was generally linked in mid-nineteenth-century America with moral philosophy. "Moral philosophy" at that time meant the integrated study of human nature

in all its aspects. The art of persuasion naturally required an understanding of human motivation and social relationships, as well as
knowledge of right and wrong, all of which moral philosophy
supplied. Moral philosophy occupied an important place in college
curricula and was often said to be the most valuable of academic
subjects.[10] Other subjects, including history, classics, and the natural
sciences, were treated as exemplifying the lessons moral philosophy
taught in the abstract. In attempting to understand Whiggery
through its value system, one can hardly do better than begin with
an examination of moral philosophy. There a distinctive and integrated value system found explicit and coherent expression.

Moral philosophy, as its name implied, was first and foremost a
study of ethics; joined to it were what we term the various social
sciences, treated within an axiological framework. The dominant
school of moral philosophy in the United States was Scottish Common Sense, which had been introduced during the mid-eighteenth
century and had since spread to practically all American colleges. In
this school, ethical norms were considered objective, immutable
principles. They were studied in a context that was hortatory as well
as analytic; the ethical relativism prevalent in academic circles today
was rejected.[11] This concept of morality, permeating the political
discourse of the period, called attention to value judgments instead
of emphasizing, as ethical relativism does, questions of means and
the technical implementation of policies. A Whig journal, condemning John Tyler's apostasy, admonished its readers: "BE TRUE!
Falsehood, unfaithfulness, dissimulation, treachery—these may *seem*
to prosper for the moment, but the eternal laws of the Universe are
against them and *must* prevail."[12] Historians have often noted such
moral absolutism in the language of the abolitionists. However, it
was peculiar neither to them nor to the debate over slavery.

A majority of academic moral philosophers in the United States
seem to have been Whigs, and Whig political rhetoric was certainly
more influenced by moral philosophy than was Jacksonian rhetoric.[13]
The absolutism of Scottish moral philosophy constituted both an
advantage and a danger to the Whigs. It was an advantage to them in
their efforts to impose certain moral reforms upon American society;
it was a danger when it got out of hand and threatened the whole
social order. We are mistaken if we suppose that all aspects of a world
view are necessarily integrated and harmonious; life is not so tidy.
Within Whiggery, social conservatism dwelt uneasily alongside ethical absolutism. The unresolved contradiction was bared in the debate
over the Fugitive Slave Act of 1850, which pitted Webster Whigs

against Seward Whigs, the claims of stability and Union against the claims of morality and the "higher law."[14]

Of all the aspects of moral philosophy, the one that exerted the most influence on Whig political values was faculty psychology. The moral philosophers conceived of human nature as consisting of a hierarchically arranged series of powers or faculties: the "mechanical" (reflexes over which there was no conscious control), the "animal" (instinctive desires and emotions), and the "rational" (prudence and conscience). It was the task of the rational powers to order the rest, not by crushing them altogether but by regulating and balancing them to produce a harmonious personality. Conscience was rightfully the highest power of all, before which even self-interest should bow.[15]

Within faculty psychology, the highest value was balance, that is, the proper expression of each human power but the excessive indulgence of none. The ideal was not easily implemented. All the faculties had legitimate objectives, entitled to fulfillment, and balance could be attained only by careful self-control. Unfortunately, the strength of the faculties varied inversely with their position in the sequence of rightful precedence. Left to themselves, the lower powers would escape control and wreak havoc. An unregulated faculty—whether pride, licentiousness, or some other appetite or emotion—was called a "passion." The good life entailed continual self-discipline, as one sought to "suppress his passions" or "cultivate and improve his virtues." The animal powers present in everyone were "captives impatient of every subjection, and ready every moment to mutiny and throw off the yoke."[16]

Like countless others before them, the American Whigs drew "the analogy between the human system and the social and political system"; Webster could liken the circulation of blood in an organism to the circulation of money in the marketplace. An essential feature of the analogy for the Whigs was the parallel between regulating the faculties within an individual and regulating the individuals within society. Faculty psychology taught an ideal of harmony within diversity, each of the human powers performing its appropriate function within an integrated whole. The model ruled out laissez-faire as a social philosophy, emphasizing instead the mutual responsibility of individuals and classes.[17] The ideal society, like the ideal personality, improved its potential in many directions. Economic development promoted a healthy diversity, which "furnishes employment for every variety of human faculty." The conception implied an active, purposeful central government, "administering the affairs of the nation according to its best judgment for the good of the whole, and all parts of the whole."[18]

Both the freedom of the individual will from divine determinism and the freedom of the body politic from government tyranny were asserted vigorously in America at this time, by Whigs as much as anyone. Yet, Whigs insisted, this freedom brought with it responsibilities and duties. The Scottish philosopher Thomas Reid had declared that a man was free only when following the dictates of reason and conscience; otherwise he was a slave to his own lower nature.[19] The American Whigs agreed. Their political discourse frequently reflected concern for the due precedence of the rational faculties. "No deeper degradation of the soul can be conceived than the complete mastery of Man by a base appetite," declared a Whig newspaper, editorializing on behalf of the temperance movement.[20]

The hierarchical sequence of the faculties, in which the lower appetites and emotions were subordinated to higher conscience and reason, had specific application to human society. Many years before, John Locke had written that people who lacked the opportunity to cultivate their higher faculties (such as women and the poor) could not become fully rational and therefore justly held subordinate positions within society. The conservative eighteenth-century English constitutionalist Bolingbroke, claiming to represent the collective "reason" of the commonwealth, had accused Sir Robert Walpole of stirring up a party based on "passion."[21] The American Whigs were less explicit than Locke, but they shared his general view that those who had not had the opportunity of education should defer to the leadership of those who had received it. And, like Bolingbroke, they identified with the cause of "reason" against the party of "passion." As one of them put it in retrospect, "The Whigs placed their whole hopes on the right and justice of their cause, while their antagonists sought theirs in the passions of the multitude."[22]

Much of the apprehension the Whigs felt regarding conspiracy and corruption can be traced to their fear of inflamed passions subverting good order. "We live in times of turbulence and change," observed the *North American Review*, times of danger from demagogues, "men compounded of ignorance and wickedness, wholly unfitted to guide the passions which they are able to excite." If Americans were misled by the class-conflict appeals of the Jacksonians against the national Bank, Webster warned that they would "cease to be men, thinking men, intelligent men, [and become] slaves to their own passions."[23] Democratic politicians were not the only people whom many Whigs suspected of pandering to the lower impulses in human nature. Masons, Catholics, and immigrants were accused of giving in to their baser selves. The antislavery movement, when it came along, also attracted support by its condemnations of the licentious, lazy, tempestuous slaveholders, whose absolute power corrupted their natures.[24]

The task of the statesman in this system was to maintain the orderly balance of society, analogous to the orderly balance of the individual faculties, and he did this largely through his rhetoric. Rhetoric gave concrete application to the abstractions of faculty psychology, addressing and stimulating the various elements in complex human nature. An orator had a delicate assignment: to arouse the emotions enough to motivate action but not so much as to destroy the primacy of rationality. A great statesman-orator could restore human nature and convert his audience from "a tumultuous herd" into "men—into a nation."[25] A demogogue, of course, performed the converse.

Faculty psychology, a hierarchical model of society, classical rhetoric: these expressed habits of mind that had provided the basis for a politics of deference in colonial America. They were the elaborate articulation of deep feelings of respect for custom and status, the tip of the cultural iceberg, so to speak. Such inherited modes of thinking, both explicit and implicit, go far to explain why even free landowners in a New World continued so long to accept the leadership of the affluent and classically educated.[26] It was this longstanding culture pattern that Andrew Jackson defied—not by his "spoils system" itself, for in appointing his supporters he was only doing what administrators and patrons had always done, but by justifying his policy on grounds of equalizing opportunity. Jackson's opponents rallied to the defense of the politics of consensus and deference, and his challenge to the cultural heritage shaped the course of the political debate.[27]

Though the Whigs made use of an old-fashioned elitist view of politics and society, they did not really want to return America to a preindustrial state of isolated agricultural communities. Instead, they applied their hierarchical conception to the new commercial, industrializing social order they were trying to introduce. Old-fashioned elitism not only coexisted with their economic innovations but actually helped the Whigs justify them. It provided the rebuttal to those who complained that economic development was fostering inequality. The Whig party represented those people who, for one reason or another, expected to do well out of economic development and were working to hasten it. In the process, they were able to take traditional ideas about social roles and obligations, about paternalism and duty, and adapt them creatively to the new society. They poured the new wine of commerce and industrialization into the old bottles of deference, patriarchalism, Scottish moral philosophy, and classical rhetoric.[28]

When John Bell of Tennessee announced in 1835 that he was joining the Whig party, he declared: "We have, in truth, in the last eight or ten years, been in a continual state of moral war."[29] With such moral pronouncements Whig leaders reached out to their followers. The party's economic program was quite clearly designed to appeal to "haves" rather than "have-nots." A protective tariff would most directly benefit northern factory owners and the large-scale planters of certain southern staples like hemp and sugar, while a national bank would be of greatest use to businessmen in all parts of the country. As for internal improvements, these "could vitally concern only those producers, of whatsoever, who produced more than they could use themselves or sell locally." It is scarcely surprising that most rich men in America were Whigs.[30] What is more remarkable, and requires more explanation, is the party's broad support in the electorate. Many men voted Whig whose economic stake in Whig policies was no clearer than that of their Democratic neighbors. To persuade them, the party relied heavily on moral appeals.

Probably all political parties take moral stands at least occasionally, but for the Whigs these had particular importance. Moral appeals were the Whigs' substitute for party loyalty. Less well knit than the Democrats by patronage and organization, the Whigs emerged as a party only intermittently, at election time. This gave their campaigns something of the flavor of religious revivals. If the Whig party won over most rich men by its economic program and some poor men by its ethnic identity, its moral appeal was particularly effective for those in between, the large middle class.[31] Most voters, of course, would not have sorted out economic, ethnic, and moral appeals into separate compartments but would have taken note of the overall persuasive effect. To borrow a term from psychology, their voting patterns would have been "overdetermined" by many factors.[32]

In making their moral appeals, the leaders of the Whig party were addressing widely shared values; if they had not, they would not have remained leaders of a major party for long. By studying the political careers of several leaders, we shall be learning something about the constituencies that accepted them as spokesmen. Of course, all Whig voters did not share all aspects of the Whig value system; many would not even have been fully aware of all of them. For ordinary Whig voters, the values must often have been implicit in their lives rather than the product of much self-conscious reflection. From the leaders we can derive the fullest, most detailed picture of this value system. Probably every culture known to mankind possesses such a system; the Whigs, however, asserted their values with unusual insistence. Indeed, the first aspect of Whig culture deserving attention is this: it was didactic.

This aggressive didacticism of theirs was something new. It was probably related to the rise of the missionary spirit in religion that accompanied the Second Great Awakening and sent Protestant emissaries all over the world in search of converts. There had been different "political cultures" even in the eighteenth-century American colonies, it would appear. The political culture of the coastal and urban areas was more elitist, commercial, and "cosmopolitan"; the remote areas were more democratic, agrarian, and "localist."[33] To some extent the political culture of nineteenth-century Whiggery represented a continuation of this colonial "cosmopolitan" culture. A number of monographic studies have shown a tendency for more economically developed counties to vote Whig, except as concentrations of ethnic blocs distort the pattern.[34] But no one (so far as I know) has claimed that the cosmopolitan culture of colonial times was allied to, or transmitted by, the First Great Awakening as nineteenth-century Whig culture was propagated by the Second Awakening. Indeed, a powerful argument has been made for the reverse proposition: that the evangelical and cosmopolitan cultures were hostile to each other in the eighteenth century.[35]

The Whig party's electoral campaigns formed part of a cultural struggle to impose on the United States the standards of morality we usually term Victorian. They were standards of self-control and restraint, which dovetailed well with the economic program of the party, for they emphasized thrift, sobriety, and public responsibility. E. P. Thompson has called the evangelical reformers of early nineteenth-century England the "disciplinarians." It is a term that fits the American Whigs too. They looked upon the Democratic voters as undisciplined—men who had escaped the institutional controls of European society but had not yet learned to impose internal restraints on themselves.[36] The Whigs wanted to teach these people that liberty has no real value without responsibility and order. The objective was well stated by the great English Victorian, John Stuart Mill: "The test of what is right in politics is not the *will* of the people, but the *good* of the people, and our object is not to compel but to persuade the people to impose, for the sake of their own good, some restraint on the immediate and unlimited exercise of their own will."[37]

Running through Whig political appeals was the concept of consciously arranged order. This was characteristic of their reliance on government planning rather than the invisible forces of the marketplace. It was characteristic of their economic program, so carefully contrived to integrate tariff policy, land policy, internal improvements, and federal revenue-sharing. It was characteristic of the standards of personal morality that the evangelical reformers promoted. It was even characteristic of the formal, not to say pedantic, arrangement of ideas that constituted Whig rhetoric and moral philosophy. In the absence of order, the threat of a Hobbesian state of nature, where men behaved like "famished, infuriated animals, goaded by instinct and unrestrained by protective hopes and fears," seemed very real to the Whigs.[38]

The American Whigs' dedication to order was never more apparent than in their response to the European upheavals of 1848. The great Rabbi Isaac M. Wise recalled how, when he first heard of the revolutions, he fairly burst with excitement and began to make plans to return to his native Bohemia and participate. Then he took counsel with William H. Seward, who warned him: "The peoples are not ready for freedom and the revolution will end in the supremacy of the army."[39] Such caution typified the Whigs' reaction, and events only confirmed them in it. As one commentator put it, "We cannot see that Americans are any more bound to sympathize with every radical movement in Europe which dignifies itself with the name of republican than we should be to lend a favorable ear to the ravings of our own demagogues." Even the New York Tribune, most progressive of Whig organs, after initial sympathy in the spring, drew back in horror from the Paris working-class uprising in June.[40]

Like John Stuart Mill, American Whigs typically assumed moral responsibility for others. They called this assumption "rectitude": the love of virtue, by whomever manifested. To them, it seemed proof of their sincerity. To many of the others involved, it seemed meddlesome at best, coercive at worst. The debate over whether Whig moral reform should be condemned as middle-class repressiveness—a debate that historians still carry on—was begun by contemporaries. When Lyman Beecher's church on Hanover Street burned down, the volunteer fire companies, who hated his temperance crusading, refused to fight the flames. Instead, it is reported, they watched and sang: "While Beecher's church holds out to burn / The vilest sinner may return"—a parody of a hymn.[41]

There were many, like those firemen, who resisted the moral didacticism of the Whigs. A network of what sociologists call "negative reference groups" existed in America, and, since there were only two major parties to choose between, political alliances were often made according to the venerable principle that "the enemy of my enemy is my friend." So the Irish Catholic immigrants became the most loyal of Democrats in reaction against Whig Protestantism, and the blacks voted Whig in reaction against the Irish, who hated them. In Louisiana, where the French Catholics were prosperous and long-established sugar planters, they were the Whigs, while the Protestant small farmers who resented them were the Democrats. On the whole, however, the Whigs were the more homogeneous party because they drew upon the most powerful single culture in the society, evangelical Protestantism. There is much to be said for applying to cultural politics the interpretation that Arthur Schlesinger, Jr., has applied to the politics of economic interests: the Whigs sought to strengthen the hegemony of the dominant group, while the Democrats represented all those out-groups who resisted.[42] As the more heterogeneous party, the Democrats were naturally more inclined to tolerate cultural differences.

One of the postulates of this book is that social tensions mirror individual tensions. By examining the lives of individual Whigs, we can locate problems that the party as a whole confronted. Whig prescriptiveness illustrates the principle. Very likely many Whigs wanted to suppress in others the impulses they had suppressed, at considerable psychic cost, in themselves. Beecher said that the Democratic party in Connecticut "included nearly all the minor sects, besides the Sabbath-breakers, rum-selling tippling folk, infidels, and ruff-scuff generally." Greeley put it more strongly: "the haunts of debauchery and vice" voted Democratic.[43] Hence the Whigs' conviction that they were the party of reason and the Democrats the party of passion. The Whigs may well have exaggerated the extent of Democratic lawlessness, because, like other people, they projected upon their enemies what they disapproved and denied in themselves. The political scientist Robert Lane has suggested that people afraid of their own inner impulses find a politics and morality of order congenial. He adds: "And who is to say they are not right? Men who are afraid of themselves may indeed be better off in conservative, moralized societies."[44]

The object of Whig didacticism was redemption: to make people better. One of the greatest Whig reformers explained it this way: "I look for the harmonizing of Desire with Duty, not through the blotting out of the latter, but through the chastening, renovating, and purifying of the former." If people were made to want to be good, there would be nothing to fear from their freedom.[45] The Democrats, by contrast, wanted liberation: to get rid of every vestige of oppression, at least as far as white men were concerned. The reactions of the two parties to the extinction of the national debt during Jackson's administration typify these orientations. The Democrats welcomed the chance to liberate people from the burden of taxation. The Whigs favored redeeming the people by retaining the taxes and spending the money on worthwhile improvements; a society that did not respond positively to such an opportunity for collective self-improvement would become "a community of self-degradation," warned John Quincy Adams.[46]

The recurrent controversies over public education in antebellum America displayed the contrasting value systems of the Whigs and Democrats. Whigs correctly perceived that the diversified, capitalistic social order they wanted required a population that was literate, ambitious, and disciplined. The public-school systems they organized and supported throughout the country promoted these ends.[47] The public schools represented a massive institutionalization of the Whig dedication to redeeming people. Horace Mann, the greatest educational reformer of the day, was a Whig and employed the vocabulary of moral philosophy in expounding his objectives. He urged that children be taught to cultivate their higher faculties and to subordinate their passions. A believer in uniformity and conscious planning, Mann wanted more centralization in school systems. Democrats, resenting higher taxes and loss of local control, frequently opposed Mann and other Whig educational reformers. Particularly in the South, Democratic politicians could be blatantly antiintellectual. When Democrats supported public education (and they did so less consistently than Whigs), it was out of commitment to equal opportunity, not because they desired to refashion human nature. Even when Democratic and Whig policies converged, it did not mean their values were the same.[48]

The Whigs assumed that human nature was malleable. It could and should be shaped by schools, benevolent societies, reformatories, asylums. But the wise person shaped his own nature. This promise is what gave Whig values their appeal for those who did not find them coercive or patronizing. Self-denial, self-help, self-control: these were all part of the process of self-culture. It was not an ideal peculiar to the American Whigs but one they shared with many middle-class European contemporaries. A European intellectual historian has described it well. "The really free man," in this system of values, "is not the man who can choose any line of conduct indifferently—this is being rather a frivolous and weak-willed man—but the man who has the energy to choose that which is most conformable to his moral destiny."[49] Democrats rejected the ideal of self-culture, often implicitly, occasionally explicitly. What the Whigs called "culture" they thought "artificial." It was desirable to remove artificial impediments and assert the rights of the natural man and his freedom to act.[50]

The reforms the Jacksonian Democrats fought for were the kind of reforms people undertake for themselves in pursuit of greater liberation and greater participation in decision-making. They included reapportionment of state legislatures, popular election of judges and presidential Electors, dismantling the national banking monopoly, and some early efforts at labor organization. Whig reforms, by contrast, were frequently altruistic efforts to redeem others rather than examples of self-help. Whigs supported Dorothea Dix's campaign for federal aid to mental hospitals; Democrats opposed. Whig prison reformers sought to make prison a place of redemption as well as retribution (from this hope comes our word "penitentiary"); Democratic prison reformers, on the other hand, were usually concerned with economy, efficiency, and deterrence.[51]

Redemptive Whig reform was benevolent yet restrictive. The two aspects are well illustrated in the opposition to both flogging and the grog ration in the U.S. Navy.[52] Ralph Waldo Emerson, a perceptive if uninvolved observer of the political scene, satirized Whig didacticism and anxiousness to redeem people by calling the archetypal Whig an overprotective physician, whose "social frame is a hospital." He dresses everyone in "slippers & flannels, with bib & pap-spoon," and prescribes "pills & herb tea, whig preaching, whig poetry, whig philosophy, [and] whig marriages."[53]

If the Whigs could be officious, the Democrats could be callous. They were interested in the liberation of free white men but cared little for others. There was more debate over slavery within the Whig party than within the Democratic party, just as, in the 1960s, there was more debate over the Vietnamese War within the Democratic than within the Republican party. In both cases the national party leadership would have liked to keep the troublesome issue quiet but could not make its policy of silence stick. Some Whig congressmen, like Adams and Giddings, persisted in bringing up questions related to slavery until northern Whig opinion swung round to supporting them. By contrast, the party of Jackson started out by being almost unanimous in its hostility to antislavery, even in the North, and was slower to feel the impact of the issue.[54]

Belief in white superiority, of one kind or another, characterized nearly the entire spectrum of white American opinion before the Civil War. Caucasians typically regarded nonwhites with a mixture of hostility and condescending paternalism. Inside this broad framework, different emphases can be distinguished among different whites. The most important determining variable was probably geography, but party affiliation was relevant too; there is considerable indication that the paternalistic attitude was stronger among Whigs than among Democrats. Within limits, Whig legislators showed greater willingness to support measures like trade with Haiti and civil rights for free Negroes.[55] The deferential concept of society that Whigs generally shared can plausibly explain this willingness: Whigs could help blacks without having to acknowledge their equality. On the other hand, the Democrats' egalitarianism seemed to force them to deny the very humanity of nonwhites lest they have to confront them as equals.

Even antislavery Whigs did not think so much in terms of liberating the blacks as of redeeming them. Lyman Beecher, a good example, was preaching temperance to black congregations before he preached emancipation to white ones.[56] Of course, the black ministers invited him to come. A philosophy of "improvement" and "uplift" was supported by many black intellectuals in the prewar period—by more of them, in fact, than were actively involved in abolitionism. The black community's affiliation with the Whigs was not simply a negative reaction to the hatred they experienced from Democratic groups like the Irish-Americans or southern poor whites; it also expressed, quite accurately, the cultural program of these black leaders.[57]

There was a tradition of long standing among whites that nonwhites, like women and children, had natures more "passionate" than "rational." The American Whigs were influenced by this tradition.[58] Still, they emphasized acquired characteristics, that is, culture, more often than innate characteristics like race. "In the great wants of their moral nature all men are alike. All were born in want of culture," declared Daniel Webster. "The wholly untutored white man is little better than the wholly untutored red man," Edward Everett agreed. (The slight advantage of the white, he added, was due to his "living in an enlightened community.") The task of good government, explained the *North American Review*, is to facilitate the "improvement" of the inhabitants, that is, the full development of their potential. Blacks were specifically included.[59] Two prominent Whig journals, examining certain racial theories that were beginning to be discussed at midcentury, emphatically maintained that, although different races of mankind can be distinguished, "their unity is incomparably more prominent than their diversity." The *National Intelligencer* simply dismissed Democratic talk of the "Anglo-Saxon race" and America's "manifest destiny" as "political clap-trap."[60] When John C. Calhoun came out against the conquest of territory from Mexico because the inhabitants were racially incapable of liberty, the Whig *American Review* welcomed his stand but not his grounds. "Free institutions are not proper to the *white* man," it insisted, "but to the courageous, upright, and moral man."[61]

As we know, the Whigs were a political party with a large British-American constituency, both old Yankee and recent immigrant. Some of the party's appeal was based on ethnic identification. Not surprisingly, the Whigs' language included celebrations of this heritage. However, their ethnocentrism was more cultural or ideological than genetic. "I am no great believer in the natural excellencies of Anglo-Saxon blood, but I have great faith in the acquired excellencies of Anglo-Saxon institutions," declared one moral philosopher who was an especially outspoken Whig. Daniel Webster at Plymouth Rock praised the many achievements of the English-speaking peoples, but he affirmed that their highest glory was dedication to "the freedom of human thought and the respectability of individual character"—principles he maintained were applicable to all humanity, "I care not of what complexion, white or brown."[62] Henry W. Bellows, writing in the *American Whig Review*, actually welcomed intermarriage on the ground that it would improve the genetic stock of the Anglo-Saxons while facilitating the extension of their culture. He also looked forward to the time when all South Americans would speak English and be converted to Protestantism and the common law. The converse of such hopes for cultural imperialism was the fear of cultural degeneracy. An eminent divine writing on behalf of the American Home Missionary Society warned that the Boers of South Africa illustrated just such a process. They had become nomads, practicing lynch law and torture, neglecting education, letting "their women do the work." As a result, "They are now a race of nominally christian barbarians—barbarians under the Synod of Dort, a standing proof that Protestants, and they too of

Saxon blood, may drop out of civilization. . . . Let no American that loves his country refuse to heed the example."[63]

The contrasting positions of the two major parties on race and culture are dramatically illustrated in the controversy over government policy toward the Indians. This issue was actually second only to banking in provoking the polarization of parties under Jackson.[64] The controversy was provoked by the removal of the Cherokee Nation from Georgia to Oklahoma. The Cherokees had adopted sedentary agriculture, commerce, Christianity, constitutional government, and—thanks to Sequoia—literacy. Although they were by no means assimilated, they were showing great progress in becoming what the Whigs considered "redeemed" and were referred to as one of the "Five Civilized Tribes" of the Southeast. "They are civilized, not in the same degree that we are, but in the same way that we are," explained Edward Everett. The "truly benevolent" policy was to encourage this "improvement." As long as the Indians remained nomadic hunters and gatherers, they had no right to their land that could not be extinguished by compensation from settlers who represented a higher stage of cultural development, John Quincy Adams believed. When, however, they became settled agriculturalists, they acquired an absolute right of domain and could justly refuse to sell. This was what the Cherokee Nation had done, and its rights were guaranteed by a federal treaty of 1785.[65]

When the state of Georgia determined to expel the Cherokees despite their treaty rights, it arrested Samuel Worcester and Elizur Butler, two white missionaries living with the Indians, who had defied the state's claim to authority. The evangelical united front swung into action to support the missionaries, organizing mass protests and condemning Indian removal as appalling and disgraceful. "He must be worse than savage who can view with cold indifference [such] an exterminating policy." A leading evangelical organ, examining the Cherokee case as one instance of a historical pattern, concluded that white Americans were all implicated in a gigantic crime.[66] But the Georgia authorities were not without their supporters, too. Heading the list was President Jackson, renowned for his hatred of Indians and the contempt for international law he had displayed during the First Seminole War.[67] White settlers throughout the Deep South coveted the rich lands of the Five Tribes, with their cotton-growing potential. The Democratic-party press encouraged them by popularizing theories of the ineradicable inferiority of the nonwhite races, which taught that hopes for civilizing the Indians were delusive. The debate continued for a generation. Despite opposition from a number of Whig writers, including the great anthropologist, Lewis Henry Morgan, the new "scientific racism" proved increasingly attractive as a rationale for dispossession.[68]

Chief Justice Marshall delivered the judgment of the United States Supreme Court in *Worcester et al.* v. *Georgia* on March 3, 1832. He found Georgia's action unconstitutional: the state had no right to legislate for the Cherokee Nation, whose autonomy was guaranteed by federal treaty. But Georgia defied the Court's decision, kept the appellants in prison, and went ahead with its expulsion of the Indians. Jackson made it clear that he would never enforce the Court's mandate, and loopholes in federal appellate procedures enabled him to avoid doing so. Meanwhile, he used the Army to facilitate the dispossession of the Indians, not to protect them. Jackson's re-election later in the year sealed the doom of the Cherokee Nation in Georgia.[69]

The opposition in Congress protested eloquently but vainly on behalf of morality and the supremacy of the Constitution. Then, during the winter of 1832–33, the Nullification Crisis forced a truce between Jackson and the National Republicans (who had not yet adopted the name Whig), since both wanted to sustain national authority against Calhoun's South Carolina. Vice-President Van Buren negotiated the release of Worcester and Butler from the hardships of their captivity. They requested a pardon from the governor of Georgia, which was granted, terminating their legal case. The Cherokees set forth along the grisly Trail of Tears that led the survivors to the West. Some escaped into the mountains of North Carolina.[70]

The dispossession of the Cherokees did not mark the end of the "Indian Question" as a political issue; other tribes had their confrontations in the years to come. Calvin Colton, one of the most prominent spokesmen for Henry Clay, debated at length against Lewis Cass, spokesman for the administration, in defense of tribal rights in the Old Northwest. Colton vigorously asserted the innate equality of the red and white races and maintained that the Indians should be accorded equal protection of the laws in their existing location while they acquired Christianity and Western civilization. Of course, his arguments were futile.[71] Later, the Second Seminole War in Florida brought the cause of red and black people together in resisting white aggression. Antislavery Whigs joined with abolitionists to denounce the conduct of the war. The Supreme Court, however, became less sympathetic to Indian rights after Jackson had replaced John Marshall with Roger B. Taney as chief justice.[72]

The Whigs' sympathy for the Indians was congruent with their preference for restrictive land policies that would keep the white population relatively concentrated in the East and facilitate industrialization. However, a simplistic reduction of all their moral concern to hypocritical self-advantage will not do. Horace Greeley defended the rights of the Indians even though he was an early convert to the cause of western homesteads. Davy Crockett, Tennessee frontier Whig, put moral principle and party loyalty above the wishes of his constituents and opposed Cherokee dispossession; he lost his seat in Congress at the next election.[73] People act out of many motives, and if some Whigs stood to benefit by curtailing the dispersion of white settlement, they or other Whigs stood to lose if the Deep South and the Northwest were irretrievably alienated from their party. In the end, prudential considerations dictated Whig acquiescence in the removal of the tribes.

To be sure, the contrast between Whig and Democratic attitudes toward the Indians was not absolute. There were some Whigs who favored removal, particularly among the Conservative Democrats who joined the Whig party in 1835–36. Nor did the Democratic party altogether disavow humanitarian objectives.[74] Still, the Whig party never lost its reputation for being less hostile to the Indians than its rival. Though William Henry Harrison had originally become famous as an Indian-fighter, during his long preparation for the election of 1840 he published a sympathetic history of the northwestern Indians, and in the campaign itself his supporters were careful to portray him as humane and just toward them.[75] In 1844, when Henry Clay let the Whig convention freely ballot for the vice-presidential candidate, the delegates chose Theodore Frelinghuysen of New Jersey, an ardent evangelical well known for his spirited and unquestionably sincere defense of the Cherokees. As for the Democrats, they elected as vice-president in 1836 Richard Mentor Johnson, vaunted killer of Tecumseh, whose mounted riflemen cut razor strops out of the dead chief's skin. And in 1848 their presidential nominee was Lewis Cass, who, as secretary of war, had borne heavy responsibility for the atrocities committed on the Trail of Tears.[76]

Three

John Quincy Adams, Nonpartisan Politician

As the elections of 1830 drew near, Joseph Richardson, retiring congressman from the Twelfth District of Massachusetts, inquired of former President John Quincy Adams whether he would accept a draft for the federal House of Representatives. The suggestion was unprecedented, but National Republican leaders were anxious to secure an outstanding candidate to succeed Richardson. They could expect opposition from both Jackson men and Federalists, since the latter were not yet defunct in the commonwealth. Massachusetts law required an absolute majority for election, so with three candidates there was chance of a deadlock that would leave the district unrepresented. The sixty-three-year-old Adams found the invitation balm for the wounds of his defeat by Jackson in 1828. He accepted and won handily in November. "My election as President of the United States was not half so gratifying to my inmost soul," he confided to his diary.[1]

Election to Congress began the third career of John Quincy Adams (1767–1848). During the first career, a series of distinguished diplomatic posts had culminated in his tenure of the State Department under Monroe, when Adams dominated the administration. Then, as Monroe's successor in the White House, Adams had formulated a far-reaching program of federally sponsored economic and intellectual development only to fail of reelection. Now, in 1830, nearly eighteen years as a member of the House of Representatives lay ahead of him. During this time he would become a leader in the fight for civil liberties and against slavery.

Just before his election to Congress, Adams finished reading in Latin the complete works of Cicero. Years before, as professor of rhetoric and oratory at Harvard, he had defended the "immeasurable superiority" of ancient over modern rhetoric but held out the hope that the republican virtues and republican rhetoric might be reborn and flourish in America. The highest model for imitation he had offered his students was Cicero. All his life Adams retained his admiration for the man he termed "not only the orator, but the moral philosopher of Rome." His conception of politics was essentially that of Ciceronian civic humanism. Indeed, he identified himself with the old Roman and projected the dangers to the state embodied in Cicero's adversary, Caesar, upon his own rival, Jackson. Rereading Cicero now was for Adams a labor of love, though a disciplined, well-ordered love: it had taken him two hours a day for ten months.[2]

All Adams' accomplishments bespoke the same tireless energy and versatile determination. He knew seven languages (Tocqueville was impressed by his fluency in French), double-entry bookkeeping, and shorthand. He was conversant with the mathematics, science, and scholarship of his day in almost every field. President of the American Academy of Arts and Sciences, a conscientious member of the Harvard Board of Overseers, he was a connoisseur of fine wines and a prolific poet as well. Adams recognized that his verses displayed no poetic talent, but he wrote them anyway, apparently because doing so was part of the role of the man of letters, which he scrupulously cultivated.[3] His meticulous regimen included regularly swimming naked in the Potomac while president of the United States and walking daily from the White House to the Capitol and back, regardless of the weather, while in his seventies.

Adams was not an easygoing man, nor is understanding him an easy task. The television series The Adams Chronicles portrayed his stiffness better than his intensity, his sense of responsibility better than the violent drama of his congressional career. Even most of Adams' contemporaries found him remote. He never became the focus of a personality cult the way Webster, Clay, and Jackson did. He was not handsome or charismatic enough to be idealized as an orator; yet he had been professor of oratory at Harvard and could more than hold his own in debate by dogged courage and mastery of parliamentary procedure. He felt ill at ease among strangers, and this manifested itself in a defensive formality. Only among intimates could he relax, and only people whose moral integrity he respected could become his intimates. With such people—like James and Lucretia Mott—he could be warm and witty.[4]

John Quincy Adams dedicated himself to painstaking regulation of all activities, public and private, by conscience and goal-oriented rationality. The ambitious scheme for integrated national development that he announced in his first State of the Union Message in 1825 was his own daily program for self-development writ large. Fundamental to both his public and private programs was a hierarchical conception of order derived from moral philosophy: the disciplining of the passions by the higher faculties. The individual should subordinate his inclinations to the prescriptions of conscience; government should represent the conscience of the body politic.[5] There was a remarkable congruence between Adams' didactic personality and the didactic political culture of Whiggery.

Everything Adams did he recorded in his massive diary, still never published in its entirety. The diary of John Quincy Adams is, as he intended it should be, a treasure-house of American intellectual history; in the words of Harriet Martineau, it was "the greatest and most useful of his deeds, and his most honourable monument." Through its entries he struggled each day for immortality. The diary was an indispensable instrument in his program for self-control; a man who keeps one has "a perpetual guard over himself," he explained to his ne'er-do-well son George.[6] Often lonely and misunderstood, Adams longed for vindication by posterity—specifically, his own posterity, for the diary was written principally for his descendants. That a famous son of a famous father should manifest strong family pride is scarcely surprising, but Adams' sense of family was an intensified version of a feeling common to most of the Whigs studied in this book and to their counterparts throughout Western civilization. Very likely the Whigs' tendency to view society in organic paternal metaphors arose from their applying to the larger world the family relationships they felt so deeply in their lives.[7]

Adams' diary is famous for its mordant comments on his contemporaries and for his equally unsparing self-criticism. Yet, because the diary was part of his self-discipline, and because it was addressed to his posterity, Adams dared not let his guard down in it. Thus he was not altogether candid even there. For example, on the day of his crucial conference with Henry Clay prior to the presidential runoff election in the House of Representatives, there is a blank space in the diary manuscript, suggesting that he debated with himself over how much he should set down in his account of it.[8] Some of the most revealing, passionate, and earthy language of John Quincy Adams appears in his off-the-cuff congressional debates—and frequently these must be consulted in the *National Intelligencer* because hostile House officers kept them out of the official record. Even the *Intelligencer* did not always report him fully. (He would sometimes complain and publish his speeches in pamphlet form.)[9] All this has compounded the difficulties of those who would know him.

The first thing that needs to be understood about John Quincy Adams is that he was a political person who spent virtually his whole adult life in public office. His actions had political objectives, the most important of which was that he wanted the United States to be a strong and successful example of liberty. From this major objective stem his formulation of the Monroe Doctrine, his expansionism vis-à-vis the Spanish Empire, his devotion to economic development at home and American commercial aggrandizement abroad. Especially in his youth, Adams could be a tough American imperialist in the name of antiimperial idealism.[10] Yet, when he became convinced that American ideals were being betrayed by the slave power, Adams turned against expansionism, opposing the expropriation of the southern Indians and the annexation of Texas.

Adams was not only a political man, he was a politician who wanted very much to win. His unwillingness to campaign publicly for the presidency reflected the conventions of his time. Yet he was not at all above trying to promote his prospects. He had, in Thurlow Weed, a New York campaign manager who was as shrewd as any politician of his generation. Adams himself was no babe in the woods. In his pursuit of the presidency he displayed (as a recent biographer has put it) "a natural aptitude for political maneuvering that was as inspired as some of his diplomatic efforts." Indeed, thanks to Ernest R. May's reconstruction of the making of the Monroe Doctrine in 1823, we can now perceive in Adams' greatest diplomatic triumph the workings of his political ambition.[11]

During the campaign of 1824, Adams first sought, unsuccessfully, alliances with both Jackson and Calhoun by offering each second place on the ticket with him. Then, when the electoral votes showed no candidate with an absolute majority, he refused to bow out gracefully in favor of the front-runner, Jackson. Instead he waged an aggressive fight for support in the House of Representatives, calling on every possible congressman and discussing such matters as the award of government printing contracts. Though Henry Clay's personality had rubbed him the wrong way in the past, Adams now proved himself able to reach an elusive but famous understanding with the Kentuckian.[12] At the runoff election in the House, with votes being cast by state delegations as units, Adams held onto the delegations from the seven states he had carried in the general election. The bargain he had struck with Clay—whether it was "corrupt," as the Jacksonians charged, or "statesmanlike," as Richard Hofstadter has termed it[13]—brought him the three states Clay could deliver. His own diligent congressional calls had won over the votes of three other states carried by Jackson. With thirteen states, Adams was elected, and his victory marked him a master of what might be called the political "old-boy network."

Why should there be anything surprising about terming one of our presidents a politician? Adams acquired the reputation of being a nonpolitician for two reasons. In the first place, he did not like to admit his political ambition even to himself, and his diary, with its self-conscious posturing, reflects the guilt he felt over it. The psychiatrist David F. Musto, in a sensitive paper, has argued that John Quincy Adams could not accept his feelings of ambition because he compared himself with the myth of selfless devotion his mother Abigail had created to describe his father John, absent in Europe while the boy was growing up.[14] Thus Adams preferred to believe that high office was a moral reward rather than an object of competitive striving. "*Detur digniori* is the inscription upon the prize," he told Henry Clay in 1822, applying the words of the traditional award for academic excellence in Harvard College to the presidency of the United States. "The duty shall be assigned to the most able and the most worthy."[15]

The other reason why we do not always recognize the politician in John Quincy Adams is that the dominant mode of the political art in the United States has changed since he practiced it; indeed, it was changing even as he was practicing it. Adams was not an effete snob, as the Jacksonians charged, not a weak politician or a nonpolitician. He was an antiparty politician, seeking to perpetuate the Era of Good Feelings that had been known under President Monroe. The politics he understood was a politics of regions—regions with vertically integrated social structures that accepted and deferred to their "natural leaders." In such a region he had his own power base; with such leaders he knew how to deal. While president, Adams was baffled by the beginnings of a new sort of politics, a politics of mass-movement parties. In Andrew Jackson's conduct he could see only base ingratitude, demagogy, and "unnatural passions."[16]

As a politician, Adams remained in the tradition of the eighteenth-century "country party," a political heritage with a long history in his native New England. His concern with "the character of the good ruler" was one he shared with generations of Yankees and Puritans before him.[17] The eldest of the representative Whigs examined in this book, he was, not surprisingly, more old-fashioned than the others in certain ways. For example, he sometimes continued to oppose "virtue" and "commerce" in the country-party rhetorical style, citing the authority of Milton on the corrupting dangers of prosperity. Even though he strongly supported economic development, he despised sordid motives and remained essentially unsympathetic with the businessman's outlook. When the banks suspended specie payment during the Panic of 1837, Adams suggested a law to authorize jailing the bankers.[18] It was left to his son Charles Francis to marry Abigail Brooks and thereby unite the Adams family to urban wealth. It was likewise left to younger members of the Whig party to effect a fuller reconciliation between political virtue and moneymaking.

Unlike such Whigs as Webster or Clay, Adams was little influenced by the wishes of the business community; that his economic program coincided with their desires was incidental as far as he was concerned.[19] To him economic development was "a solemn responsibility," undertaken in an austere spirit of self-improvement, and not to be confused with making life easier. As the national debt neared extinction, he warned, "it would neither be a wise nor a salutary policy to relax into languor and inactivity the energies which have been exercised for the accomplishment of that end." The nation, like the individual, had the duty to be vigorous and purposeful, to "exercise the faculties" and develop its potential. After the frustration of his presidential program, Adams bitterly remarked, "The American Union, as a moral Person in the family of Nations, is to live from hand to mouth." But, though his plan was defeated politically, Adams' identification of community economic development with individual moral striving reflected an attitude that was widely shared. In the vocabulary of the day, the word "improvement" was commonly used in connection with both economic and moral projects.[20]

Adams tried to make his presidency a continuation of James Monroe's. The judgment of a contemporary politician seems justified: "the administration of John Quincy Adams blends so intimately with that of Monroe, in which he was chief minister, that no dividing line can be drawn between them."[21] The policies of tariff protection, federally sponsored internal improvements, and national banking that were later to become known as the "American System" took coherent shape in the years between 1816 and 1828 and were identified with the "national" wing of the Republican party. Adams saw himself as a Republican in the same activist, nationalist spirit as his two predecessors. His eulogy of Monroe contains this prose hymn to internal improvements: "Rise! before your forefathers here assembled, ye unborn ages of after time. . . . Rejoice! that for you every valley has been exalted and every mountain and hill has been made low. . . . Rejoice! that for you Time has been divested of his delays and Space disburthened of his obstructions."[22]

In his old age, Adams gathered together his thoughts on human progress in an essay entitled "Society and Civilization." The theory of the phases of history he there presented was indebted to the Scottish moral philosopher Adam Ferguson. Adams identified four stages of human development: hunting, pastoral, agricultural, and civilized. The stages are characterized not only by economic and technological improvement but also by spiritual and moral advance. In religion there is a progression from primitive animism in the first stage to idolatry in the second, polytheism in the third, and monotheism in the fourth. The relationships between the sexes change from promiscuity in the first to polygamy in the second and monogamy in the third. Adams emphasizes that the status of women improves with each stage; one might therefore expect him to add that genuine equality between the sexes would eventually be achieved, but Adams seems not to have carried his thinking this far. He is carefully explicit, however, in stating that the highest stage of human development necessitates a mixed urban-rural society with a complex, diversified economy.[23]

Upon assuming the presidency in 1825 Adams left almost all of Monroe's appointees in office. This policy need not be attributed to passivity or impracticality. Adams realized his vulnerability as a minority president. What was more logical than to emphasize the connection between the preceding administration and his own by attempting to rally its varied supporters to himself?[24] In selecting Henry Clay for secretary of state, Adams was committing himself to one of the most prominent spokesmen of Madisonian Republicanism, already well known for his strong views on national banking and internal improvements. During the decades to come, not only National Republicans but also their Whig heirs would continue to emphasize the early Republican origins of their program. When John Tyler vetoed recharter of the national bank, Clay berated him for his failure "to occupy the Madison ground" and for betraying "the great republican school." In the campaign of 1844, the Maryland Whig John Pendleton Kennedy still appealed to what he called "the Madisonian Platform": national banking, a protective tariff, internal improvements, and limited executive authority. Jefferson, in his later years, had also provided the Whigs with some justification for invoking his name on behalf of economic diversification.[25]

Linked as he was with the Monroe administration, Adams inevitably inherited many of its enemies. Important among these were the "Old" Republicans, who had nearly carried Pennsylvania against Monroe in 1820 and were to become a source of strength to the Jackson movement.[26] Adams' efforts to appease Crawford and Calhoun were in vain. But one signal political success of his must be acknowledged: he won over most of the Federalists, who had hated him ever since he had supported Jefferson's Embargo. Having opposed him in the general election, they supported him in the House runoff and remained thereafter a component of the Whig coalition. The alliance of former Madisonians with former Federalists had its effect on the rhetoric of the second party system. While the Whigs themselves pointed with pride to their Jeffersonian antecedents, their Democratic rivals invariably accused them of being Federalists in sheep's clothing.[27]

The frustrations of Adams' administration were largely a consequence of the failure of his brand of nonpartisan politics. In his inaugural address he rejoiced that the "baneful weed of party strife was uprooted."[28] Somehow, the weed was reborn and overran the garden. Adams steadfastly refused to purge his political foes from office, because, he explained, it would entail an "inquisitorial scrutiny" into the personal opinions of the whole civil service.[29] (Indeed it would have, in the absence of party designations.) Precedent was on the side of restraint in such matters; Monroe had kept William H. Crawford on at the Treasury when Crawford was at odds with him and was even personally disrespectful. In any case, it is by no means clear that a purge would have helped Adams politically. The image of being above party was not without advantages; it would later be exploited successfully by Zachary Taylor (and by Dwight Eisenhower).

Adams' strategy for 1828 was the traditional one, based on regional leaders. He failed of reelection because his secretary of state, Clay, and his running mate, Richard Rush of Pennsylvania, failed to deliver their regional constituencies. Adams' plan, plausible though it was, could not withstand the popularity and organization of the

Jackson movement. Even so, he managed a better showing than Clay did four years later—though legend has it that Clay was a consummate politician and Adams a blundering one. Adams held onto his own regional base of New England in the election. New England, significantly, was destined to become the heartland of Whig political culture, from which it often spread elsewhere with migrating Yankees.

Adams' aversion to political parties had a firm intellectual basis. In most of the political theory then current in the Anglo-American world the legitimacy of parties was not accepted, and the principal "country" authorities, Harrington and Bolingbroke, were explicit in their disapproval. Though Edmund Burke was admired by Adams and many other Americans, his defense of parties in *Thoughts on the Present Discontents* was less influential than his observations on the American and French Revolutions. The persistence of antiparty attitudes during colonial and early national times, despite the gradual emergence of political parties as functioning entities, is one of the great anomalies of that age.[30] The so-called Era of Good Feelings under Monroe actually witnessed much strife, as we know, including sectional controversies, personal political rivalries, and the Panic of 1819 and its ensuing depression. Yet, notwithstanding these troubles, the era took its name from the absence of political parties, because contemporaries regarded that as a sign of civic health. In later years National Republicans and Whigs continued to look back fondly on the Era of Good Feelings. Bolingbroke, long before, had welcomed the end of the party divisions of the later Stuart reigns and celebrated an era of nonpartisan consensus that, he charged, was disturbed only by the rise of Walpole's office-hungry spoilsmen.[31] The American Whigs, idealizing Bolingbroke, applied the same interpretation to their own history. They romanticized the lost Era of Good Feelings and resented Jackson as a latter-day Walpole.

The historian Ronald P. Formisano, who has uncovered the widespread antiparty sentiment in American public opinion before the Civil War, has written that antiparty thinking "began with society rather than the individual." It posited "a hierarchy of classes" and "social harmony, not conflict." Describing the half-articulated feelings of ordinary antiparty voters, he says they felt political parties "mocked the idea that government existed to promote the common weal."[32] In a sophisticated person like John Quincy Adams such attitudes took on philosophical form. Adams rejected out of hand the Utilitarian principle that government should promote "the greatest good of the greatest number," calling it "jesuitical." He felt the true task of government was to balance all interests so that none of them was harmed. "This is the only principle to seek—'the greatest good of all.'" There was no place for partiality or partisanship in such a scheme. The development of political parties Adams could regard only as a threat to consensus and an opening toward conflict.[33]

During the bitter campaign of 1840 Adams worried that "parties are falling into profligate factions." This was always the danger with parties. In contemporary usage, a "faction" was a party that pursued its self-interest to the detriment of the common interest. The terminology was widespread and sanctioned by time; Bolingbroke and *The Federalist* had employed it. The formation of factions was considered a stage in the degeneration of a republic. Thus, the provocative course that the Polk administration followed with respect to Mexico could be attributed to the spirit of faction: it was selfish, reckless of the true national interest, and subversive of the Constitution.[34]

Historians have usually agreed that the Democrats accepted the legitimacy of party sooner than the Whigs, though even Democrats expressed occasional misgivings. Martin Van Buren's *Inquiry into the Origin and Course of Political Parties in the United States*, defending the concept of party competition, is a landmark in the evolution of American opinion.[35] From the viewpoint of most Whigs, parties posed a threat to the proper social order. They "challenged custom, dissolved deference, fettered leaders, and elevated conflict to a public virtue."[36] Party organizations raised up "demagogues" to rival the established "natural" leaders of the community. Demands for party loyalty seemed to entail a dangerous abdication of personal responsibility; the Protestant clergy were particularly concerned about this.[37]

Resistance to the idea of party and fear of faction were profoundly conditioned by the faculty psychology of the day. A faction represented a group of people not under the sway of conscience and prudence; it was a collective form of "passion." American moral philosophers consequently continued to warn against the evils of parties after the politicians had made them a fact of life. Adams, dedicated as he was to subordination of the passions within the individual, not surprisingly deplored the emergence of factions in the body politic. Even more scrupulously devoted to self-discipline than most Whigs, he took longer than most to become reconciled to the idea of political parties.[38] To varying degrees, however, Whigs manifested the same misgivings about partisanship and passion that Adams displayed in extreme form. They tended to think of themselves as nonpartisan defenders of reason against the passions of the

crowd. In the heat of the campaign of 1840, a Whig manifesto declared: "General Harrison cannot be properly considered the candidate of any particular party." Afterwards, most Whigs probably
would have agreed with the *New York Herald* that Harrison's victory
was "a triumph of intellect over prejudice—a triumph of mind over
passion—a triumph of free thought over party despotism."[39]

Whig leaders regularly included condemnations of "party," "faction," and "passion" in their speeches. The principal Whig newspaper in the country averred that "To mere Party, and its power, the
Intelligencer has never professed any devotion, even when acting the
most heartily with that body of citizens whose practice as well as
avowed principles seemed to it to offer the steadiest and sincerest
hope of a wise, good, and moderate government." As late as 1850
Horace Greeley could explain that the Democrats were, "strictly
speaking," the only political party in the country; the Whigs were
simply a group of concerned citizens.[40] To us, accustomed to the idea
of a two-party system, such claims sound absurd, probably hypocritical. Yet it would be a mistake to dismiss them as "mere" rhetoric,
bearing no relation to reality.

In 1836 the Whigs refused to hold a national party convention and
instead placed several regional leaders in the field against Van Buren
and his running mate, Richard Mentor Johnson. The strategy failed
(though it did force Johnson into a Senate runoff), but it typified the
Whig approach to politics. More often than not, the Whigs' distaste
for party hampered them in the competition for office. Recent research has indicated that the Whigs were, on the whole, slower to set
up political organizations than their Democratic counterparts and
had more difficulty in getting out their vote.[41] However, to view the
matter only in these terms is to adopt the standards of party success
that the Whigs were rejecting. In an era when such abuses of party
organization as massive vote fraud were widespread and blatant,
conscientious men might well have doubted the benefits to be
gained from the rise of political parties.

Even when parties were honest, they conjured up evil associations. Their avowed partiality made them only marginally different
from "conspiracies," in the loose sense in which that term was then
used. Parties seemed to impose a quasi-military discipline on their
members and certainly brought a quasi-martial spirit of conflict to
society. It is no accident that politicians came to speak of waging
"campaigns" or of Jackson's "war" on the national bank.[42] The difficulty of accepting party in politics was also related to the difficulty of
accepting denominationalism in religion during this period. John

Quincy Adams, significantly, was a Unitarian, a member of the most antidenominational denomination in the country. The Unitarians for decades resisted pressures from their adversaries to set up a separate organization of their own; they maintained that theirs was an ecumenical movement of all "rational" Christians. Partisanship in religion was no more acceptable to them than partisanship in politics.[43]

As time went by, most Whigs became reconciled to the idea of party, provided the party was based on issues. What continued to bother them was the concept of party based on patronage. The *American Review* explained in 1845 that, whereas a "party" was organized around principles, a "faction" was patronage-oriented. The Whigs were a party and the Democrats a faction, it added.[44] Interestingly enough, recent scholarship is inclined to agree, though attaching a different value judgment. The Democrats, we are told, were modern men who understood the importance of building a political organization; the Whigs were moralistic fuddy-duddies.[45] It was indeed perfectly logical for the "spoils system" to become an issue between two such parties. However, it is highly questionable that the mid-nineteenth-century American political spoils system contributed to improving the efficiency of government as claimed. In practice, it fostered a rather primitive politics based on personal fealty to local bosses, consanguinity, and ethnic identity. The Whigs were never able to do more than deplore the spoils system in general and then practice their own version of it whenever they won office; they developed no real alternative to it. It was left for a later generation of neo-Whigs, after the Civil War, to devise a program of civil-service reform for the United States.[46]

A major contributor to the antiparty strain within Whiggery was the Antimasonic movement. In 1826 a former Mason named William Morgan, living in western New York State, threatened to reveal certain secret rituals of the Order. He was arrested on flimsy charges by local officials who were Masons and, while in their custody, disappeared. It was widely believed, then and since, that he had been kidnapped and murdered by Masons, but no one was ever brought to justice for the killing. Those who agitated unsuccessfully for a thorough investigation became convinced that they were confronted with a Masonic conspiracy to hush the matter up, and in reaction they founded the Antimasonic movement. The object of the movement was to expose the secrets of the Masonic Order, including those surrounding the Morgan case, and to limit its political influence by opposing its members when they ran for office. The Antimasons had already become a force to be reckoned with in New York during the campaign of 1828. Since the president and his state manager, Thurlow Weed, showed sympathy, while Andrew Jackson was a Mason, the Antimasons went for Adams and brought him sixteen of New York's thirty-six electoral votes.[47]

When Adams ran for Congress in 1830, he was endorsed by the Antimasons of his constituency. By this time the movement had an organization in at least seven northern states and commanded much public support elsewhere as well. It had taken on the characteristics of what we would call a third party, though most of its supporters apparently thought of themselves as nonpartisan crusaders for justice. In 1831 the Antimasons were already anticipating the presidential election of the following year and took the unprecedented step of calling a convention to nominate a candidate. They were following the pattern of the conventions held by benevolent societies; the action set them apart from the established political parties, which then selected nominees in congressional caucuses. (The Antimasonic example was later copied by the major parties, and the convention was converted into the partisan occasion par excellence.) Adams carefully angled, within the accepted constraints of the day, for the Antimasonic nomination, but the convention was reluctant to back the defeated ex-president and bestowed its prize instead on William Wirt, Adams' former attorney general, in the hope that he would also be acceptable to the National Republicans. They, however, stayed with Clay, a nominal but inactive Mason unacceptable to the Antimasons. Adams preserved a delicate neutrality between Wirt and Clay in 1832 while attacking Masonry vigorously.[48] Wirt carried only Vermont, but the Antimasons had staked out a strategic position in American politics.

Antimasonry was a popular movement, strong among yeomen and tenant farmers. In social tone it was rustic, not metropolitan. Adams, it should be pointed out, had always run well in rural Yankee areas; he was literally a "country" politician in constituency as well as in terms of his intellectual heritage. His Twelfth Congressional District consisted of "middle landscape" villages and towns, quite different from urban Boston. The commercial and financial interests of Essex and Suffolk counties were always more closely tied to Daniel Webster than to him, just as they had sided with Alexander Hamilton against his father. Years later, Henry Adams would still contrast sharply the worlds of Boston and Quincy.[49] Like the Adams family, most Antimasons inhabited a world of stable moral values: to them the Masonic Order looked like a secret organization whose members were placing themselves above the law. Morgan's mysterious disappearance and the infuriating coverup afterwards became the focus of many resentments for humble but honest folk. Sometimes Antimasonry was connected with antirent agitation. Often it fed on opposition to the prototypical party machine established in New York by Martin Van Buren, the "Albany Regency" (which had ties to local Masons). Antimasonry showed that dislike of political parties was not confined to a few patricians but was firmly rooted in at least some segments of public opinion.[50]

The Antimasons have been much criticized, in their own time and since, as hypocrites, demagogues, and witch-hunters. It has become fashionable in recent years to refer to them as exemplifying the "paranoid style" of politics.[51] This concept has so captured the imagination of historians that it tempts them to neglect the solid investigations of the Masonic-Antimasonic controversy conducted by earlier scholars. What these conscientious inquirers found was that the Masons really did swear gruesome oaths of mutual aid and secrecy, that the oaths were enforced by the kidnapping and, almost certainly, the murder of William Morgan, and that the crime was in fact covered up by a Masonic conspiracy.[52] Presumably, most Masons in the country had nothing to do with the Morgan affair, yet the Order never condemned it or otherwise dissociated itself from it. The Antimasons' reaction to all this was fervent denunciation. Their language was conditioned by evangelical Christianity, the classical fear of declension in a republic, and "country-party" suspicion of power. What we too readily take for paranoia was a response to legitimate worries, phrased in the terminology of a vanished political culture.[53] The original impulse behind Antimasonry was not prejudice, not nativism, but the desire of ordinary people to be free from organized secret terror. Significantly, John Quincy Adams' attacks on Masonry were reprinted in 1875 by opponents of the Ku Klux Klan.[54]

In 1833 Adams ran for governor of Massachusetts as an Antimason and an avowed opponent of political parties. He had hoped for the National Republican nomination too, but that went to John Davis. Adams finished second in a field of four. Since no candidate had an absolute majority, the final choice devolved upon the General Court (state legislature). Adams, understandably, had no relish for becoming governor under circumstances similar to those under which he had become president. He consequently negotiated an agreement with Daniel Webster. Under its terms, Adams bowed out in favor of Davis, and, in return, the National Republicans promised a full-scale investigation of Masonry in the Commonwealth. Adams' withdrawal statement is a ringing vindication of his cause. However, the National Republicans undertook only the most perfunctory of investigations, and Adams never trusted Webster again.[55]

As the 1830s went by, the Antimasons more and more often united with the National Republicans under the banner of the new Whig party. The alliance Adams had worked toward was achieved by William H. Seward and Thurlow Weed. It would be a mistake, however, to suppose that Antimasonry was simply absorbed into Whiggery without a trace. The Antimasonic wing of the Whig party retained its crusading moralistic character under leaders like Seward and Thaddeus Stevens of Pennsylvania. Eventually this would become the antislavery "Conscience" wing of the party.[56] In the meantime, the Antimasons exerted considerable influence. They succeeded in discrediting Masonry to the extent that the number of lodges and their membership fell off drastically. In 1836 the Antimasons proved that William Henry Harrison was a strong candidate for president, thereby frustrating Webster's hope to be Van Buren's only northern opponent that year, and at the Whig convention of 1840 they played a crucial role in winning the nomination for Harrison over Clay. Sometimes politicians cast their lot with Antimasonry out of mere careerism; this seems to have been the case with the colorless Millard Fillmore, who used the movement as a stepping-stone to prominence.[57] That Antimasonry attracted more than its share of such opportunists, however, is not apparent.

One reason for the survival of Antimasonry was its association with Protestant piety. The Antimasons perceived the Masonic Order as a kind of freethinkers' church, "a substitute for religion." This religious antagonism between Mason and Antimason had deep roots. The historian Rhys Isaac, describing eighteenth-century Virginia, finds in Masonry one of the badges of a "gentry" culture, which he contrasts sharply with an "evangelical" culture. The evangelicals resented the gentry's arrogance, self-indulgence, and violence. One finds the same value judgments being made by nineteenth-century Antimasons.[58] The link between evangelicalism and Antimasonry is well typified in Charles G. Finney. The greatest revivalist of western New York, Finney had been a Mason until his conversion experience; then he quit the Order and denounced it. As late as 1869 he was still condemning Masonry in terms strong enough to provoke threats on his life. Antimasonry seems to have exerted its greatest appeal among Protestant groups whose denominational heritage stemmed from New England but which were moving away from Calvinism toward a more liberal theology.[59] Such was the religion of John Quincy Adams.

Adams knew his Bible thoroughly, appealed to it in political debate, and earnestly commended its study to others; he did not always interpret it literally, however.[60] His great diary is full of prayers, religious reflections, and spiritual struggles and takes on much of its character from them. The sentiments can seem either stiffly conventional or touchingly simple: "I deem it the duty of every Christian man, when he betakes himself to his nightly pillow, in self-examination to say, what good have I done this day?" At times his humility and sincerity are painful: "The deepest of my afflictions is the comparison of the age I have attained with the nothing I have done for mankind"; this was written in 1831, when his diplomatic career and presidency were behind him. "Whether I am or shall be saved is all unknown to me; I know that I have been, and am, a sinner."[61] Sometimes Adams wrestled with "involuntary and agonizing doubts," but he "fortified" himself against them by faithful attendance at church. He almost never failed to comment on the sermon in his Sunday entry, and the comment is often mordant; an exhortation by the chaplain of the House of Representatives reminded him of "the froth of spruce beer." A sermon on the Incarnation—"a subject for eloquence of the highest order"—was merely "cold and tame and Presbyterian." But Harriet Livermore, the unjustly forgotten woman evangelist, engaged his admiration: her "monomania" was of the kind that served the Holy Spirit.[62]

Adams' ancestral church in Quincy was among those Congregational parishes that were defining themselves as Unitarian during the first quarter of the nineteenth century. The central act of Christian life in this tradition, going back to the days of the Puritans, was a public profession of faith; Adams made his in 1826. He identified strongly with Unitarianism, though he often attended services at churches of other denominations, especially while president. His qualified support for the temperance and sabbatarian movements was typical of Unitarians, who sought to reconcile evangelical piety with Enlightenment rationalism.[63] Adams took quite an interest in controversial theology and entered a debate on the nature of eternal life while in the White House. His diary is sprinkled with acerbic judgments on the religious views of others. Jefferson and Robert Dale Owen are condemned as irreligious, while Emerson and the transcendentalists are accused of "deadly sophistry." The Calvinist theology against which Unitarianism rebelled is "a bundle of absurdities"—though its doctrine of human depravity may well be "too near the truth."[64] Adams' membership in the small Unitarian denomination constituted something of a political liability in more orthodox parts of the country. The Tennessee Democrat James Knox Polk, attacking Adams' constitutional interpretations as "latitudinarian," was also calling attention to his adversary's religion.[65]

Adams believed in a messianic age, as prophesied by the second Isaiah ("the sublimest of prophets"). The advance of civilization, technology, and knowledge were taking us closer to this long-awaited day: "Progressive improvement in the condition of man is apparently the purpose of a superintending Providence." Such had been the burden of his famous First Message to Congress in 1825. The system of internal improvements there outlined, he remained convinced, constituted a "sacred duty," imposed by God, to elevate America in the scale of civilization. The political policies of his rivals "led us back to the savage state" and away from the millennial age.[66] The contemplation of the divinely ordained glorious end of history prompted Adams to his highest flights of eloquence. When secretary of state, he had been requested by Congress to prepare a report on weights and measures. The impressive document he drew up presents a thorough justification for the adoption of the metric system in terms of scientific rationality and international cooperation. But the peroration declares the metric system desirable in the last analysis because it implements "the trembling hope of the Christian" for the unity of mankind, the binding in chains of Satan, and the thousand years of peace on earth. No more remarkable synthesis of Christianity with the Enlightenment can well be imagined.[67]

In 1834 Adams was nominated in his congressional district by the Antimasons and the newly named Whig party. His relations with the Whigs tell a fascinating tale, complicated by their, and especially his, dislike of party discipline. On the touchstone issue of the early thirties, finance, Adams sided with them and the Bank of the United States. The Bank's president, Nicholas Biddle (a fellow classical scholar), had long been his personal friend. As a member of two special House committees to investigate the Bank, Adams fought hard for its rechartering and later against removal of its federal deposits. At the time of the Panic of 1837, however, Adams became disgusted with Biddle's manipulation of credit, as did some other New England Whigs.[68]

For the first ten years that Adams was a representative, he served as chairman of the Committee on Manufactures. The Jackson men, who generally controlled the House, were willing to let him occupy this post as a sign of respect for a former president (and, one suspects, to blunt the embarrassing conflict in their own ranks between southern free traders and Pennsylvania protectionists). This chairmanship put Adams in the forefront of the great tariff struggles of the 1830s. His first task was to amend the notorious "tariff of abominations," enacted as a campaign ploy by Jackson supporters in 1828. The Adams Tariff of 1832 lowered certain duties objectionable to northeastern interests and also made one concession to the planters: a reduction in the duty on the cheap woolens used for slaves' clothing. This proved insufficient to placate the followers of Calhoun, and South Carolina nullified the tariff. Adams felt that Clay's eventual compromise conceded too much to the nullifiers.[69]

The close working relationship Adams enjoyed with the rest of the Whigs on economic issues was temporarily disrupted in 1835 by a disagreement over foreign policy. The great diplomatist chose to support President Jackson's hard line against the French in a dispute over the payment of American spoliation claims. His old-fashioned Whiggery—his antipartyism—was conflicting with the young Whig party's growing sense of itself. The party showed its displeasure by making no nomination in the Twelfth Congressional District in 1836; Adams ran under Antimasonic auspices alone and still won, though by a reduced majority. Soon he was back in the Whigs' good graces, however, cooperating even with southern members of the party in attacking the administration. In December, 1839, he used his prestige and unparalleled knowledge of parliamentary procedure to resolve an organizational wrangle that had paralyzed the House. R. M. T. Hunter, a Virginia Whig, was eventually chosen as speaker, and southern Whigs were effusive in their praise of Adams' handling of the affair.[70] But their cordiality was about to give way to dramatic conflict.

The crisis was precipitated on January 25, 1842, when Adams presented the House with a petition from Haverhill (a town in his district) for "measures peaceably to dissolve the Union of these States." The benefits of the Union were being monopolized by the South, the petitioners complained. For years Adams had been introducing petitions that angered southern congressmen, but this one was particularly excruciating for the southern Whigs. In opposition to Calhoun, they had staked their political fortunes on the sacrosanct nature of the Union. When the value of the Union was "calculated" (as the saying went) by northern extremists too, the southern Whigs felt compelled to preserve their credibility at home. If they did not dissociate themselves from this eminent northern Whig, they feared they would be ruined by the southern Democrats. Adams had shrewdly moved to refer the petition to a committee instructed to prepare an answer showing why the Union should not be dissolved. Nevertheless, southerners quickly demanded that he be censured for presenting the petition. The attack was led by President Tyler's spokesman, Henry Wise of Virginia, and Thomas Marshall (nephew of the late chief justice), a Kentucky Whig. Those few southern Whigs who defended Adams' right to introduce the petition did so at considerable risk; one of them, Thomas Arnold of Tennessee, was threatened with a bowie knife by a Democratic colleague, John Dawson of Louisiana.

Adams' defense against the proposed censure was a tour de force. The southerners had hoped to make an example of him and thereby permanently intimidate northern members. Adams turned the occasion into a major media event, widely covered by the newspapers, which mobilized northern public opinion behind the right of petition, personally mortified his leading critics, and took a step toward making the Whig party in the North openly antislavery. To remind the House that American institutions derived from the consent of the governed, Adams began by ordering the clerk to read the Declaration of Independence. By the principles of that Declaration the petitioners had the right to be heard, and he, their representative, the right to present their petition. Then, to embarrass Wise, he reminded the House that on an earlier occasion, when disciplinary action had been proposed against Wise for having participated in a duel, he had come to Wise's assistance and no action had been taken. To embarrass Marshall, he pointed out that the young man's enemies in Kentucky were accusing him of being soft on abolitionism. He quoted from a pamphlet he discovered that Marshall had written earlier, arguing that the South was less prosperous than the North because of the "cancer" of slavery. With this stroke Adams ruined Marshall's political career, and the shuddering Kentuckian knew it;[71] he would not run for reelection. Most wonderful, "old man eloquent" showed no sign of weakening. At the age of seventy-four, he could cross swords with scores of furious opponents hour after hour, day after day, and best them. Throughout the North the parties were polarizing around the censure debate, the Whigs rallying to Adams. After two weeks, fearing that the northern and southern branches of their party would split irretrievably, Whig congressional leaders decided to lay the censure motion on the table; whereupon Adams, in a gesture of triumph, presented two hundred other petitions against slavery. Thereafter, when northern Whig congressmen ventured to present similar petitions from antislavery disunionists, no one suggested censuring them.[72]

Adams played a central role in fostering antislavery within Whiggery. He had been privately hostile to slavery as early as 1820; apparently he even confided these views to John C. Calhoun while the two were still friends and colleagues in the Monroe cabinet. Eventually he reached the conclusion that slavery was contrary to his whole conception of individual and social morality. Proud as he was of his own self-discipline, Adams loathed the violent passions southern statesmen seemed to indulge. "The domineering spirit naturally springs from the institution of slavery," he observed; "the South Carolinians are attempting to govern the Union as they govern their slaves."[73] Proslavery apologetics struck Adams as "a monument of intellectual perversion"—just as abhorrent as the absolutist political theories of Sir Robert Filmer and Thomas Hobbes. There was no place for human bondage in the program of scientific, educational, economic, and moral development that Adams envisioned for America: "that the fall of slavery is predetermined in the counsels of Omnipotence I cannot doubt." In his dedication of the Cincinnati astronomical observatory in 1843, Adams sketched his vision of a free and upright society, declaring that the Founding Fathers had "pledged us, their children, to labor with united and concerted energy, from the cradle to the grave, to purge the earth of all slavery."[74]

Slavery had influenced the second party system from its inception. The Missouri controversy of 1820 alerted the slaveholders to the defense of their interest, and behind much of the political debate of the Adams and Jackson administrations there already lurked the (frequently unacknowledged) opposition between slavery and its critics. The dedication of southerners like Calhoun and John Randolph, who led the congressional opposition to Adams' administration, to restricting the constitutional powers of the national government cannot have been unrelated to their desire to avoid interference with the "peculiar institution." Such leaders could often make common cause in the Democratic party with those northern workingmen and farmers who felt threatened by the probusiness aspects of Adams' economic program. To Adams this looked as if the planters were deliberately fostering class conflict in order to divide the North and maintain their own supremacy. The election of 1828, which pitted a northern ticket of Adams and Rush against a southern one of Jackson and Calhoun, prefigured a party alignment in which the Democrats would be generally more responsive to the slaveholding interest than the Whigs.[75]

Adams expressed his resentment of the slaveholding power in terms of a conspiracy against American liberty and morality. In order to protect their special interest, he charged, the slaveowners had secured unfair favors at the Constitutional Convention, supported a more expensive military establishment than would otherwise be needed, ruthlessly expropriated the American Indians, interfered with freedom of expression both in Congress and outside it, and engaged in long-range diplomatic maneuvering to despoil Mexico of Texas. One reason why Adams fought so hard for the tariff and internal improvements is that he felt the North was entitled to some federal favors after all the ones that had been lavished on the South to benefit slavery. The attempt to censure him in 1842, preceded as it was by a secret caucus of southern congressmen, he considered a specific instance of this more general slave-power conspiracy.[76] Certainly Adams was perceiving events through the lenses of classical humanist thought and its fear of betrayal and degeneration. Like the Patriots of 1776, he had inherited this mode of perception via the political tradition of the English "country party."[77] His adversaries, who posited an abolitionist conspiracy of which he was a part, shared his manner of expression. Neither side was altogether wrong. There is good reason for believing that antebellum federal policies were often dictated by the interests of slavery more than their advocates chose to admit. There is also good reason for regarding John Quincy Adams as a crypto-abolitionist who asserted the right of petition because he wanted to push the slave power into politically untenable positions.[78]

It is arrogance on the part of historians to suppose that only they, with the benefit of hindsight, can correctly discern the tendency of events. Sometimes a prescient contemporary sees as clearly as any later chronicler; such a one was John Quincy Adams. At the time of the Missouri controversy he foresaw that the slavery issue would eventuate in the "dissolution, at least temporary, of the Union as now constituted," followed by civil war:

> The Union might then be reorganized on the fundamental principle of emancipation. This object is vast in its compass, awful in its prospects, sublime and beautiful in its issue. A life devoted to it would be nobly spent or sacrificed.[79]

The choice of adjectives was worthy of a former professor of rhetoric. During the following years Adams returned repeatedly to this bloody vision. He developed the theory that a military emergency could justify emancipation. The exercise of the war powers was the

means—otherwise constitutionally unavailable—by which freedom
would come to all Americans. Adams was not quite sure whether
Congress, the Executive, or commanders in the field would be re-
sponsible for it.[80] In the event, all three took a hand: Generals
Frémont, Hunter, and Butler, in 1861 and '62; Congress, through the
Confiscation Acts; Lincoln, in the Emancipation Proclamation.

Adams stayed in touch with abolitionist leaders and often cooperated with them. As early as 1837, in speaking to northern audiences,
he looked forward to the "extirpation" of slavery, not just to its
restriction. He wrote an introduction to the biography of the mar-
tyred abolitionist Elijah Lovejoy and intervened personally to help
restore to her anxious husband a free black woman who had been
kidnapped into slavery.[81] In 1841 he argued before the U.S. Supreme
Court the case of the Africans from the Spanish slaver *Amistad,* winning a ruling that Cinqué and his companions were free men and
could return to their homeland. The following year he tried to delete
the word "white" from the voting requirements of Alexandria, Virginia (then part of the District of Columbia). He long resisted Democratic Indian policies, calling them "a perpetual harrow upon my
feelings." In spite of all this, a scrupulous investigator can still find
evidence of racial prejudice in Adams; for example, in a literary essay
on Shakespeare's *Othello,* he assumes that interracial marriage is
wrong.[82]

Adams kept a distance between himself and the abolitionists, for
reasons they never altogether understood. Unlike them, he respected
property rights enough to feel that masters should be entitled to
compensation for liberated slaves. He preferred gradual to immediate emancipation and sponsored a constitutional amendment
that would have freed all children born after July 4, 1842. But such
proposals, he knew, had scant hope of success. This left the alternative of eventual civil war. If they realized the bloody cost he expected
America to pay for emancipation, "the sturdiest of the abolitionists
would have disavowed the sentiments of their champion," Adams
confided to a friend.[83] The aging statesman combined his moral condemnation of slavery with a veritable Burkean sense of the possible
in politics. He often criticized the abolitionists' tactics—especially
when the Liberty party contested elections against antislavery Whigs
like himself. He was determined to wage his own fight against slavery in such a way as to maximize public support. Only thus could the
aggressions of the slave power be resisted and the North steeled to
the ordeal he anticipated. Instead of making emancipation in the
District of Columbia the focus of antislavery effort, as most

abolitionists desired, he insisted that the right of petition was an issue better suited to rallying the North.[84]

The target of Adams' attacks was the "gag rule" in the House, first adopted in 1836 and tightened in 1840. It provided that petitions relating to slavery (including those applying to the territories and the District of Columbia) should be laid on the table without debate or referral to a committee. Unlike the Democrats, the congressional Whigs were always deeply divided over the wisdom of the gag. Adams considered it an abridgment of the constitutional right of petition, an opinion with more political than legal merit. A brilliant parliamentarian, he showed a small, then growing, band of antislavery congressmen how to oppose and circumvent the rule in countless ways. The gag rule may seem a purely symbolic issue (the Senate effectively buried antislavery petitions without one), but it provided an opportunity to discuss the implications of slavery in a way that brought home to white people a sense that their freedom, too, was being abridged. It also had the tactical advantage of not committing those presenting petitions to an endorsement of their contents.[85]

Petitions enabled persons not included in the electorate to make their views known. Many of these were women. While some men objected that women had no business meddling in politics, Adams argued that moral questions, like slavery, legitimately fall within the feminine sphere—a line of argument that would become the entering wedge for women's participation in public affairs during the nineteenth century. In 1837 Adams called his colleagues' attention to a petition from slaves, putting the House into an uproar. A man of profoundly hierarchical sentiments, Adams found the right of petition a congenial as well as tactically effective cause. A petition was "a prayer, a supplication to a superior being, that which we offer up to our God," he explained. "The right of petition contests no power. It admits the power." Adams was willing to defend the right of petition of women and blacks precisely because it did not force him to advocate their equality with white men.[86]

To judge from their strident vituperation on the floor of the House and from the hate mail sent to Adams, many southerners felt that petitions from slaves opened the door to full equality and race war. Before Adams had rallied northern public opinion, he spent years enduring threats to his life and the grossest personal abuse. But it was a role he was prepared for by prolonged loneliness in youth and by perennial self-discipline. "The mount of danger is the place / Where we shall see surprising grace," he quoted to himself. He lived to see his vindication: on December 3, 1844, enough northern

Democrats became angry at southern domination of their party to break ranks and enable the gag rule to be rescinded. The old warrior's reaction was characteristic: "Blessed, forever blessed, be the name of God!"[87]

During the 1840s Adams came to identify himself more enthusiastically as a Whig than he had in earlier years. He could afford to. At least in the North, his stands were defining the party's image on the subject of slavery. The succession of the turncoat Tyler to the presidency brought economic policy back to the center of political controversy. Adams found himself in the thick of the fight against Tyler for the upward revision of the tariff and for the reconstitution of a national bank. He introduced an amendment to the Constitution to enable presidential vetoes to be overridden more easily.[88] In September of 1842, Adams' constituents welcomed him home after his successful battle against censure. He used the occasion to deliver a major address, most of which he devoted to defending the Whig legislative program. The speech was avowedly partisan, rejoicing in the name Whig. At the close Adams alluded to the censure debate, but he laid all the blame for his harassment on the Democrats. The right of petition was triumphantly identified as a Whig cause. Tyler he likened to Charles I and George III.[89] Though the off-year elections of 1842 went generally against the congressional Whigs, Adams survived both this and the perils of redistricting to emerge politically stronger than ever. A vacation that he planned in the following year turned into a triumphal tour: across New York State, then from Buffalo to Cleveland, Cincinnati, and Pittsburgh. In the old Antimasonic, now evangelical, regions he had become a hero for his petition fight. He crossed the river into Kentucky, where, during the censure debate, Thomas Marshall had warned he would be lynched if he ever set foot. Instead he received a warm welcome from Henry Clay—and a conciliatory message from Marshall. Adams returned to Washington with more welcoming stops in Maryland and Virginia. They remembered his support for internal improvements along the route of the Baltimore & Ohio Railroad.[90]

The Texas question brought Adams into solid agreement with the other Whig party leaders, even in the South. In negotiating the Transcontinental Treaty of 1819 he had tried to obtain Texas from Spain and in 1825 made overtures to purchase it from Mexico. After the Texan Revolution, however, he opposed acquiring the region because it would strengthen American slavery. Annexation of an entire foreign nation also posed special difficulties of constitutional law and political theory, he felt. Should not the people of both countries have to approve such a profound transformation by referendum?[91] Since Adams endorsed the acquisition of Oregon, critics accused him of inconsistency, but he justified his course with several arguments. The same treaty with Spain that enhanced our claim to Oregon renounced our title to Texas. The American emigrants to Oregon regarded themselves as still subject to United States law; those to Texas did not. Most importantly, the American settlers in Oregon had raised the level of civilization in the area because they were cultivators, not hunters and gatherers like the Indians and the British fur traders. The American-Texans, by contrast, had lowered the level of civilization in their area by introducing slavery.[92]

In the persistent efforts of the Jackson, Van Buren, and Tyler administrations to secure Texas, Adams found much to confirm his suspicions of a slave-power conspiracy. Looking back in 1842, he felt that, if Harrison had lived, the continuity of the conspiracy would have been broken. And so, when Clay ran for president in 1844, Adams unashamedly supported him. He went so far as to make speeches for the Whig ticket in the heat of the campaign—something he had not done before, least of all for himself.[93] When Polk won the election, the same lame-duck Congress that had rescinded the gag rule also took the Democrats' victory as a mandate for Texas. Less than three months after his hour of triumph, Adams could only characterize the joint resolution of annexation, which circumvented the need for a two-thirds majority in the Senate to ratify a treaty, as "the apoplexy of the Constitution."[94] Within another three months he cast his vote against the declaration of war on Mexico.

Adams loved the Union with a profound sentiment that transcended regional loyalty. Bred to the nation's service, he had performed it all his life. He had opposed the narrow sectionalists of New England, had supported Jackson in foreign affairs, and had married a southern woman. Believing as he did in the harmony of diverse interests, he long refused to accept the inevitability of conflict between North and South. Yet, in the last analysis, the Union to him was a means to moral ends, not an end in itself. Americans should be free, virtuous, and vigorous—conditions they could best meet united and at peace. Hence the value of the Union. The dismemberment of the nation into petty warring states would entail all the ills of European militarism, heavy taxation, and autocracy.[95]

Toward the end of his life, Adams began to doubt that the Union really was serving the ends of political, economic, and moral "improvement." By 1843 he was suspecting that the Union consisted of "hostile elements," among them slavery, "which poisoned the whole composition." He hoped a historical inquiry into the confederation of four Puritan colonies in 1643 would assuage his doubts about the Union of the states, but it did not.[96] If the Union continued on the course set by the annexation of Texas, he feared it would become "a conquering and warlike nation." Then "aggrandizement will be its passion and its policy. A military government, a large army, a costly navy, distant colonies, and associate islands in every sea will follow in rapid succession."[97] Such an empire was incompatible with liberty, the classical and country-party philosophers had taught.

John Quincy Adams' last years were full of irony as well as courage. He who had been an expansionist in his youth now deplored the "perfidious robbery and dismemberment of Mexico." The great nationalist had come to look upon the perpetuation of the existing Union as an evil. "The Constitution is a menstruous [sic!] rag, and the Union is sinking into a military monarchy, to be rent asunder like the empire of Alexander or the kingdoms of Ephraim and Judah," he recorded for posterity. What he looked forward to now was the dissolution of the Union and its rebirth in freedom. Meanwhile he served his country with that highest patriotism that consists in resisting her when she is wrong. On February 21, 1848, he was smitten by a heart attack in the House chamber while opposing commendation and decorations for the generals who had led the invasion of Mexico. Thomas Hart Benton, Missouri Democrat and veteran of countless battles with Adams, observed: "Death found him at the post of duty; and where else could it have found him?"[98]

Four

The Whig Interpretation of History

News of the defeat of Union arms at Bull Run on
July 21, 1861, moved a prominent Hartford clergyman to serious thought about the nature of
American nationality. The following Sunday,
Horace Bushnell shared his reflections with his
congregation. He identified "two very distinct"
traditions in American political thought. The
first was "the historic," which saw the institutions of the state as developing organically over
time and sanctioned by God. It emphasized respect for leaders who represented historical
continuity and held office as a divine trust.
Bushnell traced the origins of this outlook to
Puritanism. The other tradition Bushnell called
"the abstract, theoretic element," which based
government on a "social compact" and the voluntary agreement of the governed. It stressed
the natural equality of all men; Bushnell traced
it to the continental Enlightenment. Though the
two political traditions had cooperated in
making the Revolution and the Constitution,
they had always remained rivals for Americans'
loyalty, struggling "like Jacob and Esau, from
the first day until now."[1] Bushnell was seeking
to blame disunion and the Civil War on the
unsatisfactory contractual model and calling for
a reinvigoration of the other model of the
state—the historic. What is most interesting in

69

his discourse, however, is his confidence that both models had long existed, providing Americans with two distinct ideological options.

Bushnell's categories provide a useful starting point for a comparison of Whig and Democratic political ideas. Americans confronted, after independence, the problem faced by all new nations of creating a sense of their nationality, and the problem was still unresolved in Jacksonian times. To define American identity, Whig spokesmen typically turned to history, Democratic ones to principle. Both rejoiced in the American Revolution, of course, but they interpreted it differently. For Democrats, it represented liberation from history; for Whigs, it was the climax of history. The Whigs' conception was more similar to European nationalisms, for it had a basis in ethnicity. The history with which they identified was that of Anglo-American Protestantism. The Democrats' conception did not preclude an interest in history, as the great Democratic historian George Bancroft proves (though most of the important American historians of the day were Whigs). Bancroft, however, defined American nationhood in terms of popular will, not in terms of tradition or the acceptance of historic limitations.

Foreigners often commented that Americans were "unencumbered with a political past." The *Democratic Review* rejoiced that it was so. "The things of the past have but little interest or value for us," the party organ declared in 1840. Two years later it was even more emphatic. "Probably no other civilized nation has at any period of its history so completely thrown off its allegiance to the past, as the American." This freedom enabled Americans to act on Thomas Paine's injunction: "Every age and generation must be free to act for itself, in all cases, as the age and generation which preceded it."[2] The Democratic appeal to principle rather than precedents reminds one of the speaker before the French National Convention who said he had tried "to preserve the virginity of [his] thought." But Horace Bushnell exaggerated the connection between "abstract" political philosophy and the French Enlightenment to suit his polemical purposes. Actually, the consensual model of the state did not require Jacksonian Americans to identify with either the English or the French Enlightenment. Bancroft's writing, for example, exalted intuition and William Penn rather than reason and John Locke.[3]

Whigs hotly disputed the assertion that America had escaped from history. "Our American liberty," Daniel Webster insisted, "has an ancestry, a pedigree, a history. Our ancestors brought to this continent all that was valuable, in their judgement, in the political institutions of England." This was why Edward Everett called the

American Revolution "the winding up of a great drama" that began with the landing of the Pilgrims.[4] The revolution could be understood only in terms of English constitutional debate and the historic struggle for "the rights of Englishmen." When the revolutionaries invoked abstract "rights of man," they had been carried away by enthusiasm. "Our forefathers had not always the best of the argument" when they did this, said the *North American Review*; "if the fathers of the Revolution had their argument to re-state, they would learn higher principles out of their successful labors." These higher principles were the lessons of experience as opposed to philosophy. The French Revolution, in contrast to the American, had "demolished all the past" in its heedless iconoclasm and consequently failed to preserve the freedoms it had won.[5] The debate over "expunging" from the Senate journal the resolution censuring Jackson's removal of government deposits from the Bank of the United States aligned the two parties with symbolic appropriateness: the Whigs defending the integrity of the historical record, the Democrats determined that the mistakes of the past could and must be obliterated. It is easy to assume from our vantage point that nothing was involved beyond a shift in the majority of the Senate from Whig to Democratic. The length, bitterness, and high drama of the debate imply otherwise; a real conflict of values was being revealed. A student of Whig thought has correctly declared: "To constitute oneself a member of the party of Memory was neither mere nostalgia nor disgruntled reaction—it was a political act."[6]

When Whig speakers addressed an issue, they typically did so by tracing its history, often going back to colonial times or the even earlier European background. In order to understand the nature of American nationhood, therefore, they examined the early colonies from which the United States was descended. "What any people can be and ought to be depends, in a principal degree, on what they have been."[7] Such an approach should not brand the Whigs as old-fashioned traditionalists. Actually, it was a sign of cultural awareness or progressivism for them to appeal to history rather than natural rights in their explication of American identity. During the nineteenth century a sense of evolution and a reliance on genetic explanations rode the wave of the intellectual future. The state was discussed more and more as an organism; contractualism and natural rights were ideas that were losing ground until, by the end of the century, they seemed positively antique.[8] The realization that political life is historically conditioned led eventually to the relativism characteristic of the twentieth century.

"Not blindly to worship, but duly to honor the past," was the objective Edward Everett set forth. What did such Whigs as he hope to achieve for American nationalism through a respectful study of the past? In the first place, they felt it could strengthen the tenuous bonds of the American Union. "Reminded of our fathers, we should remember that we are brethren."[9] Of course history could provide "models of moral excellence," as it had been doing for centuries before America was discovered. But history had special relevance for Americans in helping them preserve the fathers' "invaluable institutions" from "the Vandal spirit" of irresponsible agitation. There was more to establishing a viable democracy than a desire to shake off the chains of oppression. American history could show how popular government might avoid the pitfalls of "licentiousness" and achieve stability over time. Prospective European revolutionaries, as well as the Americans themselves, would do well to study it carefully.[10]

Whig leaders affirming the importance of history were not lonely voices crying in a wilderness. A popular awakening of historical consciousness was occurring in America; the Whig party was responding to this and helping to lead it. A number of indicators (including best-selling books, the founding of historical societies, and the composition of school curricula) show that a broad-based interest in history rose dramatically in the decades following the War of 1812 and then fell off again around mid-century.[11]

Rejecting Thomas Paine, Whigs maintained the right and duty of one generation to bind another. In an era when the repudiation of state bonds was often an issue between the parties, this was no merely academic matter. William Henry Seward argued the Whig case eloquently in recommending to the state legislature of New York a system of internal improvements that would benefit (and mortgage) future generations. He and other Whigs sought to imbue Americans with a proper sense of responsibility, both toward previous generations, whose sacrifices had made freedom possible, and toward subsequent generations, who depended on present exertions.[12] "Standing thus, as in the full gaze of our ancestors and our posterity, having received this inheritance from the former, to be transmitted to the latter," a Whig orator could proclaim that "no temporary impulse shall induce me to yield." Perhaps these words of Webster's were "only" rhetoric, but when John Quincy Adams confided to his diary that "the freedom of the human race" was at stake in the annexation of Texas, the sense of responsibility was deeply felt.[13] It goes far to explain the moral determination that historians often seem to find puzzling in Whig politicians.

Whigs prided themselves on their empiricism. They often claimed that the protective tariff enjoyed the sanction of "experience," while free trade was a mere "theory." Likewise, they dismissed the states'-rights principles of John C. Calhoun and the hard-money principles of Andrew Jackson as "theories" ungrounded in practice.[14] But this does not mean that the Whigs were apostles of a mindless "muddling-through"; there was an emphasis on conscious control of people and events in their outlook. Wise public policy dictated the integration of planning with practicality. The word that best captures the combination of planning and practice the Whigs favored is "experiment." The United States itself could be viewed as the grandest experiment of all: "the steamboat of moral and political being," as Adams put it. Like the mechanical inventor, the statesman could make mistakes. But the hope for great achievement was still there, just as there was hope in the technological innovations of the time.[15]

To make a proper use of past experience, Whigs believed it was necessary to recognize that history constituted the gradual unfolding of a pattern. To divine the secret of this pattern would be to possess the key to understanding the destiny of America and all mankind. The pattern that Whig commentators most often discerned, especially in Anglo-American history, was one of gradual improvement in the human condition, of increasing political liberty, increasing power over nature, higher moral standards, a richer quality of life. Behind this pattern they sometimes glimpsed "the finger of God." They called the pattern "progress."[16]

Antecedents of the American Whig view of history may be located in the writings of the Scottish moral philosopher Adam Ferguson. Ferguson broke sharply with the contract theory of society. He considered man a social or political animal who could fulfill his destiny only in an evolutionary "progression" from "rudeness" toward "civilization." The highly ordered and differentiated state of civilization permitted greater development of the various human aptitudes ("faculties"), i.e., greater realization by individuals of their humanity.[17] Ferguson's writings were well known in the United States, though this does not in itself explain why American Whigs found them congenial. The fact is that step-by-step progress toward a more fulfilling social state was a concept they encountered in everyday life. Henry Clay described it in homely language:

On the same farm you may sometimes behold, standing together, the first rude cabin of round and unhewn logs and wooden chimneys; the hewed log house, chinked and shingled, with stone or brick chimneys; and, lastly, the comfortable brick or stone dwelling, each denoting the different occupants of the farm, or the several stages of the condition of the same occupant.

The social theory of Adam Ferguson corresponded with the personal experience of many Americans, especially those living in developing areas, where the Whig party was strongest.[18]

What the Whigs called progress was a pattern of ordered change in which order and change were equally important. A sensitive observer of one group of Whigs explained it this way: "It was their conviction that institutions embodied the moral sense of the race thus far, and that any further progress must be made gradually by the increase and spread of just ideas, not by sudden or violent convulsion."[19] The agents of progress were often the enlightened few rather than the tumultuous many. By their "steadiness of principle, just moderation, and unconquerable perseverance," true progressives strengthened the forces of conscience and reason in society. The outcome of this kind of benevolent social change was greater order, not less. The whole process mirrored an individual's patient struggle for rational self-control and proper self-development.[20]

Sophisticated Whigs did not, of course, imagine that everything that happened constituted progress. Some of the best American Whig historians (Prescott, Ticknor, Motley) wrote on Spain, a country whose history did not embody progress in their sense, and found a fascination in locating where the Spanish had gone wrong. The Spanish served as a negative referent in countless ways: they were cruel to the Indians, persecuted Protestants and Jews, oppressed the Netherlands, failed to industrialize, never rationalized their finances, and did not evolve democratic institutions.[21]

Even republics could fall into evil ways and let their hard-won progress unravel. Aristotle, Polybius, and Cicero, the standard classical writers on politics, had all warned of this. The American Whigs were heirs to a long tradition of developmental political thought, much of it cyclical. Cyclical theorists, of whom the greatest in modern times was Machiavelli, had declared that degeneration, the converse of progress, was just as natural and inevitable. Adam Ferguson himself believed the eventual decline of every nation, if not unavoidable, was at least a strong possibility.[22] Small wonder then if, ever since the establishment of the United States, people had wondered how long it could last. The optimism that Whig faith in progress seems to imply was severely tempered in actuality by the warnings of the cyclical philosophers. The organic metaphor in which Whigs usually discussed politics had compelling implications for the future;

for if "nations are intelligent, moral persons," then they "grow, mature, and decline." Perhaps to stave off the decline was all that one could hope. "There is a law of dissolution to which all the works of man are subject. Even this land, like Italy and the Peloponnesus, like Carthage and Syracuse, must one day own the sway of tyrants. . . . It is ours to do all that in our day and generation may be done, that this catastrophe may be long postponed."[23]

The American Whigs were poised uneasily between two contrasting views of history. The legacy of classical political thought, stretching across continents and centuries, had made use of history (in words attributed to Thucydides) as "philosophy teaching by examples." History was a great storehouse of lessons—for the most part, cautionary tales with grim endings. Such had been the use the authors of *The Federalist* had made of history. By the nineteenth century, however, the idea of long-range improvement in the human condition, of history as progress, was also appealing. How the Whigs balanced these two rival conceptions is a complicated matter. Eventually, as later chapters will relate, evangelical religion tipped the scales in favor of belief in progress. But confidence did not come easily for the Whigs, and their struggle to attain it will be one of the recurring themes in this book.

Whether the historical pattern of progress could be indefinitely extrapolated into the future was the ultimate question confronting the nation's statecraft. Tocqueville concluded his great examination of the American political and social system with a warning that its implications were ambiguous; it could lead "to servitude or freedom, to knowledge or barbarism, to prosperity or wretchedness." The answer might depend upon Americans' willingness to take the lessons of history to heart. Like causes would produce like effects at any point in time; if America repeated the mistakes of the past, the outcome would be a foregone conclusion. "In Greece, in Rome, in Venice, in France, men have called on the Goddess of Liberty," Rufus Choate noted, "but they were not wise enough, they were not virtuous enough, for diffused, steady, lasting freedom."[24] Wisdom and virtue, then, were the crucial elements. Wealth and power could be taken for granted, given the natural advantages of the United States. The real question was whether the country would have intellectual and moral achievements to match its material ones; upon this would depend the duration of the material achievements themselves. Education, to disseminate wisdom, and social mobility, to recruit new virtue and weed out the "enfeebled offspring of a voluptuous parentage," provided two favorite Whig solutions to the problem.[25]

Classical political theorists had long identified two kinds of threats to republics, one economic and the other political. The first took the form of excessive "luxury," which sapped the energies and corrupted the pure morals necessary to republics. The second was the decay of institutional arrangements, leading to anarchy, tyranny, or, what was most likely, both in sequence. Democratic and Whig spokesmen in Jacksonian America, often reading the same political writers, drew different conclusions. Democrats saw the chief threat coming from economic changes and the emergence of a plutocratic elite. Whigs saw a more important threat in the perversion of the political process by demagogues taking advantage of the loss of an independent spirit among the people.[26] The historian Marvin Meyers, who has distinguished Whigs from Jacksonians by labeling the former optimists and calling attention to the misgivings of the latter, is half right. On economic issues his dichotomy works well; but the Whigs had their apprehensions too, as their positions on innumerable political and moral issues make clear.[27]

The most secure safeguard against the kind of degeneration that Whigs feared in a polity was the time-honored device of "mixed government." The objective was to introduce such "balance" into the political system that it could remain poised indefinitely in a state of equilibrium, with further motion (away from the optimal moment) suspended. "Mixed government" in the classical tradition was a balance among monarchy, aristocracy, and democracy; only in the seventeenth century did the doctrine arise of the separation and balance of executive, judicial, and legislative powers. The structure of the United States Constitution froze more elements of Tudor "mixed government" into the American political system than has generally been admitted.[28] When we ourselves speak of "balance" in the American system of government, it is usually in the context of "checks and balances," that is, of opposing forces. The Whigs generally meant something slightly different: the accurate representation of various social interests to create harmonious interaction within the institutions of government. "Balance" for them meant stability, not contention.

What is remarkable about the use of the idea of "balanced" government by the American Whigs is how often they employed it in something like the old sense of "mixed" government. In this they could invoke no less an authority than John Witherspoon, signer of the Declaration of Independence: "Pure democracy cannot subsist long," he told Princeton students in his lectures on moral philosophy; "every good form of government must be complex, so that the one principle may check the other." Within such an outlook, the purpose of government is not to implement popular will but to balance and harmonize interests. The United States Constitution was praised by a Whig writer as "a government distributed, balanced, checked, guarded, and accommodated to the actual state of society." Another (in 1842) identified the Senate as the "aristocratic" and the House of Representatives as the "democratic" element in the mixed polity.[29] A modicum of "hereditary power" could be quite compatible with American Whig ideas of good government as long as there was no "absolute" authority. Indeed, the British Constitution was termed "the finest instrument that any nation has possessed for the regulation and security of every right" in 1832—sixty-six years after independence.[30]

In the broadest sense, of course, "Whiggery" existed on both sides of the Atlantic. The American Whigs often revealed their consciousness of a community with their European counterparts. The European statesmen they admired were moderates like Lafayette, Tocqueville, and the Irishman Daniel O'Connell—reformers who steered "between the dangers of anarchy and the pressures of despotism." They applauded the French Revolution of 1830 while never ceasing to deplore that of 1789. They felt the closest affinity of all with the British who gave them their name. The years between 1832 and 1868 were a time of the classic functioning of the British Constitution on a mixed aristocratic and bourgeois basis. To the American Whigs, the system established by the Reform Bill of 1832 restored the "proper balance" to British institutions. This balance provided a model of progress synthesized with stability.[31]

The most salient characteristic of American Whig political thought was that it remained within the tradition of the "commonwealthmen," that remarkable group of English and Scottish writers whose importance to eighteenth-century American political culture has been emphasized by recent historians.[32] It was their compound of common law, Protestant piety, moral philosophy, and classical learning that constituted the American Whigs' political frame of reference. Two favorite writers in the tradition were James Harrington and Viscount Bolingbroke. Harrington provided a link between the American republic and the short-lived English republic of the Interregnum. He represented a strand of republicanism congenial to American Whigs, for he combined his belief in written constitutions, the separation of powers, and the secret ballot with acceptance of the leadership of a propertied gentry. Adams studied Harrington carefully; Beecher employed his ideas in analyzing the ancient state of

Israel; Daniel Webster took Harrington's *Oceana* as the text for two of
his own most famous speeches.[33] The "country-party" tradition of
political thought that followed Harrington was employed during the
eighteenth century by critics of the government on the "right" as
well as the "left." Bolingbroke, although a Tory, drew on the same
fund of political ideas as the Whig commonwealthmen when he
called for a restoration of England's historic "mixed constitution."[34]
Bolingbroke's felicitous expression made him a favorite exponent of
these ideas among the American Whigs. As late as the presidential
campaign of 1844, Seward could rouse a Whig mass meeting by invoking Lord Bolingbroke's authority on the need "to regenerate the
first principles of the constitution."[35]

That the Whigs, who advocated industrialization and economic
development, should have identified with a political heritage called
"country" may seem at first anomalous. Actually, however, the word
"country" was understood more in opposition to "court" than in opposition to "city." Within the English "country party" not only
landed gentlemen but also bourgeois Protestant Dissenters were
prominent; most of the writers we call commonwealthmen fit the
latter description. As a group that included both townsmen and
commercial farmers, and as inheritors of the religious tradition of
English Dissent, the Whigs found the country-party tradition congenial.

Behind the English country party lay the older political traditions
to which it was in turn indebted. One of these, we have been reminded, was the Florentine Renaissance. What Choate called the
"doctrine of liberty" contained in Machiavelli's *Discorsi* was known
and acknowledged among the more learned of American Whigs.[36]
Ultimately, of course, one reached back to the writers of classical antiquity, whose influence continued in America as long as higher
education was predicated on knowledge of classical texts. Cicero was
the most familiar, and leading Whigs were proud to call him master,
among them the great jurist, Joseph Story.[37] The pervasive vocabulary of Whig-Democratic debate—virtue, balance, luxury, degeneration, restoration—reveals the continued influence of long-familiar
patterns of classical and Renaissance political thought. That Whigs
and Democrats were both using this language helps explain why
their debate was so bitter; if they had not had such terms in common,
they might not have understood each other's accusations so well. The
Whigs, more committed to a hierarchical social structure and to using
the wisdom of the past, were probably more under the influence of
this heritage of civic humanism than the Democrats, though it is a

hazardous comparison to make until there has been more study of the Jacksonians along these lines.[38] In any case, it appears that the "end of the classical conception of politics," which at least one historian has dated at the ratification of the Constitution, actually took quite a bit longer in coming.[39]

Classical thought influenced the content of Whig-Jacksonian political discourse as well as the manner of its presentation. A clear example of this is the Whigs' oft-repeated warning against the "Caesarism" of Andrew Jackson. Remarkably, Jackson and his supporters sometimes accepted the comparison with Caesar instead of disowning it.[40] Caesarism, however, was but a special case of the general danger of corruption to republican institutions. The fear of various kinds of conspiracies against the commonweal was both pervasive and genuine among Americans during this period. Historians have devoted considerable attention to such recurrent fears in various contexts and have often used the word "paranoid" to describe them.[41] The trouble with this characterization is that it borrows a term from psychopathology to describe a cultural phenomenon that was neither deviant nor pathological for the most part. George Washington, who warned of a conspiracy to deprive the colonists of their rights, and Abraham Lincoln, who warned of a conspiracy to nationalize slavery, were not isolated cranks but responsible leaders in tune with their people. Instead of thinking of the conspiratorial interpretation of events as a mental disease, it makes better sense to treat it as a paradigm, that is, as a conceptual framework which defines problems and points to their potential solutions.[42] The fear of conspiracy, as known in America, had a respectable ancestry. It was the final elaboration of the concept of corruption and declension in a republic that had first taken shape in classical antiquity and had been transmitted to the Americans by the commonwealthmen.

Other factors besides familiarity with the traditions of civic humanism encouraged the widespread use of the conspiracy paradigm in Whig-Jacksonian America. The conspiracy paradigm arranged events into patterns and attributed the pattern to the design of a moral agent or agents. Precisely this mode of thought had long been encouraged by Christian theology as one of the means by which the existence of God could be demonstrated: natural phenomena were observed and arranged into laws, and these laws were interpreted as illustrating the providence of the Creator. So Lyman Beecher could point to the multiplication of Catholic educational institutions in the 1830s and caution his Protestant hearers: "If such complicated indications of design may exist without design, as well may the broader mechanisms of the world be regarded as the off-spring of chance." Perhaps the attribution of cause to moral agency rather than to impersonal forces was also fostered by the oral medium of politics, which (it has been argued) tends to personalize issues and encourage polemics.[43]

The internal logic of the conspiracy paradigm was compelling, given certain assumptions widely shared by both Democrats and Whigs in the middle period. Since American institutions were fundamentally good, the explanation for perceived dangers must be moral rather than structural. Since the American people were also fundamentally virtuous, the moral evils must be those of a designing minority rather than endemic in the general population. The appropriate defense against whatever danger was perceived—whether it came from the "monster" Bank and its minions or from Masons, Mormons, or slavery expansionists—was generally thought to be an appeal to public opinion, aimed at revitalizing American institutions.[44] Analyzed in this way, the conspiracy paradigm seems less paranoid, for it reveals trust as well as fear. The most common political paradigm in America today, that of competing amoral interest groups, certainly offers less hope that moral suasion can regenerate the body politic.

When Richard Hofstadter wrote that the paranoid style (i.e., the conspiracy paradigm) "has a greater affinity for bad causes than good," he seems to have been mistaken.[45] At least in American history, the good causes making use of the paradigm have been more important than the bad; the achievement of independence and the antislavery movement are of greater significance than the John Birch Society and other such organizations. Hofstadter also slipped into the genetic fallacy: to know the state of mind of a proposition's advocates, or even their motives, is not to validate or invalidate the proposition. On the other hand, if we speak of a conspiracy paradigm, we will realize that paradigms can have heuristic merit. One factor that certainly helps explain why both sides in the Whig-Jacksonian debate made use of the conspiracy paradigm is the relative accuracy with which it represented the facts. The Democrats believed that Nicholas Biddle and Henry Clay were conspiring to turn their hero out of office by manipulating the nation's finances; the Whigs believed that Andrew Jackson was conspiring to enhance the power of the presidency. Both, as it happens, were right.

The word "conspiracy" puts us off, but we must overcome this reaction if we are to take American political discourse during the early and middle periods of our history with the seriousness it de-

serves. Like many words, "conspiracy" once had a broader definition than it has since acquired; it could be used to mean any "union
or combination (of persons or things) for one end or purpose." In this
sense, society itself was spoken of as a "conspiracy in virtue."[46] But
most lesser political conspiracies, including political parties, were
frowned upon. A careful student of conspiracy ideas in Jeffersonian
America has noticed that "anything which caused a man to seek
some lesser goal—money, power, love of section—at the expense of
his allegiance to the Constitution" might be called a conspiracy.[47] In
the Whig-Jacksonian period, the assertion of a slave-power conspiracy could mean simply that the political influence of slaveholders,
pursuing slaveholders' interests narrowly conceived, was perverting
America's free institutions. Joshua Giddings had something like this
in mind when he predicted that the Polk administration would wage
aggressive war on Mexico for Texas and would compromise with
Britain over Oregon. When the events befell, he pointed out the predictive power of his conspiracy paradigm.[48] Such a concept of conspiracy might resemble our own concept of an "interest group,"
except for the fact that it was conceived in personal and moral terms.
As long as the competition of interest groups was not accepted as legitimate, conspiracies would be presumed a danger to the general welfare; they were very much like the "factions" against which the
Federalist Papers had warned.[49] While the classical model of a balanced republic persisted, the conspiracy paradigm was bound to
continue, as its logical corollary, to describe threats to that ideal. The
paradigm seems paranoid only to those who have imperfectly mastered the language of politics in pre–Civil War America.[50]

There are remarkably few references to John Locke in the writings
of the American Whigs. Still, it would be a mistake to conclude that
Locke had no influence on their thinking about history and politics.
When one examines what Whigs said about the origin of government, one finds a fascinating synthesis of Lockean contractualism
with organic developmentalism. The dichotomy set up by Horace
Bushnell, as he looked back after that first defeat at Bull Run, turns
out, on close inspection, to have been a bit too facile. Of the two
strands, however, the organicist is predominant in Whig political
thought; no more is conceded to contractualism than the facts of the
American case necessitate.

A number of Whig accounts of the origins of government reveal
the same features. A sharp distinction is drawn between constituent
power and political power, and the contractual model is strictly confined to the former. At a certain moment in history, popular

sovereignty—or, more precisely, the sovereignty of society—is called into existence. It exists just long enough to consent to a fundamental law, by which it binds itself forever after. As soon as this constituent act has occurred, sovereignty disappears. So far, this is all in accord with Locke. But the fundamental law does not arise *ex nihilo* for American Whigs, at least not if it is to be workable. It must embody the previous history of the people for whom it is intended. "Nor are all times or all occasions suited to such great operations. It is only under the most favorable circumstances, and only when great men are called on to meet great exigencies, only once in centuries," that the right constituent moment occurs. The Democrats, by contrast, treated popular sovereignty as a continuing force within politics and regarded their hero, Jackson, as embodying it. For this reason a Whig accused the Democrats of "indulg[ing] men in a perpetual revolution, cutting off the past from the present, and the present from the future, . . . deriving their authority from acclamation."[51]

Behind every government there was a society, and to this society government owed its existence. In Whig doctrine, it is society that is sovereign—not the people as an undifferentiated mass, but the people organized, with their families and property, their various abilities, training, and social roles, their language, customs, and traditions. Society is natural, indeed essential, to man; human nature could not develop, particularly in moral and intellectual dimensions, without it. One does not *choose* either society in general or the particular society into which one is born; it is simply given.[52] Every people needs a fundamental law of its own, to suit its own distinctive society and culture. "The conclusion to be drawn is, not that the Constitution of the United States is, in the abstract, the most perfect system of government conceivable for all countries, but that it is admirably suited to the precise purpose in America for which it was created." The experience of the Latin American countries confirmed it: their attempts to copy the U.S. Constitution had been unsuccessful (said Webster) because their social structure and traditions were different.[53]

Both society and government had their constitutions, that of society being necessarily unwritten, that of government either unwritten or written. Locke had spoken of two compacts, one establishing society, including the family, and a second, establishing government.[54] American Whigs sometimes followed him in this usage, even though insisting that the former "compact" was based on human nature and tradition rather than conscious choice. John Quincy Adams showed how an American Whig could explain the two compacts in 1842.

Going back to the seventeenth century, he scrupulously defended
Locke and Sydney against Filmer and Hobbes. Society, he said,
exists prior to government and has the right to establish it; but he
undertook to explain at length that the consent of society needed to
institute a valid government is not simply the present consent of all
persons. It is part of the constitution of society that a majority should
be able to bind a minority and that one generation can commit its
posterity. Since society was in existence before government, the parties to the second compact are really families rather than individuals.
Adams proved from Scripture that families must consent as units and
that the husband-father is their legitimate spokesman. Property, resi-
dency, religious, or other voting tests might or might not be expedient. The whole people are bound "by that portion of them capable
[through nature and custom] of contracting for the whole." The constitution of government should reflect the constitution of society; this
is what "balanced" government achieves. Adams insisted that the
United States had a "mixed" polity: "It is not Democracy—nor Aristocracy, nor monarchy, but a compound of them all." The audience
took this speech as a condemnation of the recent Dorr Rebellion (it
was delivered in Providence, Rhode Island); Adams said he had
written it two years before and that its applicability was fortuitous.[55]

It is well known that the Whigs maintained that the national government was created by the people of the country as a whole and not
by the individual states.[56] It is not so well understood just how they
conceptualized this. In the first place, by the "people" they meant
organized society, working through "natural leaders." Next, the
Whigs were claiming that there had not been thirteen separate social
and economic systems, thirteen different cultural identities, but a
common American one in 1787. Twentieth-century scholarship lends
considerable substantiation to the view that the Constitution was the
work of the nationwide "people" in the Whig sense (i.e., an articulate leadership group) and not that of the states.[57] Yet in many respects it was undeniable that the states were autonomous; they had
elected delegates to the Constitutional Convention and had ratified
its work individually. How then could one avoid the conclusion that
the central government was their creature? The concept of "mixed
government" provided a handy solution. Just as the ideal classical
polity was neither monarchical, aristocratic, nor democratic, so the
government of the United States was "neither wholly federal nor
wholly consolidated" but "of a mixed nature."[58] The sovereign
people had created a complex structure of two concomitant layers of
government, each with its own jurisdiction, to balance each other.

Since sovereignty was located in society, it would follow logically that it must not be located in government. And in fact one does find Whigs denying repeatedly that sovereignty can properly be found anywhere within the structure of American government. It is always difficult if not impossible to reconcile the idea of fundamental law with the idea of sovereign power in government. Chief Justice Coke had made the point: "Magna carta is such a fellow, that he will have no sovereign."[59] Of course, the Whigs denied that the states were sovereignties. Moreover, they were usually suspicious of sovereignty wherever they encountered it and felt more comfortable with fundamental law. For example, even the sovereign society could be considered limited by the divine principles of morality, which stood in somewhat the same relation to society as fundamental law did to government.[60]

To say that government owes its origin to some kind of act of consent is not to say that continuing consent is necessary for its legitimacy. In 1826 the youthful Edward Everett asserted that a presumed ancient consent could not legitimate a government in defiance of current public opinion.[61] After the birth of the Whig party, however, its spokesmen were much more likely to claim a prescriptive right for existing institutions of government. The nullification crisis proved a transforming experience. Webster's resistance to the rule-or-ruin statecraft of the nullifiers will always remain his finest hour. There is no "middle course between submission to the laws, when regularly pronounced constitutional, on the one hand, and open resistance, which is revolution or rebellion, on the other," he declared in his debate with Hayne. If the South Carolinians were to resist the law, they would have to invoke a right of revolution, because there were no constitutional grounds for either nullification or secession. The crux of Webster's argument was this: "The Constitution, Sir, is not a contract, but the result of a contract"—that is, it did not depend upon assent being continually renewed. "The people have agreed to make a Constitution; but when made, that Constitution becomes what its name imports. It is no longer a mere agreement." This made the existence of government rather than its origin the question.[62] In later years Seward inherited Webster's mantle as the defender of the prescriptive rights of the federal government. The Union does not exist by mere "voluntary consent," he insisted; it is "the creature of necessities, physical, moral, social, and political." In the greatest speech of his career, in which he alluded to the divine and moral law as "a higher law than the Constitution," Seward also declared: "The Union, then, IS [his capitals], not because merely that men choose that it shall be, but because some government must exist here, and no other government than this can."[63]

The Dorr Rebellion in Rhode Island provoked much heated debate over fundamental questions of political philosophy. The state entered the 1840s still operating under its colonial charter of 1663, a basic law long since antiquated. A patrician Whig named Thomas W. Dorr, having led a movement for constitutional reform that had failed, turned to more radical measures. As the nature of his cause changed, Dorr's affiliation and power base switched from Whig to Democratic. He found that many Rhode Islanders were willing to appeal from their existing institutions to the sovereignty of the people (what the eighteenth century had called "the people out of doors"). His followers set up a rival government in 1842 with claims to the support of a majority of adult white males. It was quickly crushed by the established authorities, and Dorr himself was sentenced to prison.[64] While many Democrats all over the country expressed sympathy for the Dorrites, Whigs were unanimous in deploring the uprising. Henry Clay, in one of his most important addresses, declared that the Dorr Rebellion was the climax of a long pattern of usurpations by Democrats, endangering "the permanency and stability of our institutions," that included the expunging resolution in the Senate, repudiation of state bonds, cheating in elections, and, of course, nullification. Even Horace Greeley, the most progressive voice in the Whig party, denounced the Dorrites in language reminiscent of Burke's on the French Revolution.[65]

Out of the Dorr Rebellion came one of the landmark cases in American constitutional law, *Luther v. Borden*. Benjamin F. Hallett, a prominent Democrat, appeared for the appellants; Daniel Webster argued the case for the charter government. "We are not to take the will of the people from public meetings, nor from tumultuous assemblies," Webster declared. "What is this but anarchy?" The sovereignty of society could be expressed only through the modes known to law, unless government were to "abdicate" its authority as James II had done. (Here Webster slipped unwittingly into the Tory rather than the English Whig theory of the Glorious Revolution.) Even the Revolution of 1776 had been "marked by a peculiar conservatism."[66] By the time the case reached the U.S. Supreme Court, Rhode Island conservatives had accepted a measure of constitutional reform (they included black suffrage, to spite the Dorrites, who had not wanted it); the cause of Dorr's shadow government as a practical matter was lost. Chief Justice Taney avoided having to sanction Webster's political philosophy by ruling on narrow grounds: the federal executive and the Rhode Island state courts having already chosen to regard the charter government as the authentic one, the Supreme Court was in no position to challenge their determination.[67] This meant that the judiciary would not recognize the right of revolution unless the revolution were to succeed. The sovereignty of the people had been shoved, where the Whigs wanted it, farther into the background of American political life. The struggle over popular sovereignty was not over; in the next decade Stephen Douglas would revive its claims to a place in the interstices of institutional authority with his famous Freeport Doctrine. But the outcome of the Dorr Rebellion can be seen as one step in that strengthening of institutionalism that has been a long-term tendency of American history in the nineteenth and twentieth centuries.

The direction in which Whig political thought was moving is indicated in a philosophical address given in 1846 by a former congressman named Daniel D. Barnard, a follower of Millard Fillmore. Barnard began with Aristotle's description of man as by nature a political animal and then synthesized this classical conception with nineteenth-century historicism. For Barnard, what Aristotle called the *"polis"* was what the nineteenth century called the "state." And, by the "state," Barnard meant society, not government. The state is a moral entity, a "moral person," embodying what we might call a collective value system. (The denial of the moral identity of the state Barnard called "political materialism.") The state can exist through changes in government; it can even survive geographic relocation.

> The State in this country, familiar as we may think ourselves with its origin, has a history which reaches far enough behind that of the first colonization of the country, running back into the opposite continent, and finding in the Norman, the Dane, the Saxon, the Roman, the old Briton, the links of a chain terminating only, if it were faithfully traced up, with the first age and the first family of mankind.

The family (he specified the "patriarchal" family) is the ultimate origin of the state.[68] Barnard may well have been reading *The Manual of Political Ethics* by Francis Lieber, a German political scientist forced to flee Prussia and come to the United States. Lieber distinguished society from government and described the former as natural and organic. An admirer of English constitutionalism, he infused the political tradition already familiar to American Whigs with German historicism. A suggestion of his influence may be found in the fact that Barnard, like Lieber, called society "the state." Lieber believed in virtual representation and mixed government, though he used a different terminology. (He translated "mixed government" into Greek and came up with "hamarchy.") The views that had made Lieber dangerously liberal in Prussia placed him in a conservative position in the United States. He was bitterly attacked by the radical Democrat Orestes Brownson in the *Boston Quarterly Review*.[69]

But we must not get ahead of the story. German ideas did not have their main impact in the United States until after the demise of the Whig party; the staple of Whig political culture remained the Anglo-American "country-party" tradition. Everything in the logic of their situation conspired to make this so. For most of their history the Whigs were in opposition to the occupant of the White House; it seems inevitable that they should make use of this great tradition of opposition rhetoric. A "court-party" ideology of interest groups also existed; it might have been employed to defend the Second Bank of the United States the way Alexander Hamilton earlier had used something like it to defend his financial program.[70] But the strain of Protestant moralism was too strong in the culture of the Whig constituency to sanction this. The country-party tradition was just right: it sanctified property rights while viewing the world through the eyes of English Protestantism. This is not to say that the country-party political heritage supplied the *motives* of the Whigs; it supplied their way of dealing with their situation, their vocabulary, the patterns into which they placed events. It even seemed natural to the Whigs to use country-party rhetoric to disparage popular sovereignty. "What the sycophant, the courtier is to the Sovereign Prince, the demagogue is to the Sovereign People. The maxim that 'The King can do no wrong' is as mischievous in a free state as in any other."[71]

Of the components of mixed government, the one that historically had most often threatened the others was monarchy or the executive. The usurpation of power by the executive was such a common cause of the recurring cycle of republican degeneration that it had to be forestalled if at all possible. Andrew Jackson's military past and reputation as a strong-willed leader impatient of restraint did nothing to reassure Whigs on this score. The analogies to Napoleon and Cromwell, who had betrayed their respective revolutions, were still strong in people's minds. Back in 1818, when Jackson's unauthorized invasion of Florida was being debated in Congress, Henry Clay had warned:

Beware how you give a fatal sanction, in this infant period of our republic, scarcely yet two-score years old, to military insubordination. Remember that Greece had her Alexander, Rome her Caesar,

England her Cromwell, France her Bonaparte, and that if we would escape the rock on which they split, we must avoid their errors.

When Jackson became president, his avowedly partisan distribution of the "spoils" of office, his confrontation with the Supreme Court over Cherokee rights, his unprecedented use of the veto (and pocket veto), and, finally, the "Bank War," all combined to revive these fears. By the end of 1833 Clay was charging that "we are in the midst of a revolution, hitherto bloodless, but rapidly tending toward a total change of the pure republican character of the government."[72] The circumstances of the controversy surrounding the removal of government deposits from the Bank were such that resistance to Jackson came from the cabinet (where two Treasury secretaries lost their jobs for not obeying orders) and the Senate (which, for the only time in history, voted censure of a president). From these origins arose the Whig party's durable policy of defending the independent power of the cabinet and Congress vis-à-vis the president.

What could be more natural, then, that in early 1834 Clay and his followers should adopt the name Whig?[73] (They tried simultaneously to stigmatize their rivals as Tories, but that label could not be made to stick.) The term "Whig" was still a living symbol, rich in its associations; in that same year the English Whig party for the last time confronted a constitutional crisis with a reigning monarch when William IV dismissed his cabinet. The whole range of "country-party" iconography and vocabulary lay open to Clay and his supporters: the warrior Jackson was cartooned as the wicked Richard III, the patronage-dispenser Jackson was attacked in the Whig press as a corrupt Sir Robert Walpole. After Van Buren succeeded Jackson, Clay commented: "We have had Charles the First and now we have Charles the Second." The expunging resolution of 1837, he warned, would revive the Stuart doctrines of "passive obedience and non-resistance."[74] That audiences apparently did not find such allusions obscure must say something about the state of historical consciousness in the United States at the time. The explanation probably has to do with the constituency of the Whigs, and not simply in terms of their socioeconomic class or educational level. Since they were a party predominantly composed of British-Americans (both Yankees and more recent Protestant immigrants from the British Isles), it is not surprising that the Whigs should view American history as an extension of English history and invoke examples from the English past. Well might John Pendleton Kennedy of Maryland proclaim: "When we say we are WHIGS, we refer to a whole volume of past history for the identification and description of our faith."[75]

A peculiarly sensitive aspect of English history was seventeenth-century Puritanism. The nature of Puritanism and its relation to modern America were sometimes the subject of debate between Democrats and Whigs. When William Cullen Bryant's Democratic *New York Review* declared that "our civil and religious liberty exist, not in consequence, but in spite of the spirit and genius of Puritanism," the Whig *North American Review* responded with a defense of Puritan courage, self-discipline, and resistance to tyranny.[76] During this period New England Societies were being formed in many parts of the United States by migrating people of Yankee extraction wanting to preserve their identity in a new home. The societies made the Pilgrim Fathers objects of a self-conscious cult and observed the anniversary of their landing every December 22. Though they admitted anyone of New England birth, they were dominated by prosperous businessmen.[77] The Whig party, like the New England Societies, was helping keep alive the Puritan tradition. All this seems broadly congruent with Lee Benson's description of Whigs as neopuritans and Democrats as nonpuritans in religion and values; however, there were many complexities within Whig attitudes. Cromwell, for example, was a highly ambivalent figure, praised for leading the Puritan revolution and condemned as a military tyrant. Later, when antislavery became more militant, the positive aspect of Cromwell was emphasized; in 1855 Seward called for a new Republican party "like that army which Cromwell led, that established the commonwealth of England."[78]

Arthur M. Schlesinger, Jr., correctly perceived that the American Whig fear of the presidency contained within it a fear of democracy. The dangers to mixed polity "from the monarchy or the military despotism, on the one side, and from licentiousness and anarchy on the other" had long been recognized. But Jackson, as a popular hero, typified both these dangers at once. He successfully appealed to the voters directly, over the heads of those who considered themselves the natural leaders.[79] Such charisma threatened the social order. Ralph Waldo Emerson, though he avoided active involvement in politics, confided this Whiggish observation to his journal: "The Best [sic] are never demoniacal or magnetic but all brutes are. The Democratic party in this country is more magnetic than the Whig. Andrew Jackson is an eminent example of it." Daniel Webster, noting the conduct of Jackson, Van Buren, and Tyler, observed that the executive power had "a strong tendency to make [the incumbent] consider himself, in some vague sense, the representative of the American people, clothed with a certain undefined authority, as if he were above the Constitution." Charles Francis Adams warned that the concentration of popular attention on the occupant of the White House could have but one consequence in the long run: "pure democracy."[80]

Yet opposition to an overmighty executive was not confined to an embittered, displaced elite. It was the most common Whig appeal to the electorate, and it proved effective enough to win a big victory in 1840. The Whig campaign of that year hammered away at the theme of executive encroachments. Harrison promised to set a good example of restraint: to exercise the veto sparingly, to poll his cabinet on decisions, to put a stop to the worst abuses of the spoils system, and not to run for reelection. He even promised to defer to the wishes of Congress on the Bank issue (a safe enough commitment if a Harrison victory elected a Whig Congress on his coattails—as it did).[81] One reason historians have disparaged the alleged lack of issues in the 1840 campaign is that they have refused to take opposition to the executive seriously as an issue. They have seen only the self-interest of the "outs" and have been oblivious to the cultural power of the country-party tradition that "outs" had been exploiting for hundreds of years. If some Whig politicians exploited it opportunistically, they were doing no more than many observers have suspected Bolingbroke of doing in the eighteenth century. In any case, like Bolingbroke, they recognized the strength of the tradition and contributed to it. But Whig opposition to a strong executive extended beyond tactical opposition to Democratic incumbents. During the 1840s Whigs consistently opposed granting strong powers to the executive in the state constitutional conventions of the Old Northwest.[82]

We are often told that the Whigs, in favoring a weak executive, were reversing the earlier conservative position in America; such a reversal appears, however, only if one assumes the Whigs to have been a continuation of the Federalists.[83] Viewing the Whigs within a country-party tradition puts the matter in a different light. Both Whigs and Democrats claimed to be heirs of the Republican party of Jefferson though both in fact contained some former Federalists. Ex-Federalists like Daniel Webster became willing to cite Jefferson as an opponent of executive power once they had identified themselves as Whigs.[84] The closest ideological predecessors of the Whigs seem to have been not the Federalists but the "moderate" or "nationalistic" wing of the Republicans. This group combined, as the Whigs did later, a country-party respect for constitutional balance, legal tradition, and executive restraint with belief in federally sponsored economic development and government "for" rather than "by" the people.[85] The archetypal representative of this brand of Republicanism, and the patron saint of Whiggery, was James Madison. It is well known (or it should be) that Jefferson disapproved of Jackson's candidacy in 1824; it is even more significant that Madison and Gallatin, who were still alive in 1832, when the issues of the Jacksonian era had been clearly drawn, supported Clay for president that year.

On March 3, 1841, William Henry Harrison repeated all of his campaign pledges in an elaborate inaugural address, full of classical allusions, that he had written himself but permitted Webster to edit. He coupled his promises of executive restraint with admonitions to the people. They should remember that they had limited their sovereignty by fundamental law. They should not allow themselves to be misled by "designing men," who would play upon their "passions" and pretend to protect them from aristocracy. Actually, Harrison assured his audience, history proved there was no danger that a constitutional republic would degenerate into an aristocracy; "the tendency of all such governments in their decline is to monarchy."[86] It was a day of bitter cold, and the speech went on much longer than most inaugural addresses. Perhaps the new president wanted to lay to rest any doubts that the "log cabin and hard cider" slogans might have created about his background and to display his classical education. But the proud old man had refused to wear an overcoat for the occasion. He caught the fatal chill that led to pneumonia. William Henry Harrison's dedication to the classical republican tradition and to the image of the heroic orator cost him his life.

The bitter confrontation that ensued between Harrison's successor, Tyler, and the congressional Whigs, led by Clay, confirmed all the Whigs' resentments of presidential power. Lacking a two-thirds majority in both houses, they could neither override Tyler's vetoes nor amend the Constitution, as they threatened, to permit veto-overriding by a simple majority. Robbed of the fruits of their triumph, some Whigs fell to envying the British Constitution, which allowed the legislative body to vote an executive out of office. Even more than under Jackson, the cabinet resisted the president's will. The dramatic coordinated resignation of all Tyler's cabinet save Webster reflected something of the British example of collective responsibility. Tyler counterattacked through his patronage powers, seeking to build up a following of his own; these officeholders went through the motions of a convention to renominate him in 1844 but failed to attract a significant constituency. Such behavior could only remind the Whigs of the shameful machinations of a "court party." Tyler was also carrying on other, more momentous, machinations, which have been recorded by the most meticulous of American historians, Frederick Merk. These achieved their purpose in the annexation of Texas through the flagrantly unconstitutional device of a joint resolution of Congress after Whig opposition had prevented Senate consent to a treaty.[87]

Eighteen forty-four was a vintage year for Whig campaign pronouncements as the party rallied round its grand old leader, Clay. "The Hampdens, the Sidneys, the Vanes, and Miltons" were invoked with vigor. Calvin Colton produced a series of Whig position papers called "the Junius tracts" after a set of anonymous English commonwealthman letters that had enjoyed a wide circulation in the colonies during the 1760s.[88] The Marylander John Pendleton Kennedy (noted for his plantation novel *The Swallow Barn*) wrote a spirited defense of the congressional Whigs' opposition to Tyler. In it, Tyler, surrounded by "obsequious flatterers" and working to circumvent the Constitution, is likened to the Stuart monarchs. Kennedy's pamphlet offers what may be the most lucid summary of the relevance of the country-party tradition to the American Whigs.[89] Different Whigs had different motives for opposing the annexation of Texas (hostility to the extension of slavery and fear of disturbing the sectional balance were prominent), but they agreed in seeing Tyler's conduct as subversion from above. Joshua Giddings of Ohio called it "treason against the Constitution—and treason against humanity itself."[90]

The Whig defeat in 1844 entailed consequences of imponderable magnitude, leading as it did to war with Mexico and exacerbated sectional antagonism. War was traditionally an evil in country-party ideology, dreaded not only for its cost in blood and money but because it provided an occasion for executive aggrandizement. President Polk's devious and provocative conduct, both before and after the beginning of hostilities, provided plenty of confirmation for such fears.[91] Though Polk's own margin over Clay had not been great, he brought in a Senate that was Democratic by 30 to 24 and a massively Democratic House of Representatives—144 to 77. These majorities pushed through the declaration of war he requested with a minimum of debate. (Exasperated by Polk's blockade of the Rio Grande, Mexico had declared war on the United States several days before, but no one in Washington knew this.) The Whig caucus in the House, fearful of being denounced as unpatriotic, decided not to oppose the declaration they were powerless to stop. Fourteen Whig members voted against the war anyhow; they all came from safe districts and had little cause to worry about Democratic challenges. Perhaps the Whig congressmen were too timid, as politicians often are. Public opposition to the war turned out to be substantial and increased as Polk's partisan conduct of it—displayed in his jealousy of Whig generals and his use of the Army as a giant patronage machine—became apparent. Though antiwar sentiments were strongest in the North, the South was not without its own vocal critics of the conflict.[92] The midterm elections of 1846 severely rebuked the president's party, but, under the ponderous Constitution of that era, the new Congress did not meet until December, 1847, by which time the main campaigns of the war had been fought.

The extent of Whig congressional opposition to the Mexican War has been amply demonstrated by historians who have examined votes in addition to the declaration itself.[93] The "spot resolutions" introduced by Representative Abraham Lincoln, questioning the defensive nature of the war, reflected common Whig opinion. Most Whig congressmen felt that patriotism required them to support military appropriations once the U.S. Army was actually engaged, but they began to try to end the war as quickly as possible: John J. Crittenden of Kentucky proposed sending peace commissioners within a month of the outbreak of hostilities. They also hoped to avoid the acquisition of territory by conquest. Representative Alexander H. Stephens of Georgia expressed the Whigs' feelings well. Stephens was no "enemy to the extension of our domain," he explained, but American expansion should be accomplished peacefully, the way Webster had recently settled the boundary between Maine and New Brunswick. To transform ourselves into a warlike, imperial power would undermine our republican character. Expansion through war constituted a grotesque perversion of the Whig ideal of progress; *"downward progress,"* Stephens called it. "It is a progress of party—of excitement—of lust for power—a spirit of war—aggression—violence and licentiousness. It is a progress which, if indulged in, would soon sweep over all law, all order, and the Constitution itself. It is the progress of the French Revolution."[94]

Even more outspoken was Senator Thomas Corwin of Ohio, one of the few Whig congressmen to oppose war appropriations, though he was not otherwise radical. In a ringing speech he described the president as a "monarch" with a "court," his military-appropriations bills as contrary to the spirit of the Settlement of 1688, and his justifications for war as a "feculent mass of misrepresentation."* The war seemed to portend a degeneration, not only of our mixed form of

*The adjective "feculent" is derived from the noun "feces."

government, but of American society and values. "The desire to augment our territory has depraved our moral sense," Corwin warned the Senate. "If I were a Mexican, I would tell you, 'Have you not room in your own country to bury your dead men? If you come into mine we will greet you with bloody hands and welcome you to hospitable graves.'"⁹⁵ That a respected party moderate like Corwin would use such language indicates the chasm that separated the administration from its critics.

Leadership in the Whig opposition to war outside of Congress came from the same Daniel D. Barnard who was also a prominent organic social theorist. In a series of forceful articles in the *American Review* he condemned the aggression against a "sister republic" as "emphatically an Executive War," brought about by "the most flagrant and alarming Executive usurpations." Barnard interspersed his country-party rhetoric with the vocabulary of evangelical Protestantism: "a civilized and Christian people engaged in an unnecessary war in the middle of the nineteenth century is a spectacle of backsliding and crime over which angels may weep." But his articles contain analysis as well as denunciation. Barnard's account of Polk's conduct is informed throughout by his knowledge of constitutional law and political theory; he sees the dangerous precedents being created by Polk's use of his powers as commander-in-chief to order the Army into an area disputed between Texas and Mexico even before the annexation of Texas had been consummated and to provide himself with an independent revenue by levying taxes in the occupied areas of Mexico.⁹⁶ The rest of the Whig press opposed the war with near unanimity and occasional insight. When the population of New Mexico rose in rebellion against the United States army of occupation in early 1847, the *New York Tribune* pointed out the hypocrisy of resubjugating them in the name of popular sovereignty. There were a few calls for the impeachment of President Polk, but there was never any actual chance of this.⁹⁷

Despite the vigor with which many Whigs opposed the war, there remained much confusion among them about the party's proper course. The role of a political opposition in wartime is always tricky, and the fate of the Federalist party after the War of 1812 did not set an encouraging example. Apart from prudential considerations, there was a genuine conflict of loyalties. Actually, few Whigs could help but rejoice in American victories, especially when these were won by Whig generals like Taylor and Scott. While they might explain that "We toast the *men*, but not the cause," in practice this was a difficult distinction to draw.⁹⁸

Yet, all in all, the Whigs provided opposition at least as effective as that raised by any party in the course of an American war. This is the more remarkable in view of the fact that in the Mexican War (unlike the war in Vietnam or the War of 1812) American arms were uniformly successful; successful enterprises are much more difficult to oppose than unsuccessful ones. When the Thirtieth Congress at last assembled, the slender Whig majority in the House of Representatives passed a resolution—on a strict party vote—that "the war with Mexico was begun unconstitutionally and unnecessarily by the executive government of the United States." Polk concluded that he could no longer count on congressional support for his war; the next month he reluctantly accepted a peace that had been negotiated in defiance of his orders. Senate Whigs were unhappy at the territorial acquisitions provided by this treaty, but they lost on a vote to delete them. Eventually a majority of Whigs consented to ratification for fear that prolonging the war would encourage superimperialist Democrats like Sam Houston and Jefferson Davis, who were demanding even more of Mexico. The Whig mood was well captured by the *National Intelligencer*: it is "a Peace which everyone will be glad of, but no one will be proud of."[99]

In February, 1848, a Whig journal published a brief piece entitled "The New Machiavel." It warned of the dangers to internal liberty in a country that allowed its executive to deceive it into waging so-called "little" wars.[100] By the twentieth century the country-party tradition in political thought had been forgotten. The English constitutional struggles with the Stuarts and the teachings of classical or early modern authors no longer constituted, as they had for the Whigs, resources for helping to recognize threatening contemporary political trends. By coincidence (or not), American historians were rediscovering the country-party tradition at about the same time that the nation as a whole was rediscovering the dangers of presidential usurpations and executive wars.

Five

The Entrepreneurial Ethos

In or about the year 1843, a sensitive observer set down this description of a "New England Capitalist":

What are his machines
Of steel, brass, leather, oak, & ivory,
But manikins & miniatures,
Dwarfs of one faculty, measured from him,
As nimbly he applies his bending self
Unto the changing world, thus making that
Another weapon of his conquering will?
He built his mills, &, by his politics, made
The arms of millions turn them.
Stalwart New Hampshire, mother of men,
Sea-dented Maine, reluctant Carolina,
Must drag his coach, & by the arts of peace
He, in the plenitude of love & honor,
Eats up the poor,—poor citizen poor state.
                    Much has he done.
Has made his telegraph,
Propeller, car, post office, phototype,
His coast-survey, vote by majority,
His life assurance, & star registry,
Preludes & hints of what he ventures next;
Now let him make a harp!

Here technology is portrayed as a novel extension of the human "faculties," providing instruments for man's power and "conquering will." The poet acknowledges the accomplishments of his capitalist (listing majoritarian democracy among them), yet he expects still others; he demands some commensurate aesthetic achievement. Emerson's poem was not published until the mid-twentieth century, but one could search a long time and find no more apt brief commentary on economic development in the young American republic.[1]

The New England capitalist Emerson encountered was the product of an evolution. His predecessor had been the Puritan merchant, a preindustrial, premodern capitalist, who had difficulty reconciling the claims of religion and trade. During the eighteenth century the New England merchants had gradually legitimated themselves and had even become leaders of their society. Then, in Emerson's lifetime, the most important change of all took place: the merchant became an industrialist. The shift from commerce to industry entailed momentous consequences. Industry provided more of a spur to technology, for innovation in navigation and shipbuilding had been comparatively slow through the centuries. Industry was also more compatible with democratization, since it catered to a mass market rather than to the small affluent clientele that had consumed most of the luxury goods brought in by traders. The industrialist was in general a more dynamic influence, for he frequently altered social and economic arrangements to suit his insatiable ambitions for raw materials, workers, or markets. The old-time merchant had been engaged in many activities that were hard to justify: smuggling, traffic with the enemy in time of war, the slave trade, privateering, and piracy.[2] The industrialist may not seem much of a moral improvement from our perspective, but many of his contemporaries celebrated him as the trader had never been celebrated. Everyone had always known that the trader owed a lot to luck; the industrialist, in the prime of his glory, was thought to have attained his wealth through merit. Industrialism, in fact, became the focal point of a whole reorientation of values and life-styles for a civilization.

One businessman of this period exemplifies many of the changes that were going on at the time and provides a convenient window for us to look in upon them. He is Nathan Appleton (1779–1861), a merchant turned industrialist, banker, philanthropist, and congressman. His friend and fellow Whig, Robert C. Winthrop, lauded Appleton after his death as a model self-made man who had first arrived in Boston with his belongings tied up in a large handkerchief. Actually, the handkerchief was more an indication of the young Appleton's thrift than of penury. Son of a New Hampshire deacon, he came from a distinguished and affluent family who had been prominent in New England affairs since the seventeenth century and could trace their ancestry back to Suffolk landed gentry. That his eulogist chose to dwell on the bulging handkerchief rather than the fourteenth-century "Appulton" family crest tells us something about the bourgeois value system that had come to prevail by the time of Appleton's death.[3]

Though admitted to Dartmouth College, young Appleton decided to enter his older brother's business instead. Samuel Appleton was a wholesale merchant, a middleman between overseas importers and country storekeepers and peddlers. Nathan's choice of a brother as employer was natural. Business in the last years of the eighteenth century had not yet become impersonalized; commercial relationships, like most relationships in the premodern world, followed ties of blood. Family connections located one within a community. When the corporation developed out of the kinship group, it would be one of many institutions to take over functions from the family.[4]

The talents Nathan brought to his brother's firm lay not in any specialized skill (though he mastered double-entry bookkeeping quickly) but in his agile mind and imagination. Daniel Boorstin has aptly called Nathan Appleton one of the "versatiles."[5] Emerson's line, "As nimbly he applies his bending self," suits him perfectly. Being so flexible, Appleton was well fitted to take advantage of an age of transition. We must be careful to avoid attributing to him a stronger sense of direction than he actually possessed. His purposes mingled innovation with tradition, and often his means were more original than his ends. Appleton did not start out as an industrialist, any more than he started out as a Whig; he came to these identities through energetic trial and error. The shift of Appleton and other New England businessmen from free trade to protectionism is usually taken simply as an illustration of their selfishness. It shows this, of course; but it also shows their remarkable adaptability. Just two years after the looms began operation at Waltham, a member of Appleton's company was in Washington lobbying successfully to get cotton textiles included in John C. Calhoun's protective tariff of 1816.

Whether to seek government assistance was not a difficult problem for Appleton and his associates. The question of "private enterprise" versus "public enterprise," which has loomed so large in the twentieth century, was not then an issue. The question was rather one that concerned enterprise in general: how important was the economic development of the country? To men like Appleton, who became Whigs, it was an urgent priority. The very word "enterprise" was laden for them with heroic connotations.[6] Like most developing nations, the antebellum United States mingled public with private enterprise. It was the age of "mixed" public-private corporations (among them the Smithsonian Institution and the Bank of the United States), in which state and federal governments alike participated. The line between public and private corporations had never been clear; after all, some of the colonial governments themselves had begun as private English corporations. Churches, colleges, grist-mills, banks—all had long been conceived as mixed public-private enterprises. Whigs saw nothing wrong with helping private interests when these coincided with public purposes. "When any one of our merchants displays a spirit of enterprise and humanity," Henry Clay declared, "it is very proper on the part of the government to encourage such efforts."[7] The conception of an individual having an irreconcilable "conflict of interest" was alien to the Whigs. They trusted mixed corporations to balance and resolve different interests, just as the structure of "mixed government" did. It was the Democrats, in their concern to avoid favoritism, who eventually broke down acceptance of the mixed corporation.[8]

Samuel Appleton's merchandising business prospered, and when Nathan came of age in 1800 he was admitted to partnership with his brother. The Appletons took full advantage of the Napoleonic Wars and the mercurial fortunes of international trade that the next dozen years brought. Then came 1812, and opportunities in shipping were foreclosed for the duration of the war with Great Britain. What happened next was a classic event, as if life imitated textbooks.[9] In 1813 Francis C. Lowell and his brother-in-law, Patrick T. Jackson, approached Appleton for an investment in a water-powered loom, the idea for which they had acquired in Lancashire. Appleton contributed $5,000 toward their enterprise. All the initial investors were either relatives or neighbors of Lowell and Jackson. (Although they incorporated as the Boston Manufacturing Company, the firm was run much like a partnership.) Here is how Appleton told of the first operation of their revolutionary device:

> It was not until the new building at Waltham was completed, and other machinery was running, that the first loom was ready for trial. Many little matters were to be overcome or adjusted, before it would work properly. Mr. Lowell said to me that he did not wish me to see it until it was complete, of which he would give me notice. At length, the time arrived. He invited me to go out with him and see the loom operate. I well recollect the state of satisfaction and admiration with which we sat by the hour, watching the beautiful movement of this new and wonderful machine, destined as it evidently was, to change the character of all textile industry.[10]

Reading this account, so familiar in our own day, of getting the "bugs" out of a new machine and then of its proud trial run, we realize that we are in the presence of the birth of industrial society. The series of inventions that made possible the mass production of cotton textiles constituted the first technological innovation to have a major impact on American life since the coming of the Europeans.

Appleton's prose was restrained, but his feeling was strong. Others voiced their excitement in more florid language: "The music of the water-wheel is heard on the banks of our thousand rural streams," Edward Everett rhapsodized within a decade. Applied science "is conferring on us that dominion over earth, sea, and air which was prophesied in the first command given to man by his Maker," a famous preacher rejoiced. "Arkwright deserves to be regarded as a benefactor of mankind," Daniel Webster agreed. Webster even developed a new natural theology, using the achievements of science and technology to celebrate their creator (man) and, in a more remote way, their creator's creator (God).[11]

Our own jaded era finds it hard to recapture the sense of wonder and joy these early technological achievements could arouse. Interestingly, they were not welcomed as labor-saving devices, at least not explicitly, for the proponents of industry did not praise leisure. It was not even the promise of an improved standard of living (of better clothing for millions of people, in the case of the loom) that altogether accounts for the enthusiasm. Technology represented an inspiring triumph of mind over matter, of mankind over nature. "Mind, acting through the useful arts, is the vital principle of modern civilized society. The mechanician, not the magician, is now the master of life."[12] There was still confidence that the human being, not the machine, would be in fact the master: Emerson called the machines "dwarfs" rather than "giants."

Not that the enthusiasm for technology was unanimous. Working people—both those who toiled at the mills and those whose labor the mills supplanted—had reason to question the benefits being bestowed.[13] Marvin Meyers, as noted earlier, has distinguished Whigs from Democrats in Jacksonian America on the basis of the degree of optimism they displayed, and in their reception of technology the Whigs were indeed the optimists of their time. "Truly this is almost a miraculous era," Webster declared in 1847; "the progress of the age has almost outstripped human belief."[14] To men like that, Nathan Appleton was a culture hero. (Emerson, whose poem warned of the cruel exploitation accompanying the exciting transformations of industrial capitalism, remained aloof from both Democratic and Whig parties.)

The Whigs thought of economic progress as providing the basis for all other kinds of progress. The "idea of progress," said a speaker at a Whig rally in 1848, is "twofold"—"to bring out the material resources of America; and next to improve the mind and heart of America." For Whigs, the first led to the second. Democrats might worry about the consequences of economic development, such as urban squalor, inequality, or moral relaxation. Whigs took account of these hazards, then decided: "If prosperity is dangerous, [economic] decline is well nigh fatal."[15] By keeping the economy strong, Whigs felt they were helping to elevate the intellectual and moral level of society. "There never was, and never can be, an intelligent and virtuous people who at the same time are a poor and idle people, badly employed and badly paid." To make use of the material for ideal or spiritual ends was the doctrine of Whig moral philosophers, and it was a doctrine broadly congruent with the avowed purposes of Whig politicians and businessmen.[16]

The Whig justification of prosperity may appear superfluous because we so often regard prosperity as an end in itself. The Whigs could not; they had to overcome the idea that "commerce" was opposed to "virtue" and constituted a threat to it. This had been a major convention of classical-Renaissance-commonwealth thought, and it remained powerful in Jacksonian rhetoric. Significantly, earlier programs for American industrialization had been advocated on the grounds that they would keep people frugal and independent of the "luxuries" of Europe.[17] The Whigs were resolving an age-old polarity in the country-party tradition by arguing that commerce could nourish virtue.

Whigs regarded the machine as an agent of redemption. Improvements in communication and transportation facilitated peace among nations and the spread of the Christian gospel. At home, they helped cement the Union and facilitate the working of democratic politics. "Popular government follows in the track of the steam-engine and the telegraph." The West in particular stood in need of salvation by technology: "The sooner we have railroads and telegraphs spinning into the wilderness, and setting the remotest hamlets in connexion and close proximity with the east, the more certain it is that light, good manners, and christian refinement will become universally diffused."[18]

The Whigs justified not only the new technology but the system of industrial capitalism on the grounds of moral benefit to society. They never employed the argument later apologists for American business would sometimes use, that profitability itself is an indicator of social utility. Appleton could call on capitalists to invest in the early railroads out of "enlightened public spirit," whether these seemed profitable or not. Whigs generally explained the advantages of industrial capitalism in terms of improving the quality of life and giving wider scope for the employment of talents and savings. Industrialization, therefore, was "intimately connected with the moral welfare" as well as with the "highest prosperity of a country."[19] That Daniel Webster's speeches regularly joined the promotion of business interests with high ideals comes as no surprise. But it is worth noting that such objectives were not confined to public pronouncements. Business activity is "the most efficient civilizer of our Barbarous race," a Whig politician confided to a friend.[20] Industrial capitalism was the high point of civilization from the Whig point of view. Edward Everett told a fairgrounds audience in New York City that it was technological achievement and business enterprise, not innate racial characteristics, that gave the whites their favorable position among the peoples of the world.[21]

The mills at Waltham proved so profitable that by 1821 Appleton and his associates were ready to begin another operation, their most famous one, on the Merrimack River. Like old-time merchants incorporating each voyage anew, they formed another joint-stock company, the Merrimack Manufacturing Company, to undertake it. Appleton and P. T. Jackson named the town around the new mill sites Lowell, in honor of their now-deceased comrade. It was Appleton who conceived the object of making Lowell a showpiece of industrialization. Waltham had already displayed aspects of company paternalism; these were intensified at Lowell. The company built homes for the households of its male supervisory employees and boardinghouses for its unmarried female operatives; it supplied the town with a school, a hospital, and a library, whose resources made possible the magazine the employees put out, the famous *Lowell Offering*. It was by no means sufficient for the proprietors to provide what they thought were wholesome working and living conditions at Lowell. They desired to "preserve the morals of the people there to be gathered."[22] With this in mind, they built or subsidized eight churches, exercised strict supervision over the workers' private lives, and founded a savings bank, where employees could practice thrift with safety. Far from feeling guilty about their dividends, which averaged 12 percent, or their astronomical capital gains on lands bought secretly from unsuspecting farmers, the capitalists of the Merrimack Manufacturing Company enjoyed the peace of conscious virtue. When Edward Everett came to Lowell to deliver the Fourth of July oration in 1830, he surveyed the scene before him and saw in it a tribute to the energy, talent, and morality of "progressive Christian civilization."[23]

Lowell, Massachusetts, represented social innovation as much as technological innovation. In its original conception, it was to be not only a company town but also an experimental utopia. Rational planning promised to guarantee the community a bright future. Though their technology was pirated from England and their social ideals were influenced by Robert Owen's New Lanark in Scotland, the proprietors defined their aim as the avoidance of British mistakes. Instead of the grotesque urban sprawl of Birmingham, there was to be an attractive town of controlled size, where working and living would form an integrated whole. Well might Henry Clay declare: "Lowell will tell whether the Manufacturing system is compatible with the social virtues."[24]

Lowell illustrates the Whig desire to remake the world. Rather than rest content with the "putting-out" system of domestic industry, already widely practiced, Appleton and his associates built a whole new model community. It was an artificial world, a "total institution," where most of the workers were isolated from their families and lived regimented lives of hard work, chastity, and diligent uplift.[25] The recognized social dangers of a propertyless proletariat were avoided by what was (within the framework of prevailing ideas) a stroke of genius: the workers would be women—who couldn't own property anyway! By hiring women, the Merrimack Manufacturing Company could pay lower wages than British industry was paying men[26] and yet avoid invidious comparisons. Like the black slaves of the South, the "mill girls" of Lowell constituted an unacknowledged American proletariat.

As a consciously directed social experiment, Lowell lasted about thirty years. Why not longer? To answer this question one must look more closely at the motives behind its establishment. In the first place, the social innovations at Lowell were dependent on the economic objectives of the proprietors. It has recently been argued with much persuasiveness that these were (a) security for the fortunes made in shipping and (b) as high a rate of return as was consistent with safety. Once the mills were set up, there was little motive for reinvestment of profits and much desire on the part of these family-oriented businessmen to transmit dividend-paying operations to their heirs.[27] These objectives dictated occasional work speedups and resistance to demands for a ten-hour day. So, despite company paternalism, there were sporadic strikes and other signs of labor unrest in Lowell from the mid-1830s on. During the 1840s two antimanagement workers' journals appeared in Lowell, *Factory Tracts* and the *Voice of Industry*, to challenge and rebuke the *Lowell Offering*. In the second place, the social ideals of the Lowell proprietors, for all their innovativeness, were undoubtedly constraining. They wanted Lowell to be a hierarchical society, with clearly defined classes, and they placed it under the supervision of one Kirk Boott, a stern disciplinarian who was a veteran of Wellington's army.[28] Two analogies suggest themselves: Lowell was to be run like a large family, with the women employees treated as children; Lowell was to be run like an efficient plantation, with a work force defined by sex rather than race. But the model that influenced the founders of Lowell most of all was the preindustrial New England village, with its traditional patterns of deference made more rigid by a corporate table of organization. Such an elitist vision was bound to encounter opposition from more egalitarian aspirations in the age of Jackson— which was also the age of Sarah Bagley, the labor organizer.

After the influx of Irish immigrants, the Lowell company increasingly shifted over to them as its source of labor, apparently because their bargaining position was weaker than that of Yankee farm women. The original ideals were never explicitly repudiated (Appleton himself affirmed them all his life), but in practice they were gradually abandoned. The Whig generation of businessmen was replaced by members of a new, less paternalistic generation, who took over active direction of the corporation during the 1850s. Lowell, then, was a transitional phenomenon. Its particular coincidence of self-interested and altruistic motives, and the paternalistic utopia envisioned there, did not outlive the Whig party.[29]

Lowell's blend of innovative means with conservative intentions inside a corporate structure was not unique. The quest for investments that would combine security with income was widespread in the United States at the time. Traditionally, capital could be put either into highly speculative investments, like voyages or unimproved land, or else into more secure forms that yielded no income, like gold or works of art. The ideal solution, large tracts of productive real estate, constituted a viable investment option only if the acres were fertile and there were people to till them. The joint-stock company seemed to provide an alternative answer, for by pooling capital it shared risk, especially after the introduction of limited liability. But the business corporation, despite centuries of experimentation, was still an ill-defined organization, frightening to many people.[30] In reply to Democratic charges that corporations were conspiratorial and elitist, Whig defenders of corporations (mixed or private) insisted that they conferred great benefit on savers of modest means by allowing them to participate with the rich in the profits of incorporated business. This was why John Quincy Adams could speak of "the truly republican institution of joint stock companies."[31] Those at the top of the existing social ladder had little reason to be worried and required less reassurance. The new corporations did not at first threaten traditional local communities with their social hierarchies. The Bank of the United States, for example, customarily worked through the local power structure wherever it maintained branches. No other business in the country was more than middle-sized by later standards, and most were family-controlled.[32] Truly big corporate business, impersonal and bureaucratic, did not arise until the middle of the nineteenth century; only then was *Gemeinschaft* more completely displaced by *Gesellschaft*. During the time of the Whig party, economic innovation and social stability could still seem compatible.

Among the many transitions in Appleton's life, none was more important than that from "speculation" to "investment" (in the vocabulary of the day)—from acquiring money in high-risk enterprises to preserving an existing fortune in such a way as to live off the income. Appleton became the moving spirit behind the Boston Associates, an organization of the more prominent business and professional men in the city, whose purpose it was to consolidate control of the textile industry and related economic activities like insurance. Most of the Boston Associates lived in proximity to one another on Beacon Hill and gathered for social intercourse as the Friday Evening Club. Inside this intimate circle, personal character could be known and trusted. Outside it lay uncertainty. "Excessive competition," Appleton's pastor explained to a working-class audience, "generates fraud. Trade is turned into gambling, and the spirit of mad speculation exposes public and private interest to a disastrous instability."[33] The Boston Associates did what they could to foster interlocking directorates and to minimize competition. Very much the same group provided leadership for the Whig party in the state, which was run, a recent historian has noted, like a "private club." When the slavery controversy came to pit some younger members of this club, men like Wendell Phillips and Charles Francis Adams, against Appleton, Winthrop, and the rest, the division was felt with keen regret.[34]

Appleton pursued stability through new forms of business organization in banking as well as industry. Banking had long been a haven for commercially created fortunes, as the merchant-bankers of the

Italian Renaissance illustrate; Appleton and his associates showed their originality by creating the Suffolk banking system. Member banks in many New England towns would deposit sufficient funds to guarantee their notes at the Suffolk Bank in Boston. In consideration for the use of their money, the Suffolk Bank would redeem the notes of the out-of-town banks at par instead of discounting them. Thus a uniform circulating medium and banking reserve requirements were maintained within the region served. Suspensions of specie payments, periodic elsewhere, were generally avoided within the Suffolk system. This was important to Appleton: "The effect of a suspension of the banks is immediately apparent [on] the moral sense of the community, as regards the obligation of contracts."[35] The system also kept "wildcat" banks out of business and had the effect of retaining control of New England banking in the hands of a few well-established capitalists. The Suffolk system operated independently of the Bank of the United States and in fact rendered its services superfluous in the area. For this reason such New England Whigs as Appleton and Adams could afford to take a detached, sometimes critical, view of Biddle and his operations.[36]

The class of which Appleton was a representative has often been loosely called "aristocratic," by contemporaries as well as by historians. It would seem more accurate to term it a bourgeois patriciate, not only because of its urban base and commercial origins but also because of certain typically bourgeois values it endorsed, like sexual restraint, education, and self-improvement in general.[37] The group bore a number of similarities to the southern planters who were their contemporaries. Both were paternalistic toward their workers and emphasized ties of kinship among themselves; the experience of shifting from a "speculative" to an "investment" outlook was also common among both groups. Their ideals of social service differed somewhat; for although both often entered politics, the Yankees were more likely to endow institutions like hospitals, libraries, and colleges.

Appleton lived up to the ideals of his class. He did not merely patronize religion and learning with money; he devoted effort to them himself. He was a faithful parishioner of William Ellery Channing's church on Federal Street and took his religion seriously enough to engage an Anglican clergyman in public theological debate.[38] Although he had given up his chance for college, he dabbled in science and scholarship, even publishing a paper in geology.[39] His daughter Fanny married Henry Wadsworth Longfellow, and the proud father made them a present of a beautiful house in Cambridge, ever after associated with the poet. Appleton answered the call to political leadership as well. He served several terms in the General Court (state legislature), moving from Federalist to National Republican. In 1830 he won election to the federal House of Representatives as a protectionist against an unrepentant maritime free trader and played an important role in shaping the high Adams tariff of 1832. A decade later he was again elected to Congress (to fill an unexpired term) and once more proved an effective spokesman for protectionism in helping to pass the Tariff of 1842. No wonder Appleton came to typify the Boston patriciate in the minds of friend and foe. Francis Bowen, an admiring Harvard economist and moral philosopher, called Appleton "one of the most eminent living representatives of a highly honored class, the merchant princes of Boston," and dedicated his *Principles of Political Economy* to him. And when George McDuffie, South Carolina congressman, denounced protectionism, he cast his argument as a personal challenge to Nathan Appleton.[40]

Whatever one's views on the capitalistic system he helped create, it is impossible to withhold respect from some of Appleton's personal qualities. He could be refreshingly ingenuous. Despite all the flattery he heard and the honors he received, he never believed in his own genius, candidly admitting that his first investment in textiles had been a stroke of good luck. "The truth is, that my mind has always been devoted to many other things rather than money-making," he told a friend near the end of his life. "Accident, and not effort, has made me a rich man."[41] It was the old-time merchant, not the modern industrialist, who could talk thus. Perhaps it was one reason he took his responsibilities of stewardship more seriously than some have done who thought they fully deserved their wealth. Appleton did believe in the efficiency of his mills, however, and he boasted that they could turn out goods as cheaply as the British. When a free-trade newspaper seized on this as evidence that the tariff was unnecessary, Appleton was embarrassed.[42] This plain-spoken businessman admitted he had no talent for the flowery oratory then in fashion, but his speeches possess a directness we can perhaps appreciate better than his contemporaries.

Appleton was what would later be called "a team player." He was loyal to his class, to his party, and to his country, and he always strove to submerge personal differences in the interest of the group. In Boston he mediated the rivalry between Abbott Lawrence and Daniel Webster; in Washington he swallowed his distrust for Biddle out of loyalty to Clay's general program. An advocate of "harmony of interests," he consistently maintained that "the cotton planter has an interest in the protective system as direct and positive as the cotton manufacturer." Nullification he of course dismissed as "an absurd theory."[43] Appleton was willing to compromise on the slavery question if by doing so he could help save the Whig party and the Union. He counseled moderation to Conscience Whigs and remained in touch with southern Unionists to the end in a vain effort to prevent secession.[44]

Appleton and his associates brought modern industrialism to the United States, yet they themselves were not fundamentally modern in their outlook. They were paternalists and *rentiers* who regarded their factories much as old-fashioned gentry might regard their estates. Appleton had stumbled upon industrialization; it was for others to make industrialization a conscious objective. Henry C. Carey was one of these others.

On April 15, 1859, there was a testimonial dinner in Philadelphia. Banners were hung in the banquet hall bearing the slogans "Harmony of Interests" and "Protection to American Labor." The mayor of Philadelphia presided, and among those present were prominent political supporters of protectionism, including Republican Senator Simon Cameron and Senator John Bell of Tennessee, who still thought of himself as a Whig. The guest of honor was Henry C. Carey (1793–1879), and this dinner formed part of his triumphal tour of Pennsylvania. The commonwealth was recognizing one of its foremost citizens.[45]

Carey's admirers found no praise too extravagant to describe his contribution to economics. "Ricardo and Malthus will be to Carey as Ptolemy to Copernicus," Rufus Griswold wrote in the *American Whig Review*.[46] Academics like Thomas Hill of Harvard accorded him respect, but Carey also appealed to a wide audience through his columns in the *New York Tribune*, whose weekly edition circulated nationally, for economics had not yet become inaccessible to the general literate public. In Pennsylvania, a bastion of protectionist sentiment, Carey's popularity transcended party lines. Elsewhere he was idolized by Whigs and Republicans; in 1853 he declined the Whig nomination for governor of New Jersey. Carey was the first American economist to acquire an international reputation. Works by him were translated into French, German, Italian, Spanish, Swedish, Portuguese, Russian, Magyar, and Japanese. *Harmonies économiques*, by the noted French economist Frédéric Bastiat, was heavily in his debt.[47] But nowhere were Carey's ideas accorded more recognition than in Germany. Like the Americans, the Germans were struggling to consolidate their nation of recalcitrant states, and the supporters of the *Zollverein* (customs union) established in 1833 found that Carey's economic nationalism spoke directly to their needs. Friedrich List, who spent four years as a political exile from Württemberg sharing Carey's company and views in Philadelphia, helped transmit his influence to the Germans.[48]

Widely read and discussed in his own day, Carey had been almost forgotten by the beginning of the twentieth century. Even before that, assessments of his work in the 1890s had manifested a remarkable sense of distance from him.[49] Simon Patten, whose sympathy for protection and optimistic conviction that the basic human condition was abundance rather than scarcity make him seem a latter-day Carey, was not in fact influenced by him (according to Patten's biographer).[50] To understand the changing fortunes of Carey's reputation, one must learn what his message was, how it was formulated, and to whom it was directed.

Henry Charles Carey was the son of a distinguished father. Mathew Carey, an Irish Catholic, fled political persecution and came to the United States in 1784. In Philadelphia he set up a publishing firm and became well known as a writer on political and economic questions. He eventually identified himself with what might be called the commercial wing of Jeffersonian Republicanism, advocating internal improvements, a protective tariff, a national bank, and reconciliation with the Federalists—in short, the "Madisonian Platform." Henry followed his father into the publishing company, which gave him a good start in life, comparable to Appleton's family connections, though Carey never built it into anything like Appleton's eventual wealth.[51] (The family remained intellectually prominent in the next generation too, for Henry Charles Lea, the great historian of the medieval Inquisition, was Henry's nephew and Mathew's grandson.)

More than Mathew, Henry Carey assimilated into the American mainstream. He converted to Protestantism and seems to have retained little of his Irish heritage beyond a resentment of the English. Though he often expressed indignation at the oppression of the Irish in the old country, Henry (unlike Mathew) took no special interest in the situation of the Irish in America. He was more concerned with the good opinion of Yankee businessmen and during the 1840s cultivated Nathan Appleton and Amos Lawrence in particular. Like Appleton, Carey had an authoritarian streak (he admired the reforming despotism of Alexander II of Russia), but he differed from Appleton in being a narrow, zealous man, lacking cosmopolitan culture or patrician manner. He also had nothing of the cameraderie, humor, or "blarney" people expected of an Irishman; instead, contemporaries commented on his intensity and tactlessness.[52]

Carey invested the profits of the family publishing firm in Pennsylvania coal and iron, identifying his self-interest with the cause of the tariff he advocated so energetically. He pursued his interests—and those of his state, his nation, and his party—with a single-minded devotion worthy of altruism. No doubt he thought of himself as an altruist. Sometimes his self-interest is quite apparent, as in his opposition to an international copyright law that would have benefited foreign authors at the expense of American publishers.[53] (It is but just to add that Carey's firm paid royalties to British authors even in the absence of such a law.)

In many ways Henry Carey was typical of millions of Americans of his time, and not least in the ardor with which he promoted his own interests. He had a burning ambition for his nation to prosper and escape economic dependence on Britain; he was confident that a higher standard of living for the average person could be achieved; he simplified complicated questions; he worked hard. At times he challenged oppression. Our own generation owes much of its material comfort to nineteenth-century Americans of his kind.

Henry Carey was more a generalized social scientist than an economist in our technical sense. Since his discussions were often normative as well as descriptive, he might be called a "moral philosopher" in nineteenth-century terms, though he lacked the grounding in metaphysics and formal ethical theory usually associated with that calling. Perhaps Carey can best be described as a social myth-maker, one whose myths were specific and systematic, not abstract or vague. The vision of the good society he postulated was widely shared in the America of his time (especially in the free states). What Carey did was to construct an integrated rational system linking common aspirations with particular political policies—a protective tariff, internal improvements, and (eventually) the containment of slavery. His writings organized the Whig economic program into an ideology. Carey shows the uselessness of the contrast often drawn between the "pragmatic" and the "ideological" person. He was an ideologue who was anything but impractical.

Sir Isaiah Berlin has made historians familiar with the distinction between the hedgehog and the fox. The fox knows many things; the hedgehog knows one big thing, that is, he pursues "a single central

vision."[54] Henry Carey was a hedgehog. He believed America would
be a better place to live if it could industrialize. It was by no means a
foolish premise.[55] Everything else in Carey's system depended on
this insight. Even tariff protection was a dependent variable (Carey
supported Clay's compromise of 1833 while it lasted). Carey operated
within a tradition of all-encompassing social science that moral
philosophy had long fostered. He repeated Sir Francis Bacon's
metaphor of the "tree of knowledge," showing the relations of all
branches of learning to one another.[56] Carey's works show a progressive straining after universality, as he wrote first on wage theory,
then on economics, then on the social context of economic life, and,
finally, in old age, on the unity of all knowledge.[57]

Beginning with his first work (*Essay on the Rate of Wages*, 1835) and
continuing throughout his career, Carey emphasized that an
economist must consider the society he treats as a totality and must
do so with a regard for maximizing true "happiness," not merely
"wealth." He rejected the abstraction of the "economic man," that
hypothetical person who wants only freedom to pursue material advantage.[58] In this he was typically Whig, for it was one of the distinctions between Democrats and Whigs that the Whigs considered a
much wider range of human activities relevant to public policy than
their opponents. Of course, wealth and happiness were not mutually
exclusive. The important nonmaterial goals would follow from a right
organization of material existence. Carey was not an economic de-
terminist, for he strongly believed that people were free to order their
affairs properly. Among these affairs, however, economic ones were
basic.

Carey realized that underdeveloped countries were plagued by
what we would call underemployment; that is, the productivity of
labor was often low, and vast numbers of people were engaged in
activities with little to show for their efforts. Genuine full employment was both the means to economic progress and, for Carey, the
end of economic progress. His reasoning is circular, yet his vision is
compelling: one of well-paid, productive workers with jobs that
satisfy them. "Highest, therefore, among the tests of civilization," he
declared, is whether society "enables all to find demand for their
whole physical and mental powers." Because people's powers differed, "diversity of employments" was essential. Only a diversified
economy that included industry could provide such varied career
opportunities.[59] This was Carey's application of the worldwide
bourgeois principle, "careers open to talent." For the careers to be
available to talent, they first had to exist.

For Carey, economic development was a means to human redemption. Addressing himself to women in particular, he argued that economic diversification held out the promise to them of liberation from the role of farmer's wife and fulfillment of their individual talents. (Carey deplored the oppression of women in the factories of Britain; such stultifying proletarianization was not what he had in mind for American women.)[60] When people had interesting, productive work, they themselves grew accordingly—they "developed their faculties," in the language of the day. This in turn fitted them for "the higher enjoyments of life," as Carey put it. "The more perfect is [a person's] development the greater is his desire for knowledge, the greater his love for literature and art, the greater his desire to see for himself the movements of the world, and to learn from those who are capable of affording him instruction."[61]

Was it curious that someone who himself lacked broad culture should thus celebrate it? The contrast between Carey's narrow, dogmatic, materialistic personality and the scope and enlightenment of his goals is striking. It was, however, common among American Whigs that their reach should exceed their grasp. They more often praised "the higher enjoyments" than appreciated or partook of them. This should serve to remind us that Whig ideals had an existence independent of individuals' inclinations. They were accepted as objective, and it was the individual's responsibility to acknowledge them and try to shape himself to them.

The economic system that Carey felt offered the best prospect for economic development was, of course, capitalism, but he was quite willing to call on government to help the process along. Technological innovation and population increase, fueled by unrestricted immigration, Carey acknowledged important. Government policy should add to these dynamic influences what is today called social overhead—a transportation network and an educational system. To keep the economy expanding, the burden of taxation should not become oppressive, but in the United States in Carey's time there was little danger of this. Carey laid the most stress on a plentiful money supply and a protective tariff to prevent this money from being drained off in payment for imports. Taken together, these policies would secure investment capital, increase productivity, and raise wages.[62]

Carey's contribution to the Whig campaign of 1840 was a pamphlet on the currency issue, supporting free banking and general laws of incorporation and defending the utility of bank notes against Democratic calls for hard money. Through the years he continued his insistence that the government permit bankers to create abundant money.[63] To the extent that state and federal governments followed such advice, they tended to speed up the economic development of the country as Carey intended they should. Considered as rigorous economic analysis, Carey's discussions of money were over-simplified and flawed, but his instincts about the effects of easy credit seem to have been right.[64] While Carey's monetary policy emphasized expansion, Appleton's, as exemplified in the Suffolk system, emphasized stability. Appleton became spokesman for a group seeking security above all, the preservation of existing wealth; Carey represented the much more common American man-on-the-make. Fortunately for the Whig party, the area of agreement between them was large.

Carey's optimistic assessment of the possibility of a better life for all is his most salient characteristic, both as an economist and as Whig myth-codifier. It is this optimism, far more than mere dis-agreement over the protective tariff, that set him apart from the Man-chester School. If so many inhabitants of the earth eked out a bare subsistence, Carey attributed this to political causes that people were free to change, not to an "iron law of wages" or other economic inevitability. The Manchester economists had a much more vivid sense of the conflicting interests of classes than Carey. He looked to technology to resolve the differences between capital and labor; by increasing productivity it would provide for increases in both profits and wages. He disagreed with Nassau Senior, who saw the intro-duction of machinery as opening the way to lower wages.[65] Carey retained the faith of his Jeffersonian father in human ability to master circumstances. Underlying his sanguine outlook was not only a positive estimate of human nature but also an assumption that the natural resources of the world were virtually inexhaustible.

Thomas Malthus often came in for criticism by American Whigs, but none of the critics was more severe than Carey. Where Malthus saw additional people as more mouths to feed, Carey saw them as so many pairs of willing hands. Malthus' rule that population expands geometrically while food production increases only arithmetically was elaborately refuted by Carey. But of all the aspects of Malthus' system, the one that most horrified Carey and other American Whigs was the claim that charity is futile because it merely encourages the poor to breed faster.[66] The repeated references to Robinson Crusoe in Carey's writings provide a clue to his basic assumptions. He con-ceived the human condition as that of an ingenious but lonely indi-vidual who welcomes a companion for the task of exploiting the paradise around him. This attitude is understandable, given Carey's time and place. Actually, Malthus himself readily admitted that the United States faced no population problem in the near future. Carey's response to the ultimate Malthusian question, What happens when all the productive land on the globe is taken up? was simply to say (a) that the event is too far away to worry about and (b) that, when it does occur, we can rely on human resourcefulness to limit population. Carey evidently had no objection to birth control as such.[67] He also attacked David Ricardo's theory of diminishing returns from agriculture, again employing the American experience to make his case.[68]

Carey's arguments against Malthus and Ricardo demonstrate his preference for history over theory. In this he was a typical American Whig. He claimed to be an inductive empiricist and criticized the Manchesterians for creating deductive systems that sacrificed life to logic. He admired Auguste Comte and considered himself an economic "positivist."[69] Actually, however, the spirit of Carey's writings was alien to that of Comte because of its Christian and moral tone. Carey was convinced that economic laws must follow the principles of natural theology, that is, they must illustrate the wisdom and beneficence of the deity. "If the doctrines taught in the English school are right, then has the Creator made a serious blunder" in so condemning the mass of humanity. More likely the economists, not God, had made the mistake.[70] This visceral conviction that Manchester economics was not only false but wicked imparted a fervent moral tone to Carey's treatises. Only if people were persuaded that improvement was possible would they strive for it. Carey therefore resisted arguments that economic hardship was inevitable. When the Democratic editor William Cullen Bryant commented, during the Panic of 1857, that nothing could be done to avoid or relieve such depressions, Carey demanded: "Can it be that a beneficent Providence has so adjusted the laws under which we live that laborers *must* be at the mercy of those who hoard food and clothing with which to purchase labor?"[71]

Like Herbert Spencer, Carey believed that human society evolves into ever-increasing complexity and interdependence, though he rejected Spencer's disposition to deny that deliberate action can speed the process along. The great French sociologist Emile Durkheim acknowledged his own indebtedness to Carey's ideas on social evolution.[72] Carey termed this tendency in human affairs "the law of association" and likened it to the law of gravitation in physics. He packed a great deal of Whiggery into his concept of association:

The more [man's] power of association, the greater is the tendency toward development of his various faculties; the greater becomes his control of the forces of nature, and the more perfect his own power for self-direction; mental force thus more and more obtaining control over that which is material, the labors of the present over the accumulations of the past.

As is evident from this passage, the law of association was normative as well as descriptive. If Americans were to fulfill it properly, they must guard against dispersing themselves thinly across the continent. Instead of exhausting the soil to produce export staples and then moving on, American farmers should practice diversified agriculture for a home market and clear additional lands in the East to keep transportation costs low. Carey supported conservation measures and opposed territorial expansion and government inducements to westward migration. When someone moved away from civilization to the frontier, Carey looked upon the value of his labor as lost to society, at least until the settler reentered the market economy.[73]

The society for which Carey strove was one in which moral values he approved would be rewarded. A head of household with foresight, thrift, and conscientious application would have not only a variety of career choices but also the opportunity to rise from wage-earner to employer. The existence of a wage-earning class posed no danger as long as its work was wholesome and avenues for upward social mobility remained open. Success within this scheme was not itself a moral end but an appropriate reward for moral effort. Such a society would require agriculture, commerce, and industry, all in proximity to each other. Carey's ideal was neither an arcadia of yeomen farmers nor a big city but a "middle state" between rural and urban life. Temperate in life-style, stable yet progressive, this middle state was widely celebrated by Americans of the nineteenth century, especially by those within the Whig tradition.[74] It was not a homogeneous "middle," however, that the Whigs praised, but a heterogeneous one; the terms "mixed" and "balanced" recur as frequently in Whig economic writing as they do in Whig political writing. Nor was it a static "middle"; in fact, Carey's ideal society was very similar to the one John Quincy Adams had portrayed as "civilization" in his outline of human progress. The famous Whig symbol of 1840, the log cabin, was the perfect image for this society, expressing, as it did, not permanent poverty but the coming of civilization and gradual improvement through human effort.[75]

Though Carey and the Whigs favored industrialization, they

were not generally enthusiastic about large-scale urbanization. The political philosophers who shaped their habits of mind—Cicero, Harrington, Bolingbroke, et alia—had generally celebrated the countryside. The very name "country party" conjured up associations of rural virtue resisting metropolitan vice. When John Quincy Adams used the phrase "rabble of a populous city," it was a cliché he invoked automatically. When Lyman Beecher spun a cautionary tale about a youth falling into temptation, he automatically made him a country boy new to the city.[76] Whiggery was an outlook more appropriate to villagers or townsmen than to either frontiersmen or city dwellers. Kenneth Lockridge has wisely pointed out the enduring influence of the town ideal in American history, and in many parts of the country where the Whig party was strongest it was associated with a longing to recreate the early New England town settlement pattern. Such a town could interact constructively with the surrounding countryside without dominating it. (Carey, never finicky, pointed out that if a town were not too large its street manure and human waste could profitably be put to use by neighborhood farmers.) Two of Carey's disciples, Eli Thayer and John C. Underwood, actually organized a model community in Virginia to practice his principles of association.[77] In a more general way, of course, the small industrial towns, like the early Lowell and Eli Whitney's Whitneyville, Connecticut, illustrate the Whig objective.

Whig endorsement of industry did not preclude support for agriculture. In a country still predominantly agricultural, the Whigs could hardly have ignored rural interests and attained major party status. "Our agriculture is our greatest interest," Henry Clay affirmed in 1824. "It ought ever to be predominant." He went on to argue, as Carey would also do, that the best way to promote agriculture was to foster a strong home market for its products by encouraging industry. Whigs continued to respect the farmer, not only for his contribution to a diversified economy, but also as custodian of moral values. "Large commercial cities tend to great orderliness and decency of manners and morals. But they also tend to very low and barren views of moral excellence," the first issue of the Whig *American Review* explained. If the country were ever to lose all contact with the rural way of life, something noble would vanish.[78]

Marvin Meyers has identified a nostalgia for rustic simplicity with the Jacksonian Democrats, but such feelings were common among the Whigs, too. Daniel Webster and Horace Greeley, to take prominent examples, always praised country life even when supporting protection for American industry. Webster's home at Marshfield and Greeley's at Turtle Bay gave both men a chance to practice as well as preach the rural virtues whenever they sought escape from their city offices.[79]

The Whig party existed at a pivotal moment, and it looked both forward and back. The period from 1820 to 1860 witnessed the greatest relative growth in the size of cities in American history. Whig candidates generally outpolled Democrats in these growing urban centers. The irony of a party with a "country" political heritage that nevertheless did well in cities was not lost on Henry Clay. "In our Cities, where we had most to apprehend from political corruption, we have found most public virtue; whilst in the Country, where we had a right to expect the most opposition to misrule, and wild and dangerous theories, they have received an alarming degree of countenance."[80] There were a few Whigs who, perceiving the direction urbanization was taking, welcomed it wholeheartedly as the triumph of civilization and the fulfillment of God's plan for man. Rufus Choate sought an urban historical sense as an alternative to the "country" tradition; he surveyed the cities of ancient Greece, medieval Germany, and Renaissance Italy and found them, not the rural areas, the authentic bearers of political liberty.[81] More often Whigs tried to retain a mediating position between city and country, but this mediating position itself was creeping in the direction of larger communities, from village to town; the "mixed" social ideal did not specify the precise proportion in which its elements should be mingled. Edward Everett best expressed (as he so often did) the Whig ideal as a synthesis of rural morality with urban economic dynamism:

> Society is in its happiest state when town and country act and react upon each other to mutual advantage, when the simpler manners and purer tastes of rural life are brought to invigorate the moral atmosphere of the metropolis, and when a fair proportion of the wealth acquired in the city flows back, and is invested in landed improvements.[82]

The Whig desire to preserve rural values within an urban context eventually led to important developments in urban park and cemetery landscape architecture, culminating after the Civil War in the genius of Frederick Law Olmsted.[83]

Although Carey's assessment of the human potential was optimistic, he was by no means a Pollyanna. The critical edge to his social science and its true significance have, however, generally been neglected. Carey drew a vital distinction between intracommunity

economic exchanges, which he called "commerce," and extracommu-
nity ones, which he called "trade." Within a community, commerce
was simply the economic dimension of association, the mutually
beneficial interaction between human beings. But trade between
two different communities was typically exploitative. While commerce arose within friendly society, trade generally originated and
perpetuated itself in warfare. The slave trade and the Anglo-Chinese
Opium War provided Carey with well-chosen examples of the predatory, destructive nature of trade.[84]

Trade develops, according to Carey, out of a distortion in the
natural process of association, like a cancer on an organism. Speciali-
zation of function is carried too far, and raw materials are brought to
a metropolitan center from distant points. Parasitic middlemen appear. Armies are raised to conquer new lands to supply the metropolis, and armies require taxation. The population of the colonies
is reduced to poverty and often to actual serfdom or slavery. In his
own ancestral home of Ireland, Carey saw the tragic effects of English
"trade" policy: Ireland, deliberately prevented from developing a
diversified economy of its own, had seen its population systematically impoverished and degraded.[85] Carey pointed to the sugar islands of the West Indies to show the evils of trade most dramatically.
The people of the islands had long been unable to create a normal
society, being divided into a mass of slaves and a tiny group of
planters, who were not really local leaders but agents of an external
metropolis. The colonies were means to the ends of others instead of
healthy communities in their own right. The southern United States
was but another instance, less extreme, of the same perversion.
There, too, agriculture concentrated on export staples, while slavery
prevented the emergence of a significant home market. Conservation
was consequently disregarded, and population was too thinly spread
for optimal social life.[86]

The same Carey who praised the small-to-medium-scale capitalism
of the town deplored the large-scale capitalism of the metropolis. A
trading economy corrupted its own society as well as others. Swollen
megalopolises emerged. Within these cities, a submerged "proletariat" (Carey never minced words) appeared, just as truly
exploited as the distant laborers who produced the staples. Carey's
analysis of trade bore a remarkable resemblance to the analysis of
capitalism by his great contemporary, Marx. The trading class lived
by "appropriation" of wealth created by others. The impoverished
urban populations of trading empires would eventually cease to be
able to consume the finished products of their own labor, Carey

predicted.` Wars would ensue as the trading nations competed for markets.[87]

The difference between Carey and Marx is apparent, however, in the relative ease with which Carey felt the evils of trade could be overcome. A protective tariff was the answer. The simplicity of Carey's solution to the gigantic problem of oppression he so graphically described must seem incongruous; it can only be explained in terms of his optimism, reasserting itself. Although a tariff would raise prices in the short run, in the long run it would lower them by keeping transportation costs low. There being less chance for middlemen to rake off profits, the share of national income that would go to the actual farmer or laborer ought to be higher. A more important justification for protectionism, as we have seen, was social rather than economic: a diversified economy would provide a healthy human environment for varied talents. John Stuart Mill, English free trader that he was, acknowledged the power of this argument of Carey's.[88] But protection (as the name itself indicated) was most valuable as a defense against alien exploitation, against what Carey called "trade." It enabled local people to organize their own industry instead of being forced into dependence on distant monopoly capitalists. A now-forgotten spokesman for peoples who felt their communal identity threatened by economic colonialism, Henry Carey found that his message was welcomed wherever nations were industrializing and British economic hegemony resented.

Carey's case for a diversified economy rested, significantly enough, on the same ground as the traditional "country-party" defense of a yeomanry: the need to secure people's independence against intimidation. Henry Clay placed the "mixed" economy within the context of "country-party" ideology quite aptly: "A judicious American farmer, in the household way, manufactures whatever is requisite for his family. He squanders but little on the gewgaws of Europe. He presents, in epitome, what the nation ought to be *in extenso*."[89] In this image of the nation as a family farm writ large, protectionism becomes a political and moral objective, the fulfillment of national independence. The apparent paradox of the Whigs' combining "country-party" values with "mixed" economic policies turns out to be explicable after all: the means of defense against the corruptions of the metropolis has changed, but the end is still there.

Carey, like his German counterpart List, argued that the protective tariff was but a temporary device, designed to see a country through the phase of industrialization. Once the economy had become strong and diversified, there would be no reason to fear foreign domination. Then duties could be lowered or removed, and international commerce (instead of trade) could flourish, at last, on terms of equality.[90] This, the "infant-industries" argument for protection, was a staple of Whig discourse. Henry Clay foresaw a time when "our manufactures shall have acquired a stability and perfection which will enable them successfully to cope with the manufactures of any other country." One of the justifications for the Compromise of 1833 was that it provided a transitional phase during which American industry could see whether it was ready so to cope.[91] (In 1842 Whigs decided it was not and raised the tariff.) Carey's emphasis on the economic advantages of a home market stemmed from his elemental recognition of what economists today term the multiplier effect. The profits to particular businesses from export trade were, he felt, outweighed at this stage of American development by the broader advantages to the economy as a whole of spending money within the country. The latest evaluation of Carey's protectionism in the light of twentieth-century economics concludes, despite qualifications, that there was substantial merit in his position as applied to developing countries.[92]

Carey lived long enough to become a Republican, though that party never captured his loyalty as fully as the Whig party had. He campaigned for Frémont in 1856; still, he tried to preserve a good relationship with his fellow Pennsylvanian, Buchanan, until the president deserted his protectionist home state in the low tariff of 1857. Carey was careful to avoid the stigma of abolitionism because he never gave up hope of conciliating the southern Whigs. In 1860 he even toyed with the Constitutional Union party of his old friend John Bell.[93] The Kansas-Nebraska Act had outraged Carey as it did so many northerners; yet he always felt free soil to be a subsidiary issue. The true long-range solution to the slavery problem was industrialization, because masters, finding that free workers had more incentive, would consent to emancipation. A mixed economy would also be better for the freedmen, offering them varied employment options. In the more immediate future, the same solution also applied to the slave trade, because, if labor-exporting regions like West Africa and Virginia (and Ireland, he added) industrialized, they would create a demand for their workers at home.[94] Believing as he did that southern industrialization would have resolved the sectional conflict, Carey could insist as late as 1867 that if Henry Clay had been elected president in 1844 the Civil War need never have been fought. In the final defeat of the Confederacy Carey saw the vindication of his many years of criticism of southern one-crop–free-trade policies.[95]

The great triumph of Carey's life came with the passage of the Morrill Tariff of 1862, commencing a century of American protectionism that would last until the Kennedy round of economic conferences. Yet instead of a decentralized "middle zone" of opportunity and morality, economic consolidation and further urbanization characterized the high-tariff era. The idea that protection was only a transitional phase for "infant" industries was ignored. The huge companies that dominated the new social order were not "mixed" corporations, with directors representing the public participating in their decisions, but private ones benefiting from government favors. Carey realized quickly that his dream was being betrayed. He had never been blind to the dangers of monopoly in America. Even before the war he had attacked the Camden & Amboy Railroad, exposing its tax frauds and charter violations.[96] After the war he identified federal monetary policy as the heart of the problem. By retiring the greenbacks and restoring the gold standard, the government was enriching creditors at the expense of debtors. Carey's judgment was not off the mark. A recent economic historian says of the postwar deflation: "Human ingenuity would have had difficulty contriving a more perfect engine for class and sectional exploitation."[97]

The policy of deflation originated during Andrew Johnson's administration with Secretary of the Treasury Hugh McColloch, a former Democrat who finally had the opportunity to put into practice the hard-money principles of his youth. Carey bitingly called him a "finance minister" instead of a Treasury secretary, accusing him of being in effect an agent of British interests. "War now exists" between alien capitalists and American workers; "on which side does the Administration propose to fight?" he demanded.[98] As deflation continued, Carey received his answer. "The Treasury [is waging] war upon all who have the misfortune of being obliged to use the money of others." Unless the economy of the defeated South were restructured with the aid of easy credit, the aged economist insisted, the landowning class that had led the rebellion would revive. But the government, he recognized, had become the captive of northeastern creditor financial interests. These interests, like the prewar planters, represented international "trade" rather than local "commerce." In his last major work, the comprehensive *Unity of Law* (1873), Carey decided that the real issue was no longer "protection" against trade, but "resistance."[99]

In recognizing Carey's innovative qualities, we must not lose sight of his links with predecessors. He was the last American social thinker in the tradition of Adam Ferguson. He remained a moral philosopher at heart, celebrating, as Ferguson had, the small organic community made self-sufficient by its people's virtues and diverse talents. In the alien element of trade he recognized a source of corruption endangering his ideal of progress. He was not mistaken.

Two causes explain the rapid oblivion to which the once-influential Carey was consigned after his death. One is that during the 1870s economics underwent an important conceptual change: it ceased to be taught as a branch of moral philosophy and became a separate discipline. The broadly humanistic approach to economics Carey had always practiced now seemed old-fashioned. The other is that the "greenback" cause he espoused and his criticism of "trade" were not respectable within opinion-shaping northeastern circles. Boston's *North American Review* gave an early signal in a savage attack on Carey in 1866.[100] The gold standard was the new orthodoxy; American capitalism had come of age and no longer needed Henry Carey.

Together, Appleton and Carey illustrate the range of possibilities within the Whig entrepreneurial ethos: Appleton the genial paternalist and Carey the compulsive striver. They were practical, adaptable, and shamelessly self-seeking businessmen who were also idealists. Together, such entrepreneurs labored to create a new America. The society they envisioned would be designed to encourage talent and virtue. It would be economically diverse but morally uniform, industrialized but not urbanized, innovative but stable. In parts of the country something like the mixture of industry, commerce, and agriculture these Whigs worked for came into being. One such area was Springfield, Illinois, where the young Whig Abraham Lincoln studied law and then applied his hard-earned training to the causes of railroads and banks. But the Whigs' ideal proved transitory. Capitalist economic development did not turn out to be compatible with the social order as they knew it. The world of Appleton and Carey passed into history, a phase in larger developments they helped set in motion but understood only imperfectly.

Six

Henry Clay, Ideologue of the Center

The career of Henry Clay (1777–1852) is unique in the history of American electoral politics. It spans over fifty years, for more than forty of which he was an important national figure and decision-maker. A leading contender for the presidency in 1824, 1832, 1840, 1844, and 1848, he served as speaker of the House longer than anyone else in the nineteenth century and was the most influential member of the United States Senate during what is universally regarded as the golden age of that body. Abraham Lincoln, in his eulogy for Clay, pointed out that "the infant nation and the infant child began the race of life together" and that the history of each coincided in many ways with that of the other. This was so on many levels of meaning. Clay's nationalism was personal as well as patriotic, for all his political ambitions were at the national level. (For example, he never ran for governor of Kentucky.) Clay spoke the truth in his first Alabama Letter of 1844: "If anyone desire to know the leading and paramount object of my public life, the preservation of this Union will furnish the key."[1]

Clay could arouse almost fanatical devotion in his followers. After the Civil War, Horace Greeley still remembered his charisma. "I have admired and trusted many statesmen: I profoundly loved Henry Clay." Even those who met him briefly often fell under his captivating spell; Charles Dickens confessed "a wild attachment" to him. It is a fair judgment that, given such charm and his long experience as a parliamentary leader, Clay would have become prime minister under a different system of government.[2] Yet the presidency always eluded him.

As a political tactician Clay was the victim of his own ambition. He was always trying to devise some artful stratagem. John Quincy Adams got it right in his diary: "In politics, as in private life, Clay is essentially a gamester."[3] Clay eventually ceased to be a gamester in private life, but he never quite ceased to be one in politics. His elaborate scheming made him even more numerous enemies than his magnetic personality won him admirers; as the English would say, he was too clever by half. And yet there was a serious statesman in him along with the gamester-politician; behind his never-ending series of plausible expedients there was a consistency of purpose.

Clay the exponent of a coherent vision of America's future was actually far more perceptive than Clay the self-seeking politician. As a politician he was forever blundering. He blundered when he accepted the State Department from Adams, imagining it would be a steppingstone to the White House; when he persuaded Nicholas Biddle to apply for recharter of his Bank four years early; and when he helped block Martin Van Buren's confirmation as minister to Britain. They were blunders when he denounced the abolitionists in 1839 and tried to mollify southern expansionists at the last minute in 1844. Clay has been overrated as a politician and underrated as a statesman. He never won the presidential prize he coveted, yet his vision of America as economically diverse, commercially powerful, and politically integrated came to be fulfilled. This is the proper gloss to place upon Clay's oft-quoted remark that he would rather be right than be president: though never president, he was often right; and he would have been right even more often had he wanted to be president less.

Clay's utterances were invariably addressed to specific and immediate issues, not to philosophical abstractions. Yet, in the aggregate, his statements reveal a coherent political program and philosophy, particularly from the time he accepted office under Adams in 1825 until his death in 1852. Henry Clay was an ideologue of the Center, just as there are ideologues of the political Left and Right. The combination of ambitious politician and dedicated ideologue, after all, is scarcely unique in the modern world.

To understand Clay's ideology, one must realize that "compromise" and "principle" are not necessarily opposites. For Clay, compromise was itself a principle; that is, he believed saving the Union was a matter of continual adjustment of competing interests. Today we are conscious that Clay's sectional compromises did not last and that they attempted to buy peace for whites at the cost of indefinite postponement of freedom for blacks. But they were rooted in a typically nineteenth-century ideal of progress. Christopher Dawson's verdict on the social order of the English Victorians can be applied to Clay's statesmanship. "It is easy to criticise this Victorian achievement as an illogical and philistine compromise, which sacrificed political ideals to material interests and allowed social evils to go unredressed so long as they did not interfere with the interests of the dominant class," he writes. Nevertheless, "the Victorian compromise was the work of idealists."[4]

The kind of progress Henry Clay believed in was the same kind of progress John Quincy Adams believed in, one of stability and order. Their ideals of balance and harmony were the same. But whereas Adams relied on conscience to impose order, Clay relied on the other rational faculty of the moral philosophers, prudential calculation. Hence his dedication to compromise and to commercial development. Businessmen were famous for prudence, and Clay felt the country needed this. He wanted prudence and conscience to be allies, just as he and Adams were allies. Together they would overcome the "passions," exemplified for Clay in Andrew Jackson.[5]

The battle against passion was one Clay had to fight on a personal as well as a political level. By nature he was himself a passionate man, "free and wild as the elk of the forest," who exulted in his triumphs and despaired in defeat.[6] In youth he had been a hothead: a war hawk, duelist, and gambler. But by the time he formed the Whig party, he was in his fifties and had long determined that the statesman in him should prevail over the "gamester." Renouncing the belligerence of 1812, he had opposed the invasion of Florida in 1818. In 1824 he foreswore the code of honor and thereafter opposed dueling whenever it came up as a political issue.[7] His personal habits while he was secretary of state never annoyed Adams as they had done a decade earlier, when the two had been negotiators at Ghent. Harriet Martineau, that shrewd judge of character, observed in 1835: "Mr. Clay is a man of an irritable and impetuous nature, over which he has obtained a truly noble mastery. His moderation is now his most striking characteristic; obtained, no doubt, at the cost of prodigious self-denial on his own part." She noticed that the struggle for self-mastery sometimes imparted a certain stiffness to his discourse, and one who has read much of his correspondence will agree. No doubt he was anxious to live down his early reputation, and from the age of forty-seven on, he claimed to be "growing old."[8]

Clay's enemies determined not to let him get away with developing a new image of sober moderation. John Randolph of Virginia, brilliant and savage leader of the antiadministration forces in the House of Representatives, baited him mercilessly. The Adams-Clay alliance joined "Blifil and Black George," he sneered, "the puritan with the blackleg."[9] In Fielding's Tom Jones, Blifil is a sanctimonious hypocrite, Black George an irresponsible scamp. "Blackleg" meant a dishonest race-track tout or cardsharp. Like all really cruel insults, this one had enough truth in it to hurt. Clay was beside himself with rage. Notwithstanding his renunciation of dueling, he issued a challenge to Randolph. Neither was wounded in the exchange of shots, but Clay had played into his opponents' hands by regressing to violence.[10]

Clay's decision to join forces with Adams had been perfectly logical in terms of philosophy and tactics, since they agreed on the issues and Adams did not cut into Clay's western support, as Jackson did. Yet, for the rest of his long life, Clay would be hounded by the charge that he had made a "corrupt bargain" with Adams by trading his vote in the House for the State Department. The fact that the issue would not die requires some explanation from the cultural historian. If Clay thought he could work with Adams and supported him in return for a place in his government, why should this be so terrible? The answer lies in the legacy of attitudes from the colonial past. Adams was doing what the king had often done in Parliament and what royal governors had tried with less success to do in colonial legislatures: gaining support by bestowing offices. In the eighteenth century these had often been lucrative sinecures that legislators accepted while continuing to sit for their constituencies. Country-party spokesmen had called the practice "corrupting" the legislature.[11] The parallel, while not exact, was close enough to damage Clay. Jacksonians, like the Whigs, found the country-party tradition available and exploited it.

In his psychological studies of Luther and Gandhi, Erik Erikson has proposed that leaders may undertake to solve for their society at large the difficulties they encounter in their own lives. Wrestling with a problem on a personal level, the leader finds he must confront it on a social level too. This hypothesis can illuminate the life of Henry Clay. His private struggle to attain self-mastery mirrored a statecraft whose objective was the substitution of compromise and rationality for violence and passion. Eriksonian psychology bears out the insight of a contemporary:

[Clay] was ardent, bold, generous, and even ambitious; and yet, with a profound conviction of the true exigencies of the country, like Alexander Hamilton, he disciplined himself, and trained a restless nation [as well] . . . to the rigorous practice of that often humiliating conservatism which its welfare and security . . . so imperiously demanded.[12]

In Clay's case, the relationship between personal and social objectives would have been reciprocal. If his quest for psychological order prompted him to pursue a politics of order, it is also true that the political culture he identified with encouraged the individual to control himself.

There is no denying that violence and related forms of disorder constituted a major social problem in Jacksonian America. The decade of the '30s saw race wars (Nat Turner's revolt and the Seminole War), major urban riots, political murder (Elijah P. Lovejoy), and Georgia and South Carolina defying the federal government, in addition to the chronic violence associated with slavery, dueling, Indian expropriation, and lynching.[13] "It is believed abroad that property is less secure among us, order less stable, law less revered, social ties more easily broken, religion less enforced, life held less sacred, than in other countries," William Ellery Channing told Clay. He illustrated the point with "the burning of a colored man by a slow fire in the neighborhood of St. Louis." Other thoughtful contemporaries warned against "the bowie-knife style of civilization" and wondered if "the dark ages are threatening to return upon us."[14]

Meanwhile, the early decades of the nineteenth century were witnessing a dramatic decline in violence, both legal and illegal, in Great Britain. One of the leading objectives of the Second Great Awakening was the achievement of a comparable decline in this country. Feeling accordingly rose against lynching, corporal punishment, child and animal abuse, drunkenness (which was associated with violence), particular wars, and warfare in general. Henry Clay acted through political means rather than moral agitation, but his objective was parallel to the evangelicals': to lower the level of violence. "All legislation, all government, all society, is formed upon the principle of mutual concession, politeness, comity, courtesy," he declared in one of his rare generalizations.[15]

It is well known that there was a sectional difference between North and South in the toleration of violence and that certain ethnic groups were accused of being more violence-prone. But the conflict over conflict, if we may call it that, also had a partisan dimension. Whigs tended to be more critical of violence than Democrats. Whigs saw themselves as the party of "all who love law and order and peace and prosperity"; their ideal of progress entailed the substitution of moral suasion "over mere brutal force." The Whig Congress elected with Harrison outlawed dueling in the District of Columbia; the Whig administration of Fillmore outlawed flogging in the Navy. Southern Whigs generally defended freedom of speech more than Democrats did in a context where illegal violence often suppressed free speech.[16] Clay repeatedly accused the Democrats of encouraging social disorganization and violence, as when he blamed the Dorr Rebellion on them or opposed the periodic preemption acts that gave retroactive legal claims to the squatters on government land.[17]

The Whig condemnation of violence often developed slowly (as in Clay himself), and it could take any number of forms. When the second party system was taking shape, those political leaders on their way to becoming Whigs generally began to take more pacific stands on a variety of issues. Some who had cheered the Greek Revolution in the twenties were conspicuously unenthusiastic about the European revolutions of 1848. Adams turned away from the aggressive expansionism of his youth and gradually became more sympathetic to the Indians. Clay's views on Indian policy underwent a dramatic evolution, from private acceptance of dispossession in 1825 to eloquent defense of the Cherokee Nation in the thirties.[18] One wonders whether this change of heart on the part of so many men involved some kind of generational conflict; certainly their fathers and grandfathers had had a high tolerance for violence in many forms, including riots and drunkenness. To be sure, the Whig party never uniformly came to repudiate violence, any more than Clay himself could. Sometimes Whig leaders regarded rioting for conservative objectives, such as that by vigilantes or antiabolition mobs, with conflicting feelings.[19]

In April, 1832, Congressman William Stansberry of Ohio was badly clubbed by Sam Houston, former congressman from Tennessee, whom he had accused of rigging an Indian contract. Both men had previously been Jackson supporters, but the National Republican press denounced Houston's deed, while the president openly befriended Houston and remitted a $500 fine levied on him by a District of Columbia court. The event helped establish a pattern: the violence that marred congressional life in this period tended to be perpetrated by Democrats and southerners upon Whigs and northerners. Preston

Brooks's attack on Charles Sumner is only the best-remembered of many such episodes. President Adams' son was assaulted by a Jackson supporter while in the Capitol, where he had come to deliver a message from his father. Horace Greeley was beaten by an Alabama Democratic congressman, Albert Rust. Not all the incidents involved slavery. They seem to have reflected two rival value systems, a Democratic-southern one that honored violence as a sign of manhood and a Whig-northern one that placed a higher value on self-possession and expressed anger verbally instead of violently. A southern Whig like Clay was caught in between, which helps explain the inner drama of his struggle.[20]

One other party issue relating to violence and social disorder deserves mention: vote fraud. Of course each party accused the other of frauds, but there is at least some reason for believing that the Democrats committed more. The fact that voter registration was a Whig-sponsored reform probably implies that the Whigs expected to gain from more honest elections. Clay's narrow defeat in 1844 may well have been due to massive Democratic ballot-box stuffing in New York, Georgia, and Louisiana.[21]

The pursuit of peace and good order was not the only aspect of Clay's political program with origins in personal experience; the same could be said of his belief in purposeful progress and in the complementarity of diverse interests. For a full understanding of Clay's ideology, one must look at his life. Clay's antecedents were firmly upper middle class. His father was a Baptist clergyman, by no means as impecunious as many of them, and his mother owned 464 acres and 18 slaves in her own right. The Reverend John Clay died when Henry was four, and his widow remarried. In later years Clay and Whig propagandists made much of the idea that he was a "self-made man"; indeed, Clay has been credited with inventing the expression.[22] Though his family background was scarcely humble, Clay was in fact self-educated and in that sense self-made. Like all too many southern children, he received practically no schooling. As manhood approached, he came under the benign influence of George Wythe, a Virginia gentleman and former tutor of Thomas Jefferson. Wythe imparted to Clay an appreciation for classical learning and encouraged him to read law. The mature Clay was capable of an occasional apt literary allusion, but he always regretted his lack of formal education.[23]

To us, the idea of a "self-made man" stands for individual as opposed to collective effort. For the Whigs this was not an important distinction; the accent was on "effort," not on "individual." They posed the alternatives as purposeful progress versus drift toward chaos. Concern with self-improvement sparked a dedication to public improvement. Clay supported public education so that others might benefit where he had not. The very speech in which he first praised the manufacturers as "self-made men" was one on behalf of a tariff to provide collective encouragements to their efforts.[24]

In 1797 young Clay moved from Virginia to Kentucky and set up a practice of law. Like most frontier lawyers, he took all kinds of cases; one that brought him notoriety was the successful defense of Aaron Burr at his treason trial. But the real money lay in corporation practice, and Clay made his representing clients like the Kentucky Insurance Company and the Bank of the United States. In 1799 he married, advantageously, Lucretia Hart, daughter of the leading businessman in Lexington and a lady of poise and taste. That same year he embarked on his political career by serving in the Kentucky constitutional convention. In 1803 he was elected to the legislature and in 1810 to Congress. There were practically no Federalists in Kentucky, but the Republicans divided on issues involving corporations and the judicial system. When the state supreme court invalidated debtor-relief laws, an angry legislature repealed the statute organizing the court and set up a whole new one. For a time there were two supreme courts in the commonwealth, each claiming sole legitimacy. Clay supported the "old court" (which eventually prevailed), and so did most of those who went on to become Whigs later. The "new-court" faction—including Amos Kendall, Francis Blair, and Richard Mentor Johnson—provided the nucleus for the future Democratic party in Kentucky.[25]

The district Clay represented in Congress contained not only the town of Lexington but also the richest agricultural land in Kentucky. Clay invested the money he made from his law practice in a beautiful plantation, Ashland. There he raised horses and flowers and enjoyed "a two-hundred-acre woodland park that Lord Morpeth, who visited Ashland, said was the nearest approach to an English park of any he had seen in this country."[26] But Ashland was more than a showplace. It was a working model for the American economy. The cash crop was hemp, a staple protected by tariff against Russian imports. Like other hemp-growers, Clay invested in the Louisville rope industry that used his raw material. Agriculture and manufacturing complemented each other in his opinion, which was shared by many contemporary Republican nationalists. Finding a term to characterize a person like Clay—planter, businessman, and professional—is not easy, but perhaps the best is one that E. P. Thompson has applied to the eighteenth-century English gentry: "agrarian bourgeois."[27]

The kind of planter Clay typified was not so different from the kind of industrialist typified by Nathan Appleton. In both cases capitalist economic enterprises served the owner's patriarchal social values. The plantation, like the company town at Lowell, tried to combine efficiency with quasi-familial cohesiveness. Plantation slaves, like Lowell "mill girls," were thought to benefit from the benevolent discipline of paternalism. Robert F. Dalzell's comment on Lowell will do for Ashland too: "We are left in the end, then, with a curious hybrid: a strikingly modern combination of resources and methods, but one devoted to maintaining the existence of a quite traditional class of leisured, public-spirited *rentiers*."[28] Only by such an interpretation can we resolve the conflicting evidence regarding the nature of the American plantation system. One set of historians has shown that slave plantations were economically capitalistic, while another has emphasized their traditional, hierarchical social system.[29] Actually, the juxtaposition of aggressive capitalism with old-fashioned elitism was not peculiar to the Old South or to the institution of slavery. The fact that many northerners—especially Whigs—were also anxious to preserve a deferential society helps explain their frequent fascination with the plantation as a social ideal.[30]

Clay's political program was generally attractive to southerners like himself—the business and professional men of commercial areas and those planters who were part of the commercial nexus, particularly ones with diversified subsidiary investments. The protective tariff had a special appeal for agricultural producers whose primary market was domestic rather than foreign, such as growers of hemp, sugar, wool, and cereals; the coal-, iron-, and salt-mining interests of the South also supported it. In the economic interests it served, the Whig party of the South differed little from its northern counterpart.[31] However, there was less immigration into the South from Europe and consequently less ethnic diversity among the white population. The place of ethnic rivalries in southern politics was taken by intrastate geographical rivalries. Often these pitted commercial and cosmopolitan Whig regions against less-developed Democratic ones; the twenty-three cities of the South voted Whig by two to one. Occasionally, an undeveloped region would support the Whigs out of hope for economic aid. Eastern Tennessee was one of these; it needed transportation facilities and investment capital to develop its iron and coal. In Virginia and North Carolina the regional rivalries were especially intricate.[32]

Lexington, Kentucky, variously called the "emporium" of the frontier and the "Athens" of the frontier, was both a commercial and a cultural outpost. Besides his professional activities, Clay found time to serve as trustee for Transylvania University in Lexington. Southern Whig leaders often supported education along with economic development, especially in the Upper South.[33] Yet we know that, on the whole, the South lagged behind in education and industry, just as it lagged in suppressing violence. The preindustrial values of the Democrats were stronger in that largely rural section; they appealed to subsistence farmers and to those planters who idealized self-sufficiency and did not identify themselves as businessmen. In place of the Whig ethic of self-improvement, the Jacksonians emphasized group loyalty, reinforcing it with political patronage and fierce racial pride. They saw black slavery as guaranteeing a kind of equality among white men—what can be called (by analogy with the Afrikaners) *Herrenvolk* democracy. With their defensive egalitarianism, the Jacksonians resented efforts to change their world, particularly the Whig didacticism they associated with northern outsiders.

The Whig party in the South did contain many emigrants from the North, just as the Democratic party in the Old Northwest contained many emigrants from the South. Often southern Whigs looked to these northerners for intellectual leadership. Sergeant Smith Prentiss, the famous orator and tariff advocate of Mississippi, had been born in Maine. William Holmes McGuffey, professor at the University of Virginia, whose influential schoolbooks propagated Whig values, was an Ohioan born in Pennsylvania. Francis Lieber of South Carolina College, whose political and legal theories appealed to Clay, came from Germany via New York. In 1818 Clay visited New England himself to see his son at Harvard College; years later he recalled being most favorably impressed by the Yankees' morality and industriousness.[34] But it was a sign of the weakness of Whig values in the South that transplanted northerners played the role they did.

In the South, implementation of Clay's vision of progress depended heavily on the willingness of planters to innovate and diversify. There was an example in those English landowners who supported sophisticated central banking, allied themselves with urban entrepreneurs, and gave Americans the name Whig. And yet the planters did not respond to the call as well as Clay or other southern evangelists of industrialization would have liked. The plantation was too perfect. Combining capitalist economic advantages with patriarchal personal gratifications, plantation agriculture fulfilled the aspirations of its owners even better than Lowell did. While some southern planters experimented with scientific agriculture or invested in railroads, many—particularly in the cotton belt—simply lacked a compelling reason to tamper with a good thing.

Clay argued that industrialization was compatible with southern slavery. Historians have shown that indeed slaves could be, and were, successfully used in industry.[35] But the dispossession of the Civilized Tribes, by opening the way to rapid and single-minded expansion of cotton agriculture, doomed Clay's hopes for a diversified southern economy. The southern population remained too dispersed to provide the attractive home market Clay wanted. What is more, many contemporaries, both southern and northern, suspected that the kind of industrialization Clay envisioned would pose a threat to the slave system. When it came down to it, their suspicions about Clay were justified. If industrialization should undermine slavery in the long run, Clay could accept this.[36] In the long run, he did not believe in perpetuating slavery.

Clay's attitudes on slavery, like his hopes for economic development and his fears of executive power, took shape while he was still a Jeffersonian Republican. Throughout his long career, he consistently advocated gradual, compensated emancipation and "colonization" of the freedmen in Africa. He supported this at the Kentucky constitutional convention of 1799; he still supported it at the Kentucky constitutional convention of 1849. The details of his program, as he set them out in the latter year, provided that all slaves born after a fixed date should become free at age twenty-five. During their last three years of servitude, they would be hired out and the wages set aside to pay the cost of their transportation to Liberia. Thus Kentucky would "acquire the advantage of the diligence, the fidelity, and the constancy of free labor" while avoiding the danger of racial strife. Of course the commonwealth did not adopt his plan, but in his will Clay provided it to his own slaves and ordered that they be taught reading, writing, and arithmetic in preparation for their ultimate freedom.[37]

Clay often expressed regret that slavery had been introduced into America. For a time he was a personal friend of the leading abolitionist James G. Birney; another prominent abolitionist, Cassius M. Clay, was his cousin. Northern Democrats, in their typical fashion, accused Henry Clay of favoring racial amalgamation.[38] Actually, his position was that of a prudent slaveholder whose views were conditioned by Whig political theory. He explained it well on a visit to Indiana in 1842 when a Quaker in his audience confronted him with a petition asking him to free his own slaves at once. Clay regarded the statement "All men are created equal" as an abstract truth applicable to humanity in the state of nature. Once society was constituted, inequality became inevitable as a consequence of diverse social roles. Large numbers of people, such as "women, minors, insane, culprits, [and] transient sojourners," were always subject to others. By the same token, when two races lived together, one would inevitably subjugate the other. If the blacks were set free and left to live with the whites, a "struggle for political ascendancy" between the races would ensue, leading to bloodshed and war. Clay was defending slavery not on grounds of anthropology or the new "scientific racism" but on grounds of a hierarchical concept of society and sheer prescriptive authority. Until they should be sent away, it was important to keep the blacks in slavery, not because they were inferior but because they were *not* inferior. If they were given the chance, they might do to whites what the whites had done to them. As Clay candidly admitted on another occasion: "Whenever it is safe and practicable, I desire to see every portion of the human family in the enjoyment of [liberty]. But I prefer the liberty of my own country to that of any other people, and the liberty of my own race to that of any other race."[39]

The apologetic defense of slavery where it already existed as a means of controlling race relations enabled southern Whigs like Clay to go on working with antislavery Whigs from the North. But in the 1820s and '30s more militant southern sectionalists began to describe slavery as a "positive good." This school of thought, nurtured by John C. Calhoun and other South Carolinians, arose less as a response to northern abolition than out of a desire to discredit southern moderates like Clay. Those who wanted to unite the South could do so best by pressing hard for the expansion and protection of slavery. Clay had every reason to deplore their strategy, which was incompatible with his own.[40] Southern Whigs hoped to avoid a confrontation with the northern wing of their party over the expansion of slavery by avoiding war with Mexico. Northern party moderates reciprocated by telling their people that if the South were left alone, slavery would die out. (If southerners like Clay had prevailed, perhaps it would have.)[41]

Clay's views on the problem of slavery reflected the central dilemma in all Whig thinking about society: how to reconcile redemption with social control. An ideologue of the Center, he rejected both abolitionism and the "positive good" of slavery. The former manifested an extreme commitment to redeeming both whites and blacks from the sin of slavery; the latter, an extreme commitment to social control, implying that slavery might be good for white workers.[42]

Between Scylla and Charybdis, Clay steered for the African colonization movement. It embodied in a specific program just the right
combination of redemptiveness with the preservation of order. In
their ancestral continent, former slaves could safely redeem not only
themselves but others. From being the victims of Western civilization, they would become its evangels. They would propagate Christianity and Western technology and nip the slave trade in the bud.
Meanwhile, their departure preserved order in America. Emancipation could be accomplished without white Americans having to
share political power with the freedmen. The Civilized Tribes of
Indians could be left where they were, in Whig opinion; they had a
distinct territorial base and legal autonomy. The colonization program would provide the blacks with these in Liberia (or Haiti or
other locations the movement considered). The cohesive social ideal
of the Whigs contained no place for a huge unassimilable free
minority group within American society. Yet to allow free Negroes
genuine assimilation would mean allowing them to intermarry with
Caucasians, a prospect virtually all whites regarded with horror.
Colonization resolved this critical difficulty. Interestingly enough,
the proponents of colonization attributed the problems free Negroes
encountered in the United States to white prejudice more often than
to black deficiencies, but they had the cultural conservative's respect
for prejudice and did not seek to change it.[43]

In the best of all Whig worlds, transporting the freedmen might
not have been indicated. For example, in 1844 Clay and his beloved
butler exchanged the highest compliment each could pay the other:
the senator emancipated Charles, and Charles chose to continue in
his former master's employ. But such ideal reciprocity within a deferential structure was rare, as everyone knew. Class as well as racial
fears were present among the Whigs; perhaps the class fears were
even more important. Liberated blacks might well fall prey to demagogues, who would excite their passions. Trying to control the
turbulent passions of the white working classes was hard enough
without adding a new black proletariat.[44] If conscience indicated
emancipation, prudence indicated colonization. Logistical difficulties were real but not insurmountable, Clay was confident. To trans-
port the entire black population of the United States would not be
necessary; if enough blacks left to lower their proportion in the
population significantly, that would suffice to reduce white "apprehension" over emancipation.[45]

The colonization movement in the United States got under way in
1816, when thirty-eight passengers were taken to the British colony

of Sierra Leone by a merchant named Paul Cuffee, who was himself half-Negro and half-Indian. What began as an experiment in self-help was quickly taken over by white paternalists. Henry Clay presided that same year over the first meeting of the American Colonization Society in Washington. An American version of Sierra Leone was created and named Liberia. Though a private organization, the Colonization Society hoped for federal cooperation. It was to be a mixed public-private enterprise, like so many others of that era.[46]

The high point in the hopes for colonization came in 1832. Clay incorporated it into his comprehensive Distribution Bill, providing federal funds to the states for education, internal improvements, and colonization projects. If government support had been forthcoming, perhaps colonization could have achieved a conjunction of purpose with the antebellum black separatist movement represented by the physician and ex-slave Martin R. Delaney. But this is sheer speculation. In the Senate, Clay's bill overcame opposition from the Deep South and Southwest, which wanted a large supply of slaves to expand production into new areas. To get Distribution through the House, the specified ends had to be dropped and the states given total discretion in spending the money they were to receive. Then Jackson killed the bill anyway, with one of his famous "pocket vetoes." Like the rest of the American System, of which it was an integral part, the colonization program presupposed a degree of government consolidation and conscious social planning that was anathema to Democrats. Besides, it looked like a disguised subsidy to the merchant marine.[47]

Clay and the other Whigs did not give up on colonization easily. The plan became closely identified with Clay's political fortunes and no doubt would have been revived if he had become president. Daniel Webster and Edward Everett were among the many Whigs still advocating it in the 1850s, as was Abraham Lincoln. Millard Fillmore composed a long proposal for federally financed colonization to put in his Message on the State of the Union in December, 1852, but was persuaded to forgo it. By then, positions on slavery had become more polarized, and it seemed best not to disturb the fragile peace of the Compromise of 1850.[48] The American Colonization Society struggled along as a private philanthropy, and after James Madison's death in 1836 Clay became its president; but no one expected that without massive federal funding the society could provide anything more than a pilot program.

The colonization plan was awesomely ambitious, rigorously logical within its Whig presuppositions, and—let it be said—ruthless in its intended manipulation of humanity. As its leader, Henry Clay revealed the mindset of a genuine ideologue. There was nothing diffident about his "moderation." The same boldness characterized his entire program, to which he gave the immodest name "the American System." Of all major figures in American political history, Clay had the most systematic and multifaceted program. If he had been able to implement it (that is, if he had been as capable a politician as he was an ideologist) he would have changed the course of United States history in the nineteenth century. Even apart from the colonization project, there would have been much more precedent for government intervention in the economy and for planned response to social problems in general.

The American System was a highly organized articulation of Whig political culture. The leading values of the culture, such as order, harmony, purposefulness, and improvement, found expression in the form of an economic program. Through this System, the future of America would be shaped in accordance with those values. Clifford Geertz has suggested that ideologies appear in new nations to replace their traditional cultures, but the case of the American System was somewhat different. The ideology did not so much replace as summarize and embody much of the cultural inheritance of Whiggery.[49] Even so, the American System reminds one of those bold development programs, sometimes called five-year plans, by which new nations often seek to achieve full independence. The name "American System" distinguished Clay's economic nationalism from the "British system" of laissez-faire. To permit free trade would keep the United States subservient to British economic colonialism, Clay warned.[50]

The American System began to take shape while Clay was still a Jeffersonian Republican. In 1818 he secured passage of a resolution stating the sense of the House of Representatives that Congress possessed constitutional power to finance internal improvements. Having supported the tariff bills of 1816 and 1820, he announced a full-blown doctrine of protection for developing industry and national self-sufficiency in 1824. By the latter date he had begun what was to be a lifelong association with the economic principles of Mathew and Henry Carey.[51] Before long Clay figured out how to circumvent the scruples of the strict constructionists. He hit upon the device of revenue-sharing, or, as he called it, "distribution" of federal money to the states for specified purposes. This would have the added benefit of forestalling the state bankruptcies and repudiation of bonds that were playing havoc with investors at the time.

A land policy was integrated into Clay's System. Because it kept out some imports, a protective tariff raised less money than a tariff for revenue only. To make up the difference, Clay favored selling the public lands rather than giving them away to settlers. The public lands were a "great resource" for the whole nation, he explained. If they were given away, only the recipients benefited; if they were sold, the proceeds could benefit all the people.[52] Very likely this policy would result in slowing westward migration, but Clay agreed with Henry Carey that population dispersion should be discouraged. Too rapid settlement of the West would outrun the transportation network, draw the work force away from manufacturing, and keep the country at a more primitive economic stage. It would also create more conflicts with the Indians and a higher level of violence generally. The System, which took all these elements into account, was beautifully logical—officious, its enemies thought.

Clay intended his American System to foster national integration and inhibit sectionalism. Economic diversification and good transportation, by creating domestic markets, would encourage commercial bonds of interest. Patriotism, put on a material basis, would enlist the prudence of the businessman in its service. Americans would become "one free, Christian, and commercial people." Meanwhile, the policy of distribution would knit the Union more strongly together by turning the states into eager clients of the federal government instead of its jealous rivals.[53] Ironically, some of Clay's fellow southerners were promoting economic development for precisely opposite motives. John C. Calhoun and J. D. B. DeBow urged industrialization upon the South because they wanted the section to become more independent of the North.

The American System was predicated on the basis of a harmony of interests. Whigs conceived such harmony to be providential. Thus, when southern free traders insisted that their interests were contrary to those of the North, John Quincy Adams replied, "It cannot be true." In the large scheme of things, it simply *had* to be that interests were reconcilable.[54] Just as the Whig party liked to think of itself as nonpartisan, it also liked to think of itself as transcending locality and section. Certainly it did harmonize the interests of some western and southern agrarians with those of the northeastern business community. The American System also claimed to reconcile the interests of classes, a more questionable proposition. The argument has become familiar to twentieth-century Americans: if the economic pie is enlarged, everyone can have a bigger piece of it. The Whigs insisted that economic development bestowed advantages on all; class conflict was a "delusion," an attempt to pit the worker's "passions against his interests."[55] In the early 1830s a Workingman's Party existed, which accepted the harmony-of-interests doctrine and allied with the National Republicans; around 1834, however, it went over to Jackson. The Democrats tended to view economic change as a "zero-sum game," in which one group's advantage comes at the expense of another. Although historians have yet to investigate the matter, one would suppose that the harmony-of-interests doctrine sounded most plausible to workers when there was an ethnic identity between them and their employer. Doubtless, in the long run, the average American's standard of living did improve as a consequence of the Industrial Revolution, but the latest findings also indicate that economic growth did nothing to mitigate the extreme inequality of wealth distribution in Jacksonian America.[56]

In 1832 Clay faced the unenviable task of trying to figure out how to prevent Jackson's reelection. He hit on the scheme of making the recharter of the Second Bank of the United States his issue, hoping that the Bank's popularity would prove greater than the Old Hero's, especially in Pennsylvania, where the Bank was headquartered. In this he miscalculated. Jackson won reelection and even carried the Keystone State. Here is not the place to retell the protracted and complex maneuverings of the "Bank War." Clay and the Bank's president, Nicholas Biddle, resorted to ever more desperate expedients in trying to force renewal of the charter, including an artificial contraction of the country's credit. Clay showed himself to be a dangerously irresponsible as well as unsuccessful politician, but it would be wrong to think of the Bank issue as nothing more than a politician's ploy. If it had been, it could not have polarized the American electorate for over a decade. The Bank issue brought into sharp focus the conflict between two views of the nation's destiny: Clay's vision of economic development planned centrally by a capitalist elite and the Democratic vision of a land of equal opportunity. Even after the Bank's charter finally expired in 1836, banking and currency remained the subject of bitterest partisan debate.[57]

The Bank War displayed Clay at his worst; even some Whigs became disgusted toward the end. But right in the midst of it the Nullification Crisis brought out the statesman in him. The Adams Tariff in 1832 proved very unpopular with the cotton-growers. South Carolina took the drastic and unprecedented action of calling a convention to consider nullifying it, that is, declaring sections of the federal statute book unconstitutional and void within the state. Clay showed himself capable of rising above his animosity toward Jackson by cooperating with the president in the interests of the Union. The result was a policy at once firm and conciliatory: the

Force Act showed that the central government meant to enforce the law, and the Compromise Tariff of 1833 gradually lowered duties over the next nine years.[58]

In the spring of 1835 Clay took a much more conciliatory line than Jackson on the settlement of the debts France owed the United States. While Jackson was threatening to seize French assets to pay the American claims, the Whig party advocated patience. Eventually the French paid up and the excitement passed, but the issue was symptomatic of a recurrent difference between the two parties and their leaders with respect to international relations. The personal animosity between Clay and Jackson went back to 1818–19, when Clay had led the congressional critics of Jackson's unauthorized invasion of Florida. Clay deplored *Machtpolitik*, whether directed against European powers, Indian tribes, or sister republics of the Western Hemisphere. The peace negotiations of 1814, not the war fever of 1812, set the pattern of his career. Clay regarded the preservation of international peace as part of the general struggle against violence and disorder that he also undertook in domestic politics and on a personal level:

> War unhinges society, disturbs its peaceful and regular industry, and scatters poisonous seeds of disease and immorality, which continue to germinate and diffuse their baneful influences long after it has ceased. Dazzling by its glitter, pomp, and pageantry, it begets a spirit of wild adventure and romantic enterprise, and often disqualifies those who embark in it, after their return from the bloody fields of battle, from engaging in the industrious and peaceful vocations of life.[59]

The American peace movement took root in the opposition to the War of 1812, revived during the confrontation with France in 1835, and persisted from then on in opposition to the belligerent policy of the United States toward Mexico. Throughout this time it was associated with Federalist-Whig domestic politics, nor was the alignment mere coincidence. The two parties' views on foreign relations reflected their different value systems and visions of national destiny. Democratic aggressiveness, glorified as the fulfillment of the nation's "manifest destiny," displayed a strong commitment to racial supremacy, an acceptance of unrestrained competition, and a high toleration for violence. The Whigs were more anxious for America to become a responsible member of a community of nations recognizing international law and substituting diplomacy for violence. Nations, like individuals, should impose restraints on themselves.[60]

The Whigs' dedication to peace was selfish as well as principled. Taking land from Mexico and the Indians did not particularly coincide with their interests, and strained relations with European countries were bad for business. Europe, especially Britain, supplied valuable investment capital, on which much of the Whigs' hope for economic development rested.[61] During the recurrent Anglo-American disagreements of the era—the *Caroline* affair, the Maine–New Brunswick boundary dispute, the Oregon question, the Clayton-Bulwer Treaty and its interpretation—Whigs were generally more eager than Democrats to seek accord with Britain. To be sure, the Democrat Polk proved willing to settle for a partition of Oregon rather than wage two wars at once, but the Whigs would never have risked the wars in the first place. American Whigs agreed with Tocqueville: "Commerce is naturally adverse to all the violent passions: it loves to temporize, takes delight in compromise, and studiously avoids irritation."[62] Nineteenth-century capitalism could be warlike, as in the notorious Anglo-Chinese Opium War, but the Whig party in the United States manifested a pacific form of capitalism. When the Hungarian revolutionary Louis Kossuth visited in 1851 to seek American intervention in central Europe, he found Democrats more willing than Whigs to entertain the possibility. Clay, by then ill and bedridden, begged Kossuth to desist and not involve the United States in a European war.[63]

As the election year of 1840 approached, Clay's thoughts turned again to presidential strategy. It seemed expedient to dissociate himself from the abolitionists, so he gave a speech in which he berated those of them who renounced the Constitution and also declared his opposition to emancipation in the District of Columbia.[64] With this anti-antislavery move, Clay outsmarted himself. At the Whig convention, Thurlow Weed of New York and Thaddeus Stevens of Pennsylvania, appealing to the northern Antimasonic reform wing of the party, were able to block Clay's nomination and substitute that of William Henry Harrison. Harrison's preferences, like Clay's, were for colonization, but he had kept on good terms with the antislavery movement.[65] The magnanimous Harrisonians then asked Clay to suggest a vice-presidential nominee, but he, despondent, refused to answer. It was a costly fit of pique; for without guidance from Clay headquarters, the choice fell upon John Tyler of Virginia, who had been supporting Clay against Harrison but had no commitment to Clay's program. When Harrison died, a month after his inauguration, Tyler succeeded to the presidency.

Before he died, Harrison had summoned a special session of

Congress to consider the Whig legislative program. The Whigs held a commanding majority in Congress, and Clay's power over it led to his being nicknamed "the dictator" (a word whose connotations were not quite so evil then). However, it turned out that the Bankruptcy Act of 1841 and the Tariff of 1842 were the only major pieces of legislation the Whigs were able to enact. The new president, Tyler, broke with the party and frustrated its program. Tyler belonged to a small faction of Old Republicans dedicated to states' rights. He had associated himself with the Whigs as a means of opposing Jackson. Having become president, he seems to have hoped that he could remake the Whig party in a states'-rights image through the use of executive patronage and then win election in his own right. Accepting the Whig legislative program would have conceded Clay the dominant role in the party and made him the likely nominee in 1844.[66] Like many later historians, Tyler misjudged the nature of the Whig party. Being fundamentally issue-oriented rather than office-oriented, it could not be turned around so easily. Clay's program had broad appeal within it, and only a tiny minority of Whigs, even in the South, sided with the president. The midterm elections of 1842 practically annihilated the little band of Tyler followers in Congress.

Clay has been criticized for not reaching an accommodation with Tyler over rechartering a national bank. In fact, a meeting of minds between the two was impossible. Tyler rejected two recharter bills; by the time the second one reached his desk, it contained every concession he had demanded. Still he vetoed it, perhaps because he had recently been insulted by a pro-bank Virginia Whig named John Minor Botts, perhaps because he never intended the concessions he demanded to constitute binding commitments on his part. What is most likely is that no compromise bank could have satisfied both Tyler and Clay.[67]

The conflict between Tyler and Clay was a classic case of "court" versus "country" party, between executive patronage and a legislative majority. (The little clique of southern politicians encouraging Tyler, the strong odor of administration corruption, and even the ostentatious White House social life after the president's second marriage suggested a "court" all too strongly.)[68] Just as the confrontation between "court" and "country" in England under George III produced the pioneer legitimation of party politics by Edmund Burke in 1770, the comparable situation in America in the 1840s produced the real birth of avowed party solidarity among the Whigs. Henry Clay, like Edmund Burke, started from "country" premises and eventually decided that political parties were good because they could counterbalance the power of an unresponsive executive. By putting the new idea of a party system into the service of the old antiexecutive objectives of the "country" tradition, Clay showed himself an imaginative political ideologist.[69]

Though Martin Van Buren is usually credited with developing the modern party system in the United States, a measure of that credit belongs to Henry Clay. What is more, while Van Buren's party was based on patronage, Clay built his around a program and in opposition to the White House. After Tyler's second bank veto, every member of the cabinet save one resigned in a dramatic display of party unity. The holdout was Secretary of State Daniel Webster, reluctant to accept Clay's leadership and new-fangled ideas about party responsibility. Tyler then tried to pursue his ambitions within the Democratic party—an equally unpromising strategy, for that organization looked after its own and was not about to give the juiciest plum of all to an outsider.

Besides frustrating Clay's domestic program, Tyler had another grand objective, the annexation of Texas. Northern Whigs had feared this prospect ever since the Lone Star Republic won independence in 1836. The addition of Texas would expand the area of slavery in the United States. When Webster failed to dissuade Tyler from pursuing its annexation, he too resigned from the cabinet. A few northerners even called upon their section to secede if Texas joined the Union.[70] But opposition to Texas was more a party issue than a sectional one. Reservations about Texas were shared among southern Whigs, for not all cotton-growers welcomed competition from new lands beyond the Sabine. Besides strengthening the Southwest against the Northeast, Texas was also expected to strengthen the Democratic party against the Whigs.[71] Apart from their specific objections to Texas, Whigs were generally less interested in continental expansion than the Democrats. Since they preferred a relatively slow and orderly settlement of the West, on both economic and moral grounds, they felt no pressing need for additional territory. Their primary concern was the qualitative development of American society, both economically and morally, not its mere quantitative extension. The conventional Whig view had been stated early by Webster: "No nation ever had less to expect from forcible aggrandizement" than the United States. "The mighty agents which are working out our greatness are time, industry, and the arts. Our augmentation is by growth, not by acquisition; by internal development, not by external accession."[72]

Clay knew that Tyler and his new secretary of state, John C. Calhoun, wanted Texas in order to strengthen the slaveholding interest. He himself had no desire to expand slavery, and he recoiled from the war with Mexico he expected annexation to provoke. Naturally, he opposed Texas. His Democratic counterpart, Martin Van Buren, reached the same conclusion; he too resented the schemes of Tyler and Calhoun. Van Buren visited Clay's plantation in May, 1842, where the two great party-builders seem to have agreed (no record of what transpired exists) to keep the Texas question out of the next campaign. On April 27, 1844, both leaders issued statements opposing annexation. But the best-laid plans go oft awry; expansionism had too great an appeal among Democrats. Their convention denied Van Buren the nomination he had expected and bestowed it instead on James Knox Polk of Tennessee, who wanted to press for Texas and easily bought off northern Democrats by including a claim to all Oregon in the platform. Continental expansion was America's "manifest destiny," the northern Democratic press trumpeted. The Democratic campaign was unashamedly imperialistic and threatened war with Britain over Oregon and with Mexico over Texas.

Unlike Van Buren, Clay enjoyed the support of a united party and was nominated without opposition. During the summer, however, Clay became worried that his stand on Texas was costing him votes in the Deep South, where Calhoun had succeeded in making annexation a test of sectional loyalty. By custom, presidential candidates were entitled to remain silent and let local supporters make arguments on their behalf, but Clay could not resist trying to mend his fences in the Gulf states. He penned two "Alabama Letters," hoping to explain his position in such a way as to mollify expansionists there. Back in 1827, as Adams' secretary of state, Clay had offered to buy Texas from Mexico. Now he stated that he would again be willing to acquire Texas *if* it could be accomplished "without national dishonor, without war, with the general consent of the States of the Union, and upon fair and reasonable terms." In the present situation those conditions could not, of course, be met. As an exposition of the logic underlying Clay's statecraft his assertion was accurate, for on expansion, as on most subjects, Clay was a genuine Centrist, not a mere trimmer. As an election tactic, however, the Alabama Letters created an impression of equivocation. They conceded too little to strengthen Clay much in the lower South but enough to lose him vital votes in the North.[73] One cannot confidently attribute the result of a close election to a single tactical mistake, but it is a fact that enough voters turned to the unambiguously antiannexationist Liberty party in New York and Michigan to give Polk pluralities in those states. The Democrat eked out a narrow but momentous victory.

After Polk's war with Mexico came, Clay deplored it. He had resigned from Congress to run for president, but in a major speech at
Lexington he declared that "no earthly consideration would have
ever tempted or provoked me" to vote to raise an army against
Mexico, supported as the measure was by the untruths of the administration, "falsely attributing the commencement of the war to
the act of Mexico."[74] Clay had long been the leading advocate in the
United States of good relations with Latin America. He had ardently
supported the republics in their revolutions against Spain and had
favored extending them arms for their struggle as well as prompt
diplomatic recognition. As secretary of state he had supported the
prototypical inter-American conference at Panama in 1826. Peaceful
commerce within the Western Hemisphere was a logical extension of
the American System, in Clay's mind.[75] In Mexico, the bourgeois
federalista party also hoped for peace and commerce between the two
neighboring countries. Statements by Clay and other Whigs endorsing harmonious relations had been translated and reprinted
south of the border.

Despite all he had done to avoid the war, Clay was called upon to
bear his share of its suffering. Among the soldiers killed at the Battle
of Buena Vista was Henry Clay, Jr. The father's grief was compounded by the knowledge that "this Mexican War was unnecessary
and of an aggressive character. My poor son did not however stop to
enquire into the causes of the War. It was sufficient for him that it
existed in fact, and that he thought the Nation was entitled to his
services."[76] In his bereavement Clay sought the consolations of the
Episcopal Church. Another leading critic of the war, Daniel Webster,
also lost a son in it.

On March 10, 1848, Senate Whigs gave grudging consent to ratification of the Treaty of Guadalupe Hidalgo, by which the United
States acquired New Mexico and California as well as Texas. And,
almost immediately, Whigs reconciled themselves to the new acquisitions. Within a few months they even nominated war-hero
Zachary Taylor for president, frustrating for the final time the hopes
of Henry Clay. Taylor's nomination was the work of an ambitious
group of middle-level Whig politicians (among them, Abraham Lincoln of Illinois) who still believed in the American System but felt the
party needed a new face. The Taylor campaign showed that the
Whigs were not altogether immune to the temptations of imperialism. Clay's own Alabama Letters had betrayed their secret:
outside New England, most Whigs did not object to expansion as
such; it was the concomitant price in social disruption and dishonor
they minded. Now the price had been paid. If the guilt was borne

mostly by Democrats, so much the better. The Whigs took no perverse pleasure in self-flagellation. The fruits of the Mexican War were too rich to be spurned, especially when gold turned up in John Sutter's millrace. Even Daniel Webster decided that "my apprehensions over California and New Mexico have not been realized."[77] After all, the Whigs had also reconciled themselves, in the end, to the dispossession of the Civilized Tribes.

In April, 1849, the *American Whig Review* printed an article on California welcoming not only its wealth but its advantageous location. The United States was now a two-ocean power and could expand its commerce with Asia as well as Europe. "America must become the center of the world." Of course, Americans must exercise their new greatness wisely, and this they could do only by rededicating themselves to Christianity.[78] The conjunction of commerce with Christianity was typical of the Whig version of imperialism. Whereas Democratic imperialism took political and military forms, Whig imperialism took economic and religiocultural forms. If the West could be redeemed, expansion would not be so dangerous. Perhaps, through the efforts of businessmen, educators, and missionaries, the West could be made more like the East. As time went by, the power of commerce and Christianity to overcome violence and disorder seemed encouraging. Influenced by evangelical tracts like Lyman Beecher's *Plea for the West* (1835), as well as by the economic development Clay promoted, eastern Whigs gradually adopted a more positive attitude toward the frontier. Acceptance of the Mexican Cession was only one indication of their changing views.[79]

As president, Zachary Taylor proved responsive to this new spirit within Whiggery. The Mexican Cession forced Whigs to choose between two goals: acceptance and redemption of the West or compromise of North-South differences. Taylor opted squarely for the former; he stood ready to welcome California and New Mexico into statehood. Although a Louisiana slaveholder himself, Taylor was undismayed by the prospect of two new free states. Many other southerners, however, felt differently and feared they were losing the fruits of military victory. Southern Democrats took advantage of the situation to demand that a federal slave code be enacted for the territories.[80] Taylor summoned a special session of Congress to confront the issues before the nation, as Harrison had done, but his administration controlled neither house. The president was powerless to implement his policy, straightforward and statesmanlike though it was. Meanwhile, California and New Mexico remained in political uncertainty. New Mexico, with a population mainly Indian and Mexican, was threatened with invasion by an army from Texas, which claimed all land east of the Rio Grande. Taylor declared that he would lead the Union army to defend New Mexico against Texas; though he had achieved his fame fighting against Mexico, he did not intend to stand aside while Mexicans who had become United States citizens were despoiled or massacred by an insubordinate state.[81] Taylor's attitude makes an interesting contrast with Jackson's in the Cherokee-Georgia dispute; there was a difference between a Whig old soldier and a Democratic old soldier. Just when it looked as if civil war might break out in the Southwest, President Taylor suddenly died. He was the only president between John Quincy Adams and Abraham Lincoln whose policies were not proslavery.

Clay had not given Taylor the support the late president deserved; his disappointment at having been passed over for the nomination in 1848 ran too deep to be set aside. He could not bear to see another man defining Whig policies.[82] Where Taylor had committed the government to securing order and morality in the new lands, Clay chose to pursue a more cautious version of Whiggery. Taylor's death and the succession of Millard Fillmore opened the way for Clay's program, which included the following proposals. (1) California should become a state, but New Mexico should remain a territory. (2) Territorial governments for New Mexico and the Mormon community of Utah should be established without congressional legislation on slavery; neither the northern-backed Wilmot Proviso, forbidding it, nor a code of laws enforcing it would be enacted. Instead, the matter would be left to the territorial legislatures. (3) Texas should renounce her extravagant claims to half of New Mexico and be compensated by federal assumption of the debts contracted during her independence. (4) One other concession was offered to each section: the interstate slave trade (though not slavery itself) was to be abolished in the District of Columbia, and a new Fugitive Slave Law was to be enacted to provide federal rather than state administration of recovery procedures.

In advocating his comprehensive compromise, Clay admitted the force of northern arguments that the expansion of slavery was incompatible with his vision of national progress. He told his fellow southerners that the expansion of slavery into the territories was "an effort to propagate wrong." If it provoked a civil war, "we [southerners] should have no sympathy, no good wishes, and . . . all mankind would be against us." Before matters came to that pass, Clay wanted one final effort made to substitute persuasion for violence. The appeal to prudential calculation sprang from the depths of his being. "I go for honorable compromise whenever it can be made. Life itself is but a compromise between death and life, the struggle continuing throughout our whole existence until the great Destroyer finally triumphs." He spoke as an old man who had known many disappointments.[83] In defense of his plan, Clay invoked the time-honored formulas of Whig moral philosophy: "Mr. President, it is passion, passion—party, party, and intemperance—that is all I dread in the adjustment of the the great questions which unhappily at this time divide our distracted country." He called upon his hearers to subordinate their personal feelings to the organic unity of society:

> Mr. President, what is an individual man? An atom, almost invisible without a magnifying glass—a mere speck upon the surface of the immense universe. . . . Shall a being so small, so petty, so fleeting, so evanescent, oppose itself to the onward march of a great nation, to subsist for ages and ages to come—oppose itself to the long line of posterity which, issuing from our loins, will endure during the existence of the world? Forbid it, God![84]

To the end, Clay's political skill was unequal to his vision. The "omnibus" bill embodying the provisions of his compromise was defeated. Support for the compromise came mostly from northern Democrats and southern Whigs, for by now the Whig party in the North and the Democratic party in the South had become almost entirely polarized over the extension of slavery. After Clay had departed, weak and heartsick, the compromise was passed piecemeal by the maneuvers of Stephen A. Douglas and other northern Democrats.[85] In the form which its Democratic managers finally enacted, however, the compromise conceded more to slavery than Clay had originally intended. His affirmation that the Mexican law prohibiting slavery would continue in the Cession area unless specifically changed was dropped. His provision for a jury trial of alleged fugitive slaves also disappeared. Finally, the Texas–New Mexico boundary was revised to favor Texas somewhat more.

The compromise measures of 1850 were Clay's final contribution to his country. They manifested his faith that true progress comes through peaceful accommodation. This Whig vision of progress appears in every aspect of his career. The steadily increasing imposition of order upon turbulence was his ideal in both his personal and his political life. He hoped to reconcile morality with harmony as goals, but, being primarily a man of prudence, he inclined more toward preserving political harmony. He intended his last compromise to grant the country "repose" and salved his conscience with the comforting thought that the Southwest would prove geographically unsuited to plantation slavery if Congress left the matter alone. Perhaps he repressed the memory of earlier occasions when he had shown how slave labor could be used in any number of economic activities.[86]

Clay's last parliamentary effort took place at the beginning of March, 1851, when he spoke on behalf of a bill for improving riverways and harbors. The bill, like so many others Clay had supported, was defeated.[87] By the time Congress met again, Clay was incapacitated by tuberculosis. He died June 29, 1852, having failed to win acceptance for the American System, to recharter the national bank, and to become president. The Whig party itself would not long outlive him.

Of course the Compromise of 1850 did not settle the slavery issue, and the bloody civil war Clay hoped so desperately to avoid occurred. In these and many other ways Clay's statecraft was a failure. Yet the compromise did buy a decade of time during which the forces of Union and freedom gathered strength. The action that upset it was the Kansas-Nebraska Bill of 1854, introduced by the same Stephen A. Douglas who had managed the Compromise of 1850. But Douglas was a Democrat, and he understood neither the moral issue of slavery nor the moral claim of precedent. Clay's statesmanship compares very favorably with that of Douglas. In the long run, the triumph of the Union in 1865 and the rise of the United States as an industrial nation may be taken to award Clay a posthumous success. If so, it was Clay the man of vision rather than Clay the politician whom events ultimately vindicated.

Seven years after Clay's death, one R. McKinley Ormsby was writing a *History of the Whig Party*. He described what he thought was the ideal Whig personality type. A Whig, he wrote, is one who

has not the gratification of a present passion in view; but crushes out and sacrifices private feelings and interests, and compromises with antagonistic views, to secure the stability of the country, develop its resources, and place its future on a safe and enduring basis. His ideas are not formed on partial views, nor inspired by local interests; but are liberal, enlarged, comprehensive, and are the growth of long-continued and mature reflection.[88]

It is exactly how Clay would have liked himself to be.

Seven

The Evangelicals

Lyman Beecher (1775–1863) was a central figure in the great evangelical movement, which constituted an important dimension of Whiggery. Today people find it difficult to come to terms with him. Beecher's reputation as a reactionary crank is not merely a distortion, it is a total misconception of his place in history. Beecher and the evangelical movement to a large extent shaped the dominant culture of nineteenth-century America—what has been called "American Victorianism." During the twentieth century, many cosmopolitan intellectuals have been struggling to free themselves from this culture. Perhaps, at last, the battle has been won enough so that a new generation of historians can study Beecher and what he stood for without having to renew the fight.[1]

Beecher himself loved a good fight; yet he learned to control his combative temperament in the interests of higher strategy. In the world of his time he was a moderate reformer and practiced the arts of compromise. Indeed, as a mediator of great personal magnetism with a grand vision of his country's destiny, Beecher might be called the Henry Clay of the ecclesiastical realm. Like Clay, he was emotional, impulsive, an ardent man who knew the price of self-control. Both were beloved of their partisans and mistrusted by their enemies.

Beecher's sermons, like Clay's speeches, depended a great deal on the charm with which they were delivered; their words in print do not convey all the power that contemporaries felt in them. In the end, like Clay, Beecher felt personal triumph elude him.

The son of a blacksmith, Beecher fathered one of the truly great families in American history. Among his five daughters and eight sons were Harriet the novelist, Edward the abolitionist, Henry Ward the preacher, Isabella the suffragist, and Catharine, the founder of home economics.[2] His own father had been stern and unloving, but Lyman involved himself wholeheartedly with his children. He encouraged them in both intellectual and religious seeking and succeeded in imbuing them with his strong sense of mission. In an age when education for women was a novelty, Beecher devoted as much concern to his daughters' minds as to his sons'. His drive for himself, his family, and the cause of Christ knew no bounds.

The Autobiography of Lyman Beecher (a compilation of letters and reminiscences pieced together as a collective family enterprise during the patriarch's old age) is full of illustrations of his warm humanity and shrewd practical sense. Harriet recalled a "household inspired by a spirit of cheerfulness and hilarity." Lyman played the fiddle, and since several of the children could play the piano and flute, the house often rang with happy music. He installed parallel bars, climbing ropes, and other gymnastic equipment in the back yard and performed on them with "as much apparent delight and pride as [he took] in any of his intellectual exertions." In everything he was intense, and he admired intensity in others wherever he found it. He could be moved to tears by Milton's heroic portrayal of Satan, and he loved Byron's poetry and felt sure he could have converted that famous infidel if given the chance. He thought Napoleon Bonaparte "a glorious fellow" ("the Bourbons [were] not a whit better morally, and *imbecile* to boot"). His eccentric rusticity, his sense of humor, and his argumentative conversation sometimes suggest Dr. Samuel Johnson (whose home town, incidentally, was the one for which Beecher's Litchfield was named). But Beecher was a Yankee of Yankees and a consecrated evangelical. One who knew him well observed: "He had no small ambitions."[3]

Beecher's grandest ambition—and it could hardly have been grander—was to prepare the way for the Second Coming of Christ. He had encountered in his reading of Jonathan Edwards the idea that this event might occur in the New World; and though at first the notion seemed "chimerical," he eventually became persuaded of its plausibility.[4] The tradition of Edwardsean eschatology had been transmitted to Beecher via Timothy Dwight, Edwards' grandson, who became president of Yale during Beecher's undergraduate years there. The continuity of evangelical thought remained unbroken during the time of the Whig party; the providential interpretation of history that one finds in Edwards' accounts of the Reformation or the Glorious Revolution reappears in the writings of Whigs as late as the 1840s, though the latter have a more specifically patriotic tone.[5] Like Edwards—and John Quincy Adams—Beecher believed in postmillennialism, the doctrine that the Second Coming will occur at the end of the thousand years of peace foretold in Scripture. Human exertion to bring about this happy social state therefore contributes to hastening the day of the Lord. (Premillennialism, the alternative doctrine, teaches that Christ's return will precede the thousand-year peace, implying that the millennium will occur through divine intervention and not as part of human history.) The Second Coming was not far off, Beecher believed, and his efforts to win souls and reform society carried the urgency of this conviction. One last big effort would do it—or rather two: the establishment of foreign missions to complete the conversion of the world and the moral renovation of American society to give Christ a beachhead for His return.[6]

The importance of postmillennial theology for Whig political culture lay in its optimistic view of history. It provided an alternative to the cyclical theory of classical republicanism. The secular writers on politics whom the Whigs read generally espoused a very limited view of the possibilities for human achievement; Adam Ferguson, though he analyzed human history in terms of progression toward complexity, carefully hedged his predictions for a brighter future, while the ancient and Renaissance authors were even less sanguine. From religion, however, the Whigs could draw on a fund of more hopeful ideas. Most people since the beginning of history have lived in "barbarism and despotism," Beecher acknowledged before the Connecticut state legislature, but through the interpretation of Scripture we can derive assurance of transcending this ("Behold, I make all things new"). We can dare to believe that "our nation had been raised up by Providence to exert an efficient instrumentality in this moral renovation of the world." With the invocation of Providence, the evangelicals escaped the constraints of the civic humanist tradition and opened the way to a vision of unbounded progress for America.[7]

The hopes and consolations of eschatology were especially precious to Lyman Beecher, who suffered from recurrent bouts of melancholia (origin undiagnosed). He found personal religion "a war which the Christian is destined to maintain for life, in which there is neither sleep, truce, nor rest." Within the framework of evangelical cosmic optimism, periodic reverses and disappointments could be accommodated: "Instead of fainting under the stroke, we are animated by it, to double confidence in God and double diligence in this work."[8] As already noted, Henry Clay's personal struggle to subordinate the violent passions in the interests of harmony mirrored a problem confronting American society as a whole. Likewise, Beecher's long battle to overcome depression replicated a struggle by American culture to achieve confidence in itself.[9]

Condorcet, Paine, and the other writers of the Revolutionary Enlightenment might, of course, have provided an ideology of progress, but in practice they were not invoked by American Whigs. The condemnation of the French Revolution by the American clergy in 1795 turned out to mark a lasting turning point in the history of opinion.[10] Whigs carefully distinguished the American from the French Revolution, condemning the latter for atheism, and they often went all the way back to the Reformation era to find their sources of inspiration. (Beecher and his coworker, Nathaniel William Taylor of Yale, called their journal *The Spirit of the Pilgrims*.) The historian David Brion Davis has put it very well: "We have not sufficiently appreciated that for many American Protestants, the Reformation, even more than the Revolution, was the model of a timeless, archetypal experience that had to be reenacted, in almost ritualistic fashion, if freedom was to be preserved." Even a religious liberal like Edward Everett dated "the entire cause of modern political reform" to the Protestant Reformation.[11]

The evangelical movement supplied Whiggery with a conception of progress that was the collective form of redemption: like the individual, society as a whole was capable of improvement through conscious effort. Nineteenth-century evangelicalism, even more than eighteenth-century evangelicalism, demanded the moral regeneration of society, not simply of the individuals within it. Beecher accordingly urged that Christians never elect duelers to office (the abolitionists later applied his principle to slaveholders).[12] But for all its moral urgency, social redemption was still a gradual and historical process for evangelicals within the Whig fold. Slowly but surely, people would come to grasp what the immutable divine law implied for the conduct of their lives. If one wished to express the difference between Whigs and Democrats in the vocabulary of theology, one could say that, while the Whigs were political postmillennialists, working for redemption through history, the Democrats were political premillennialists, who did not see history as a process of

conscious moral improvement but as a legacy of suffering and oppression from which they desired liberation.

Postmillennialism synthesized ancient Christian theological conceptions with the activist mood of modern times. It could coexist
comfortably with the Industrial Revolution and the kind of economic
progress Clay advocated. When Lyman Beecher declared that "the
stated policy of heaven is to raise the world from its degraded condition," he had in mind not only its spiritual but also its intellectual
and material condition. The means providence would employ were
"the facilities of art, the increase of capital, and men of enterprize,
who will use this world as not abusing it, and appropriate their
income under the guidance of the wisdom which is from above." The
evangelical movement practiced what Beecher preached by bringing
"men of enterprize"—laymen from the business world—into prominent roles in its philanthropic and missionary activities.[13] Though
the old distrust of affluence died hard, the evidence indicated that
economic development favored the kind of morality that clerical
Whigs wanted to promote. "What encourages us," William Ellery
Channing wrote to Jean Charles de Sismondi, "is that public morals
do not seem to decline, but rather seem to improve, amidst this rapid
accumulation of the means of self-indulgence." With intellectual and
moral greatness "cherished in the bosom of wealth," the growth of
prosperity, so characteristic of the modern world, could be welcomed
as laying the foundation for "the millennial condition of society."[14]

The evangelical movement in Britain and America has often been
viewed as a reactionary response to the French Revolution. That the
French Revolution played an important part as its catalyst need not
and cannot be denied. But to see the evangelical movement simply as
a "great retrogression" is to misunderstand its real nature.[15] There
were, to be sure, a number of genuinely reactionary movements in
nineteenth-century Europe, including some religious ones, like the
Ultramontane and Oxford movements, but the evangelical movement was not among them. The Anglo-American evangelical movement was both a bourgeois and a popular movement at a time when
the bourgeoisie was a dynamic and progressive force. The dynamic,
progressive aspects are particularly evident in the American branch
of the evangelical movement.

In 1846 an international convention of the Evangelical Alliance met
in London. Among those in attendance were Lyman Beecher and
Horace Bushnell. Beecher played the more prominent part; he gave
major addresses on temperance and antislavery. But Bushnell was an

acute observer, and what struck him about the gathering was its antiaristocratic modernity:

No bishops in their robes of office, no papal nuncios clad in the symbols of God's viceregency, no princes in trappings of royalty, no military at the door, nor prison hard by where the heretics are chained waiting their trial, no scholastic dogmas proposed, no contests of logic, no intrigues on foot to secure some ecclesiastical promotion....[16]

The evangelical movement manifested a resurgence of middle-class Protestant culture that had been subordinated in England ever since the Restoration of 1660 and the defeat of Monmouth's rebellion in 1685. It represented the religious aspect of that culture, just as the commonwealthman tradition had represented the political aspect. The evangelical reinvigoration of middle-class Protestant culture in the early nineteenth century created the preconditions for much that was characteristic of the Victorian era in Britain. The English author Lucy Aikin saw what had happened clearly enough in 1847:"[The evangelical party] at length became great enough to give the tone to society at large."[17]

In the United States, the evangelical movement represented an analogous cultural reinvigoration. It could be found in all parts of the country, East and West, North and South, yet it played the largest role in regions corresponding to the band of New England Yankee settlement. What we think of as New England culture was the American distillation of middle-class English Protestant culture, which had acquired a geographical focus by the Puritan migration of the 1630s. Though the impact of the French Revolution was felt less powerfully across the Atlantic than in Britain, the evangelical movement in the United States can still be viewed in terms of challenge and response. The principal challenge here was the continually renewed one of population migration. The American evangelical movement was marked by a reaffirmation of the values of New England culture and by their geographical extension across the Mohawk Valley into the upper Old Northwest and into many urban centers all over the country.

Beecher's home town of Litchfield, Connecticut, "a town of small businesses, where the carding of wool was largely done in families," with its academy and law school, typified in many ways the New England ideal.[18] It was what we have called a "middle landscape." But Beecher's social ideals were not merely a reflection of what in fact existed around him; they also drew on the seventeenth-century community ideal, which he consciously revived to mitigate the social evils entailed in both the growth of cities and the dispersion of the frontier. The labors of Beecher and a generation of other pioneering missionaries across the land taught Whigs to take a more optimistic view of the chances for redeeming the frontier and the cities.

Lyman Beecher's "Lectures on Political Atheism" (1829; revised in 1835 and 1852) express much of his social philosophy. They are dedicated "To the Working Men of America" and show the identification with the common man that the blacksmith's son never lost. (Of course, he felt free to quote Virgil and Milton and to debate the opinions of Hegel and Hume, for he was not ashamed of having obtained an education.) Beecher begins by arguing that Christianity is the ally of social progress and liberty. "It is *your* cause that the Christian revelation espouses. No other religion ever cared for the common people. . . . In all Pagan, Mahometan, and Papal lands, they are in deep darkness and in chains." Biblical Christianity, that is, Protestantism, promotes schools, morality, economic enterprise, and relative social equality. At the same time, it preserves the "attractions of heaven," without which, Beecher is convinced, "society will dissolve." He recurs to moral philosophy: the "bad passions" in human nature are very strong, and it is only by constant effort that the virtuous are able to keep them under control. Good men employ various institutions—"the law, and schools, and families, and religious institutions"—to keep the bad passions under control, but it is never easy. Evil men ally themselves with the bad passions, and this gives them an advantage over the virtuous, who are trying to strengthen conscience and reason—inherently weaker aspects of human nature. Among the bad men are "ambitious demagogues, who care not by what ladder they rise." They make extravagant promises but leave desolation in their wake. The "political atheism" they preach, explicitly or implicitly, threatens religion, the conventional family, and private property.[19]

The stakes are high in the conflict Beecher depicts, yet this does not justify any restriction of freedom of opinion. "Free inquiry is the birthright and the duty of man," the true principle of the Reformation; and "if the friends of truth cannot, or will not, maintain their cause, they ought to perish in its ruins." If the good can successfully create an enlightened public opinion, "the nation will be a safe depository of liberty forever." There is no need to fear that America must decline like other republics, Beecher assures his audience. What will be needed to bring in the long-awaited millennium?

Beecher is specific: (1) universal land reform, to give ownership to actual cultivators; (2) representative democracy in all countries; and (3) worldwide freedom of thought and expression. He is not so naive as to think these can be easily achieved. Those enjoying privileges will fight to keep them, he knows, and the ensuing conflicts will be bloody and awful. In all of this the United States has a crucial role to play, being the advance guard of progress. In order to fulfill their destiny, Americans should venerate their historic legacy, support education and philanthropy, engage in ecumenical evangelism ("no *one* denomination can do it"), and secure the cooperation of the state in the cause of moral reform. To achieve this last, Christians must not abandon politics; they must reward friends and punish enemies at the polls (though with an inconsistency typical of Whigs, Beecher also hopes to "banish party spirit"). He ends his lectures on a note of confidence. "The means of preservation *will* be used, and the God of our fathers *will* make them effectual."[20]

Beecher was a man of action, and he moved about the country organizing efforts to put his principles into practice. With his daughter Catharine he mobilized public opposition to Indian removal. In 1840 he publicly campaigned with William Henry Harrison. More often, however, he worked outside the party system—or, rather, alongside it. He carried the Christian gospel from the small-town ambience of his youth to the big city (Boston in 1826) and then to the West (Cincinnati in 1832). In the growing urban areas and in the burgeoning West, Americans were building new societies; Beecher wanted to give a spiritual dimension to the material civilization being constructed. The agencies through which he and his comrades operated included churches, journals, and educational institutions, but, most of all, they relied on specialized "voluntary associations."

Voluntary benevolent societies were not new. They had flourished in colonial America and, before that, in Puritan England. Yet they achieved an unprecedented importance in Beecher's day, such that the French visitor Tocqueville marveled at their ubiquity. Tocqueville (who tended to share the viewpoint of his mainly Whig informants) saw these associations not as competing interest groups but as nonpartisan agencies through which the common good was promoted by public-spirited volunteers.[21] A well-known fact about Lyman Beecher is that he fought hard to retain the establishment of religion in Connecticut but, after losing that fight in 1818, became rapidly reconciled to disestablishment. The benevolent societies served the purpose of collective religious and moral dedication more effectively than an established church, he decided. Beecher was not mistaken. One reason why the Whigs were able to keep insisting on the evil of political parties is that the benevolent societies (mainly led by Whigs and promoting the kind of reform Whigs wanted) provided them with an alternative mode of organizing in pursuit of their social objectives. The rise of political parties, along with the danger that they would become patronage-oriented, could only tend to undercut the influence of the cause-oriented voluntary associations.

A good example of Beecher's activities is the temperance movement. Temperance was a new cause in the history of Christianity; Beecher could recall that, as late as 1811, ministerial ordinations had been occasions of considerable convivial drinking. At first the temperance advocates restricted themselves to encouraging moderation in drinking (hence the word "temperance"); in this phase they condemned only distilled liquors, not beer and wine.[22] Beecher's *Six Sermons on Intemperance,* first given in 1826 and republished many times in later years, helped push the movement in the direction of total abstinence. Liquor caused countless social problems, especially in law enforcement, Beecher argued, and it consumed a vast amount of capital and labor. The people engaged in the liquor business were not particularly evil, but they might more constructively be employed in other pursuits. Not everyone who drank, of course, was destroyed by it, but the incidence of harmful consequences was high enough to warrant regarding alcohol as too dangerous to use. This was a case for collective responsibility. Yet, with commendable sense, Beecher repudiated legal prohibition as unenforceable and relied entirely on changing public opinion.[23]

Beecher first became persuaded of the merits of temperance by the medical reports of Benjamin Rush, the distinguished physician. He made his own presentation in strictly rational terms; indeed, Beecher's entire case against liquor was based on a commitment to reason and the supremacy of the rational faculties. Liquor deadens a person's self-control, he argued, leaving him a "prey to animal sensation"; it panders to those parts of our nature that moral philosophy teaches us should be carefully subordinated. Temperance, like many other aspects of the evangelical movement, was predicated on the assumption that each person has a potential and is morally obliged to develop it. Dependence on liquor threatens "dissipation," that is, loss of focused energy and talent.[24]

Here an element of paradox enters. In order to create the conditions for self-realization, Beecher and his colleagues had to act collectively. As one shrewd historian has observed, "Believers in the self-reliant, independent spirit, they created societies to produce conformity."[25] To resolve the paradox, we must realize that what the evangelicals really valued was not freedom per se but freedom to shape one's life rationally and religiously, according to the principles of moral philosophy. The kind of freedom they approved was equivalent to self-discipline.

The literature of the temperance movement was vast, and it encompassed every genre: fiction, poetry, songs, and drama, as well as lectures and sermons. Of all the novels published in the United States during the 1830s, more than one in eight dealt with the theme of temperance.[26] To read through even a small fraction of this material is to encounter over and over again the affirmation of rationality, calmness, "plodding industry," foresight—all the classic bourgeois virtues. The evangelicals' objective, in the last analysis, was to win souls for Christ, but along the way they were promoting values conducive to industrialization. The voluntary societies, by both their precepts and their organizational example, were helping to create a modern capitalist social order.[27] Temperance illustrates well the broad congruence between economic development and the evangelical movement. Not surprisingly, historians who have looked at cities and states across the land are in agreement that the Whigs were the party of temperance.[28]

The evangelical reinvigoration of New England culture proceeded along two dimensions, the social and the intellectual. The social dimension was the "evangelical united front" of interdenominational benevolent associations; the intellectual dimension was represented by New Haven Theology, otherwise known as New School Calvinism. This carefully wrought reconciliation of divergent elements was constructed at Yale Divinity School, largely by Nathaniel William Taylor, building on the work of Timothy Dwight.[29] Taylor undertook to provide the rationale for the work of his good friend, Beecher. He was one of the great American intellectuals of his age, though his achievement can be appreciated by few today. He addressed himself to the perennial concern of theologians, the reconciliation of reason with a traditional faith, and also to the central concern of the Whig-Jacksonian era, human nature and its potential. He wrestled with the problems of moral responsibility and moral conditioning at a time when the balancing of freedom and control had taken on a new urgency.[30] The objective of New School Calvinism was to blend the activist, voluntaristic, ambitious, fluid attitudes of nineteenth-century America with the religious doctrines of the Reformation. Broadly stated, this meant formulating into a religious ideology the culture associated with Whiggery.

American religion in the time of Taylor and Beecher had much in common with politics. Both were dominated by moral philosophy as a mode of thought and by oratory as a medium of expression. Besides the moral nature of man, another focus of theological attention was revivalism, which raised questions about legitimate techniques of persuasion. The revivalists were controversial oratorical innovators. Some stimulated the emotions to a dangerous extent. In his own preaching, direct and simple though he kept it, Beecher was careful to observe a classical balance between rational and emotional appeals.

Beecher, Taylor, and their associates prided themselves on being "liberal," "catholic" (i.e., ecumenical), and "unsectarian."[31] Far from assuring peace and quiet, however, this commitment involved them in complex ecclesiastical maneuverings. It placed them in direct competition with the Boston Unitarians, who were also claiming to provide the basis for a new ecumenicism and who regarded the Calvinist theological tradition as bankrupt. With the Unitarians declaring that Calvinism was incompatible with a respect for human moral agency, it was essential for the New Haven–based group to refute them and to insist that Calvinism was not ugly, tyrannical, and outmoded.[32] Moreover, a confrontation with the Unitarians offered the opportunity to rally all the Calvinist denominations in the country against a common enemy. The Unitarian controversy of the 1820s, carried on at the immediate level of winning converts as well as at the academic level of theological debate, took Lyman and Edward Beecher to Boston and halted the spread of Unitarianism.

While Beecher was defining a front against the Unitarians, however, he was also trying to join forces with potential allies. Among these was Charles G. Finney, a lawyer-turned-itinerant-evangelist of the "burned-over district" in upstate New York. The more cautious of the New England clergy, led by Asahel Nettleton, were distressed by Finney's bold methods, which included praying by name for prominent individuals he considered "unconverted" and use of the "anxious bench" to pressure waverers into a decision for Christ. Beecher, however, was determined to reach an accord with Finney that would enable them to make common cause. In July, 1827, they met at New Lebanon, Connecticut, for negotiations. Eighteen ministers were present, nine from each party to the talks. The conferees succeeded in reaching a consensus on every aspect of revivals save one: whether women should be allowed to lead public prayers. The Seneca Falls Convention was still in the future, but the western New Yorkers already took women's rights seriously. Beecher's moderates were not prepared to go so far, and the meeting broke up without issuing a common platform. The New Lebanon Conference has been dismissed as a failure, but actually it laid the basis for future understanding and cooperation. By May, 1828, Beecher and Finney were ready with a short mutual statement (it did not mention women), and in the summer of 1831 Beecher invited Finney to preach in Boston.[33]

What no one seems to have noticed about the New Lebanon Conference is its importance in laying the groundwork for a coalition that would become central to the Whig party. Beecher's New Englanders were ex-Federalist National Republicans, but Finney's New Yorkers represented an Antimasonic constituency. Their accord in religion presaged an accord in politics a few years later, though tensions would remain, since the New Yorkers were more antislavery and less nativist. (One reason why the political significance of New Lebanon has eluded historians is the misidentification of Finney as a Jacksonian Democrat.)[34]

A still larger religious party with whom Beecher was anxious to cooperate consisted of Old School Calvinists. They formed a majority within the Presbyterian church, a denomination linked with Beecher's own Congregationalists by the Plan of Union of 1801. The continuation of this ambitious experiment in ecumenicism was essential to Beecher's ecclesiastical strategy. On it rested his hopes for the redemption of the West. Beecher was convinced that the American national character would be shaped in the West (in this anticipating Frederick Jackson Turner), and he wanted a hand in the shaping.[35] In 1832 Beecher came West to assume the presidency of the new Lane Theological Seminary in Cincinnati, a Presbyterian institution. He qualified for the post by being received into the Third Presbytery of New York, a procedure permitted by the Plan of Union and arranged for him by his Finneyite allies. But the Old School Presbyterians already had a seminary in Pittsburgh, and they regarded Lane as a New School intrusion.

The West was an appropriate arena for Beecher: it was large, exciting, and vigorous. "When I first entered the West, its vastness overpowered me with the impression of its uncontrollable greatness," he admitted, but he rose to the challenge. Since the West needed help in becoming civilized, the East should supply it in the form of teachers and ministers, just as the East itself had drawn on the resources of Europe. The West would determine "whether the perpetuity of our republican institutions can be reconciled with universal suffrage," Beecher declared. Because the West was growing fast, time was of the essence. "Half a million of unprincipled, reckless voters in the hands of demagogues, may, in our balanced elections, overrule all the property, and wisdom, and moral principles of the nation."[36] Extending New England influence into the Ohio Valley was thus an act of national political significance, as was its extension into Kansas a generation later, with encouragement from Lyman's son, Henry Ward Beecher.

The West was a land of sharp contrasts in religion as in politics. Both Democratic egalitarianism and Whig aspirations for economic development and diversity had strong appeals. Both wildcat banking and hostility to banks were extreme. In religion, the conflict lay between the social activism of the benevolent organizations and a dour doctrinal orthodoxy willing to enter into a tacit alliance with secularism and irreligious hedonism to frustrate the initiatives of an ecclesiastical imperialism they all resented. Underlying both political and religious rivalries was a clash of cultures that resulted from parallel zones of influence across the Old Northwest, one following the Yankee path of migration across the Great Lakes, the other representing southern migration across the Ohio. In 1863 the evangelical journal *Home Missionary* looked back over this culture conflict and termed it a "thirty years' war." The Yankees were more self-conscious about trying to propagate their culture; the migrant Yankee, a contemporary observed, often thought of himself "as a sort of religious, political, industrial, agricultural, and commercial missionary."[37] The strategy of the other side (like the economic policy of the Democratic party) was more often defensive and negative. Beecher's hopes for cooperation in promoting Christian objectives looked to the Old School like Yankee subversion.

There was a basic difference in outlook between the Old School and New School Calvinists that was destined to frustrate Beecher. The New School represented an activist religious orientation, variously labeled "pietist" or "devotional," that emphasized the conscious structuring of life—both one's own and others'—in terms of the perceived divine will. The Old School represented what is best called a "confessional" religious orientation, which emphasized loyalty to orthodox doctrine. The divergence in world views of these two religious orientations has been shown by sociologists and historians to have wide ramifications. "Where devotionalism is dominant, a dynamic potential for social change is present," one investigator has concluded; "where orthodoxy prevails, this potential for change is lacking." The devotionalists are more likely to pursue social mobility, as conventionally defined, and are more likely to seek to control the behavior of others. The confessionalists are more concerned to preserve their faith (and, by implication, their own special identity as its custodians) in a world they have largely written off as irredeemable.[38] Often in American history the confessionalists have resisted efforts at assimilation by the pietists. An extreme concern for the purity of Calvinist orthodoxy, especially the doctrine of predestination, has been convincingly associated with resistance on the part of the nineteenth-century "Antimission Baptists" to the spread of New England culture and attendant social reforms.[39] Beecher encountered analogous opposition from the Old School Presbyterians.

Beecher was anxious to include as wide a spectrum of Protestants as possible in his evangelical united front because of the threat he perceived from the expansion of Roman Catholicism in the United States. According to an interpretation widely current, Beecher's concern over Catholicism was "paranoid": he was projecting on Rome and its hierarchy his own feelings and designs.[40] It would be more accurate to say that he was (in psychiatric terminology) "projecting into reality," that is, he was sensitive to the import of Catholic policies because they were in fact similar to his own. Gregory XVI, former prefect of the Propaganda Fide, began an aggressive missionary program when he ascended the papal throne in 1831. Nor were Beecher's counterparts among the American Catholic clergy passively awaiting persecution. Though in a minority, they were as ambitious and purposeful as he—and no less convinced of the exclusive claims of their faith. They resembled the Protestant nativists in being sometimes tactless, sometimes shrewd, and sometimes willing to resort to coercion in pursuit of their objectives.[41] Beecher's complaints about the Catholic clergy are reminiscent of the complaints made of the Masons: they were an exclusive, well-organized male society, privy to secrets, with special property interests, exerting influence presumably hostile to republican institutions. The possibility that he might exaggerate the danger from Catholicism did not worry Beecher. Like anyone waging a vigorous campaign, he felt it important to "run scared." Besides, the use of fear to prompt action was a time-honored evangelist's device. Whatever purposes Beecher's crusade against Catholicism served for his own psyche, it had a powerful ideological and strategic justification. It was a matter of deepest conviction, yet it was also a tactic to unify American Protestantism. In New England, Calvinists of every hue had joined in denouncing the Unitarians. Perhaps another common enemy, Rome, would rally them anew.

Within a few years, massive immigration from Catholic Ireland caused Beecher's warnings to be widely echoed within the Whig-voting constituency. The ethnic and religious hostilities of the nineteenth century need to be taken seriously. In view of the magnitude and suddenness of the Irish influx (1.2 million people in a decade), the wonder is that social conflict was not even greater.[42] Since the Whigs identified political freedom with a cultural matrix of which Protestantism was an important part, they found the growth of Catholicism disturbing. Concern that the Church of Rome was less than enthusiastic about free institutions cannot be dismissed as irrational Protestant bigotry; Gregory XVI and Pius IX were not John XXIII. American Whig criticisms of the papacy, though placed on the *Index*, were welcomed by Italian nationalist revolutionaries. And Beecher's charges that Catholic educational and proselytizing activities in the United States were being financed by Metternich's Austria, far-fetched as they sound, have been partially substantiated.[43] Catholic immigrants sided overwhelmingly with the proslavery wing of the Democratic party. Their political impact was felt quickly as a result of the Democratic policy, implemented in many states, of enfranchising resident aliens. The American Catholic Church even supported the war against Catholic Mexico that the Protestant Whigs were opposing. Some Irish-American soldiers, however, switched sides to form the celebrated St. Patrick's Battalion in the Mexican army.[44]

On August 11, 1834, Beecher was in Charlestown, Massachusetts, speaking on the dangers of Catholicism and urging support for Protestant educational institutions in the West. That night, the city's Ursuline convent and its school were burned by a Protestant mob. The rioters were not in Beecher's audience, and his speech played no role in inciting the violence. Respectable Protestant opinion was shocked. The episode illustrates an important fact about what we loosely term "nativism": it was composed of independent elements. The Charlestown rioters were working-class Protestants, fearful that Catholic immigrants were taking away their jobs; they bore a marked similarity to the anti-Chinese rioters on the West Coast in later years.[45] On the other hand, the nativism of men like Beecher was more ideological than socioeconomic and was directed more against Roman Catholicism than against immigration per se. Contemporaries recognized the distinction well; in some places the ideological anti-Catholic nativists were called "Jonathans" and the antiimmigrant nativists "Sams." The Jonathans were more likely to be antislavery and moved readily into the Republican party after its formation.[46]

Beecher belongs in the Jonathan category. He was not so worried about the presence of immigrants as about their political power. His quarrel with the newcomers was ideological rather than racial. Unlike the advocates of immigration restriction in later generations, he did not combine his anti-Catholicism with anti-Semitism. In fact, he was something of a philo-Semite, who endorsed nineteenth-century Zionism and expressed admiration for the bourgeois virtues of European Jewry. (Worried about Catholic power for obvious reasons of their own, American Jews sometimes supported the nativist movement.) In his famous *Plea for the West*, Beecher was careful to specify that he would not "consent that the civil and religious rights of the Catholics should be abridged or violated. ... *The Catholics have a perfect right to proselyte the nation to their faith if they are able to do it. But I too have the right of preventing it if I am able.*"[47]

While Beecher was in the East, trying to raise funds for Lane as an outpost of the Protestant crusade, the school itself was riven asunder by the slavery question. One of the great student rebellions of American history, led by Theodore Dwight Weld (a Finney convert) broke out in 1834 when the trustees acted in response to complaints from Cincinnati townsfolk that the students were associating with blacks as equals. Beecher had known of Weld's abolitionism and had admitted a former slave to the seminary as a student: James Bradley, a native of Guinea. Beecher had hoped that Lane would incorporate both the major versions of antislavery—abolition and colonization—in a kind of ecumenicism of reform. Hastening back to Ohio, he found the situation beyond his powers to mediate. The trustees (fearing attack by white-supremacist mobs) were adamant; and Beecher, much as he admired Weld, could not persuade him to stay under those conditions. Weld and most of the first-year class left to found Oberlin, where Finney joined them. Beecher managed to prevent Lane's total disintegration and stuck it out at the institution. He gradually realized the impossibility of developing an antislavery program that would bring together the colonization movement and abolition, and he opted for the latter.[48] Probably Beecher would have come out directly for abolition sooner had he not feared that this would wreck the other aspects of his religious and social program. It is said that in 1830 he offered to make William Lloyd Garrison "the Wilberforce of America" if the younger man would defer to his leadership; Garrison, of course, refused.[49]

The Old School Calvinists took advantage of Beecher's embarrassment at Lane to press charges of heresy against him. The principal accuser at his trial in 1835 was Joshua Wilson, a Kentuckian who had moved to Cincinnati and was later the author of proslavery writings. The trial record shows Beecher and Wilson confronting each other on the issue of whether it would be just for God to condemn sinners who did not possess the ability to obey His laws. Beecher maintained that it would be "oppressive" for God to do so. He marshaled a host of theologians to sustain the orthodoxy of his viewpoint, and in the end the court voted to acquit him. Some of Wilson's charges were rather vague and amounted to assertions that Beecher was encouraging the Finneyites. Beecher always claimed that his antislavery and other social views had really prompted the accusations. The trial was part of a pattern of Old School prosecutions of New School ministers for heresy that signaled the coming breakup of the Presbyterian denomination.[50]

The Schism of 1837 was provoked by an alliance between northern theological conservatives and southern proslavery men to drive the New School, which threatened both, out of the denomination. The Old School–New School division reflected many factors in addition to religion itself: geography, ethnicity (Scots-Irish versus Yankee), and class (the Old School was stronger among working-class Presbyterians and the New School among entrepreneurs, at least in Philadelphia).[51] As the second party system developed, many Old School Presbyterians opted for the Democrats—Andrew Jackson himself among them. In the election of 1828, Ezra Stiles Ely, a Pennsylvania Old School minister, sought to rally Calvinists of all denominations behind Jackson as the "Christian" candidate against the Unitarian Adams. The clergy were seldom so overt as Ely in their electioneering, but an Old School Presbyterian tradition in the Democratic party has been traced from Jackson to Grover Cleveland.[52] Impressionistic evidence is overwhelming that the New School, in contrast to the Old, was Whig. (Data for later years in the Midwest show that New School Presbyterians predominantly voted Republican and the Old School, Democratic.)[53] Perhaps the strict literalness of Democratic constitutional interpretation and the looser, more evolutionary approach of the Whigs to the Constitution owed something to the Old School–New School debates over the meaning of the Reformed creeds.

The evangelical united front, which Beecher hoped would include both Finney on the left and the Old School on the right, proved unstable. In its place a different alignment of religious groups emerged. Most of the "devotionalist" Protestant groups—the Unitarians, Finneyites, "perfectionists," and New School Calvinists, as well as Quakers, Free Will Baptists, and others—learned to ignore their differences and cooperate in the interests of national redemption. The end of Beecher's campaign against Unitarianism coincided with the birth of the Whig party, within which they all found a place.[54] As early as 1830 the *Spirit of the Pilgrims* found it necessary to distinguish William Ellery Channing's "valuable" political opinions from his "unscriptural and absurd" Unitarianism. Eventually the cooperation reached the point where the distinguished moderate Calvinist theologian Moses Stuart could be one of the most loyal friends and political associates of the Unitarian Daniel Webster.[55] Opposing this alliance were the "confessional" bodies in the Democratic party, an even more incongruous assemblage of Roman Catholics, German Lutherans, Dutch "True" Calvinists, Old School Presbyterians, and Antimission Baptists; with them should probably also be listed the small organizations of freethinkers, who honored the memory of Thomas Paine. What these disparate groups shared was a grim determination to survive in the face of pressures to assimilate. If historians have yet to establish a clear association between Methodism and either major party in this period, it may be because the Methodists, while predominantly "devotional," remained outside the evangelical united front and concentrated more on individual than collective redemption.

Henry Clay failed to become president, and Lyman Beecher's ecclesiastical politics did not succeed as he had intended either. Yet both the American System and the evangelical movement had contributed to the shaping of a new bourgeois society. In 1850, at the age of seventy-five, Beecher at last retired from Lane. He remained vigorous long enough to encourage the birth of the Republican party. Then his mental powers gradually failed, though his energy and enthusiasm were still undaunted. At his son's famous Plymouth Church in Brooklyn the old man had this to say: "If God should tell me that I might choose . . . whether to die and go to heaven, or to begin my life over again and work once more (straightening himself up, and his eye kindling, with finger lifted up), I would enlist again in a minute!"[56]

At the age of forty-one, Joshua Reed Giddings (1795–1864) was born again in Christ. From being an ordinary small-town lawyer, he was transformed into a crusader for liberty and a righteous society.

Giddings represents the western wing of the evangelical movement, which was more populistic than Beecher's. His career was also more overtly political. His eleven consecutive terms in the House of Representatives set a record, for that body was far more volatile in the nineteenth century than it has since become. As a congressman, Giddings carried on his "work of reformation" with a single-minded courage that earned the respect of his bitterest foes. The Whigs' impulse to universalize their values, to stop others from drinking or to Americanize immigrants, received one of its greatest expressions in Giddings' campaign to eliminate all federal support for slavery.[57]

Like Lyman Beecher, Giddings was forced to choose between opposition to slavery and the rest of his desired program, but he showed much less hesitation in giving primacy to antislavery among his evangelical goals. For Giddings as for Beecher, the evangelical movement was the climax of a world-wide revolutionary process begun with the Protestant Reformation and continued in the revolutions of 1642, 1688, and 1776. It had suffered periodic setbacks—like the betrayal of the French Revolution to atheism and militarism or the crushing of the forty-eighters—but it would ultimately prevail. Though the Anglo-Americans had pioneered the way, the divine principles of liberty were intended for all peoples, including blacks, Latin Americans, or Louis Kossuth's Hungarians, and Giddings was emphatic about this universal applicability.[58]

Joshua Giddings was born in Pennsylvania, the son of a chronically unsuccessful Yankee farmer. The family moved first to upstate New York and then to the Western Reserve of Ohio; both were frontier areas when Joshua was growing up. In Ohio he lived just two and a half miles from an Indian village, and, like his Indian neighbors, young Joshua dressed in deerskins; perhaps his later battles on behalf of Indian rights had a basis in these early impressions. The boy grew into a husky six-foot-two-inch man—an advantage for one destined to face down many an angry threat. Giddings never received any formal schooling, but at the age of nineteen, having seen action briefly in the War of 1812, he got a part-time job as schoolmaster. Keeping one page ahead of his students, he discovered that he liked education. Soon he married another teacher and read law in the office of Elisha Whittlesey. For eighteen years Joshua and Laura Giddings led a conventional life of hard work and child-rearing. Like Beecher and most of the other Whig leaders treated in this book, Giddings was very much a "family man"; his extensive and candid correspondence with his wife, daughters, and sons constitutes a valuable source for understanding him.[59]

Aspiring to upward social mobility, Giddings practiced law in successively larger towns. Finally he won the big case that made his reputation (a malpractice suit against a physician). He joined the organizations Yankee pioneers so typically founded: a Bible society, a debating club, and a branch of the American Colonization Society. He also joined the Masons, but in 1832 he quit the order and called for its suppression in Ohio. He served a term in the legislature and, working with his former mentor Whittlesey and with his law partner, Benjamin Franklin Wade, helped put together the Whig party in Ohio. Investing his legal fees in real estate, he became wealthy. Then, just when the American Dream had come true for Joshua Giddings, the Panic of 1837 wiped out the investments and ruined the law practice.

An unsympathetic historian has called Giddings' mind "commonplace."[60] In a way this is an accurate characterization, though it seems better to divest it of pejorative connotations and call him "typical." Giddings was not unusual in his background, aspirations, values, or limitations. Like most of the settlers in the Western Reserve, he and his wife were of New England descent; the town where he grew up (Wayne) replicated the traditional New England village. In religion he was a Congregationalist/Presbyterian within the Plan of Union; he once served as delegate to a New School General Assembly. His hopes of affluence and their disappointment were, of course, all too common. Nor did his Whig politics set him apart, for the Whiggery of the area was more a matter of its people's cultural identity than of their class position. In the early 1820s they had been divided between Adams and Clay in their loyalties; after those two leaders allied, the region became overwhelmingly National Republican and Whig.[61] The people of the Western Reserve were known for antipathy toward slavery, and Giddings was destined to become an ardent antislavery crusader. But Giddings practiced a cultural style that was far more widespread than abolitionism, one of crucial importance to Whiggery: evangelicalism. Through evangelicalism the Whigs were able to reach out beyond what seems their obvious social base in the urban bourgeoisie and rally many "commonplace" people to their side.

Giddings' response to his personal crisis in 1837 was conditioned by his evangelical culture. He rode off alone into the woods toward the West and spent the summer communing with God through nature. There he restored his sense of wholeness and composure. His comments on the wilderness in writing to his wife suggest a common man's counterpart to the nature religion of Jonathan Edwards (or

Thoreau).[62] He had already come into contact with Theodore Dwight
Weld, the evangelical abolitionist who had left Beecher's Lane Seminary for Oberlin in the Western Reserve. After his solitary conversion experience, to put his newly renewed faith into practice by
seeking the redemption of American society seemed imperative.
Back from his sojourn in the forest, Giddings quit the colonization
society and joined one of Weld's abolitionist groups as well as the
local temperance organization. As it happened, Elisha Whittlesey
chose this moment to vacate a seat in the House of Representatives,
and he endorsed Giddings as his successor. Giddings secured the
Whig nomination and, running on a platform that included opposition to the gag rule and slavery in the District of Columbia, easily
defeated his Democratic opponent at a special election in 1838.

Giddings' twenty-one years in Congress were often stormy. The
more he identified himself with the cause of freedom, the more he
encountered violent hostility. In February, 1843, he was threatened
with a bowie knife by J. B. Dawson, a Louisiana Democrat. In
January, 1845, Edward Black, a Georgia Democrat, charged at him
with upraised cane and had to be wrestled back into his seat by those
with calmer heads. Later the same day Dawson again threatened
Giddings, this time with a gun. Though Giddings had been attacking slavery, the five congressmen who rushed to shield him on this
occasion were three northern and two southern Whigs; the four
who rallied to Dawson's side were all Democrats. These confrontations exemplify in exacerbated form a conflict between a didactic,
evangelical cultural style and an older culture that countenanced
violence. The Whig disapproval of violence, which, as we have seen,
led Henry Clay to repudiate the gentry code of honor, reappears. In
April, 1848, Giddings faced threats again, this time by an armed mob
when he visited a Washington jail to make sure that two men who
had aided the escape of fugitive slaves were not lynched. Thereafter
he seems not to have encountered violence, perhaps because he had
proved his courage.[63]

Such experiences put Giddings' composure to severe tests. The
man's large frame belied his sensitivity and self-doubt. Robert C.
Winthrop, a bitter political enemy, declared after Giddings' death
that he had been in search of martyrdom. On the contrary, it appears
that Giddings longed for approval.[64] But in spite of all that happened
to him, Giddings did not give way to self-pity or magnify his perse-
cutions. Instead of projecting all evil onto his opponents, he conceived of the sin of slavery as collective. "We are all involved in the
dread responsibility," he told the House. Not long after the confron-

tation at the jail, this estimate of Giddings' personality was made by a colleague who knew him "on the most intimate footing," the scholarly John Gorham Palfrey: "With perfect firmness and some impetuosity, he has rare gentleness and delicacy of character, and all sustained by an enlightened and fervent piety. He looks rough, but the mildest elements are mixed up in him, and he fears God, and nothing else."[65]

The theme linking most of Giddings' speeches in Congress, and the writings of his later years as well, is the exposure of a slave-power conspiracy. The northern public was not aware of the extent to which the general government was being exploited in the interests of slaveholders; Giddings undertook to reveal these "ulterior designs."[66] The conspiracy paradigm came naturally to one of Giddings' background. A shrewd historian has recently pointed out that the perception of evil in personal terms, of "conspiracies" rather than "forces," is typical of face-to-face societies in which not everyone reads.[67] Joshua Giddings grew up in such an environment and did not acquire an education until he was an adult. His transition from oral-aural to literary culture was no simple matter, as is indicated by his early awkwardness in practicing law, the poor spelling he used all his life, and his persistent diffidence regarding his manner of public speaking. Giddings' speeches were more colloquial than those of literary politicians like Webster and Everett; he sometimes related to his audience in the "call-and-response" pattern so typical of non-literary revivalism.[68] Perhaps the popular style of Giddings' rhetoric explains why many southerners regarded him as even more of a threat than the erudite Adams.

Of course, Giddings' "acculturation" to literate Whiggery would have done nothing to shake his belief in the danger of conspiracies against liberty. He could quote the Bible and warn of the retributive wrath of God against a sinful community. He was also exposed through his legal training to the political thought of the "country party," and was capable of defending his opposition to the Mexican War by citing the example of British parliamentary Whigs like Burke and Fox in 1776. His frequent warnings that the nation was losing "the virtue of our better days" show that the cautionary lessons of classical republicanism had entered his consciousness. His denunciation of President Pierce's "executive influence" at the time of the *Black Warrior* crisis is firmly in the tradition of Old Whiggery.[69]

From the time Giddings arrived in Congress, he worked to turn the Whigs into a party avowedly hostile to slavery. His desire for "a reconciliation between the abolitionists and other friends of Mr.

Clay" was comparable to Lyman Beecher's hope for cooperation between the abolitionists and colonizationists. On February 13, 1839, Giddings threw the House of Representatives into an uproar by declaring he would oppose all appropriations for the District of Columbia as long as the gag rule protected the slave trade there. His strategy was to portray the gag as a Democratic party measure, ignoring its appeal to some southern Whigs. Clay's anti-antislavery statement of the same month came as a disappointment to Giddings but did not budge his party loyalty. He supported the successful Whig nominee for speaker, R. M. T. Hunter of Virginia, though the latter was a strong supporter of the gag rule. Out of impatience with such faithful Whiggery, the Liberty party was organized in Ohio; the Liberty men repeatedly fielded a candidate against Giddings in his constituency. In 1840 Giddings campaigned vigorously for the Whig ticket. One of the most powerful evocations of the "log cabin" symbol is a speech Giddings gave in June, 1840.[70] Harrison had befriended Theodore Dwight Weld in the Cincinnati area and enjoyed good relations with the antislavery leaders. However, just before inauguration day, Giddings raised another storm in the House by denouncing the proslavery aspects of the Second Seminole War. Harrison thereupon felt it necessary to dissociate himself from antislavery and, during his short presidency, sought to reassure southern Whigs.[71]

Giddings' devotion to Clay's economic policies was sincere and helps to explain his support of the Whig party. When the special session of Congress called by Harrison met in the summer of 1841, Giddings forbore to raise the gag issue in order not to obstruct consideration of the Whig economic program. Most of the time, however, he felt that antislavery was the logical complement of the American System. He grouped them both together as "northern rights." Slavery, Giddings complained, was a drag on the economy. Emancipation would help promote economic diversification and stimulate manufacturing because the freedmen would have a higher standard of living and would thus offer a better home market. Giddings saw nothing sordid about combining a moral appeal against slavery with an economic one. ("There is no argument so strong as that adressed [sic] to a man's pocket," he once remarked.)[72] His constituents found that his synthesis of evangelicalism and practicality suited them well. Whenever Giddings' right to speak for the Whig party was challenged by southern members, he would reply with pride: "The congressional district which I have the honor to represent gives the largest Whig majority of any in the United

States." If southern Whigs would deny Giddings the chance to denounce slavery, then, he told them, they were properly *"no whigs."*[73]

Giddings' close friendship with John Quincy Adams is a touching tribute to the integrity of both men and their ability to transcend their widely divergent backgrounds and personalities. Adams' mind was legalistic and formalistic, his style precise and impersonal. Giddings was more emotional and impulsive, and his public manner was rough and plain. The learned ex-president's sensibilities had been shaped by the categories of Ciceronian rhetoric and Scottish moral philosophy, the rude westerner's by the fervor of revivalism. Together they exemplified the two great sources of Whig ideology: the commonwealthman tradition and the evangelical movement. What united them was a mutual commitment to purifying American society, to making it moral. Specifically, of course, they shared a profound commitment against slavery. Besides, both were lonely men who welcomed a friend to whom they could confide hopes and plans. Before long they came to realize they could trust each other implicitly. Seldom has a union of "head" and "heart" been more effective or more firm than the friendship of these two doughty legislators. As the years went by, Adams came to look on Giddings as his natural successor, and Giddings called the older man "Father Adams."[74]

With Adams as his mentor, Giddings developed into an excellent parliamentary strategist, adept at circumventing the gag to get in criticisms of slavery before being called to order. Twenty-eight years younger than Adams, Giddings felt more at home in the hurly-burly of nineteenth-century partisan politics and proved a valuable coadjutor for him. Encouraged by Adams' example, Giddings was able to come to terms with the hatred he encountered. He even learned to take advantage of the southerners' anger: baiting them could be a form of filibustering. More importantly, Giddings and Adams were talking over the heads of their colleagues to northern public opinion. They intended by their legislative maneuverings to rally dormant antislavery sentiment. Their preoccupation with shaping public opinion was thoroughly typical of evangelicals and Whigs.

Once Giddings went too far for his colleagues. Soon after Adams had beaten off the attempt to censure him in 1842, Giddings pressed the attack by introducing a set of resolutions relating to the *Creole*, a vessel engaged in the coastal slave trade. The human cargo had rebelled, killed a crew member, and sailed to the Bahamian port of Nassau, where British law held them free. Giddings' resolutions (written by Theodore Dwight Weld, who was serving a group of antislavery congressmen as legislative aide) declared that slavery did not exist in United States waters outside the jurisdiction of an individual state and that the mutiny was therefore justified. The House quickly passed, by a vote of 125 to 69, a motion of censure, calling Giddings' resolutions "shocking to all sense of law, order, and humanity." Democrats had no difficulty supporting censure, 77 to 10; but the Whigs' vote, 44 in favor and 59 against, revealed a sectional division. (Four unaffiliated representatives voted for censure.)[75] Unlike Adams, Giddings had been accorded no opportunity to defend himself. His response turned reproach into victory: he resigned his seat, returned to Ohio, and was overwhelmingly reelected by his constituents. But before he left Washington, Giddings ran into Henry Clay in the Capitol. The senator "held out his hand to Giddings, thanked him for the firmness with which he had met the outrage perpetrated upon him, and said that no man would ever doubt his perfect right to state his views."[76]

The object of Giddings' legislative battles, frequently avowed, was to get the federal government to stop aiding slavery. Among the federal actions he opposed were the Army's campaigns in Florida to recover fugitive slaves, the Navy's protection of the coastal slave trade, the payment of claims that involved compensation for slave property, the embargo against commerce with Haiti, the enforcement of the fugitive-slave acts, negotiations with Canada and Mexico for the recovery of fugitive slaves, and, of course, the maintenance of slavery and the slave trade in the District of Columbia and the territories. The iniquities of the Second Seminole War were a theme Giddings took up early and recurred to often. He exposed the fact that the Army was trying to separate Indians from Negroes among captured Seminoles—sometimes splitting up families in the process—and was treating the Negroes as slaves, to be disposed of by the government, rather than as prisoners of war. The plan was to give the captured blacks to the Army's Creek Indian allies as booty, the Creeks in turn to sell them to a prominent slave-trader. The scheme fell apart when General Zachary Taylor refused to implement it.[77]

Giddings held that the federal Constitution, because it contained no explicit reference to slavery, could not be construed as recognizing it. The Constitution embodied the history that had gone before it, which included the affirmation of human equality in the Declaration of Independence. Slavery was contrary to natural law, according to which all men are created equal; it could exist only where positive law overcame this presumption of freedom. Thus slavery must by its nature be a purely local or "municipal" institution, existing only in those states that established it. The federal government had no authority to establish it anywhere, and its existence in the territories and the District of Columbia was actually, in Giddings' opinion, unconstitutional. The Ohioan summed up his constitutional views in a series of letters published in the *Western Reserve Chronicle* beginning in November, 1842, under the typically Whiggish pseudonym "Pacificus."[78] The position was not peculiar to Giddings but was typical of that section of the spectrum of antislavery opinion that sought to justify hostility to slavery in legal terms. The view had widespread appeal among northern Whigs and Free-Soilers. Its originator may have been Theodore Dwight Weld; among its influential proponents were also Charles Sumner and Salmon P. Chase.[79]

Like a good Whig, Giddings recognized the power of institutions, and he felt that slavery could be most effectively combated within the context of existing arrangements. He wanted to work through the Constitution, the two-party system, and the major religious denominations. The elimination of federal aid to slavery would not only absolve northerners of complicity in its crimes but would bring on the demise of slavery, Giddings believed; for it was an economically inefficient system that could exist only as the beneficiary of artificial encouragements. "When northern freemen cease to uphold that institution, its death will be inevitable."[80] Southern leaders clearly shared Giddings' opinion that the long-term existence of slavery was dependent on a friendly federal government.

There was a world of difference between Giddings' antislavery Whiggery and the abolitionism of a radical like William Lloyd Garrison. Giddings' argument that the Constitution was not a proslavery document implied in the largest sense that the foundations of American society did not rest on slavery, that slavery could be excised like a tumor, leaving a healthy body behind. Garrison, on the other hand, was saying that the nation had been built on slavery and that a truly drastic pulling-down of these supports was necessary. Angry southerners did not notice the distinction, but the abolitionists did. At a camp meeting in Ohio in 1847, Giddings debated against Garrison the subject of whether antislavery men should support disunion. Giddings saw himself as claiming no more than the restoration of the attitude of the Founding Fathers toward slavery.[81] He was an evangelical bent on regenerating American society through what has been termed a "cultural purge." At the same time, he was a lawyer and legalist who felt that "wild ultraism" was a liability rather than an asset to antislavery. It was a typically Whig combination. In his conscientious service as chairman of the House Claims Committee, Giddings indulged both his affection for the common man with a grievance and his relish for the legal system.[82]

In 1844 Giddings campaigned with desperate earnestness, not only for his own reelection but also on behalf of Henry Clay. The annexation of Texas was a dreadful possibility, and the only way to prevent it was to elect Clay. "Thanks to a Whig Senate," which had rejected the treaty of annexation, "we are yet free," he pointed out, and, if Texas could be kept out of the Union, the eventual doom of slavery was sure. Giddings was one of many people under the spell of Henry Clay's charming personality; he was also convinced that the Kentuckian, although a slaveholder himself, would divorce the federal government from its subservience to the slave power. Votes thrown away on the Liberty party, Giddings warned, would only ensure the election of Polk. Giddings imported Henry's antislavery cousin, Cassius Clay, to help him stump Ohio, and he succeeded in carrying it for the Whigs, only to see his worst fears come true when defections to the Liberty party in New York enabled Polk to carry that state and, with it, the nation.[83]

Giddings correctly predicted that the Polk administration would make concessions on Oregon while pressing for all of Texas. The southerners were afraid of war with Britain, he taunted them—afraid of a black West Indian expeditionary force that might rally American slaves (as the British had done during the Revolution) with an offer of freedom. Giddings also predicted that Texas would tip the balance of economic power in Congress in favor of the South, a prediction borne out when Texan votes enabled the tariff reduction of 1846 to pass.[84] The confirmation of such warnings began to have an effect on northern public opinion, an effect that found expression in the demand for the Wilmot Proviso. While speaking on the proviso, Giddings declared: "There can be no compromise between right and wrong."[85] The Whig party had been built on compromise, on a delicate balance between social morality and social stability. Giddings' days as a member of the party were drawing to a close.

The Mexican War occasioned some of Giddings' most eloquent denunciations of government criminality and aggression.[86] It also permanently alienated him from moderate Whigs like Robert C. Winthrop, who insisted on voting supplies even for a war they agreed was unjust. As a result, Giddings and two others (but not Adams) would not vote for Winthrop as speaker when the Whig Congress of 1847 assembled. Winthrop never forgave Giddings. When "Father Adams" died in February, 1848, Winthrop refused to name him to the memorial committee—a spiteful act toward one who felt himself the dead man's son in spirit.

In June, 1848, Giddings asserted at the Tremont Temple in Boston that "from the 11th of May, 1846 [the date war was declared on Mexico], the Whig party have ceased to have the characteristics of a party." The Whigs had allowed themselves to become implicated in the policies of their opponents. On July 30, back in Congress, Giddings proclaimed his refusal to support the Whig nominee, Zachary Taylor, for president. The old soldier's attachment to Whig principles—among which Giddings counted the denationalization of slavery—was too uncertain. What if he turned out to be a "Whig" like John Tyler? For himself, Giddings insisted, "I shall adhere to my whig sentiments, until I become satisfied that they are erroneous."[87] Thus Giddings took his leave of the Whig party, insisting, in doing so, that he was being faithful to true Whiggery. When the Free-Soilers nominated his long-time adversary, Van Buren, Giddings was unhappy, but he backed the new party anyway. His persistent distaste for cooperation with Democrats, however, cost him election to the United States Senate. When the Free-Soilers won the balance of power in the Ohio legislature, most of them wanted Giddings for senator, but the seat went eventually to another Free-Soiler, Salmon P. Chase, who was more willing to negotiate for Democratic support.[88]

After leaving the Whig party, Giddings became more unorthodox in both religion and politics. The spiritualism of the Fox sisters and the perfectionism of John Humphrey Noyes engaged his concern. His political warnings were becoming even more urgent and passionately religious in response to the aggressions of the Fugitive Slave Act and the repeal of the Missouri Compromise. "We are 'a city set upon a hill,'" he reminded his countrymen. The preservation and extension of slavery were betraying this historic mission. Americans had to prove "our faith by our works" and halt the spread of oppression.[89] Only such theological language seemed to Giddings adequate to the momentousness of the occasion. In Jesus Christ he found his model "agitator." While he had been a Whig, Giddings had viewed economic self-interest and morality as compatible. Now, however, he came to regard them as opposing forces, and he denounced slavery as the creature of base selfishness. By 1858 Giddings had conceptualized the impending crisis as a "conflict between religious truth and American infidelity."[90]

The more deeply interested Giddings became in theology, the more relevant it seemed to be to politics. "Nothing more directly

marks the age in which we live than the application of the doctrines
of our holy religion to the political duties of government," Giddings
told his constituents in 1853. The political divisions of the time corresponded, he claimed, to theological divisions. The freedom of the
slave from bondage to his master became a cause parallel to that of
freedom of the will from bondage to predestination: "No real distinction can be drawn between that infidelity which denies the responsibility of human action, and that political conservatism which
maintains a traffic in human flesh." Giddings was carrying the assault on Old School Calvinism into the realm of politics.[91]

The Kansas-Nebraska Act stung Giddings to two of his most
eloquent protests, "The Appeal of the Independent Democrats," an
open letter to the northern public, written with Salmon P. Chase and
Charles Sumner, and "The Moral Responsibility of Statesmen," a
speech he delivered in the House on May 17, 1854. In the latter
Giddings spelled out what he meant by the application of truth to
political duty: "Were I a resident of the territory, and slaves were
held in bondage around me, I would do by them as I would have
them do by me, were I in their condition—I would supply them with
arms and teach them to use all the means which God and Nature has
[sic] placed within their control to maintain their freedom and their
manhood."[92] Whether Giddings actually ever armed slaves or not, it
was an open secret that he fed and sheltered fugitives. By the 1850s
he was advocating equal rights for blacks in many areas of life; for
example, he sought to amend the homestead bill that passed the
House in February, 1854, to eliminate the racial-restriction clause.
(His proposal drew laughter and was overwhelmingly defeated.) If
one statement sums up Giddings' politics in the 1850s, it is this: "I
wish that gentlemen would learn to treat colored people as *men*."[93]

Yet growing numbers of northerners were coming to agree with
Giddings, if not on racial equality, at least on the principle that the
extension of slavery must be stopped. The Republican party, based
mainly on a northern Whig constituency and dedicated to the containment of slavery, was in fact the kind of political organization
Giddings had once hoped to make of the Whig party. The midterm
elections of 1854 returned a House in which the new party commanded a plurality. When their candidate, Nathaniel P. Banks, was
elected speaker, Giddings, as senior representative, was accorded
the honor of administering the oath. It was the proudest moment of
his life. The "moral revolution" for which he had worked seemed
fulfilled, and he wrote to his constituents: "I am satisfied." From our
perspective, the self-congratulation seems amazingly premature. But

to Giddings, who had labored so long in a small minority, it was immensely gratifying to feel that he finally had a preponderance of public opinion on his side. Now that public sentiment had been shifted by him and his coworkers, he had no doubt that an eventual solution to the slavery problem could be found.[94]

Giddings acted as the conscience of the Republican party. To him it was the agency of a "reformation" more important than any since the sixteenth century. Not all Republicans shared this evangelical vision, and in 1858 party moderates used his age (sixty-three) and his history of heart trouble as excuses to deny the eleven-term veteran renomination. But the man still had fight in him. At a dramatic moment during the national convention of 1860, Giddings forced the party to adopt a plank affirming belief in the equal rights of the Declaration of Independence.[95]

Lincoln appointed Giddings U.S. consul general at Montreal—in effect, American ambassador to Canada. From this vantage point the aging crusader urged the president to implement John Quincy Adams' doctrine that civil war legitimated emancipation by executive order. He also spent much time working on a carefully researched *History of the Rebellion*. While the interpretation of sectional conflict he presents in this work remains, of course, one of slave-power conspiracy, the tone is surprisingly calm. Now that the North was actually fighting, Giddings obviously felt that a sober, well-organized presentation rather than further exhortation met the needs of the country. Yet he did not neglect the future in his concern for the past and his own vindication. He was determined that the rights of the freedmen should be protected.[96] The tradition of Conscience Whiggery would need to be perpetuated, and Giddings had his eye on a successor. When the old warrior fell ill, Charles Sumner came to visit. Giddings, feeling his time had come, whispered the same words to him that he had received from the lips of the dying Adams: "I have more hope from you than from any other man."[97]

The evangelical movement, as represented by Beecher and Giddings, enlisted countless common people of America in the cause of propagating Whig values. It was surely one of the most massive conscious efforts at social control ever undertaken in human history. To affirm this, however, should not be to damn the evangelicals. Beecher and other pioneering missionaries encouraged Americans to redeem the frontier and the cities from squalor and violence. Giddings and other courageous agitators gradually mobilized public opinion against the indefinite extension of slavery across space and time. To be sure, Beecher and Giddings were enthusiastic proponents of the Whig economic program, and the values they inculcated were capitalistic.[98] But their capitalism was still young and vigorous, and they identified themselves with the forces of progress in the world, not with those of reaction. The evangelicals wanted people to break with folk tradition and shape their lives anew. They taught people to overcome the doubts engendered by Old School Calvinism and civic humanism, to have faith in themselves and in their country's future.

Eight

The Modernizers

"What has always struck me most in my country," Alexis de Tocqueville told a friend, "has been to see ranged on one side the men who value morality, religion, and order, and on the other, those who love liberty and equality before the law. This seems to me most extraordinary, and most deplorable." The bifurcation Tocqueville deplored has preoccupied historians who have tried to label the Whig party either "conservative" or "liberal." Actually, like Tocqueville himself, the American Whigs tried to transcend these alternatives and embrace what Edward Everett called "an enlightened and liberal conservatism."[1] As long as the party remained viable, it remained committed to "equitable and peaceful progress," eschewing both "violence" and "stagnation." Historians can borrow a term from lawyers to describe the Whig objective: "ordered liberty."[2]

The Whigs' commitment to institutions helped them synthesize order with freedom and change. Democrats of this era often perceived institutions as being opposed to liberty; freedom was to be secured through breaking down institutions that were repressive, such as established churches. The Jacksonian assault on the Bank of the United States derived much of its power from this fundamental assumption. Whigs, however, felt that institutions provided the structures that made freedom meaningful. Institutions could evolve to cope with changing circumstances; they could serve as instrumentalities for redemption, as the benevolent societies did. Whig institutionalism was by no means incompatible with antislavery, since Conscience Whigs like Giddings and Adams did not think of slavery as forming an integral part of the institutional fabric of the country.

European conservatives in the nineteenth century sometimes found that progressive legislation suited their purposes, as Bismark and Disraeli well illustrate. Lord John Russell put their policy nicely: "There is nothing so conservative as progress."[3] This attitude—that a measure of progress is desirable to forestall more drastic upheavals—was certainly not unknown among the American Whigs. "It behoves [sic] the friends of good order and moderation to be up and doing, lest much that is valuable and can never be replaced . . . be swept away," a young Whig orator declared. "True conservatism," a party spokesman affirmed, "operates not by indiscriminate resistance to change, but the intelligent and seasonable combination of Order and Improvement."[4]

Yet Whig progressivism cannot be reduced to a mere tactical device. Though Whigs sometimes thought of social progress in terms of avoiding the dangers of radicalism, many of them—like Clay, Carey, and Abraham Lincoln—had a strong positive concept of the national destiny, a concept they hoped to implement. The spirit of Whig innovation was by no means merely preventive; it was also constructive. To understand how the Whigs combined innovation with order and freedom with redemption, it is helpful to relate them to the concept of modernization. "Modernization" is a term applied by social scientists to economic development and certain concomitant cultural changes considered to reinforce it, such as secularization and the assimilation of ethnic differences. Societies undergoing modernization are usually characterized by industrialization, technological innovation, population growth, increasing literacy, growing national self-awareness, and value changes in the direction of greater time-thrift and productivity.[5] Such a society was nineteenth-century America.

The early phases of modernization typically occur under some kind of elite auspices. The economic, social, cultural, and moral program of the Whigs can be characterized in a broad sense as that of a modernizing elite, a bourgeois elite that was open to the talents of an upwardly mobile Lincoln or Greeley. Recently a number of scholars have challenged the applicability of modernization theory to non-Western societies, arguing that it is derived from a historical model that is distinctively American, assimilationist, bourgeois-reformist, and even imperialist.[6] These very objections to the universal application of the concept of modernization, however, underscore its special relevance to the Whigs, who were, after all, Americans, assimilationists, archetypal bourgeois reformers, and, in their way, imperialists.

Lynn Marshall, in a seminal article, placed the party battles of the Jacksonian era within the context of modernization. He saw that the "voter-oriented" Democratic party was one of many large bureaucratic organizations coming into existence at this time, and he argued that the Democrats were the principal "modernizers" of their era, while the Whigs, because of their distrust of parties, must have been opposed to modernization.[7] What Marshall did not recognize, however, was that most of the other important organizations of the day—voluntary associations, school systems, and business corporations in particular—were run by Whigs, men like Joseph Tuckerman, Horace Mann, Nicholas Biddle, William H. Ashley, and the Tappan brothers. The Democratic party itself was indebted for many of its modes of operation to evangelical revivalists and to the proto-Whig Antimasonic party. In fact, the modernizing of social organization during this time was pioneered to a great extent by paternalists. The idea of people as interchangeable parts was not a part of their ethos; they were trying to preserve and foster inequality. Jackson declared war on this group when he vetoed recharter of the Bank of the United States. He and his Democratic party were primarily defending a society of independent yeomen and artisans, who were threatened by the kind of modernization the Whigs envisaged.[8]

In the case of the Whigs, it is important to distinguish what was intended from what was actually achieved. Just as Whig social reforms could serve conservative purposes, so other forms of modernization could represent means to old-fashioned ends. John Quincy Adams supported measures favorable to business enterprise out of a dedication to the classical humanist ideals of discipline and self-improvement. For a patrician manufacturer like Nathan Appleton, modernization was a means to preserving the family fortune. Such rationalization of production as took place on Henry Clay's property was adopted in the interests of a patriarchal social ideal, the plantation. It is clear that the modernized bureaucratic benevolent associations of evangelicals like Lyman Beecher were means to the ancient end of converting souls to Christ. But not everyone in the Jacksonian era stumbled into modernization as the unintended by-product of other efforts. There were some for whom modernization had become an end in itself, although they did not use that word for it. They called it "progress," by which they meant much the same thing as modernization, plus a positive value connotation.

As exemplars of Whigs who were deliberate modernizers, Horace Greeley and William Henry Seward serve well. In their activities, modernization seems to have become secularized and even divorced from the aspirations of a rentier class. It has taken on a life of its own, in much the same way that, according to Max Weber, the "spirit of capitalism" finally developed out of, and became differentiated from, the "Protestant ethic."

Perhaps the least understood of all prominent American political leaders, Horace Greeley (1811–72) has been laughed at for genera- tions since his death as an impractical, fuzzy-minded eccentric. His contemporaries took him more seriously, and did so rightly. A hard-driving, methodical man, a consistent Whig, he was the most influential journalist of his time, a major shaper of American public opinion for over thirty years, and a presidential candidate. Yet there is no satisfactory intellectual portrait of Horace Greeley. The two best studies of him are Glyndon Van Deusen's biography, which focuses on his politics, and Constance Rourke's portrayal of him as a pic- turesque figure in American social history. Both authors emphasize the confusion and lack of realism they find in his outlook.[9] Greeley's reputation for impracticality is ironic. He considered himself a su- premely practical man, and with reason, for had he not built the most successful newspaper in America from scratch? He looked down on reformers who lacked practical experience in the business world, who did not know what it was to meet a payroll.[10]

Greeley came to fame and power from obscure origins. He grew up in a remote township of New Hampshire, whose hard-scrabble farm- ers in the election of 1828, as he later recalled, cast 334 votes for John Quincy Adams and 4 for Andrew Jackson.[11] His father's bank- ruptcy and loss of the family homestead were traumatic experiences for the young boy. It did not occur to him, then or later, to blame the Panic of 1819; he blamed Zaccheus Greeley's drinking, and for the rest of his life Horace Greeley retained a horror of both alcohol and debt. Like Henry Carey, Greeley learned the printer's trade, but, unlike Carey, he had no family business to enter. In 1831 Greeley came to New York City to seek his fortune, as countless thousands of others had done and would do. Becoming a living example of success wrested from fate by talent and application, Greeley not surprisingly celebrated the American way.

John Greenleaf Whittier called Greeley "a second Franklin," and the comparison is an instructive one.[12] Both made their fortunes as big-city printers, turned their attention to philanthropic projects, and worked to build a united and prosperous America. Both were modernizers, for Franklin believed in popular government, rational problem-solving, and social engineering as much as Greeley. Yet from the differences between them we can acquire a feeling for the changes that had occurred in American bourgeois culture between the eighteenth and the nineteenth centuries. Greeley was less of a cosmopolite, for the America of his day was less intimately involved in European affairs; and of course he was not a scientist, for science by the mid-nineteenth century had achieved greater autonomy as an activity. Most interesting, however, is the subtle yet significant difference in their attitude toward the work ethic. To Franklin it was a device for getting ahead, and he was not loath to affect an industrious appearance purely for public relations. Greeley takes work (and life itself) much more seriously; he never greets us with Franklin's sly wink. Franklin was a man of the Enlightenment, but Greeley typifies the American Victorian.

In 1834 Greeley started a periodical called *The New Yorker*, a weekly with the contents of a magazine, the format of a tabloid newspaper, and a popular song printed on the back page. It achieved a circulation of 7,000—modest indeed, though the largest of any American literary magazine in 1837. In 1838 a shrewd Whig manager named Thurlow Weed hired Greeley to put out a campaign organ called *The Jeffersonian*. The Whigs won the New York state election that year, and Greeley's rise continued. In the great race of 1840 he edited another Whig campaign weekly, *The Log Cabin*, which attained the astonishing circulation of 80,000 copies an issue. The following year he began the journal that was to make him famous, the *New York Tribune*, and a few months later created its spinoff, *The Tribune Weekly*. The *Weekly* reprinted the major items from the daily newspaper, and, by means of it, Greeley reached beyond New York to a nationwide audience. In 1850 a European edition was created. The circulation of *The Tribune Weekly* grew until, by the eve of the Civil War, it had reached 200,000. Together with his Democratic rival, James Gorden Bennett of the *New York Herald*, Greeley ushered in modern American journalism.[13]

April 10, 1841, marked by coincidence both an important end and an important beginning in the history of the Whig party. It was the day of William Henry Harrison's funeral and the day the *New York Tribune* began publication. To read the paper is to appreciate both the seriousness of politics in the Jacksonian era and the high standards of the editor. Among those who wrote for the *Tribune* were not only distinguished Whig intellectuals like Henry C. Carey, Richard Hildreth, and Bayard Taylor but Karl Marx and Friedrich Engels, Walt Whitman and Ralph Waldo Emerson. Works of Dickens, Carlyle, Thomas Moore, and Victor Cousin appeared in its pages. Margaret Fuller, chief literary critic, carried on a vigorous dialogue with such other journals as *The Dial*, Brownson's *Quarterly Review*, and *Blackwood's Edinburgh Magazine*. Proceedings in Congress and major trials were covered closely; important political speeches and proposed treaties were printed verbatim. The *Tribune* was passionate in its causes, conscientious and thorough in its reporting, and minced no words in condemning its adversaries.[14] The editorials, written by Greeley himself, breathed fervent Whiggery. The popularity of the *New York Tribune* is hard to reconcile with a notion of politics in the middle period as a mere diversion for a mindless populace being manipulated by a few office-seekers and having no interest in issues.

The man behind this newspaper was nothing if not earnest. Greeley's moral seriousness is well typified in a story he told of the French Revolution. A member of a revolutionary assembly calls out, "Mr. President, I move that *all* the knaves and dastards be arrested!" Greeley observes that he can sympathize with the man's feeling, but what is really needed is not punishment but redemption: "their thorough cure of knavery and cowardice." We must labor constantly, he instructs us, to eliminate vice in ourselves and in others.[15] Greeley was an intensely didactic man, who considered the world "a seminary" and education a lifelong process of self-discipline. He urged college students to consecrate themselves to public service, not to selfish careerism. Like many other people of the Victorian age, he sometimes saw ethics and art as if they were opposed. "This life on which we have been launched seems a problem so grave and earnest as to afford little time or thought for either idyls or madrigals."[16] In actuality, however, Greeley was no philistine. Though self-educated, he was widely read and appreciated Tennyson and Browning, Whitman and Byron. His sympathies and appeal cut across the distinction we are accustomed to draw between "high-brow" and "popular" culture. He could contribute bad didactic verse to a mass-distribution women's gift book, *The Rose of Sharon*, yet his taste in *belles lettres* could also elicit praise from Edgar Allan Poe.[17]

Greeley called himself "a mediator, an interpreter, a reconciler, between Conservatism and Radicalism." He looked forward to the day when the "angry strife" between them would end and both would be recognized as essential aspects of true progress.[18] In a typically systematic fashion, he enumerated his reasons for aligning himself with the Whigs. (1) The Democrats overemphasized liberty at the expense of order; their celebration of popular sovereignty was demagogic. (2) "The party styling itself Democratic is, as regards Foreign Powers, the more belligerent and aggressive party." (3) Resources the Democrats devoted to war the Whigs would devote to internal improvements. (4) The Whigs favored "Protection to Home Industry." (5) Whig policy was "constructive, creative, and beneficent," while that of the Democrats was "a bundle of negations, restrictions, and abjurations." (6) As individuals, Whigs were more likely than Democrats to prefer "the ways of Virtue." (Greeley was cautious, even defensive, about making this distinction; he insisted that he was not identifying poverty with vice.) (7) The Democrats were party-oriented; the Whigs, issue-oriented.[19]

Greeley was considered a friend of the workingman in his day, though twentieth-century historians have understandably questioned this characterization.[20] What needs to be understood is that Greeley, while very anxious to help workers, thought much more in terms of redeeming them than of liberating them. He made no distinction between giving workers advice on self-help and seeking to improve their lot through legal or other collective efforts. He encouraged them to plan ahead, to be thrifty, and to limit the number of their children. He reprinted in the Log Cabin William Ellery Channing's essay "On the Elevation of the Laboring Classes," a discussion of opportunities for intellectual self-improvement by apprentice and journeymen mechanics. Greeley favored workers' cooperatives, supported the ten-hour day, and joined the printers' union; yet anything that smacked of class conflict was abhorrent to him. He advocated collective bargaining but felt that it should lead to binding arbitration rather than to strikes. Since capital and labor did not seem to Greeley to have opposing interests, arbitration commended itself to him as peaceful, rational, and just.[21]

Social reform did not, for Greeley, necessarily mean opposition to the interests or wishes of capitalists. He supported limited liability and the Whig Bankruptcy Act of 1841, admired the Lowell textile mills, and endorsed industrialization in general. He would have agreed with Lyman Beecher that economic development and the increasing division of labor that went with it were part of the "stated policy of heaven." Greeley belonged to a generation that could think of business itself as a moral cause. Among the reforms he advocated was greater use of advertising by merchants to inform consumers of products available.[22] Greeley's generation, in fact, did not often use the term "social reform"; they spoke simply of "reform," which could be either social or individual. The individual and the community should each be "self-made" in its own way, that is, should engage in conscious self-discipline and self-development. Greeley saw nothing incongruous in juxtaposing advice on self-improvement with proposals for restructuring society.[23]

The literal sense of "reform," of course, is re-shape or re-order. More than anything else, it meant during the nineteenth century the imposition of a new, more rational, order. In this sense, not only man and society but even nature stood in need of "reform." "Nature, though complaisant at seasons, is yet, in the larger view, grudging and stern toward our race, until transformed and vivified by Labor and Science," wrote Greeley. "Man, therefore, is by primal necessity a Transformer,—in other words, a Reformer."[24] The subjugation of nature, which has come to seem to many in our environmentally conscious day the very opposite of reform, seemed to Greeley (and many other Americans of his era) synonymous with it. "Reform" of nature, of the individual, and of society were, all three, components of the grand transformation of the conditions of human life that nineteenth-century modernizers hoped to achieve. When he looked about him for evidence of "progress," Greeley cited not only wider education and improved care of the helpless, but bridges, canals, and roads. Whether he was supporting a transcontinental railway, worker cooperatives, or total abstinence, Greeley was endorsing the imposition of rational order. In all three cases, it should be added, he was advocating this order for the sake of human freedom, for Greeley thought of freedom as the ability to implement rational desires, not as mere license or whimsy.[25]

Greeley was a Universalist in religion, a member of a denomination that was liberal in theology without having the odor of social exclusiveness that clung to Unitarianism. The distinctive theological belief of the Universalists was a faith that all human beings, no matter how evil, would ultimately be redeemed (possibly through finite punishment in a purgatory after death) and saved. It was an appropriate faith for one of Greeley's general outlook. He called on organized religion to participate in the progress of social reform. He was familiar with the Bible and devoted a great deal of space in the *Tribune* to religious matters, such as William Miller's prophecies of the end of the world.[26] Yet religion does not seem to have been as important a driving force in Greeley's life as it was in Joshua Giddings'.

The place of religion in Greeley's life was really occupied by work. "ATTRACTIVE INDUSTRY, the dream of the past age, the aspiration of the present, shall be the fruition and joy of the next," he hymned. Work was a means of grace, a "blessed boon of God, to alleviate the horrors and purify the tendencies of our fallen state!"[27] Belief in the redemptive power of hard work was widespread among nineteenth-century Americans, who sometimes sought out difficult or unpleasant tasks just to discipline themselves and develop their powers. Greeley gave the belief explicit and emphatic expression. The *Tribune* was full of exhortations to industriousness, as well as to related virtues like sobriety and thrift. Such an involvement in work and its concomitant values was not necessarily sordid or mean-spirited. If it suited the purpose of industrial employers, it also accorded the common man a great measure of dignity and self-respect.[28] That we find admonitions of this kind unbearably trite is in part an indication of how thoroughly modernizers like Greeley accomplished their purpose. The twentieth century has had to learn to enjoy leisure the way the nineteenth learned to enjoy work.

Greeley considered that involuntary unemployment of able-bodied workers was the unforgivable sin of his capitalist society, tragically contradicting its own high value placed on work. "Not til Society shall be so adjusted, so organized, that whoever is willing to work shall assuredly *have* work, and fair recompense for doing it," did Greeley believe justice would be done. The most important cause of his conversion to a homestead bill was his hope that it might provide a solution to unemployment.[29] But Greeley did not preach the virtues of hard work only to the "laboring classes." Like the Chinese modernizers of more recent years, he called on academics and other professionals to perform occasional manual labor in order to develop their bodies along with their minds and to foster a sense of kinship between them and the toiling masses. "I insist that the Thinking Class shall become a Working Class, in the rude, palpable sense." It would help the self-respect of people who worked with their hands to see that others did not consider it beneath their dignity.[30]

The work ethic held out the hope of collective, as well as individual, redemption. "Not individual Man only, but the Nation as an aggregate, demands that symmetric and thorough Development which is to be attained only through a many-sided Industry."[31]

Greeley fully intended the double meaning of "industry" here: diligent work in general and manufacturing in particular. Advocates of
domestic manufactures had long been in the habit of invoking the
work ethic. Back in the eighteenth century, those who called for
resistance to parliamentary taxation by nonimportation agreements
had appealed to the Puritan ethic of hard work and self-reliance to
promote the creation of a home market.[32] Greeley was a faithful
disciple of Henry C. Carey and a lifelong ardent protectionist. He
argued from historical experience that new countries that were ex-
porters of agricultural staples tended to become more prosperous to
the extent that they industrialized and diversified their economies.
Far from being a special favor to manufacturers, the tariff was simply
a device through which the competitive advantage of cheap foreign
labor was equalized. Eighteenth-century free-trade economics had
emerged out of dissatisfaction with the perverse restrictions imposed
on commerce by oppressive aristocratic regimes, but it was absurd to
assume that no regulation—even by popular governments seeking to
promote economic efficiency and the general welfare—was ever war-
ranted.[33] Northern Democrats who refused to see the logic of
Greeley's arguments of behalf of the tariff he angrily dismissed as
Jacobins.[34]

Greeley's values are highlighted in two important travel accounts
he wrote (which also display his skill as a journalistic reporter), one
of the Crystal Palace in London and another of the Arapaho Indians
he met on his transcontinental trip to California. At the Crystal
Palace of 1851, devoted to exhibits of "Universal Industry," Greeley
found "the clearest expression yet given to the spirit and aspirations
of our time." He came away duly impressed by the wealth and productivity of the British Empire and more firmly convinced than ever
that only behind a shield of protective duties could American industry develop to the stage attained in Britain. After his return to the
United States, he and a group of other American promoters paid the
London Crystal Palace their sincerest form of flattery by setting up
the New York Crystal Palace, a smaller structure that housed another
international exhibition in 1853–54.[35] If the British provided a model
for imitation, the Arapaho provided Greeley with a negative reference group. As he described them, they did not value work. The
Arapaho women did everything constructive, while the men were
strictly predatory hunters and warriors; yet all prestige attached to
the males' activities. Greeley hoped that some "humane, capable
Christian trader" and his wife could somehow turn Arapaho culture
around to value the "women's work" it had traditionally despised.

Arapaho women would have to lead their menfolk in this reorientation, he noted.[36]

Many other prominent Whigs echoed Greeley's celebration of the work ethic, and most of them were not loath to welcome the material gains that work produces. Horace Bushnell went so far as to declare that "it is the duty of every man to be a prosperous man, if by any reasonable effort he may."[37] Yet for Greeley the work itself, and learning to take pride and pleasure in it, were really more important. "The man whose only stimulant to exertion in any field is the hope of individual gain, can hardly have risen above the condition of a slave," he told a student audience. At the beginning, work should be accepted as an obligation; but as one progressed in self-discipline, it should become a joy. In Greeley's value system work was associated with freedom, dignity, and self-realization, not with servitude. The importance of such respect for work within the value system of a culture has been recognized in the developing countries of the twentieth century. David McClelland has offered extensive evidence that "achievement orientation" facilitates economic growth, not only in Western capitalist societies but also in socialist ones. The love of work, he concludes, is far more significant than the love of profit per se.[38]

Max Weber's thesis that the "spirit of capitalism" developed out of the "Protestant ethic," which has been so controversial among twentieth-century scholars, would have elicited little stir among the American Whigs. They took it for granted that the Reformed religious heritage had played a major part in developing those virtues of hard work, thrift, and self-discipline they prized in their own day. Greeley himself was of Scots-Irish Calvinist extraction and proud of it; a similar background in the Puritan or Dissenting faith was common among the other subjects of this study. It was not unusual for them to single out the "old Puritan character" as worthy of imitation and to call for a renewal of the "strenuous virtues" of the Reformation, even while regretting the fanaticism and intolerance of that epoch.[39] "There are two facts which have a great influence on our character," John Quincy Adams told Tocqueville and Beaumont; "in the North, the religious and political doctrines of the first founders of New England; in the South, slavery." Adams went on to explain the different attitudes toward work that had developed in the two sections as a result.[40]

Greeley illustrates the stage in Weber's typology when the "spirit of capitalism" emerges as an autonomous belief system. Weber carefully distinguishes the "Protestant ethic" from the "spirit of capitalism," although not all commentators on his work have kept this distinction in mind. Greeley exemplifies the "spirit of capitalism" rather than the "Protestant ethic" because his devotion to work, thrift, methodical habits, and long-range rational planning is no longer ancillary to a religious world view in which it was necessary to demonstrate election. The moral, if not the theological, significance of work remains at least as strong as ever.[41] In locating Greeley within Weberian categories, another distinction must also be made, that between the "spirit of capitalism" and capitalism itself. The latter is an economic system that may exist independently of the attitude cluster Weber identified. The biggest capitalists, in fact, can well afford to disregard the petit-bourgeois virtues of "der Geist des Kapitalismus." The "spirit of capitalism," as Greeley taught it, he intended for everybody, not just capitalists; and he himself was but an indifferent capitalist, if one can judge by the size of his estate.

Greeley practiced what he preached or, more accurately, preached what he practiced. He loved his work for its own sake, both at the *Tribune* and on the farm he purchased at Turtle Bay, a few miles outside the city. (Like Henry Clay, he thus managed to create a "mixed economy" within his own household.) Though the *Tribune* was a prosperous paper and brought wealth to his partner, Thomas McElrath, Greeley's private generosity and lack of interest in investing prevented him from amassing much of a fortune.[42] So Greeley rose from rags to fame rather than to riches. No matter; he had his reward. When, in 1868, he looked back over his career, he entitled his memoirs, appropriately, *Recollections of a Busy Life*.

The aspect of Greeley's career that has most provoked the charges of inconsistency and impracticality is his support of "Associationism." Albert Brisbane, chief American disciple of the French pre-Marxian socialist Charles Fourier, introduced Associationism into the United States in 1840 and found Greeley's response enthusiastic. Brisbane's "phalanxes" were intended to be communities of volunteers, carefully selected for skills, who would engage in a variety of economic activities, with profits to be distributed according to a fixed ratio: five-twelfths to labor, four-twelfths to capital, and three-twelfths to skill. By living in a single large building (the "phalanstery"), the participants would be able to pool child care and homemaking, thus freeing the women for tasks outside their own families. The major objective was to match every person's abilities with an appropriate job.[43]

Greeley accorded Brisbane's ideas favorable notice in the *New Yorker* and the *Tribune*, and, beginning on March 1, 1842, there was a regular series by Brisbane in the *Tribune* devoted to Associationism. (Brisbane paid Greeley for this feature, not the other way around.) Greeley also promoted Associationism through his lectures and invested money in several phalanxes. He served as vice-president of the most successful of them, the North American Phalanx at Red Bank, New Jersey, which lasted from 1843 to 1854 and earned a modest profit of 5 percent on investment. As late as 1869 Greeley showed the influence of Associationist principles in founding the "union colony" in Colorado (this ultimately became the city that still bears his name). How Greeley could reconcile these socialist enterprises with Whiggery has puzzled many, in his own time and since. His rival editor and fellow Whig, Henry J. Raymond of the *New York Courier* (later the founder of the *New York Times*), engaged Greeley in a prolonged debate in which he charged that Greeley's support for Association was Jacobinism as bad as that of the most radical Loco-Focos.[44]

Greeley's involvement with Associationism actually illustrates how much early capitalism and early socialism had in common as agents of modernization. This, after all, was still the era of the great Scottish industrialist Robert Owen, who turned from benevolent capitalism to utopian socialism. Henry C. Carey, as we have seen, used the term "association" to mean the greater efficiency that comes with collective effort and the division of labor; Greeley seems to have taken Brisbane's "Association" as an attractive special case of Carey's "association."[45] Greeley found the phalanx appealing for many of the same reasons that he admired Lowell, Massachusetts: its rational order and efficiency, its promise of uplift for the participants. As Greeley explained it, he first became interested in Association as a solution to unemployment, which he witnessed every winter among day laborers in New York City whose work was seasonal. What he liked about socialism was its organization and planning, its economies of scale, and, above all, the hope of keeping everyone busily and happily at work. The idea of equal rewards for all Greeley rejected (as did most other American Associationists); he felt it unjust that the "ingenious, efficient" person should receive no more than others.[46]

It has been charged that Associationism rejected industrialization and sought vainly to recapture the lost small community. While the appeal of a village-sized community was certainly present in the phalanx (whose ideal population was 1,645), there is no evidence of escapism in Greeley. He welcomed industrialism and sometimes defended Association and the protective tariff in the same breath,

arguing that both encouraged the division of labor and the development of a mixed economy.[47] Associationism was not a rebellion
against modernization but a peculiarly intense form of it. This was
how Emerson saw the matter, and he was right. "I regard these
philanthropists as themselves the effects of the age in which we
live," he wrote. "They [are] describers of that which is really being
done. The large cities are phalansteries; and the theorists draw all
their arguments from facts already taking place in our experience."[48]
The most useful way of looking at Greeley's Associationism is to
view it as an exaggeration of the general tendencies in Whiggery
toward the reshaping of human nature through the imposition of
artificial order.

Upon close examination, Greeley's socialism turns out to be intended as a supplement to capitalism, not a substitute for it. Greeley
expected that phalanxes would be set up by investors, who would be
paid dividends. He seems to have thought of the phalanx as just
another mode of mobilizing capital and labor, one that could conve-
niently coexist with workers' cooperatives and conventional joint-
stock companies. (His idea seems more plausible when one recalls
the fluidity of the concept of the corporation at that time and the
number of forms it could take.) Elements in Fourier's and Brisbane's
thought that were incompatible with the values of the larger society
Greeley felt free to reject. For example, in the phalanxes he approved,
he emphatically ruled out any tampering with monogamous marriage or organized Christianity. Indeed, he repeatedly argued that
Association should be classified as one of the reforms within the
evangelical movement.[49] Associationism of Greeley's variety could
act as a kind of safety valve, drawing off those desiring an alternative
social system into productive communities of their own instead of
leaving them to sow dissension. It is instructive to contrast Greeley's
Associationism with that of Parke Godwin, who came out of a
background in the Democratic party. Godwin's Associationist writings put more emphasis on class struggle and less on the compatibil-
ity of Association with capitalism. It is also instructive that Stephen
Pearl Andrews, a socialist and anarchist who was probably the most
radical American of his time, denounced Greeley with righteous indignation: "He is not a Socialist in any integral, revolutionary, [or]
comprehensive sense."[50]

It makes it easier to understand Greeley if we note his remarkable
similarity to the "progressives" of the early twentieth century. Like
them, he wanted to rationalize the existing social order and make it
more humane. Through the *Tribune* he advocated such protoprogres-
sive causes as a national presidential primary, an income tax, the

abolition of capital punishment, and the direct election of United States senators. A lifelong teetotaler, he argued for temperance on the basis of medical research detailing the harmful effects of alcohol and, of course, his disapproval of dependence on any substance making one less capable and rational.[51] Almost alone among American newspapers, the *Tribune* gave thorough coverage and serious attention to the women's-rights movement. Greeley's wife, Mary, is entitled to much of the credit for this. She taught him to respect the cause and introduced him to Margaret Fuller, whom he then appointed literary editor of the newspaper, said to be an unprecedented position for a woman. Greeley did not share Fuller's Transcendental philosophy (he called it "vague, mystical, unmeaning"), but he admired her social conscience, her powerful intellect, and, finally, the heroism of her death at sea in 1849.[52]

Conspicuously absent from Greeley's list of reforms was divorce. In fact, he engaged in vigorous debates against the slightest liberalization of the grounds for divorce and bolstered his case with appeals to Scripture. He also crusaded for the enactment of laws making adultery and "seduction" criminal offenses and for better enforcement of the laws against prostitution. In this respect Greeley was very much the prudish Victorian.[53] His stern insistence on conventional monogamy may have been influenced by the fact that the Greeleys' own marriage was preserved without being very happy. Horace and Mary were too much alike not to get on each other's nerves; she, too, was an intense person, a Yankee intellectual of humble background, devoted to improving herself and those around her.[54]

The two reform causes for which Greeley is best remembered are the Homestead Act and antislavery. During the mid-1840s Greeley moved from opposing preemption to support of the homestead principle. His shift was part of that general Whig reorientation in the direction of more positive attitudes toward the West that Lyman Beecher had pioneered and that also manifested itself in Whig acceptance of California into the Union. Like most Whigs, Greeley retained a strong sense of the moral qualities of rural and small-town life, even while favoring industrialization. The Homestead Act promised to perpetuate the values of the family farm, and Greeley also supported (without success, of course) a limitation on the amount of land that any individual could transmit to his heirs, a measure intended to prevent the consolidation of great landholdings. He was an ardent exponent (and, on his own lands, a practitioner) of scientific agriculture; even after he came to endorse westward migration, he still opposed the wasteful, soil-mining farming methods so common in America. In Greeley's scheme of things, the growth of industry would not threaten agriculture but would complement it by providing it with a home market.[55]

As the greatest celebrant of the free-labor ideology, Greeley inevitably found slavery the very antithesis of his values. The form his antislavery took, however, evolved over time. At first the colonization movement commended itself to him, but the murder of Elijah Lovejoy in 1837 and the early "filibustering" efforts to wrest Texas from Mexico caused him to shift emphasis from relocating the slaves to resisting the aggressions of the slave power. His involvement with the Whig party kept him apart from the political abolitionists, and he felt very bitter toward those Liberty-party voters who cost Clay New York and the election in 1844. (Though Clay was master of a plantation, Greeley considered him "less [a slaveholder] at heart than any of our public men.")[56] Greeley strongly backed the Wilmot Proviso, declaring that for Congress to legalize slavery in the new territories would be turning back the clock, like legalizing "Polygamy, Dueling, Counterfeiting, Cannibalism, or any other iniquity condemned by and gradually receding before the moral and religious sentiment of the civilized and Christian world." After 1854 Greeley became firmly opposed to any further compromises with slavery, and during the Civil War he resolutely pressed Lincoln to convert the war for the Union into one for emancipation.[57]

Greeley's transition from Whiggery to Republicanism was a painful process that left permanent scars. In 1848 he had toyed with the idea of backing the Free-Soil party, but in the end he stuck with the Whig nominee, Zachary Taylor. In 1850 his high regard for Clay was sorely tried by his hero's "Omnibus" Compromise, with its infamous Fugitive Slave Act. Clay's death and the crushing defeat of Winfield Scott in 1852 left Greeley feeling bereft. The progressive wing of New York Whiggery, led by Senator Seward and his manager Thurlow Weed, had become accustomed to taking Greeley's support for granted; Greeley justly felt unappreciated. When the Whig nomination for lieutenant governor went to Henry J. Raymond of the *New York Times*, a "Cotton" Whig and Greeley's bitter rival, Greeley was fed up. So in 1854 he joined the Republicans without waiting for his two long-time associates. Within a year, Seward and Weed followed suit, but Greeley maintained his independence of them, and what had been a close, mutually advantageous collaboration gave way to suspicion. At the Republican convention of 1860 Greeley withheld support from Seward, the frontrunner. While he did not succeed in delivering the nomination to his own candidate, Edward Bates of Missouri, he played a decisive role in denying it to Seward.[58]

Thurlow Weed was not a man to be crossed. The long-delayed revenge he took proved to be one of the most memorable in American history.

In 1872 the Liberal Republicans, disaffected with the Grant administration and with Radical Reconstruction, nominated Greeley as their candidate for president. The Liberal Republicans were in many ways a neo-Whig movement, with patrician leadership; they emphasized the need to recover prewar moral standards and hoped to renew their old alliance with southern white ex-Whigs.[59] Historians, knowing that Greeley was badly beaten, have often regarded his nomination as incomprehensible. Actually it was not. Greeley was put forward at the Liberal Republican convention by the practical politicians, not by the amateur reformers. Presumably, the former felt comfortable with him because of his experience and close ties to old Whiggery. Because he had been reluctant to break with the administration, Greeley lent an aura of moderation to the ticket. One of the most famous men in America, with a reputation for high principle, he would not have to build name recognition. Since he had generously put up bail for Jefferson Davis, he would be expected to run well in the South; his famous, half-apocryphal injunction, "Go West, young man," might well help him in that section too. The Democratic convention, having nowhere else to turn, gave Greeley its nomination also, but the alliance did not work well. Democratic voters were less flexible than Democratic politicians, and they remembered that Greeley had spent a lifetime denouncing Democrats. Accordingly, thousands of them stayed away from the polls.

During the campaign Greeley became the subject of what was perhaps the most vicious and certainly the most effective character assassination in American electoral history. Masterminded by Thurlow Weed and the brilliant, merciless cartoonist Thomas Nast, the regular Republican organization created a dummy Greeley, a scatter-brained incompetent, whom they gleefully poniarded. Greeley's efforts the discuss the issues proved in vain. He died within a month of the election, quite literally mortified, as Kenneth S. Lynn has put it.[60] For generations Horace Greeley was to be remembered only as the pitiful butt of ridicule.

"Mr. Seward is a power in the state," Wendell Phillips noted early in 1861. "His position decides that of millions."[61] William Henry Seward (1801–72) served the people of the Empire State as legislator, governor, and senator, and as one of their most prominent trial lawyers, for a period of thirty years before becoming U.S. secretary of state, the office he filled from 1861 to 1869. A successful politician with many constructive achievements to his credit is necessarily a shaper and a reflector of public opinion, and Seward was both. He was extremely fortunate during the Whig portion of his career to have in Thurlow Weed a political manager of consummate skill and in Horace Greeley a publicist equally skilled. The close relationship between Seward and Weed, the man of principle and the man of expedients, is particularly instructive. Historians are too apt to assume that principled statesmen must be impractical and that practical ones have no principles. Seward and Weed wedded their goals and talents very effectively, and in combination with Greeley they constituted a formidable triumvirate of progressive Whiggery.

Seward had been born into a well-to-do family of Orange County, New York, of mixed Welsh, English, and Protestant-Irish ancestry. He was educated at Union College in Schenectady and long retained a close relationship with Eliphalet Nott, the distinguished moral philosopher who was president of the college. A small, delicately featured man, Seward made a striking contrast with the tall, muscular, self-educated Weed. Though nominally an Episcopalian, Seward manifested little interest in religion; even more than Greeley, he was a secular person. There was no taint of Federalism in Seward's background for opponents to use against him; his father had been a Jeffersonian. Seward moved from the consensus Republicanism of the early 1820s to supporting John Quincy Adams. Elected to the state legislature as an Antimason in 1830, he was the unsuccessful gubernatorial candidate of the new Whig party in 1834.[62] The defeat did not sour him on politics. Life had been good to Seward on the whole, and this was reflected in his optimistic temper. In public affairs, as in private ones, he displayed a confident assumption that problems could be solved and obstacles overcome.

At the prototypical national convention of Antimasons in 1831, Seward backed Adams for the nomination, though it went to William Wirt. Seward remained loyal to Adams all his life, and took his statecraft as a model. Most of Seward's policies can readily be seen as continuations of Adams': support for economic development and education, opposition to the slave power, a strong foreign policy. When Adams died, Seward delivered two eulogies and commenced to write his biography—a task that the pressure of other commitments soon required him to turn over to a ghost writer (John M. Austin). But Seward continued to invoke Adams' precepts and example over the years; on the eve of the Civil War he recalled Adams as "the wisest statesman I ever knew." Seward's admiration for the former president was a matter of principle rather than temperament, for Seward was a genial, outgoing man who found Adams' precise, aloof manner hard to take.[63]

In 1848 Seward was invited to deliver an address before a Young Catholics' Society in Baltimore that wanted to honor him as a well-known friend of Catholic immigrants. Some in his audience may have been embarrassed by what Seward had to say, for his speech summarized his activist, optimistic, secular faith as well as any single utterance of his ever did. "Our lot," he declared, "was cast in an age of revolution—a revolution which was to bring all mankind from a state of servitude to the exercise of self-government—from under the tyranny of physical force to the gentle sway of opinion—from under subjection to matter to dominion over nature." In this dramatic yet nonviolent "revolution" that Seward saw going on around him, political freedom, public education, and technological progress were all synthesized into a comprehensive vision of modernization.

One can readily analyze the elements that go to make up Seward's world view. He assumes a metaphysical dualism in which mind takes precedence over matter and should dominate it; hence it is better to control nature than to be controlled by it. For the same reason, it is better to influence people in nonmaterial ways ("the gentle sway of opinion"), that is, to be didactic, than to influence them in material ways ("the tyranny of physical force"), that is, to be coercive. Yet to expose the skeleton of a belief structure in this way does not always serve to display its power. Reading Seward's address today, one begins to recapture something of the excitement with which he faced his country's future. What is for us an unimpassioned notion, "modernization," was for him "progress," "revolution," a new order of things, the promise of a better life for all. And the "true greatness of our country" was that America would lead the way. Of course there were doubters. "There is an opinion that our [political] system is unfavorable to great national achievements," that we lacked the disciplined staying power for long-range planning and concerted effort. Fortunately, this was an error, which came from supposing that our form of government was merely democratic, "veering with every breeze." Seward proudly demonstrated that the United States enjoyed a mixed, balanced polity and, in consequence, was sufficiently stable for world leadership.[64]

As a young state legislator, Seward had defended the Bank of the United States when his Democratic colleagues attacked it, and he was still being denounced as a lackey of Nicholas Biddle when he ran for governor in 1838.[65] This time, however, Seward won. His first message to the state legislature (1839) is to gubernatorial statements what John Quincy Adams' first message to Congress is to State of the Union addresses. He called for state aid to canals and railroads, creation of a state board of education and board of agriculture, measures to cut down on fraudulent voting in the cities, and legalization of bank notes below the value of five dollars (which the Democrats had prohibited). Each year new items were added to Seward's ambitious agenda. In 1840 it was prison reform. Seward largely abolished flogging and introduced vocational-training programs to redeem the inmates of Auburn and Sing Sing for socially useful purposes. However, the working classes were outraged when the convict labor of Seward's prison schools turned out products that competed with their own. When the Democrats eventually returned to state office, they restored the lash, cut the prisons' budget as an economy measure, and defined prison once again as strictly a place of punishment.[66] Governor Seward also supported the efforts of his good friend Dorothea Dix to reform the treatment of the insane. In after years he fought in Congress for passage of her bill for federal aid to state mental hospitals.[67]

An embarrassing issue during Seward's two terms was the Anti-Rent War of small farmers against the patroon system. It caught Seward between his obligation to uphold the law, on the one hand, and, on the other, the just cause and political strength of the protesters (most of them Whig voters). The governor made it clear that his sympathies were with the tenants and succeeded in calming them while calling on the legislature to abolish the archaic system of land tenure that had caused the problem.[68] The persistence of relics of feudalism was hardly in keeping with Seward's ambitions for his state. In 1842, just before leaving the governorship, Seward published his *Notes on New York*, an encyclopedic compendium of history, natural history, and other reflections, reminiscent of Jefferson's *Notes on Virginia*. The work celebrates New York as a paradigm of modernization for the rest of the country, in much the same way that Seward envisioned the United States as paradigm for the rest of the world.[69]

The public-school controversy tested Seward's leadership even more severely than the Anti-Rent War. It arose out of a plan to give a share of the state's aid to education to the Catholic parochial schools. To the fast-growing Catholic minority this seemed only fair, because the textbooks and instruction in the public schools were strongly Protestant in their point of view, especially in the schools operated by the Public School Society of New York City. Unwilling to expose their children to heresy in the public schools and unable as yet to find a viable alternative, many Catholic parents were providing no schooling at all for their children. Seward reminded the legislature that "education and national prosperity are reciprocal in their influence" and warned them that "the public welfare is as deeply concerned in [the immigrants'] education as in that of our own children."[70] He advocated state aid in developing a Catholic parochial-school system and on that basis formed a close relationship with Bishop John Hughes of New York. It was a plausible course of action for Seward, whose fervent belief in education was much stronger than any interest of his in sectarian differences, but the program ran into severe trouble and cost the governor heavily in votes among Whig Protestants. Religious animosities ran too deep for easy eradication; Bishop Hughes could no more deliver the votes of his overwhelmingly Democratic laymen to Seward than Seward could deliver the votes of a Whig legislature to the support of parochial schools. Democratic leaders protested that Seward's plan would violate separation of church and state. The net outcome was that the public schools were pushed away from their Protestant traditions toward secularism, while Catholics redoubled their efforts to build an educational system of their own without state help.[71]

Seward worked diligently, if vainly, to break the hold of the Democratic party in Catholic communities. He often addressed Irish-American rallies, speaking in support of repeal of the Anglo-Irish Act of Union. When other Whigs grumbled that the ungrateful Irish continued to vote Democratic, Seward would stick up for them and blame the nativists. "Irishmen abandoned the Whig party, because they were alarmed for their rights. And have not many Whigs abandoned it for a less worthy motive?" Seward enjoyed the support of Horace Greeley in these efforts, and it was the *Tribune* that first applied the derisive name "Know-Nothings" to the nativists.[72] Nor were Seward and Greeley the only Whig leaders to side with the Irish-Americans against the nativists. Clay, Webster, and Everett, for example, repeatedly welcomed immigrants from Ireland, insisted that their labor was vitally needed for industrialization, and expressed confidence in their swift assimilation.[73]

The prospects for assimilation constituted the real question between the nativist Whigs and those who, like Seward, had confidence in the ability of the country to absorb immigration. Seward wanted immigrant labor to help build his empire state and empire nation. If the truth be known, he was not particularly impressed by the actual condition of the "thriftless but contented" Irish, yet he had faith in what they might become. Ever the optimist, he was sure that education—whether public or parochial—would soon turn all manner of immigrants into useful American citizens. He was acutely aware of the diversity among New Yorkers: "We of New York are not a unique, or a primitive [i.e., original], or even a homogeneous people," he pointed out at the celebration of the completion of the Boston-Albany Railroad in 1842. "It is one of our cares, by the agency of benign and equal institutions, to assimilate all these various masses, and reduce them to one great, harmonious, united, and happy people."[74]

The Whig assimilationists did not envision a "melting pot" that would amalgamate many cultures into a new one; they expected the dominant British-American culture to absorb all the rest. Though not of Puritan descent himself, and certainly no Calvinist, Seward identified with the Anglo-American Puritan heritage in politics and morals, as most Whigs did.[75] The distinction between assimilationist and nativist Whigs was one of degree rather than kind; for the nativists did not really seek to cut off immigration, and Whigs like Seward tolerated differences only in matters they considered unimportant. Sewardites and nativist Whigs like Beecher were alike ardent promoters of education; the assimilationists were simply more convinced that they would succeed in imposing their values on others. (Beecher had to invoke divine providence to attain the degree of confidence Seward possessed by temperament.) Daniel Webster spoke for a virtual consensus among Whig leaders: "All we desire, whoever come, is that they will Americanize themselves; that forgetting the things that are behind, they will look forward [and] . . . prove themselves worthy and respectable citizens." None of the Whigs ever seemed to realize that "forgetting the things that are behind" was asking of many people something Whigs usually deplored: the denial of history. At the same time that the Whigs preserved and celebrated the cultural heritage of the British-American Protestant majority, they were telling other Americans to give up theirs.[76]

Members of ethnic minorities in Seward's America could still regard him as their champion, even if he did not espouse cultural pluralism, because of his steadfast devotion to individual rights. Since he wanted to assimilate all people into Anglo-American culture, he quite consistently wanted all people to enjoy the equal protection of Anglo-American law. "The rights asserted by our forefathers were not peculiar to themselves—they were the common rights of mankind," he told a correspondent. "Those who erected that superstructure [the Constitution] foresaw and provided for its gradual enlargement, and looked forward to the time when the same foundations would receive and uphold institutions of republican government ample for the whole human race."[77] Speaking in favor of a bill to grant homesteads to refugees from Europe, Seward was emphatically universalist:

> I am in favor of the equality of men—of *all* men, whether they be born in one land or in another. . . . There is no distinction in my respect or affection between men of one land and of another; between men of one clime and another; between men of one race and another; or between men of one color and another; no distinction but what is based, not upon institutions of government, not upon the consent of society, but upon their *individual and personal merit.*[78]

Though Seward used the notoriously ambiguous word "men" in this passage, it is worth noting that he elsewhere defended women's right to equal education. In debating a bill to authorize mining claims in California, he vigorously advocated, in opposition to the wishes of the California congressional delegation, the right of noncitizen immigrants from China and Mexico to stake such claims.[79]

When Seward was a boy, the household included two slaves. Many years later he recalled listening with fascination as a child to the lore of an old woman, belonging to a neighbor, who could remember Guinea.[80] As governor, Seward espoused a list of causes benefiting black New Yorkers, including removal of the $250 property qualification for black men to vote (no property was required of white voters). He started a long controversy with the governor of Virginia by refusing to extradite three blacks accused of helping a slave to escape. He obtained from the Whig legislature a law guaranteeing alleged fugitive slaves a jury trial and another forbidding state officials to assist in tracking them down. He went so far as to employ state agents to go South and try to recover New York citizens who had been kidnapped into slavery. The governor drew the line at outright abolitionism, but his wife, Frances Miller Seward, was a dedicated abolitionist who pressed her husband throughout his career to take antislavery stands. In return, New York blacks (it has been estimated) cast nineteen out of twenty of their votes for the Whig party.[81] Seward's racial policies went too far for some white Whigs. He and his followers in the state won the nicknames "Wooly Heads" and "Kink-heads," that is, nigger-lovers, in distinction from the more moderate "Silver Grays," who gravitated to the leadership

of Millard Fillmore. (Seward's group were sometimes called "Choc-
taws" as well, a name suggesting Indian-lovers but also connecting
them with the anti-renters, who often disguised themselves as Indians.)

But could Afro-Americans be assimilated into a homogeneous
population like Euro-American immigrants? On this question Seward's vision failed him. He could not imagine the blacks really
assimilating, but neither did his mindset provide room for their
autonomous existence. "Speculating on the ultimate destiny" of the
Negro race in America did not seem very fruitful to Seward. Of one
thing he was sure: neither Negroes nor American Indians posed any
significant obstacle to the "aggrandizement of the Caucasian family."[82] Not feeling threatened by them, he could afford to seek a
measure of justice for them.

In 1848 the Democratic party in New York split hopelessly between
the "Hunkers" and the "Barnburners," and the massive Whig victory that ensued sent Seward to the United States Senate. Seward had
been suspicious of Zachary Taylor's southern origins, but, once in
the Senate, he found himself the leading congressional spokesman
for an administration whose free-soil policies surprised many friends
and foes. Seward's maiden speech in the Senate, in opposition to
Clay's proposed compromise of 1850, voiced the feelings of most
northern Whigs, who had by that time become unalterably opposed
to any further extension of slavery. Southern extremists were arguing
that the Constitution of the United States, of itself and without need
for legislation, opened up the Mexican cession to slavery. Seward
denied this, and, he added, there was a "higher law than the Constitution" that ought to dissuade Congress from introducing slavery
into any area where it did not already exist: the moral law. "The
Creator of the Universe" (Seward preferred the most ecumenical of
names for the deity) had established this law, and it was unfolding
itself to civilized people everywhere. "The security, welfare, and
greatness of nations" depended on their recognizing and obeying
this law and on fostering "the security of natural rights, the diffusion
of knowledge, and the freedom of industry." The conclusion was
obvious: "Slavery is incompatible with all these." Seward's first and
most famous speech to the Senate grounded antislavery firmly in the
context of a call to modernization.[83]

Seward's invocation of a "higher law" captured the imagination of
a large constituency in the North; his biographer judges that well
over a hundred thousand copies of the speech were distributed

within three weeks, and, when one adds the reprints contained in
the *Tribune* and other newspapers, the total may have reached two
hundred thousand.[84] In a society whose mental habits had been so
strongly influenced by Scottish moral philosophy such an appeal
possessed undoubted power. Later, when a southern senator accused him of having advocated civil disobedience and anarchy with
his "higher law," Seward denied the charge. What he had meant, he
explained, was that "rulers, whether despots or elected rulers of a
free people, are bound to administer justice for the benefit of society." This was hardly an un-Whiggish sentiment, though it actually
did contain the germs of civil disobedience if rulers defied the principles of morality or divine law flagrantly enough. When the Fugitive
Slave Act passed, without the jury-trial provision that Seward and
Webster tried to insert, there were those in the North who felt the
time for such disobedience had come, and they sometimes cited
Seward's speech in justification.[85]

Seward's speeches supporting New Mexican statehood, much less
well known than his "higher-law" speech, are almost as interesting.
In them he points out that New Mexico has a larger population than
Ohio, Michigan, Indiana, Illinois, Iowa, or Florida had at the time of
their admission. It was being alleged against New Mexico that her
people were "unfit for self-government," being most Indians or
Mexicans. Seward says that he would not have favored annexing this
population, so different from our own in heritage, but, now that they
are under our flag, they are entitled to the equal justice of admission
to the Union. He defends New Mexico against the extravagant claims
of Texas to all land east of the Rio Grande. (The New Mexicans had
already defended themselves by routing a Texan army sent to enforce
this claim.) New Mexico fits Cicero's definition of a political community with a historic right to territorial integrity, and Seward
supplies the quotations in Latin to prove it.[86] But Seward's arguments were in vain, for he did not even speak for most Whigs. Henry
Clay conceded that the mixed population of New Mexico—
"civilized, uncivilized, half civilized, and barbarous"—were capable
of a degree of self-government but not of participation in the federal
government. "I should be utterly unwilling to receive New Mexico as
a State in her present immature condition," declared the Kentuckian,
forgetting that his own commonwealth was New Mexico's junior by
almost two centuries. Webster also preferred to wait, in the expectation that "American ideas, which are essentially and originally
English ideas, will penetrate the Mexican, the Spanish mind; and

Mexicans and Spaniards will thank God that they have been brought to know something of civil liberty, of the trial by jury, and of security for personal rights."[87]

Seward continued in Washington the advocacy of economic development he had begun in Albany. At the national level his program was linked with national expansion, with a homestead act, and with a transcontinental railroad. "Popular government follows in the track of the steam engine and the telegraph," he exulted.[88] But Seward had wider visions than these. Even more than overland projects, maritime commerce engaged his interest. He called maritime commerce "the chief agent of [this nation's] advancement in civilization and enlargement of empire." Seward was not a continentalist; his visions of American empire had more to do with ocean-based commercial domination supported by far-flung naval bases.[89] Seward wanted to beat the British Empire at its own game. Like Carey and Greeley, he was fascinated by the British, whom he admired, envied, and wanted to replace. He endorsed subsidies for the Collins Steamship Company to help it compete against the British Cunard Line and delighted in the victory of the *America* in its race on the Thames. The arena where the Americans would finally best the British would be the Pacific. To Seward, the ultimate importance of a transcontinental railroad lay in its opening up a highway to the commerce of the Orient.[90] The healthy domestic economy and growing population he wanted for the United States were intended to provide a powerful base for global commercial supremacy. And, of course, his own metropolis of New York City would become the hub of that vast empire.

Seward's interest in American commercial activity in the Pacific was not without precedent among the Whigs. Daniel Webster, when he was secretary of state, extended the scope of the Monroe Doctrine to include the Hawaiian Islands and initiated negotiations leading to a commercial treaty with China. John Quincy Adams even publicly sided with the British in the Opium War; he shocked many good Whigs by doing so but showed that he considered the national interest to lie in opening up China to Western traders. For the most part, antebellum Whigs expected American commercial penetration of the Far East to be peaceful, and they did not desire any conquest of colonial possessions. To characterize their foreign policy as *"pacific"* was a pun, as they themselves realized quite early.[91]

Much of Seward's commercial program found expression in his "higher-law" speech, where it was overshadowed by his short-range goal of stopping the expansion of slavery. Seward linked his opposition to slavery to both his desire for cultural uniformity and his desire for commercial empire. Shall disagreement over slavery cause "one great people," with all that they have in common, to "be broken in two," he demanded. To allow it would betray America's historic destiny. "The world contains no seat of empire so magnificent as this," he proudly affirmed, and he dilated upon the resources and geographic advantages enjoyed by the United States. "The nation thus situated," if only it could be endowed with "moral energies adequate to the achievement of great enterprises, and favored with a government adapted to [its] character and condition, must command the empire of the sea, which alone is true empire."[92] Other Whigs had seen the necessity for moral energy and for enterprise, public and private; few were so far-seeing as Seward in visualizing the ultimate consequences of American modernization as American hegemony.

In July, 1850, Zachary Taylor died, and Millard Fillmore, Seward's archrival, succeeded to the presidency. Fillmore's followers had long felt that Seward was too sympathetic to tenant farmers, immigrants, and blacks. The Seward-Fillmore division was more than a personal rivalry (though it was that too); it manifested the inescapable tension within Whiggery between progress and stability, between moral urgency and social order.[93] With Fillmore in the White House, the balance of power between Conscience Whigs and Cotton Whigs shifted abruptly. By signing the Compromise of 1850 into law, Fillmore intensified the bad feeling between him and Seward. Yet the other major accomplishment of Fillmore's administration was one that Seward could rejoice in: Commodore Perry's commercial treaty with Japan.

The Whig convention in 1852 was unusually bitter. In the end the Sewardites won, preventing the nomination of either President Fillmore or Daniel Webster and securing it for their own candidate, Winfield Scott. It proved a Pyrrhic victory; Scott was overwhelmed in the general election by a pro-Southern "doughface," the Democrat Franklin Pierce. In 1855 Seward concluded that the Whig party "is now manifestly no longer able to maintain and carry forward, alone and unaided, the great revolution that it inaugurated." The "revolution" Seward had in mind was the same one he had spoken of in 1848, but now he was identifying the enemy against whom it must be waged: an "aristocracy," a "privileged class"—and "the slaveholders constitute that class." Henry C. Carey (who allied himself politically with Seward) agreed. "We are in the midst of a Revolution— and a more important one, as I believe, than that of 1776," he told

Josiah Quincy in 1856. It "looks to freeing ourselves from the domination of those who believe that bondage is the natural condition of all
who live by the labour of their hands."[94] Many years later, Charles and
Mary Beard would assess the situation in much the same terms.[95]

What was needed now, Seward proclaimed, was a party openly,
avowedly hostile to the extension of slavery: the Republicans. If slavery had continued in New York State, he asked, where would our
internal improvements be? Our educational and philanthropic institutions? A whole way of life was at stake; technological innovations, the arts, a flourishing free press—all these characterized the
North but not the South. Free soil was the logical culmination of
Seward's modernization program.[96] In 1856 Seward predicted an "irrepressible uprising" of antislavery opinion; two years later this had
become an "irrepressible conflict" between northern and southern
social systems. Yet, even then, Seward did not expect the conflict to
be violent. Freedom was so superior to slavery that it could triumph
peacefully, even constitutionally. As he had said earlier, "Slavery
must give way, and will give way, to the salutary instructions of
economy, and to the ripening influences of humanity."[97] Even while
heralding a revolution, Seward did not relinquish his Whig devotion
to peace and good order.

Though Seward used the word "revolution," what he had in mind
was still the Whig idea of "progress." A revolution that would be "a
peaceful and (paradoxical as the expression may seem) a constitutional one" was his expectation. "The real authors of all benign revolutions are those who search out and seek to remove peacefully the
roots of social and political evils, and so avert the necessity for san-
guinary remedies," he once observed. "The Puritans of England and
America have given the highest and most beneficent illustration of
that conservative heroism." Seward must momentarily have forgotten, in saying this, that the Puritans had had to wage a war against
Charles I and finally behead him.[98]

It was not Seward's fate to lead the revolution he had predicted and
worked for so hard. At the Republican convention of 1860 he had too
many enemies, especially among nativists and former Democrats, to
gain the nomination he coveted. But when Lincoln was elected,
Seward believed the revolution had been consummated. He hoped
against hope that bloodshed could be avoided; there was nothing to
fight about, now that the doom of slavery, distant though it might
be, was assured. Four years of carnage exposed, as one historian has
commented, "the limits of Seward's outlook."[99]

In a sense, Seward simply looked away from and beyond the war.

After becoming secretary of state he was never again primarily interested in the sectional conflict; he looked outward, not inward. Seward's well-known memorandum to Lincoln of April 1, 1861, urging a confrontation with the European colonial powers, was not merely a desperate expedient for reuniting North and South; it prefigured his whole foreign policy.[100] Neither Civil War nor Reconstruction distracted Seward from what now became his main objective, an American overseas empire. Manfully swallowing the great disappointment of his life, his failure to win the presidency, Seward served Lincoln and even Johnson (with whom he had no personal rapport) faithfully and well. He followed up on Commodore Perry's mission, pursued trade with China, Japan, and Korea, obtained the Midway Islands, and anticipated Admiral Mahan's geopolitics. Some of his plans were prematurely ambitious: he tried to acquire a Panama canal route, Hawaii, Santo Domingo, and the Virgin Islands, tried to connect the U.S. west coast with St. Petersburg by a telegraph across the Bering Strait and Siberia. His great triumph was, of course, the acquisition of Alaska, the climax of almost twenty years of preoccupation with increasing American power in the North Pacific. To the end he remembered John Quincy Adams, though he took his inspiration from Adams the young imperialist, rather than the pessimistic elderly Adams, who had doubted whether liberty and empire would prove compatible. Upon retiring, Seward took a trip around the world and spent his last days writing it up. He played no part in the vilification of Greeley and died in October, 1872, seven weeks before his former friend.

Nine

Whig Conservatism

"There is a law and order, a slow and sure, a distrustful and cautious party—a conservative, a Whig party; and there is a radical, innovating, hopeful, boastful, improvident and go-ahead party—a Democratic, a Loco-Foco party!" declared the *American Review* in 1846. For all their innovativeness, the Whigs attached a great deal of importance to protecting property, maintaining social order, and preserving a distinct cultural heritage, three characteristically conservative concerns. I have rejected use of the term "liberal" to describe even the most progressive Whigs because of their moral absolutism, paternalism, and preoccupation with discipline. Unfortunately for symmetry, the term "conservative" cannot be similarly rejected, if only because it was a favorite contemporary appellation for the Whigs (and, significantly, for the pro-Bank Democrats who went over to the Whigs in 1835–36). As a party, the Whigs wanted "conservatism and progress to blend their harmonious action," but in practice, of course, some individual Whigs leaned more toward conservatism and others toward progress. Our inquiry into Whig political culture alternates between the "new" and the "old." From the Whig modernizers, it is only appropriate to turn to Whig conservatism.[1]

Like the modernizers, Whig conservatives were preoccupied with order. In America, however, it was hard to coerce free white men; the political community had to be influenced through persuasion. So the Whig conservatives, again like the modernizers, became didactic in the extreme. But their techniques of persuasion differed. While the modernizers appealed mainly to reason, Whig conservatives supplemented this with appeals to sentiment and prescription. Out of the appeal to sentiment came what has been called "the genteel tradition" in American literature, a major legacy of Whig didacticism. With the appeal to prescription, Whigs created a now-forgotten American vogue of Edmund Burke.

The "national" edition of Webster's works, published in 1903 in eighteen volumes, begins confidently: "Daniel Webster [1782–1852], America's greatest statesman and lawyer, and one of the world's greatest orators. . . ." At the time of his death, Webster was honored by Whigs throughout the land. It was a southerner who declared: "The whole scope and policy of American institutions, the theory and structure of our government, the very soul of American liberty, might be learned from the writings of Daniel Webster."[2] However, the cult of Webster was maintained over the years primarily through the efforts of Whig-Republicans in New England. It remained important as long as they remained in a position of cultural leadership.[3]

As a cult figure, Webster provided an alternative to Andrew Jackson. John William Ward, in his *Andrew Jackson, Symbol for an Age*, found Jackson to represent three value constellations: "nature," "providence," and "will." But not everyone in America espoused the same values. The values Webster symbolized were polar opposites to those of the Jackson cult. Instead of "nature," Webster symbolized civilization and law. Instead of the divine interposition of "providence" (sometimes used by Democrats to justify America's "manifest destiny"), Webster symbolized the nation's progress through history. Finally, instead of the iron "will" of a military hero, Webster symbolized the gentler sentiments of a peaceful negotiator.[4] The anthropologist Mary Douglas argues that people who experience structured social boundaries, such as hierarchies, are attracted by ritualism. The cult of Webster illustrates her point. Webster gloried, and was glorified, in the highly contrived situations of the courtroom and the ceremonial occasion. Defenders of a deferential social structure, his admirers seem to have found such ritualistic observances congenial.[5]

Twentieth-century historians have shaken their heads over Webster's inflated nineteenth-century reputation, and well they might.[6] Unlike Adams, Webster was never president, and unlike Clay he never even came close. His political power base was restricted to parts of New England and New York City; beyond that he achieved only fluctuating alliances. He does have to his credit the treaty of 1842 that defined the boundary between Maine and New Brunswick. He was capable of functioning in a legislative capacity: while chairman of the House Judiciary Committee in 1824–25, he drew up and saw through to passage a comprehensive revision of the federal criminal code, and he acted as floor manager for the Force Act of 1833. Typically, however, the routine of legislation bored Webster; he roused himself only for special occasions. At the risk of offending both political historians and scholars of English, I suggest that Daniel Webster's chief contribution was to American literature.

When Webster rose to deliver his great speech on behalf of Greek independence in 1824, he entertained "little or no expectation" of its leading to any action by Congress, according to his friend and fellow orator Edward Everett. Indeed it did not, but the speech was an end in itself. It was read and admired all over the world, not least in Greece; it became a literary text and a contribution to Webster mythology. Webster's orations constitute a remarkable body of American art, ignored today not only by the public but even by literary scholars, because the genre is no longer recognized as a literary form. Contemporaries, however, thought of Webster's speeches as belonging to "the permanent body of the *literature* of our language." One critic declared in 1844: "He has done what no national poet has yet succeeded in doing—associated his own great genius with all in our country's history and scenery."[7] Webster was a highly self-conscious stylist. He was well versed in the classical writers and eighteenth-century moral philosophers; Shakespeare, Milton, Burke, and Johnson also influenced him. He often revised his speeches so extensively between delivery and publication that the printed version is really a blend of oral performance with literary essay.[8] Certainly Webster thought of himself as a man of letters. He could match classical references with John Quincy Adams and pitied the half-educated Henry Clay ("I never could imagine him sitting comfortably in his library and reading quietly out of the great books of the past").[9]

Webster's orations do not lend themselves to brief quotation; their eloquence is verbose. The great ones, however—like the one at Bunker Hill Monument in 1825—are landmarks in American literary self-discovery. Indeed, they went far toward defining the dominant American literary taste of the nineteenth century.

> We come, as Americans, to mark a spot which must for ever be dear to us and our posterity. We wish that whosoever, in all coming time, shall turn his eye hither, may behold that the place is not undistinguished where the first great battle of the Revolution was fought. We wish that this structure may proclaim the magnitude and importance of that event to every class and every age. We wish that infancy may learn the purpose of its erection from maternal lips, and that weary and withered age may behold it and be solaced by the recollections which it suggests. We wish that labor may look up here and be proud in the midst of its toil. We wish that, in those days of disaster which, as they come upon all nations must be expected to come upon us also, desponding patriotism may turn its eyes hitherward and be assured that the foundations of our national power are still strong. We wish that this column, rising towards heaven among the pointed spires of so many temples dedicated to God, may contribute also to produce, in all minds, a pious feeling of dependence and gratitude. We wish, finally, that the last object to the sight of him who leaves his native shore, and the first to gladden his who revisits it, may be something which shall remind him of the liberty and glory of his country.[10]

Lincoln would bring the American patriotic oration to its perfection, but he worked within a genre that Webster had shaped.

All this is not to say that Webster's speeches were without political significance. They served nationalistic and Whig purposes, strengthening communal bonds and encouraging deference and nonpartisanship. Oratory could be an important form of action when constitutional restraints and political opposition inhibited other forms of action. Webster's words were called "half-battles, stronger than most men's deeds."[11] Clay's American System was never systematically implemented, but Webster's speeches stand as a monument to Whig values.

One important Whig value was paternalism, and the Webster cult seems to have provided a father figure in whom devotees could feel a measure of security. "People sank into repose in his presence, and felt rest and confidence in the mere fact of his existence." A favorite word used to describe Webster and his speeches was "sublime"—a key term in the aesthetics of the day, conjuring up associations of awe-inspiring power.[12] A Democratic politician, Benjamin Butler, sarcastically referred to "the god-like Daniel" during the campaign of

1840, and the name stuck. It was actually no exaggeration of the veneration in which Webster's followers held him: "He spoke like a Divinity"; "He trod the earth like a god."[13] The hero worship of Webster drew on the Renaissance tradition of glorifying the Creator through glorifying His human creatures. This impulse had just been revived by the influential New England preacher, William Ellery Channing, who encouraged people to rejoice in human "likeness to God." Whigs who saw in the "God-like reason" of Webster "the noblest gift of God to the world" were applying this line of thought to their hero.[14]

Inevitably one wants to peek behind the cult and learn something of Webster himself. He seems to have been a spoiled little boy who got his older siblings to do the farm chores and remained exploitative of others when he grew up. His manner was heavy, often abrupt and overbearing. The Englishman Sydney Smith called him "a steam engine in trousers." That he was ambitious comes as no surprise. Except when composing or delivering his speeches, he indulged an indolent streak. All sources agree that he loved luxury and good living. There was gossip about sexual affairs.[15] Suspicions regarding Webster's integrity were common and probably constituted his major political liability. John Quincy Adams considered him utterly unscrupulous, but perhaps his assessment was tinged by unacknowledged envy of Webster's ability to surround himself with flatterers. Thirty years after Webster's death, Henry Cabot Lodge concluded that his "moral character was not equal to his intellectual force."[16]

From his youth Webster hoped to "contrive some way . . . to get rich." He commanded handsome fees in his law practice and speculated heavily in western lands. However, like the stereotypical southern planter, whom his own Yankee capitalist class so often resembled, Webster habitually lived beyond his means. Consequently, he was forever borrowing money from wealthy acquaintances and then failing to repay them. Most notoriously, he became heavily indebted to the Bank of the United States, an embarrassing situation for a politician when the Bank was at the vortex of public controversy. From time to time a fund would be raised on his behalf by the Boston business community of State Street. Eventually, however, Webster had to turn over most of his western landholdings to the Bank in settlement of a debt of $114,000.[17]

Assessing the motives behind Webster's statecraft is tricky. He was not always simply bought and sold by those who supported his speculations and expensive tastes. Despite all the loans and retaining fees the BUS sent him, Webster kept trying to compromise the Bank War, contrary to Biddle's wishes, by means of a short-term recharter. This perversity may be attributed to his rivalry with Clay or to diverging interests between State Street in Boston and Chestnut Street in Philadelphia. Consistently, Webster remained the spokesman for the New England merchant-industrialist class we have seen represented in Nathan Appleton. To what extent might this have been motivated by Webster's concept of the public good as opposed to his personal advantage? The latest attempt to answer this question, Robert F. Dalzell's sympathetic study, finds the two cannot really be separated.[18] For our purposes, Webster's motives may be as shabby as one chooses to make them. His place in Whig political culture was earned by what he said and how people reacted to it, not by why he said it. If he exploited the culture by using it as a vehicle for self-aggrandizement, that was his tribute to its hold over the imaginations of his constituents. After all, Bolingbroke and Burke frequently used the country-party tradition for selfish objectives and enriched it in the process.

Richard N. Current has pointed out that Webster went through life as a role-player. Truth to tell, the senator was as much an actor as Edwin Forrest or Edwin Booth, and he employed the same broad, declamatory style as they. He treated the Senate floor and the bar of the Supreme Court as his theaters. In the presence of others he was never really off stage; Charles Dickens commented that Webster was "the only thoroughly unreal man I have seen on this side of the ocean." To his admirers, it was the public *persona* that mattered.[19]

The role Webster played was not one of his own devising; it was culturally defined. In the eyes of his contemporaries, he typified the orator. The orator was not merely someone who gave speeches; he was a public man, an embodiment of the community, an exemplar of its ideals—in short, a hero. The nineteenth century still took heroes seriously in its politics, its literature, and its writing of history. Webster and the other orators of the day were answering a felt need. "We want the orator who feels and acts with us, in whom we can confide even better than in ourselves," a professor of rhetoric explained. "We want the orator who is unmoved by the reproaches or threats that alarm us, ... who fears nothing on earth but a bad action, and regards no consideration but those of good principle." Responding to calls like this, legends of great oratory appeared, such as William Wirt's renderings of the prerevolutionary addresses of Patrick Henry.[20] In his own lifetime, Webster became the greatest legendary orator of them all.

The history of what is called the "genteel tradition" in American literature should contain an important early chapter on the New England Whig orators.[21] These orators included Rufus Choate and Caleb Cushing among the conservatives, Wendell Phillips and Charles Sumner among the antislavery spokesmen. Second only to Webster himself was Edward Everett, whose varied career as clergyman, politician, educator, and diplomat shows the many applications of eloquence in antebellum America. Their oratory, conservative and reformist alike, was explicitly didactic, and its chief concern was to impose a national character upon the United States.[22] Both Whigs and Democrats were nationalists, of course, but there was a difference: Democratic writers and mythmakers, such as Cooper and Whitman, took American nationality as a given, coming from nature. The Whig orators, and the genteel tradition that came after them, wanted to shape the national character according to conscious prescriptions. The parties' literary programs thus resembled their economic programs.

Daniel Webster acquired his political culture early in a small New England town. His father, Ebenezer, was a magistrate and represented Salisbury in the New Hampshire state legislature. Ambitious for his son, Ebenezer saw to it that the boy went to Phillips Exeter Academy and Dartmouth College. This opened the way for him to a legal career, first in Portsmouth and later in Boston. In both places Daniel gained acceptance by the business community as a defender of their interests. Though many Portsmouth businessmen were Republicans, young Webster became a Federalist like his father. His brand of Federalism accepted the necessity of electioneering and making political compromises. He had more in common with adaptable merchants like Nathan Appleton than with fanatic Federalists like Jedidiah Morse.[23]

Webster was nothing if not flexible. He switched his political career from New Hampshire to Massachusetts, switched his views on the tariff from free trade to protection, and came around to accepting westward expansion. His decision to transfer Federalist support to John Quincy Adams in 1825 played a key role in the evolution of the second party system. A quarter-century later, on March 7, 1850, he abandoned a lifelong opposition to more slave territory to the extent of supporting Clay's omnibus compromise. The method through which Webster sought to impress his views upon society also varied. Sometimes it was by influencing the interpretation of the Constitution, as when he appeared before the Supreme Court in landmark cases like *Gibbons* v. *Ogden, McCulloch* v. *Maryland*, or *Charles River*

Bridge v. Warren Bridge. Sometimes it was by seeking elective office. Subsuming both his legal and political careers was his career as an orator, a contributor to the literature of American nationality.[24]

Behind all of Webster's tactical shifts lay a constant basic assumption: government exists to protect property. Here his mentor was not Locke but the seventeenth-century English commonwealthman James Harrington, whom he called "one of the most ingenious of political writers." (Webster's debt to Harrington was pointed out in that currently undervalued classic, V. L. Parrington's *Main Currents in American Thought.*)[25] "A republican form of government rests, not more on political constitutions, than on those laws which regulate the descent and transmission of property," Webster declared. "We have no experience that teaches us that any other rights are safe where property is not safe." He went on to insist that both the Revolution of 1688 and that of 1776 had been undertaken "by the men of property for their security." After Webster changed from a Federalist to a Whig, he did not give up his belief that property gives its holder a "stake" in the political community. It was America's "happy condition" that property was widely distributed, giving a broad base of support for a government that protected property.[26]

Webster's fundamental dedication to the defense of property explains much of his apparent inconsistency. For example, he justified his conversion to tariff protectionism by saying that, although he had opposed the principle originally, to end it after it had become a government policy and industrialists had committed themselves would be unjust. The tariff had created a vested interest dependent on the tariff; once called into being, this interest had a right to continued government protection.[27] Whenever innovation was in the interests of property, Webster accepted it. He supported Henry Clay's American System and heartily endorsed technological improvements like the railroad. Eagerly pursuing wealth for himself, Webster took it for granted that government should facilitate its pursuit by the nation at large. Webster has aptly been called a "broker-state" politician who thought of government policy in terms of adjusting the claims of propertied interests to government favors. Believing in the typical Whig doctrine of the harmony of interests, he assumed that what was good for each part contributed to the welfare of the whole. In his mind, social organicism legitimated encouraging economic modernization through special favors to property.[28]

Webster took the prescriptive rights of property seriously even when the property had been acquired illegally. He angered fellow Whigs in 1838 by supporting a preemption bill to give squatters on federal lands title if they paid the minimum price. Later he embraced the cause of free homesteads to settlers. These departures from Clay's symmetrical American System reflected Webster's willingness to acknowledge the vested interests of the small landholders of the West.[29] His hopes that these stands would help his presidential chances proved vain, but they did show the way for the western-development plans of younger Whig-Republicans like Seward and Greeley. It is appropriate that Webster's own financial speculations took the form of investment in western lands; he identified the nation's interests with his own and expected westward migration to benefit both.

Alongside the protection of property, another concept central to Webster's political thinking was balance of character. By developing this intangible quality, Americans could reinforce the external controls so weak in their society. The juxtaposition of property with character was not peculiar to Webster but typical of Whigs. Balance of character, like respect for property, would guarantee balance in society. Much of Webster's oratory was devoted to praising balance of character. We can recognize here the influence of the moral philosophy he had studied at Dartmouth College.[30] Webster's favorite model, and that of many other Whigs, was George Washington. By unremitting self-discipline, Washington had acquired perfect harmony among his "faculties." Some devotees thought Webster himself illustrated the ideal character; their praises could badly distort reality.[31]

One important institution Webster valued as a means of developing balance of character was the public school. Education also helped safeguard those property rights he held dear. It would prevent the citizenry from becoming "dupes of designing men" and would postpone as long as possible that corruption of the commonwealth against which the civic humanists had long warned. In their support of free common schools, conservative and progressive Whigs were at one; literacy, self-discipline, and the harmonious development of the faculties were equally precious to both. During his governorship of Massachusetts, Webster's close associate Everett sponsored Horace Mann's modernizing educational reforms.[32] These, together with the textbooks of the moral philosopher William Holmes McGuffey, helped make the public schools effective propagators of Whig values. In place of the "rude child of nature," the educators sought to create what Webster wanted: a carefully balanced character.[33] What is more, the training in elocution they provided perpetuated the cult of Webster as orator and hero.

Webster's rhetoric displays careful application of principles of persuasion derived from moral philosophy. All Whigs agreed that balance and harmony among the human faculties were essential, but
they varied regarding which faculties they chose to emphasize in
their appeals. Where John Quincy Adams had relied on conscience to
control people, and Henry Clay on prudence, Webster invoked what
were called "the affections," that is, feelings. Though the content of
Webster's political thought remained essentially Federalist, the form
in which he expressed it was innovative. The Federalist aesthetic, as
Linda Kerber has shown, was rationalistic, austere, "Augustan."
Adams, who preferred the "ancients" over the "moderns" and
idolized Cicero, continued faithful to this classical concept of
rhetoric. But Webster struck out in newer directions. His rhetoric
resembled that of Hugh Blair, the eighteenth-century Scot who synthesized the rhetorical prescriptions of the ancients with those of
moderns like François Fénelon.[34] The result may be called "sentimental Federalism."

The Whig-Jacksonian era was a time of great economic and social changes. Unlike the Jacksonians, the Whigs generally welcomed
the economic changes. But the social changes—such as immigration, westward migration, and the decline of deference—seemed
threatening to the Whigs. Webster employed the affections to maintain traditional social and moral values. He played on the "chords of
public sympathy" as a means of social control, a device for substituting cultural restraints for institutional ones. Even while celebrating the economic changes that were fostering Gesellschaft, Webster
undertook to preserve the virtues of small-town Gemeinschaft. His
sentimentalism defended nonpartisanship, deference, organized religion, and respect for the past. These were values he had grown up
with in Salisbury, New Hampshire. But Webster's objectives were
national rather than parochial, for he consecrated his rhetoric to the
preservation of the Union. Historians have often commented on the
use of emotionalism by sectional extremists; one must remember that
it was just as important to Unionist moderates like Webster.[35]

In the closing lines of his great Second Reply to Hayne, Webster
called veneration for "Liberty and Union" a "sentiment." This was a
word with a technical meaning in aesthetics and moral philosophy.
A sentiment was an emotional regard for a rational or abstract principle, like love of beauty, love of virtue, or love of God.[36] Patriotism
was a sentiment, and Webster opened his discourse on "The
Character of Washington" with a reminder to his audience that the
emotive component of patriotism must not be underrated. Linking

the affective to the rational was the function of good oratory. "Abstractions, under the glowing genius of the orator, acquired a beauty, a vitality, a power to thrill the blood," one commentator on the Webster-Hayne Debate put it.[37]

The concept of "sentiment" implied that the affections could serve rational ends. Such was Webster's objective. In his rhetoric, he called on emotion to reinforce reason, not to challenge it. The Second Reply to Hayne consists of three parallel presentations: first, a discussion of sovereignty in the American polity (the appeal of reason); second, a reminder of the dangerous consequences of resistance to constituted authority (the appeal to prescription); and third, the eloquent emotional peroration. When, during the campaign of 1840, Webster pointed out that his older brothers had been born in a log cabin, he made use of this evocative symbol for artistic effect in the context of an argument that Democratic economic policies were not serving the interests of the common man. Similarly, Webster's famous emotional tribute to his alma mater ("It is, Sir, a small college, but there are those who love it") came at the end of a learned legal appeal to the Supreme Court.[38] Webster by no means rejected Clay's appeal to enlightened self-interest on behalf of the Union; he simply wanted to underscore it. As Webster's favorite American statesman, James Madison, had written, "The most rational government will not find it a superfluous advantage to have the prejudices of the community on its side."[39]

The capacity to respond to sentiment was called "sensibility," and it was a quality Webster's followers admired in him. His rhetoric awakened the sensibilities of others, helping them cultivate this dimension of their characters. As Webster explained at the bicentennial of the landing of the Pilgrims: "It is a noble faculty of our nature which enables us to connect our thoughts, our sympathies, and our happiness with what is distant in place or time; and, looking before and after, to hold communion at once with our ancestors and our posterity." Patriotism was not only a political device for preserving the Union; it was also a vehicle for the kind of conscious character development Whigs prized. Of course, if sensibility were to serve reason and not usurp its place, it was crucial that precisely the right balance between them be observed by speaker and audience alike.[40]

The genteel literature that Whig organs like the *American Review* and the *North American Review* praised reinforced the same values of balance and character. The emphasis on domesticity in this literature metaphorically endorsed harmony and paternalism in the larger society. Its didacticism expressed the high regard Whigs had for education and self-discipline. Its celebration of bourgeois virtues implicitly underwrote Whig economic policy and moral reform. Its transatlantic, cosmopolitan tone was the literary analogue of the Whigs' peaceful diplomacy, especially their desire for good relations with Britain. Whig literary critics considered themselves not only arbiters of taste but shapers of manners and morals. The printed word, like the words spoken by Webster and his fellow orators, was viewed by Whig opinion-makers as a means of social control.[41]

In certain ways the genteel tradition was the literary counterpart of the religious evangelism of Lyman Beecher. Both propagated Whig values by means of a careful invocation of sentiment within a framework of superintending rationality. Both provided ways for New England to compensate by cultural prowess for its declining political power. Fittingly enough, Lyman's daughter, Harriet Beecher Stowe, was a major contributor to this literature—and she was on the side of "Conscience" Whiggery, like her father, rather than the "Cotton" Whiggery of Webster. Best-remembered of the creative writers in the didactic Whig tradition are three New England poets: Longfellow, James Russell Lowell, and Oliver Wendell Holmes the elder. Some Democratic writers of the time have fared better in the estimate of later generations: Hawthorne, Melville, and Whitman. Their works are more concerned with conflict and are less explicitly didactic. However, Jacksonian values by no means necessarily produced greater art; the ultraracist minstrel shows, with their heavy freight of Democratic political propaganda, demonstrate this.[42]

Two different modes of rhetoric can be distinguished in the orations of Daniel Webster; we may term them the "forensic" and the "inoffensive." The forensic was the lawyer's mode, but it was widely used by Webster and others in legislative as well as courtroom situations. It was characterized by a historical review of the subject at hand, to discover precedents and establish trends; thus it was well suited to debating issues of constitutionality. The forensic mode was avowedly disputatious, continuing a tradition of verbal combat that extended back to classical times. For centuries it had been the principal mode of oratory, the practice of which had been confined to males and expressed male-male rivalries in ritualized form.[43]

The other influence on Webster's rhetoric was one he seems to have acquired from the New England clergy of his time, in particular William Ellery Channing. During their theological controversies with the Calvinists, Channing and the other religious liberals had cultivated the art of sustaining a cause while avoiding personal abuse.

Their example was followed by Webster in his debate with Hayne. "Hayne cast himself as a passionate Cavalier and slipped frequently into a military terminology of defense and attack. Webster was the transcendent Yankee, peaceable, cool, and deliberate."[44] The Webster-Hayne Debate was still essentially disputatious in character, but on other occasions Webster turned wholeheartedly to conciliation. The "inoffensive" preaching (as it was called) that was common among liberal ministers supplied Webster with a sentimental rhetoric of harmony. When the sectional controversy worsened, Webster found himself more and more invoking the religion of patriotism the way latitudinarian clergy sometimes employed noncontroversial piety.[45] Webster's own religious faith was bland, nontheological, and ecumenical. Depending on where he was living, he attended Congregational, Presbyterian, Unitarian, or Episcopal services. He enjoyed friendly relations not only with the Unitarian Channing but also with Moses Stuart of Andover and other clergymen prominent in the evangelical mainstream of Whiggery. He definitely lacked the sense of religious urgency to remake the world that characterized many Whig evangelicals and modernizers.[46]

In contrast to the traditional hypermasculinity of forensic oratory, inoffensive oratory cultivated a balance between what were thought of as masculine and feminine qualities. As a forensic orator, Webster could be called a "Titan" who "completely extinguished his enemy." "We never consider him as a mere debater, a mere scholar, or a mere statesman; but as a strong, sturdy, earnest man." On the other hand, devotees also declared that Webster could be "sweet and tender as a woman" and could make male auditors *"shed tears like girls!"*[47] The sentimentalism of the inoffensive rhetorical mode linked Webster's oratory with sentimental women's domestic literature, like that of Sarah Josepha Hale, which also propagated Whig values.[48]

The political ecumenicism Webster opposed to Hayne's particularism also expressed itself in a nostalgia for the nonpartisan Era of Good Feelings. After the nullification crisis he strove to continue good relations with the president he had temporarily been supporting. (It was during this time, in the summer of 1833, that Harvard awarded Jackson the honorary degree that so angered John Quincy Adams.) How far apart Webster and Jackson really were, however, was indicated by Jackson's veto of the Distribution Bill of 1833, a measure some National Republicans considered to have been part of the compromise package of that year. Any remaining chance for preventing political polarization vanished in the smoke of the Bank War.[49]

Disappointed by the rebirth of political parties, Webster still kept trying to make the cabinet a steppingstone to the presidency, as it had been during the Era of Good Feelings. His best chance for achieving this came with the election of 1840. Webster played a major role in delivering the Whig and Antimasonic nominations to Harrison; the Antimasonic convention even nominated a Harrison-Webster ticket. For his part, Old Tippecanoe promised to serve but one term, and he made Webster his secretary of state. During Harrison's brief presidency, Webster had already begun to play the role of premier and heir presumptive. When Harrison died, Webster was naturally reluctant to abandon his well-laid plans. Though all the rest of the Whig cabinet resigned in protest against Tyler's vetoes, Webster stayed on for another year and a half, trying to work with the new president. This jeopardized his standing in the Whig party and exposed him to repeated humiliations. Webster should have known better: Tyler wanted to succeed himself as president, so there was no way he would groom another as his heir. When Webster's desperate attempts to distract his chief from annexing slaveholding Texas failed, he too finally had to resign.[50]

Webster's tenure at the State Department under Tyler was nevertheless constructive, since it led to the Webster-Ashburton Treaty of 1842. In Edward Everett, Webster chose one of the best of American ambassadors to Britain, who showed the way for the eventual compromise of the Oregon question.[51] Good relations with Britain held a central place in Webster's statecraft, though as usual he allowed his personal motives to be tarnished. In the 1830s he had been on the payroll of the British banking firm of Baring while advocating measures to help the states pay off foreign creditors. Later this business contact helped smooth the negotiations between him and Lord Ashburton, a former head of the house of Baring.[52]

Webster's attitude toward Britain was conditioned by social and cultural as well as economic factors. A lawyer-turned-country-squire (like Henry Clay), Webster felt an affinity with the English ruling classes. In his patriotic orations he stressed the positive contributions the English heritage had made to America: "Bacon and Locke, and Shakespeare and Milton, also came with the colonists." It would be an oversimplification to term Webster or the Whigs in general Anglophiles. They appear so by contrast with the demogogic Anglophobia of Democrats like Lewis Cass and Stephen Douglas. But the Whig admiration for the English was tinged with envy and a desire to excel and replace the parent country. The most promising line of inquiry into Whig attitudes toward Britain will probably make

use of psychoanalytic insight regarding feelings toward father figures.[53]

Webster's last ecumenical effort came with his support for Clay's
Compromise of 1850. He stood almost alone among northern congressional Whigs in backing the Compromise, Seward's opposition
being more typical. Many people were startled that Webster would
side with Clay rather than Taylor; a year and a half earlier, at the
Whig convention, his delegation had made the opposite choice.
Moreover, Webster had a long record of opposing the extension of
slavery. For all that he had been willing to overlook in Tyler's conduct, he had finally drawn the line at Texas. He had opposed war
with Mexico and the acquisition of territory by it. More recently he
had declared himself "unalterably fixed in favor of the restriction of
slavery," called himself a "free soil man," and denounced "dough
faces."[54] Antislavery Whigs were not unjustified in feeling that
Webster had betrayed them. What was an enlightened position for a
southerner like Clay defined Webster as a conservative among Massachusetts Whigs. Had he chosen differently, Webster might have
been able to rally the northern Whig party to the kind of opposition
to the extension of slavery that the Republican party achieved a few
years later.

Three factors have to be taken into account in explaining Webster's
stand in 1850: his ambition, his constituency, and his values.
Doubtless Webster hoped that support for the Compromise would
enhance his acceptability to southerners in the presidential race of
1852; this is how most observers, then and since, have interpreted
his behavior. Probably, also, Webster was reflecting a disposition
among certain northeastern businessmen, particularly bankers and
textile manufacturers, to seek accommodation with slave-owners
who were their customers and suppliers. Fillmore, the other major
northern Whig supporter of the Compromise, had ties to the New
York City business community like those Webster had in Boston.[55]
In terms of values, Webster's decision to endorse the Compromise
reflected his preference for harmony over morality when these two
important aspects of Whig political culture came into conflict.
Webster was not the man to lead a moral crusade. His version of
Whiggery emphasized law and order, the protection of property, and
the preservation of existing inequalities. His Seventh of March
Speech on behalf of the Compromise was characterized by images of
balance and appeals to sentiment. Major aspects of the omnibus bill
he did not even mention because, unlike Clay, he was less interested
in its specific measures than in its generally soothing effect.[56]

Nothing Webster did sufficed to get him the Whig nomination in 1852: not support for the Compromise, not his return to the cabinet, not the anachronistic "endeavor to give a no-party complexion to the canvass" on his behalf. Outside New England, the Cotton Whigs preferred Fillmore, but the nomination went to Seward's candidate, General Winfield Scott, a representative of the moderately antislavery strain within Whiggery in the Upper South. Webster faced his disappointment with the bitterness of a man who had become captivated by the vision of his own grandeur. "How will this look in history?" he demanded.[57] Could he have known that a new kind of history would become relatively indifferent to the fate of heroic orators, he would have felt even worse.

Daniel Webster died on October 24, 1852. Probably it is best if he is remembered for his eloquence rather than for his selfishness. Like the operas of Wagner, the orations of Webster have an imaginative power that rises above, even if it cannot really redeem, the character of their composer. Though Webster has been lost to American history as a hero, he can still be recovered by American literature as a rhetorician and spokesman for national feeling. His last word was "poetry." His son at the bedside recited some of Gray's *Elegy*. The old man smiled, and a few hours later he was dead.[58]

The tensions and contradictions within Whig conservatism are even more apparent in the life and thought of Webster's friend and fellow advocate, Rufus Choate (1799–1859). Like Webster, Choate was a small-town New England boy who attended Dartmouth College and went on to a brilliant legal career. An energetic advocate, he argued over a thousand cases (more than three hundred of them reported) in a lifetime practice extending to virtually every branch of the law then recognized. He pioneered the techniques of arousing jury sympathy that plaintiff's lawyers in tort cases have employed ever since; for one badly injured widow he won a judgment of $22,500, a record at the time.[59]

Joseph Story once remarked that Rufus Choate saw the need to clothe the practice of law in "bewitching graces." Like George Whitefield a century earlier, Choate combined irresistible eloquence with a bizarre appearance. His saturnine complexion passed quickly from the dark handsomeness of youth to a prematurely wrinkled age; his tall, bent frame was invariably wrapped in a long cloak that created an exotic effect. To his prosaic countrymen, Choate's mind and manner seemed somehow "Oriental."[60] There was even a rumor that he used opium. He himself denied it, but the allegation seemed in keeping with his feverish bursts of energy followed by lethargy and the strangely worn look of his face. In all things—appearance, rhetoric, and life-style—Choate deliberately cultivated the mysterious, the striking, the baroque.[61]

But if Choate was a dramatic artist, he was also an authoritarian. He liked to play his role upon a delimited stage and according to a prescribed set of directions. Choate often displayed a narrow lawyer's-guild mentality. Though he loved America as a nation, as a legal and historical entity, he evinced little love for Americans as people. Perhaps because he knew human nature so well, and knew how to take advantage of its weaknesses, he had slight respect for individuals. He privately felt only contempt for jurors and took no interest in his clients beyond the requirements of his profession. He did not even have many personal friends.[62]

For brief intervals Choate held elective office, though he never enjoyed public service. He was a state legislator, a congressman, and from 1841 to 1845 a United States senator. He owed his political fortunes to the favor of the Webster wing of Massachusetts Whiggery, which he served with undeviating loyalty. When one thinks of Webster, Choate once remarked, "the idolatries of the old paganism grow almost intelligible."[63] For his part, Webster exploited Choate's devotion, borrowing money without repaying it and using Choate's oratorical powers to further his own ends.

Most of Choate's lucrative law practice concerned railroad, patent, or marine-insurance cases. Some of these cases tended to strengthen the power of the state. Choate argued successfully that the legislature had the right to regulate the use of navigable streams, as by licensing a railroad to erect a bridge, even when this resulted in severe damage to the value of the adjacent property. Later he won another case on behalf of the state police powers when he forced a railroad to put a draw in a bridge across a public highway.[64] But one must use caution in attempting to discern a pattern in Choate's briefs. As an advocate, he was under no obligation to argue consistently from one case to the next, so one finds him (for example) either broadening or narrowing, as the interests of his client dictated, Taney's celebrated *Charles River Bridge* decision.[65] He was equally adept at arousing the sympathies of a jury for or against the claims of an inventor to his patent. Senator Hoar commented, "No gambler ever hankered for the feverish delight of the gaming table as Choate did for that absorbing game, half chance, half skill, where twelve human dice must all turn up together one way."[66]

There was more to Choate, however, than the forensic talents and personal idiosyncrasies that alternately fascinated and repelled his contemporaries. This becomes evident when one passes beyond his legal arguments to what might be called his metalegal contributions: his discussions of the nature of law and its relationship to society. Choate's ambition was to make the common law and the Constitution serve his nation the way the Bible and covenant theology had once served his Puritan ancestors: as sacred doctrine embodying the ideals of the community. Then he would make the new class of lawyers the high priests of that community.

Choate intended his emotional perorations at the bar to reinforce, not undermine, the judgments of the bench; countless anecdotes testify to his respect for such jurists as Chancellor Kent and Chief Justice Lemuel Shaw of Massachusetts. Moreover, in the speeches he made as state and national legislator, as in the other addresses he gave over the years, Choate never ceased to hammer home the themes of national unity and respect for the law. He sought to bring these to a deeper level of consciousness than mere rational assent. If the great judges of the early national period may be described as the theologians of America's new religion of the law, Choate was certainly its evangelist. He called Independence Day "our great annual national love-feast" and explained the function of patriotic demonstrations in terms taken from sacramental theology. As revivalists tried to bring men to God through Christ, counsellor Choate tried to bring them to a sense of national unity through law. Summing up the purpose of his message, Choate proclaimed, "This then, is the new duty, the *opus aureum*, to cherish the Religion of the Law."[67]

Rufus Choate was an enthusiastic disciple of Edmund Burke and praised that patron saint of conservatism effusively at every opportunity, both public and private. ("Out of Burke might be cut 50 Mackintoshes, 175 Macaulays, 40 Jeffreys, and 250 Sir Robert Peels, and leave him greater than Pitt and Fox together.")[68] On the other hand, John Locke and the theorists of the social compact made Choate highly uncomfortable. They seemed to him to value individualism more than order, rights more than duties, and liberty more than law. Addressing the students and faculty of Harvard Law School in 1845, Choate cited certain "sentiments and opinions from which the public mind of America is in danger" and identified the worst as "a singularly inadequate idea of the State." The source of the pollution he found in the doctrine of "Rousseau and Locke, and our own revolutionary age . . . that the State is nothing but a contract."[69]

Burke's political writings provided Choate with a welcome

alternative to Locke. Instead of the artificiality and impermanence of contractualism, Choate put his trust in the emotions, in tradition, and in respect for "organic forms." By the latter he meant fundamental law: the United States Constitution regarded as binding not simply because it was a voluntary agreement but because it was sanctioned by usage, hallowed by sentiment, and in harmony with our national character. When Choate paid his respects to the American revolutionaries—whom he honored despite their belief in the social compact—he did so by quoting Burke and by interpreting the colonists as true conservatives, who had protected traditional rights against usurpations from London.[70]

Sometimes Choate came close to admitting that his organicism and traditionalism could only lead back, if deviously, to a contractual basis for American government.[71] He could not deny that "in the American theory" the people have the right "to make the Constitution anew"—either by peaceful amendment or by exercising their moral right of revolution. But, he insisted, no wise man "would desire to have this theory every day, or ever, acted upon up [sic] to its whole extent." As a result, he felt justified in seeking to place this theoretical right, and the contractual model of government that went with it, "rather in the background." Avowing his obscurantism with charming frankness, he declared his desire to cover the contractual origins of the American Republic with "a politic, well-wrought veil." Few people, Choate hoped, would penetrate this veil of statist mythology to find the Lockean principle underneath.[72]

Choate's objectives do not make him any the less Burkean. Burke himself, after all, had also been defending a "Lockean" political order: the Settlement of 1689 and the Whig supremacy. Burke and Locke were apologists for many of the same aspects of English society, including balanced government and protection of property; it is wrong to imagine that these two British political thinkers had nothing in common. What makes them so different, of course, is the means by which they defend their mutual Whig client; Locke defends him by reason and natural right, Burke by appeals to prejudice, sentiment, and prescription. Burke, like Choate, was seeking to envelop an increasingly contractualist society with mystical respect for established authority; it was he who first spoke of the desirability of drawing "a mysterious veil" over the source of government power.[73] Bringing Burke to America does not essentially change the matter; what distinguishes Burkeans from Lockeans, on either side of the Atlantic, is not which social order they defend but how they defend it. By this test, Choate is as much a Burkean as Burke.

A devotion to English common law comported nicely with Burkean political philosophy. Choate urged Americans to respect "not constitutional and statute law alone, but that other ampler, that boundless jurisprudence, the common law, which the successive generations of the State have silently built up."[74] This law reached back in time before the independence of the United States; prerevolutionary English precedents were part of American common law. Fortified by the traditions of the common law, Choate could afford to dismiss popular American opinion ("the national humour") with imperious sarcasm: was the state "no more than an encampment of tents on the great prairie, pitched at sundown, and struck to the sharp crack of the rifle next morning?"[75]

"The first condition in order to a sound constitution of the body politic," Choate explained (quoting this time from Coleridge), "is a due proportion between the free and permeative life and energy of the State and its organized powers." America had life and energy in plenty; one must watch, therefore, to see that its organized power, i.e., law, was kept correspondingly strong. Choate looked to the lawyers "to preserve our organic forms, our civil and social order" even amidst the chaos of geographical and economic expansion. The attorneys with their common law would provide the antidote to the poison of Locke's disorganizing philosophy. They would enable America "to withstand the pernicious sophism that the successive generations, as they come to life, are but as so many successive flights of summer flies, without relations to the past or duties to the future."[76] Of course, if the legal profession were to succeed in this ambitious conservative undertaking, it would have to guard its traditions well, especially its high academic standards and its devotion to life tenure for judges. Choate's program also implied resistance to the movement for the codification and simplification of American law. For a proponent of codification and judicial restraint like the Jacksonian labor spokesman Frederick Robinson, Choate typified the self-interested obstructionism of common lawyers.[77]

A secure bench and a learned bar would maintain "the supremacy of the calm and grand reason of the law over the fitful will of the individual and the crowd," Choate observed with satisfaction. But the "reason" of the common law Choate celebrated was highly specialized, even arcane. Chief Justice Coke had been bold enough to tell James I, when the king had meddled with legal business: "Causes which concern the life, or inheritance, or goods, or fortunes of his subjects, are not to be decided by natural reason but by the artificial reason and judgment of law, which law is an act which requires long study and experience, before that a man can attain to the cognizance of it."[78] To the untutored it might appear that law was based on will—the will of the legislature (in the case of statutes) or, perhaps, that of the courts (in the case of common law). Not so, Choate insisted; "the law is not the offspring of will at all." It is discovered by reason—albeit an "artificial" reason, in the service of which Choate artificially conscripted sentiment. Like Blackstone, Choate sought to endow the traditional common law with the prestige of rationality while simultaneously surrounding it with an emotionally impressive obscurity.[79]

Here is the irony of Choate's position: even while deploring the "artificiality" of the compact theory, he had to resort to an artificiality of his own in order to foster American national feeling. In actuality American common law was to a large extent the conscious creation of a single generation of great American jurists. However, to foster what he thought was the proper respect for their achievement, Choate declared them to be no innovators but wise men and scholars discovering immemorial truths. Choate's legal formalism illustrates and heralds that general shift among nineteenth-century lawyers that Morton Horwitz has described: they backed away from further innovation or flexibility once the law had been reshaped to accord with the interests of American capitalism. Choate deliberately cloaked a massive legal achievement in anachronistic rhetoric. He himself recognized what was happening well enough. For all his talk of "organic forms," he admitted that American nationality and American institutions were manufactured. Our national consciousness "is, to an extraordinary degree, not a growth, but a production."[80]

The hastily built American legal structure was only one aspect of the newness and thinness of American society. To Choate, it all seemed dangerously insubstantial. In words that remind one of Henry James, he bewailed America's lack of a sense of history:

> Consider how new is this America of yours! Some there are yet alive who saw this infant rocked in the cradle. . . . The authoritative prescription, the legend, the fable, the tones of uncertain harps, the acquiescence of generations, rising in a long line to life as to a gift,—where for us are they? On all this architecture of utility and reason, where has Time laid a finger? What angularity has it rounded; what stone has it covered with moss; . . . on what deformity has its moonlight and twilight fallen?[81]

Somehow, this rootlessness must be remedied. If a nation was to exist, it must have law—and if law was to exist, there must be history. The history Choate turned to almost automatically was that of classical Greece and Rome. He was an amateur classical scholar, a translator of Tacitus and Thucydides. Next to the English common law, Choate respected the Roman civil law. Next to Burke, he idolized Cicero. In the *res publica* of Cicero, Choate found the original of his own conception of the state as community.[82]

Choate constructed a fascinating and plausible historical tradition linking his own republic with the city-states of Rome and Greece. He argued that the evolution of constitutional liberty and fundamental law (the two being inseparable) must be traced from America to the Puritan-Dissenting impulse in England. From there, "the pedigree of our transatlantic liberty" led him to Switzerland and the Imperial free cities, which gave asylum to thousands of prominent Puritans during the reign of Mary Tudor. The Marian Exile formed, for Choate, the crucial link in the chain of political tradition. It was during this sojourn that the English Puritans acquired an experience of republican institutions. Describing Geneva as the exiles found it, Choate wrote: "There was a state without king or nobles; there was a church without a bishop; there was a people governed by grave magistrates which it had selected, and equal laws which it had framed." (This delineation of the republican ideal so captured the imagination of Choate's contemporaries that, we are told, it was set to music and became a popular song.)[83] "I ascribe to that five years in Geneva an influence which has changed the history of the world," Choate declared. The English Civil War, the voyage of the *Mayflower* and its Compact, the independence of America—all these were implicit in the "new politics" learned during the exile. From the city-states of early modern central Europe back to those of the Renaissance and ancient times then seemed an easy step to Choate. He had placed his country in contact with a living tradition of republicanism dating back to classical antiquity.[84] That most of the republics he encountered along his way were anything but democratic should not go unremarked.

A view of history based on the model of the life-cycle was fundamental to Choate's conservatism. The colonial era he called America's "first age" (childhood) and the generation of the Revolution and Confederation the "second age" (youth). With independence and union now achieved, the United States had apparently entered a "third age," the period of maturity, and had nowhere to go but down. Postponing this decline as long as possible became almost an obsession for Choate. A great deal of the fascination Cicero held for him derived from the Roman orator's role as the spokesman of a

doomed republican virtue. "By what means a State may be preserved
through a full lifetime of enjoyment and glory, what kind of death it
shall die, by what diagnostic the approach of that death shall be
known . . . these questions are the largest, pertaining to the things of
this world, that can be pondered by the mind of man."[85] Choate
looked back nostalgically upon the "heroic" ages, when the Puritan
settlers first organized an American commonwealth and when Alexander Hamilton and John Adams laid the foundations of the union.
The golden days of political creativity having passed, what remained
was only the second-best task of preserving the nation. Actually, the
United States had entered a postpolitical phase: "Political life is
forever ended," Choate recorded in his journal in 1850; "Henceforth
the law and literature are all."[86]

Choate saw literature, broadly defined, as creating a sense of
community. Like other American Whigs, he espoused a holistic view
of social life. Political institutions and law should be part and parcel
of a larger national culture and could not be superimposed arbitrarily. National character and national manners had to be defined so
that law could take root in them. This attitude was at least as old as
Burke and Montesquieu and in some ways much older, going back to
the Greek *polis*. Choate's conception of communal literature was didactic and rhetorical, owing much to the example of classical writers
like Demosthenes. Among the other ancients he found congenial was
Seneca, who had taught that in a time of governmental troubles a
good man must try to benefit society through nonpolitical activities.
And so Choate looked to literature and the law to strengthen the
spirit of the nation and stave off decline.

Through literature, as through law, Choate proposed to recreate,
artificially, the national strength of character and sense of purpose
that earlier Americans had possessed. Literature would accomplish
its mission by arousing the appropriate sentiments of community.
"All the discipline and customs of social life and business life, in our
time, tend to *crush* emotion and feeling," Choate observed sorrow-
fully. "*Literature alone* is brimful of feeling."[87] While the jurists appealed to the head, writers would appeal to the heart, and together
they would foster American unity. Of all literature, it was the historical epic that best suited Choate's objectives. The epic form, in which
fact, fiction, and legend are inextricably intertwined, could, he
thought, provide a people with a feeling for its collective past. He
was disappointed when he failed to make the Smithsonian Institution a literary rather than a scientific establishment.[88]

Not surprisingly, Choate was alarmed when some abolitionists
treated the Union irreverently. Their argument that moral claims at

times take precedence over legal claims was one that conflicted with all Choate stood for, and he confronted them head on. "Morality should go to school," he maintained. "It should consult the builders of Empire, and learn the arts imperial by which it is preserved, ere it ventures to pronounce on the construction and laws of nations and commonwealths." Choate was willing (as, indeed, was Burke) to make use of compact terminology when by doing so he could enhance the moral stature of government. The Constitution was a compact creating a moral obligation; therefore, one's duty to help the slaveholder pursue his property was greater than one's duty to help the fugitive (presumed not to be a party to the compact) who came seeking shelter. Thus, according to Choate, the "higher law" of superior ethical claim really favored the existing positive law. The obligation of the constitutional contract could no more be impaired than could the obligations of private contracts.[89]

Analysis of Choate's political thought reveals an apparent contradiction at the very heart of it. If the law is discovered by reason, how can it owe its authority to the state? Choate's insistence that law is discovered, not made, would seem to imply belief in some kind of natural law—presumably, in the light of his admiration for Cicero, a Stoic version. The existence of natural law entails moral standards that, being immutable, are independent of the state. But this is just what Choate was unwilling to grant. He wanted to subordinate moral values to the state while justifying the state itself in nonrational terms of tradition and emotional bonds. The same maddening ambiguity is present in Burke: occasionally he invoked natural law, but at other times he was content to rely on sentiment, prejudice, or mere "prescription," that is, the right of established might.[90]

Choate displayed his respect for constituted authority after the Anthony Burns crisis of 1854. Burns was a fugitive slave apprehended in Boston. Fearing an attempt to rescue him, Mayor Jerome Smith invoked a riot statute, called out the militia, and ordered them to clear the streets. One of the citizens arrested sued Smith and several militia officers, claiming the action of the authorities was unwarranted. Choate, appearing for the defense, dilated upon the dangers of insurrection and civil violence. He argued that the mayor's decision was "judicial, or quasi-judicial," in nature and therefore he could not be held liable for it; as for the militiamen, they were justified so long as they were obeying orders. The Supreme Judicial Court accepted Choate's line of reasoning but left open the possibility of suits against militiamen who acted against citizens without specific orders.[91]

As the years went by and the slavery controversy intensified,

Choate became deeply pessimistic about the ability of the United
States to endure. He regarded the appearance of the new Republican
party as a dire threat to the Union. In an open letter to the Whig
Central Committee of Maine, in August, 1856, Choate reversed the
party allegiance of a lifetime and announced for Buchanan. The
Democrats had become the last refuge of this ultraconservative Whig.
The moral issue of slavery extension drove John Quincy Adams and
Joshua Giddings to demand a rebirth of freedom. It had the opposite
effect on Choate. In this dramatic statement he dismissed the
philosophy of the Declaration of Independence as a collection of
"glittering and sounding generalities."[92] He was willing enough to
allow the proposition "All men are born free and equal" in the Constitution of Massachusetts, for there it could be given a legal history
and meaning; but to take the "all men are created equal" of the
Declaration as an abstract expression of natural right seemed to him
preposterous.[93]

When one explores the nature of Choate's ideal nation-state, one
discovers the significance of law for him. A true nation is a group of
people bound together by the possession of a common culture, including a common body of law. This legal heritage, passed down
from one generation to the next and embodying the national history
and character, is properly venerated. The law is not the *will* of the
nation-state; it *is* the nation-state, in its most concrete manifestation.
The duty of the legislator or jurist, properly understood, is not to
devise new laws, not even if they are convenient and accord with
current public opinion. Instead, his task is to discover the legal forms
that will capture the authentic (that is, mythic) national "genius." In
Choate's doctrine of the nation-state, the contradictory elements of
his doctrine of law are to some extent resolved. The law is discovered, to be sure, but discovered through a study of the distinctive
national character rather than by appeal to abstract principles. Thus
it is known to reason, yet not in such a way as to divorce it from the
nation-state. By dwelling on the importance of the nation-state,
Choate was carrying his Burkean principles farther than the master
had done. Nationalism, as Alfred Cobban has observed, is a logical
corollary of Burkeanism that Burke himself never really pursued.[94]

Choate's nationalism resembles that of the German romantics,
who also tried to overcome the weakness of their country's central
institutions by appeals to history and folk tradition. He may well
have come into contact with the ideas of Herder or Savigny, perhaps
through the mediation of his friend James Marsh, who translated
Herder into English. However, there is no direct evidence of such

influence, so the relationship between Choate and the Germans may be simply one of analogy. Choate's nationalistic exhortations represented an increasingly desperate attempt to foster order amidst confusion. He confronted the unenviable dilemma of a conservative celebrating a revolutionary tradition even while trying to "veil" its revolutionary aspects in mythology. The myth of unbroken authority Choate tried to propagate was indeed a myth, and none knew it better than he.

Alexis de Tocqueville remarked that an aristocratic social order and traditional manners "conceal the natural man" and throw "a pleasing illusory charm over human nature."[95] Something like this must have been in Rufus Choate's mind as he tried to create artificial constraints—prescriptive, legal, historical, cultural—for America. In a curious way, he actually relied on deception as a means of redemption. Like other figures in this book, Choate acted out in his personal life the issues he addressed in his public philosophy. His own constant posturing and masquerading mirrored his avowed desire to fabricate an awe-inspiring mystique in which to envelop the nation-state.

Yet Choate should not be dismissed as a mere cynic; the evangelist of the common law was more than a legal Elmer Gantry. Choate indeed advanced his conservative philosophy less because he thought it descriptively true than because he thought it would be useful if accepted as true. Still, it should be noted that a philosophy stressing social cohesiveness addressed itself to legitimate concerns of the time. A twentieth-century Indian political scientist adopts the same point of view the American Whigs held when he writes: "No society can live without traditions; and the challenge of modernization is to build and develop traditions of modernity both through an interaction with older traditions of secular life and by modifying the latter to suit the demands of a new age." Choate's Burkean efforts to strengthen respect for the institutions of a contractual society may be viewed as an attempt to create such "traditions of modernity." Rajni Kothari continues: "If politics is not to be made an arena of perpetual strife and tension, it is necessary that its more permanent elements should be turned into usages and conventions that are not only widely accepted but enjoy a measure of deference and sanctity."[96] Whig conservatism, seen in this light, did not contradict, but complemented, Whig modernization.

The cult of Edmund Burke, far from being peculiar to Choate, was widespread within the Whig party and helped mediate between its conservatism and its progressivism. One should scarcely be surprised that the giants of conservative Massachusetts Whiggery—Webster, Everett, and Joseph Story—enshrined Burke in their political pantheon beside Cicero. Admiration for the Irish philosopher of conservatism also extended beyond the confines of New England; southern Whigs praised him.[97] Most revealing, however, is the fact that Whig progressives like Horace Greeley and Joshua Giddings joined in paying homage to Burke. Indeed, both William H. Seward and Charles Sumner were his conscientious disciples. As for John Quincy Adams, he was old enough to have participated in the original Burke-Paine debate over the French Revolution; his "Letters of Publicola" (1791) had angered Jefferson by their attacks on Paine's view of popular sovereignty.[98]

Burke's appeal to the American Whigs was perfectly logical, though historians have perversely ignored it.[99] As a sympathizer with the American Revolution and a critic of the French one, Burke served as an authority for drawing the distinction between them, which was so important to American Whigs. Opposed, like them, to executive power, Burke had, like them, to wrestle with the problem of legitimating partisan opposition. He clung, as they did, to the ancient constitution as a limitation on the exercise of sovereignty. By endorsing reform in Britain and Ireland, he inspired American Whig reformers, while his efforts to check the abuses of the East India Company were thought to make him a paternalistic "champion of inferior races." His opposition to making war on the American colonies served as a particularly welcome precedent for Whigs opposing war with Mexico.[100]

Beyond such specifics, Burke shared the larger values and objectives of the American Whigs in his preference for experience over theory, in his willingness to invoke sentiment and prejudice on behalf of existing arrangements, above all in his respect for public opinion as a means of social control. "Manners are of more importance than law," he had declared, and the Whig culture-shapers agreed. "Manners are what vex or soothe, corrupt or purify, exalt or debase, barbarize or refine us, by a constant, steady, uniform, and insensible operation, like the air we breathe in."[101] Burke's respect for the social influence of religion particularly endeared him to the evangelicals. Of course, his reputation as an orator fascinated; he provided a favorite point of comparison for those who would praise Webster. Even his essay on *The Sublime and the Beautiful* was well received; Burke the aesthetician as well as Burke the political thinker commanded the admiration of American Whigs. The popularity he enjoyed can be measured by the fact that sixteen multivolume editions of his complete works were published in the United States before the Civil War, seven of them during the single decade of the 1830s.[102]

The enthusiasm American Whigs displayed for Burke shows how important their conservatism was to them. More specifically, it was a measure of their concern with shaping a national identity. Could a state that was an artificial, recent, and conglomerate creation, such as the United States then was, become a nation like the historic nation-states of Europe? Daniel Webster and Rufus Choate tried hard to make sure this question would have an affirmative answer.

Ten

Alexander Stephens and the Failure of Southern Whiggery

Northern antislavery Whig-Republicans like Seward interpreted the events of the late 1850s as heralding a second American revolution, in which free labor would emerge from political subordination to the slave power. Slavery itself, they hoped, would be placed on the road to ultimate extinction. But, simultaneously, another would-be revolutionary movement was also under way in America. This was the movement for southern independence, whose militant leaders demanded a central government that would be explicitly proslavery. If the nature of the existing federal Union could not be changed to make it reflect their desire, they preferred a new southern confederacy. While most northern Whigs came around to endorsing Seward's revolution by 1860 (he kept assuring them it would be a peaceful one), most southern Whigs did not approve the revolutionary movement toward independence in their own section. Yet their resistance against it proved remarkably feeble, sometimes counterproductive, and in the end unsuccessful. This chapter seeks to explain why that was so.

The South's increasing concentration on cotton production and slave labor during the years after the expropriation of the Civilized Tribes strengthened the Democratic and weakened the

Whig party. Strict construction of the Constitution, religious literalism, and white racial pride were all intensified, while the Whig
program of economic diversification became less attractive. The
mixture of town and country did not strike a balance: the South
remained an overwhelmingly rural society. Cotton planters and small
farmers shared a folk culture that valued flamboyance rather than
restraint, hedonism rather than the work ethic. It was a culture of
fierce in-group loyalties and of violence sanctioned in the defense of
honor. The Democratic party spoke for this folk culture. The Whig
party did not, and it had trouble adapting to the changing conditions. Henry Clay's agrarian-bourgeois outlook was subverted, not
only economically but also culturally. Southern Whiggery became
confused, divided in its own mind, so to speak, between the
bourgeois values represented by the national party and the premodern values encouraged by southern society itself.[1]

The torturous political career of Alexander Stephens (1812–83) was
one of many individual responses to the dilemmas and inner conflicts of southern Whiggery. Most southern Whigs followed approximately the same course through these troubled years that
Stephens did, though more passively on the whole; the extra tem-
pestuousness of his career can be explained by his unusually acute
sensitivity. They followed him in backing the Compromise of 1850.
Like him again, however, they supported repeal of the Missouri
Compromise in 1854 and sided with their states in 1861 after a secession they had regarded with disapproval. In the end almost all of
them wound up, as he did, in a reactionary postwar Democratic
party that subordinated all other issues to the preservation of white
supremacy.

Son of a Georgia country schoolmaster, Alexander Stephens always
remained something of a pedant himself. His mother died giving
birth to him, and little Aleck started life sickly, weak, and easily
frightened. The worst of many early traumas befell when he was
fourteen: his father and stepmother died within a week of each
other during a malaria epidemic. A kindly uncle, a well-disposed
neighbor, and a Presbyterian benevolent society enabled the boy to
complete his education. Later he would duplicate their paternal solicitude in his relationship with his much younger half-brother, Linton. A teacher at the local academy whom he admired bore the name
Alexander Hamilton Webster; in imitation, young Stephens adopted
the same middle name. Alexander Hamilton Stephens: he liked the
identification with the self-made hero of American conservatism.
Stephens attended Franklin College (now the University of Georgia)

at Athens, expecting to enter the Presbyterian ministry. The vocation did not materialize; instead, after an interval of keeping school, Stephens read law.

Stephens' education oriented him within the intellectual culture of American Whiggery. He acquired a love for the Greek and Latin classics, the Bible, and the major English writers from Pope to Dickens. "His attitude toward literature was 'moralistic' in an eighteenth-century way," comments his biographer, Rudolph Von Abele.[2] Stephens studied moral philosophy in college, and his categories of thought were permanently shaped by its faculty psychology and imperative to "mental improvement." He urged everyone to "suppress his passions" and "curb his propensities." The object was to develop "character" and a conscious design for the great work of life. He found the appropriate vehicle for his striving in rhetoric. A debater in college, he regarded orators as the men who "not only move masses but impress their ideas upon the world [and] control the destinies of nations." Great oratory demanded moral as well as intellectual self-discipline, he believed. Among those whom he most admired were the "accomplished and gifted Choate" and Edmund Burke—"first among orators and statesmen not only in the British Parliament but in the world."[3]

Stephens' determination to overcome his own frailty through willpower gave his exhortations to character-building profound authenticity. His daily journal and long intimate letters to his beloved brother Linton show the seriousness with which he took them. Chronically ill, Stephens never weighed a hundred pounds in his life and struggled with periodic depression. Quite possibly he was impotent.[4] He had to make up in verbal skill and high resolve what he lacked in physical strength and presence. Tragically, his quest for self-confidence never fully succeeded. He confided to Linton in 1851: "The secret of my life has been—*revenge reversed*. That is, to rise superior to the neglect or contumely of the mean of mankind by doing them good instead of harm. A determination to war even against fate, to meet the world in all its forces."[5] In practice, Stephens did not always give a philanthropic twist to his desire for revenge. Ever hypersensitive, he challenged four men to duels in his life. Like a smaller kid who cannot back away from a dare if he is to belong to the gang, he felt in no position to defy the southern code of manliness.

Stephens' rather pathetic career as a duelist can be taken as a paradigm of the awkward situation of the Whig party in the Lower South. There, as elsewhere, the Whigs were the party of the business interests and were hence potentially nationalistic.[6] All too often, however, because of an unwillingness to seem disloyal, the party was forced against its better judgment into sectional stands. Lacking the self-confidence to stick by their own values, the Whigs of the Cotton Belt eventually capitulated to the strident racism and violence of the Democratic party. Alexander Stephens' life illustrates the process. It reflects the competing claims of two value systems, one emphasizing self-discipline and the other the defense of honor. Each appealed to something deep within him: on the one hand, his commitment to education, ambition, public service, and the law, fostered by the benevolence of those who had helped him in his youth; on the other, his bitter yearning for "revenge."[7] Stephens' changing party affiliations are one manifestation of the struggle; his abortive duels are another. He issued all four of his challenges in response to imputations of disloyalty. As long as they felt such a need to reaffirm their loyalty to the white South, Whigs in the section would be vulnerable to extremist pressures and inhibited in promoting modern cultural values.

When the Whig party was organized in 1834, twenty-two-year-old Aleck Stephens joined it. The nucleus of the party in Georgia was the group around Governor George M. Troup, representing creditor and business interests. Troup's following had supported President Adams but turned against him when he refused to cooperate with the dispossession of the Creeks and Cherokees. As a result of the Indian issue, Georgia voted for Jackson with virtual unanimity in 1828 and '32. By 1834, however, dispossession was an accomplished fact, and there was little more for Georgia conservatives to gain by backing Jackson. The economic issues that had divided white Georgians politically during the Depression of 1819 reasserted themselves during the Bank War. Even Jackson's Indian policies could now suggest a dangerous tendency toward autocracy; when Stephens had a chance to discuss Indian affairs with the president in 1835, he found himself distressed by the old soldier's easy disregard for legalities.[8]

Hugh Lawson White carried Georgia against Martin Van Buren in 1836; as a former Jackson supporter, White eased the transition of the Troupites, who included Stephens, into the Whig party. Stephens himself won election to the state legislature as a Whig. His maiden speech endorsed subsidies for a railroad to connect Georgia with the Ohio Valley. He rejected nullification (reserving the ultimate right of secession) and approved the constitutionality of the Bank of the United States. Believing that moral and material progress go hand in hand, he supported state education, including Georgia Female College, the first institution of higher learning for women in the South. In 1843 he went on to the U.S. House of Representatives. There he sided with Clay against Tyler. He defended the protective tariff, insisting that "Whig principles in Maine and Louisiana, in Ohio, Georgia, and Virginia, are the same." When Georgia defied a Whig-supported federal law requiring congressmen to be elected by districts instead of at large, Stephens had the courage to declare that the House would be justified in refusing to seat the Georgia delegation, including himself. Soon afterward, John Quincy Adams inscribed a poem to him.[9]

The Texas question was the first to put a serious strain on Stephens' party regularity. He was convinced that Tyler and Calhoun risked upsetting the balance of the Union for the sake of their own ambitions. "The annexation project is a miserable humbug got up as a ruse to distract the Whig party at the South, or peradventure with even an ulterior motive—that is the dissolution of present confederacy."[10] Yet annexation had a powerful appeal in the Lower South. Like Henry Clay, Stephens was torn apart by Texas. After Clay's defeat, he met with a few other southern Whigs in Congress who felt they could no longer resist the annexationist pressures coming from their constituents. Stephens put the group's case before the House. "I am no defender of slavery in the abstract," he insisted. "If the annexation of Texas were for the sole purpose of extending slavery where it does not now and would not otherwise exist, I should oppose it." But slavery already existed in Texas, so annexation could be safely supported in pursuit of the national interest. Adams accurately termed Stephens' reasoning "sophistical," but the annexation resolution passed the House by a vote of 109 to 99, with Stephens and seven other southern Whig defectors providing the crucial margin.[11]

When the Texas problem led to war with Mexico, Stephens' Whiggery reasserted itself. He had despised the prevarications of Tyler; those of Polk were worse. The little Georgian instinctively empathized with the underdog in a fight, and he recognized Mexico as a victim of international bullying. His speeches denouncing Polk's *"masked design of provoking Mexico to war"* were charged with emotion. They also reflected his feverish perusal of classical texts and secondary authorities on the rise and fall of empires. When Stephens' patriotism was impugned by southern Democratic war hawks, he felt compelled to vindicate his honor by challenging Herschel V. Johnson of Georgia and the fire-eating William L. Yancey of Alabama to duels. Both declined, thereby affronting him further. Undeterred, he decried "the principle that patriotism consists in pliant subserviency to Executive will." He warned Polk to beware the examples of Charles I of England and Charles X of France.[12] On February 2, 1848, opposing a tax increase for war expenditures, Stephens declared, "The present Executive is the greatest enemy the people of this country have." A Whig colleague in the House, Abraham Lincoln of Illinois, called it "the very best speech of an hour's length I ever heard."[13]

The prospect of acquiring more territory from Mexico worried Stephens. Northern Whigs could be counted on to demand that such territory be free; southern Whigs would have to oppose this or become pariahs among their own people. The Democratic party did not face the problem so acutely because northern Democrats were less committed to stopping the expansion of slavery. Two Georgia Whigs, Berrien in the Senate and Stephens in the House, introduced resolutions stating that the war with Mexico was not being waged for the acquisition of any territory beyond Texas. Both resolutions were defeated on almost strictly partisan votes. Stephens remained convinced that the Mexican Cession would prove "forbidden fruit." Stubbornly he voted against appropriations for implementing the Treaty of Guadalupe Hidalgo after the Senate had consented to its ratification.[14]

In an attempt to forestall a bruising sectional battle, Whig Senator John M. Clayton of Delaware hit upon the idea of referring the question of slavery in the new territories to the U.S. Supreme Court. Stephens opposed the plan because he decided that the Court was bound to rule in favor of freedom. He agreed with Joshua Giddings and many other northerners that slavery was dependent upon positive local ("municipal") legislation for its existence. Since Mexican law had prohibited slavery, the institution would remain illegal in the absence of any new legislation.[15] Clayton's proposed compromise went down to defeat, and many in the South were outraged that Stephens should have endorsed the same line of legal reasoning as the free-soilers. Word went around that Judge Francis Cone, a Georgia Democrat, had called Stephens "a traitor to the South." When Stephens confronted Cone, the judge denied the words. Stephens responded, ungraciously, that if Cone had spoken them, he would have slapped his face. Later Cone wrote to demand that this parting shot be retracted, but Stephens refused. When the two next met, Cone did call Stephens a traitor, and Stephens hit him in the face with his cane, no doubt expecting this would lead to a duel. Instead of setting up a proper duel, however, Cone whipped out a knife and stabbed Stephens repeatedly. He climbed on top of his fallen antagonist, and, when Stephens still refused to retract anything, proceeded to slash his throat. Only then was Cone pulled off by others. Stephens miraculously survived and declined to press charges. Judge Cone pleaded guilty to wounding and was fined a thousand dollars.[16]

In 1848 Stephens backed Zachary Taylor for the Whig nomination, as did Lincoln, John J. Crittenden of Kentucky, and New York's Thurlow Weed. General Taylor's previous noninvolvement with the Whig organization proved no insurmountable obstacle, for his supporters revived the lingering Whig tradition of antipartyism in their campaign against the great party leader, Clay. Once he was elected, Taylor's conduct vindicated the political judgment of Weed: he supported statehood for California and New Mexico. Even so, most southern Whigs stuck by the administration at first, but Stephens, along with his close associate and fellow Georgia congressman Robert Toombs, broke ranks. When Henry Clay, too, came out against Taylor's plan for the West, southern Whiggery was in serious disarray.[17]

Stephens' conduct can be explained by his fear that acquiescence in Taylor's program would ruin the Whig party in the Deep South. Southern Democrats were already insisting on federal protection of slavery in the territories (the so-called Alabama Platform) and depicting Whigs as soft on abolitionism. The Mexican Cession was proving to be every bit as disruptive as Stephens had always feared, and Taylor's election was much less helpful than he had hoped. Everything seemed to be going wrong; the Georgian whom Stephens and Toombs had pressed Taylor to include in his cabinet turned out to be involved in a scandal. With Toombs, Stephens called upon the president to ask him whether he would veto the Wilmot Proviso should it pass Congress. Taylor replied no; he had made an orthodox Whig pledge not to veto any constitutional bill. Angry words passed, and, a few minutes after the two Georgians left, Taylor referred to them as "those damned traitors."[18]

Stephens was bound to be accused of treason by someone whatever he did, for he was caught in a cross fire of loyalties. In the end he would place his section and its peculiar institution above his party, his country, and his morality. This choice is the more remarkable in the light of his sentiments concerning slavery. As we have seen, Stephens defended slavery apologetically where it already existed, in much the same manner as Clay. There are hints that he sympathized with Clay's views on colonization. As a young man he had courageously prevented vigilante harassment of people suspected of anti-slavery in his own county. Even when the turmoil of 1850 was coming to a boil, he confided privately that the slave trade was "infamous," that the condition of southern slaves was "certainly not a good one," and that "the Southern Democrats are using the slave question for nothing but political capital."[19] But by this time there had grown up a marked contrast between Stephens' private doubts and his militant public sectionalism. The contrast manifested a crisis of values through which he was passing, one that mirrored the cultural strain on southern Whiggery. In February, 1850, Stephens wrote to a personal friend deploring the "braggadocio" of southern extremists; in July, however, he wrote an open letter to the editor of the *National Intelligencer* asserting that all true southerners would fight beside Texas if the national government should resist a Texan invasion of New Mexico.[20] Though his political perceptiveness told him that "the agitations at the South for several years have done more to effect [the present crisis] than all the other [causes] united," in public he affirmed the militant southern code of honor.[21]

The surprising death of President Taylor and the succession of the pro-compromise Fillmore took some of the immediate pressure off Stephens' crisis of loyalties. Despite his blustering about Texas, he was still anxious to preserve the Union and felt that nothing less favorable to the slavocracy than Clay's compromise measures would suffice. While Stephen A. Douglas was rallying northern Democrats in Congress behind the compromise, Toombs and Stephens rounded up southern Whig votes. These were forthcoming, now that Taylor's leadership was gone. After the Compromise passed, in 1850, Stephens played a crucial role in frustrating the southern extremists (almost all of them Democrats) who preferred secession to accepting it. Georgia, a key state for any southern sectional movement, had been decisive in isolating South Carolina in 1833, and in 1850 it again threw its weight behind moderation. Back home, Stephens and Toombs strengthened themselves against the disunionists in Georgia by an alliance with the pro-Compromise Democratic Congressman Howell Cobb. Finding it easier to work with Cobb than with anti-slavery northern Whigs, Stephens began to wonder aloud if the existing party alignments still made sense. He would have liked to expand the alliance with pro-Compromise Democrats to the nation as a whole, a hope he shared with Daniel Webster at this time.[22] The Democrats were strongly wedded to their organization, however, and for the presidential campaign of 1852 Stephens, Toombs, and Cobb returned to their respective party affiliations.

At the Whig national convention, Stephens served on the platform committee and saw to it that the document declared support for the Compromise of 1850. He was consequently furious when the party's nominee, Winfield Scott, refrained from explicitly endorsing the platform out of deference to northern Whig resentment of the Fugitive Slave Act.[23] Once burned, twice shy. After his experience with Taylor, Stephens did not want another free-soil Whig president. He withheld his support from the nominee and formed a splinter group on behalf of Daniel Webster. Webster had died by election time, but Stephens cast his ballot for him anyway. The futile gesture of defiance was characteristic of Stephens.

Had it not been for the slavery question, there can be little doubt that Stephens could have remained within the Whig party. His attitudes on many matters, both immediate and abstract, remained distinctively Whiggish in the early 1850s. As a lawyer, he continued to revere Chief Justice Marshall and to conceive of the law in terms of restraints upon the will of the people. He distinguished between "liberty" under law and "unrestrained licentiousness"—the political aspect of a commitment to order that found its personal expression in his advice to young Linton: "especially let not *passion* control your feelings."[24] The Compromise of 1850 seemed to Stephens the responsible, moderate course of true statesmanship; he stigmatized its opponents, both northern and southern, as "factionalists." His Washington's Birthday Address of 1852 extolled "character," "harmony," and the "moral sublime" in true Websterian fashion, not omitting an appeal to the women of the country to help maintain its "domestic tranquillity."[25] In foreign affairs, too, he pursued tranquillity, resisting both intervention on behalf of Kossuth and the movement to acquire Cuba.[26]

The Compromise of 1850 turned out to buy but a brief respite for Stephens and the nation. In January, 1854, Senator Douglas introduced his momentous Kansas-Nebraska Bill. The Missouri Compromise of 1820 had banned slavery in the Louisiana Purchase north of latitude 36'30 °. Douglas' bill proposed to repeal the famous Compromise and throw open the Great Plains to slavery if the territorial legislatures chose to establish it there. Northern Whigs hoped their party could unite in opposition to the measure. After all, it was sponsored by a prominent Democrat, embodied the classic Jacksonian principle of popular sovereignty, and was being pushed by a Democratic administration with all the power of party patronage. Against it, Whigs might have been expected to rally to the cause of tradition and a sectional compromise hallowed by association with the name of Henry Clay.

However, led by Stephens and young Archibald Dixon of Kentucky, the southern Whigs jumped at the bait Douglas dangled so temptingly before them. Dixon actually asked Douglas to make repeal of the Missouri Compromise explicit, and Douglas complied. Faced with the necessity of choosing between their party and all that it stood for against their section's desire to extend slavery, the majority of southern Whigs opted for the latter. To be sure, they were in a difficult position. "I did not ask for it," Clayton of Delaware complained, "but can a Senator whose constituents hold slaves be expected to resist and refuse what the North thus freely offers?" George Badger, a North Carolina Whig, at first objected that the Indians were again being despoiled but then changed his mind and backed the bill. Later, he was to call this switch the worst political mistake he ever made.[27] Stephens was a brilliant parliamentarian and a skillful debater. As floor manager for the Kansas-Nebraska bill in the House, he succeeded in gaining its passage by 113 to 100 votes. The price he paid was the irreparable ruin of the Whig party. An organization based upon intersectional agreement on issues, already badly divided by the Compromise of 1850, the party did not survive this second schism.[28]

In vain did Stephens attempt to hedge his apostasy by citing Whig heroes like Webster, Chatham, and Edmund Burke, by carefully embracing popular sovereignty on grounds of expediency rather than philosophy, and by claiming that the Compromise of 1850 had already superseded that of 1820.[29] Northern Whigs knew better: the Compromise of 1850 had applied to the Mexican Cession, not to the Louisiana Purchase. Stephens admitted both the novelty and the drastic importance of the Kansas-Nebraska Act in one unguarded moment. When Congress reconvened, seven months after passing the act, a northern representative asked that it be reconsidered and repealed. Stephens retorted: "Revolution never goes backward— always forward."[30] Within a few years, Stephens and most other southern Whigs would worry that the proslavery revolution was badly out of hand.

Why did Stephens and so many other southern Whigs support repeal of the Missouri Compromise? In the most immediate sense, the answer is that they did not foresee the impact it would have on northern Whigs. In a deeper sense, the explanation is probably that Henry Clay's dream of a diversified southern economy had lost out by 1854. The slave system that produced cotton for export came to seem more and more central to southern prosperity—a development boding ill for moderation in sectionalism. Values and attitudes were evolving in the same direction as the economy: an idealized version of the cotton plantation became the dominant image in the southern mind. Stephens himself had invested in slaves and land to grow cotton, as did many other southern business and professional men. He was now the proud master of a plantation he called, with unconscious irony, "Liberty Hall." He also converted to the doctrine that slavery was not merely, as he had once thought, a "stern necessity" but a positive good. And, if slavery was good, its extension was perfectly logical.[31]

The discrepancy between the proslavery political stands Stephens had been taking and his nagging personal doubts about the institution did not persist. Hypocrisy is an unstable human condition; the impulse to bring action and belief into harmony is strong. Within six months of the time he managed the Kansas-Nebraska bill to passage, Stephens finished adapting his faith to his works. He had earlier invoked Scripture and conventional prejudices to justify the enslavement of the Negro race by the Causasian, and by the winter of 1854–55 he was ready with a systematic exposition of the benefits conferred by slavery. The argument he then advanced, with the zeal of a convert, combined two aspects: the racist and the economic. In the first place, the black was innately inferior and naturally suited to the condition of slavery; as a result, "the negro population of the South are better off, better fed, better clothed, better provided for, enjoy more happiness, and a higher civilization, than the same race has ever enjoyed anywhere else on the face of the world." In the second place, slavery was an extraordinarily efficient economic system. Henry Clay had advocated economic growth and considered slavery either a liability or a neutral factor in achieving this objective. Now Stephens formulated a new version of Southern Whiggery that took slavery and its expansion as an economic asset. He appealed to the Census of 1850 to show that Georgia's agricultural yields and general prosperity compared quite favorably with those of free-labor Ohio. He was responding, in their own terms, to Henry Carey and other northern Whigs who called slavery a drag on the economy.[32] It is interesting that practically every issue historians debate relating to American slavery was also debated by contemporaries; the statistical conclusions of "cliometricians" regarding the productivity of slave labor are no exception.

With the national Whig party in ruins, its sectional branches faced the problem of where to go. At first Stephens felt that the southern Whigs should remain separate from the Democrats and cooperate with the dwindling number of northern Cotton Whigs.[33] An obvious vehicle for such a strategy appeared in the form of the Native American party, organized in reaction to the flood of immigrants who had entered the country during the preceding decade. The majority of southern Whigs affiliated with this party. Despite the scornful epithet "Know-Nothings," pinned on them by Greeley, the Native Americans also attracted many northern Whigs after Winfield Scott's efforts to woo the immigrants in 1852 proved unable to break the hold of Democratic machines. Stephens soon decided, however, that the nativist party did not constitute a satisfactory political option. Despite his enthusiasm for the subjugation of blacks, he objected to discrimination against categories of white men on ethnic or religious grounds. He also found the secret Order of the Star-Spangled Banner, nucleus of the nativist movement, distasteful. Finally, many northern nativists were also antislavery.[34] Lacking a party, Stephens planned to retire from politics but was stung (as always) by taunts of cowardice into running as an independent. By dint of Herculean campaigning efforts he won reelection to Congress.[35]

The congressional session of 1855–56 saw Stephens take the plunge and become a Democrat. In retrospect, it seems the logical conclusion to his cooperation in Congress with Douglas and, on the state level, with Howell Cobb. The Douglas Democrats had come to share Stephens' desire to encourage economic-development projects like railroads, and, in accordance with their program of popular sovereignty for the territories, they were willing to permit the expansion of slavery. The Democratic party was the one viable national organization through which the defenders of slavery could still exercise power. That Stephens nevertheless found it so hard to switch over shows how seriously people took party identities. Indeed, most southern Whigs did not make the switch until after the Civil War.

In the presidential campaign of 1856, the Native American party split along sectional lines, most of the northern members joining the new Republicans, thereby vindicating Stephens' suspicions. The others, nicknamed "South Americans," ran ex-President Fillmore, who paid little attention to nativism and campaigned as an old Whig. He gained 44 percent of the popular vote in the South but only 13 percent in the North, which showed how few real allies the southern Whigs retained there.[36] Southern Whigs who stayed with Fillmore in 1856 regarded Stephens the new Democrat as a turncoat. When one of their leaders, Benjamin Hill, compared him to Judas Iscariot, Stephens challenged the man to a duel. Hill declined with dignity: "I regard dueling as no evidence of courage, no vindication of truth, and no test of the character of a true gentleman." Stephens, in his rage, betrayed both his pitiful overcompensation for physical weakness and his obsessive need for self-justification.[37]

Stephens' support for the Kansas-Nebraska Bill turned out to be an open-ended commitment. Having assured southerners that squatter sovereignty would work to their advantage, he felt constrained to ensure that Kansas did indeed become a slave state. Continually pressed by sectionalists more extreme than himself, demanding nothing less than federal guarantees of slavery in the territories, Stephens wanted popular sovereignty to show tangible political benefits. It was as if the South had to be bribed to stay in the Union, and Stephens—still strong in his commitment to the Union—dared not default on the payments. So he fought hard for the proposed Lecompton Constitution that would have admitted Kansas as a slave state, even though he admitted privately that it had been "procured by fraud."[38] It was a distasteful role. In the end the Lecompton cause proved unsuccessful as well as immoral. Fed up with advocating his section's cause against his better judgment, Stephens retired from Congress in 1859.

On July 2, 1859, Stephens delivered his political "Farewell Speech" in Augusta, Georgia. He began with a restatement of his original Whig philosophy and support for education and industrialization. Then he undertook an elaborate defense of his conduct since leaving the Whig party, including an attempt to reconcile his support for popular sovereignty with the Supreme Court's Dred Scott decision of 1857. (Actually, the decision encouraged the extreme "southern-rights" view he had resisted for years, that slavery was entitled to federal protection in the territories.) Stephens was resolute in his advocacy of slavery as "a new order and a higher type of Christian civilization." Meeting Seward on his own ground, he acknowledged that the Constitution must be consonant with the "higher law" of the Creator. Stephens' "higher law," however, favored "graduation and subordination" and proclaimed the Negro's natural fitness for slavery. He brought the two great principles of Whig social thought, order and philanthropy, into juxtaposition and declared unequivocally for the former: "order is nature's first law." Now that Stephens had become an ardent exponent of slavery, he followed the logic of his new position remorselessly and advocated reopening the African slave trade. Now that he had become a Democrat, it was also logical that he should endorse the acquisition of Cuba and other Caribbean adventuring.[39]

Yet, along with this vainglorious sectionalism and self-vindication, there was another side to Stephens' speech. The number of slave states seemed likely to fall ever further behind the number of free states, he noted. Whether the South would remain in the Union under those circumstances might depend on the North's showing scrupulous respect for her rights. The alleged economic superiority of slavery to free labor had not enabled the South to keep pace with the North in sectional power, and Stephens could see this. A few months before, during the congressional debate on the admission of Oregon, he had conceded that the balance between the sections was "already gone."[40] He felt deeply disappointed by the split between the northern and southern Democrats (or, more precisely, between Douglas and the Buchanan administration) over Lecompton and had tried, unsuccessfully, to mediate it. His desperate efforts to make Kansas a slave state had failed, and with them his whole political strategy of proslavery Unionism within the Democratic party. Stephens' resignation from Congress, as he told President Buchanan, betokened bleak pessimism. To a friend who asked why he was quitting, he answered: "When I am on one of two trains coming in opposite directions on a single track, both engines at high speed, and both engineers drunk, I get off at the first station." On departing for Georgia, he added, "I never expect to see Washington again, unless I am brought here as a prisoner of war."[41]

Stephens had become a Democrat and a slavery expansionist by stages. As southern opinion shifted, he had moved with it, despite misgivings. If the engineers in charge of the South's train were now drunk, Stephens had been willing, from time to time, to pass them the bottle of heady sectional assertiveness. In backing Lecompton he had certainly encouraged extremism more than most southern Whigs.[42] The baneful influence of his friend Robert Toombs seems partly responsible. Toombs (in Von Abele's apt words) was a "handsome swaggerer" and "full of large emotions violently expressed." He had been born to money, but, finding Whig moderation irksome, he joined the Democratic party and became a secessionist. A man who represented everything Stephens secretly wished to be, he exerted a powerful fascination over him that sometimes got the better of his judgment. By the time Stephens openly defied Toombs in 1860, it was too late to apply the brakes to the runaway train of secession.[43]

Stephens' analysis of the political situation in 1860 was that of an old Whig: "When the passions of men are once let loose, without control legal or moral, there is no telling to what extent they will lead their victims." He blamed the breakup of the Democratic national convention that year on the "heat of passion."[44] Most of the southern Whigs shared these feelings. They rallied, one last time, under the "Constitutional Union" candidates, John Bell of Tennessee for president and Edward Everett of Massachusetts for vice-president. Their campaign deplored demagogy, party politics, territorial expansion, and the spoils system, good Whig issues all, while generally avoiding discussion of slavery.[45] Understandably, John J. Crittenden invited Stephens to join them. But to return to the Whig fold might have been construed as an admission that he had been wrong in joining the Democrats, and to cooperate with Benjamin Hill on the Bell campaign in Georgia, after their near duel, would have been mortifying. Stephens waged his struggle against sectional extremism on behalf of the northern Democratic nominee, Douglas. He knew this was a hopeless cause in Georgia, but Stephens—as on so many other occasions—seemed more concerned with self-vindication than with winning.

During the campaign, Stephens continued to oppose the demand of southern extremists that Congress enact a slave code for the territories. The important thing, he argued, was for Congress not to interfere with slavery there, whether this left it to the territorial legislatures' so-called sovereignty or to the Supreme Court's *Dred Scott* doctrine. Since the North would never consent to a territorial slave code, insistence on one must precipitate a crisis. Even in his exertions, however, Stephens was tormented by forebodings whose gloom was equaled only by their accuracy. "In less than twelve months we shall be in the midst of a bloody war," he told a friend.

> The Republican nominee will be elected. Then South Carolina will secede. For me, I should be content to let her have her own way, and go out alone. But the Gulf States will follow her example.... After that the Border States will hesitate, and their hesitation will encourage the North to make war upon us.... [We shall] be without the sympathy of the world.[46]

After Lincoln's election, Stephens and the handful of Unionist Democrats in Georgia found themselves together, willy-nilly, with old Whigs in trying to prevent secession. Throughout the South, wherever the Whig party remained a vital force, there opposition to secession could be effective. Southern Whigs were generally unenthusiastic about secession, for many reasons. The secession movement was to some extent a means of expanding slavery in the Caribbean and adjacent areas. On the whole, southern Whigs did not stand to gain much by this expansion. They tended to be urban business and professional men, often with ties to the North, or planters and politicians who were already securely established, or men whose hopes for rising in the world had more to do with government-subsidized development than with the acquisition of territory. In a broader sense, however, the southern Whigs simply placed a higher value on moderation and calm. They were less swayed than Democrats by the secessionists' militant appeals to racial pride and the defense of honor. Disillusioned by the turmoil the Kansas-Nebraska Act had wrought, they had turned against Lecompton. Most southern Whigs seem to have considered Lincoln's ability to harm their section satisfactorily limited by the constitutional restraints of "mixed government" and normal political competition. Such conservative southerners had good reason to share Stephens' fear of revolution.[47]

Secession, Stephens realized, was indeed a form of revolution. To start a revolution on behalf of slavery was to set in motion imponderable, potentially dangerous events, he warned. "Revolutions are much easier started than controlled, and the men who begin them, even for the best purposes and objects, seldom end them. The American Revolution of 1776 was one of the few exceptions to this remark." He based his "apprehensions" on history and moral philosophy. The secessionists he called "demagogues."[48] As for Lincoln, Stephens remembered him from their Whig days together in the House: "He is not a bad man. He will make as good a President as Fillmore did and better too in my opinion."[49]

Stephens appeared before the Georgia legislature to make a dramatic appeal against secession on November 14, 1860. "My object is not to stir up strife, but to allay it; not to appeal to your passions, but to your reason," he began. He was scrupulous about his choice of rhetorical devices, for his mission was one of conciliation as well as opposition. "The election of no man, constitutionally chosen [president], is sufficient cause for any state to separate from the Union." To secede before any provocation has been given will place Georgia in the wrong, he continued. Established institutions are entitled to more respect than that. "The institutions of a people, political and moral, are the matrix in which the germ of their organic structure quickens into life, takes root, and develops," he explained in good Whig fashion. "I think that one of the evils that beset us is a surfeit of liberty." Some later historians would agree with that judgment.[50]

Despite Stephens' eloquence, the Georgia legislature voted to call a secession convention. But his speech was well received by former fellow Whigs of the North, among them Abraham Lincoln. The president-elect promptly wrote Stephens a complimentary letter requesting reprints. In the correspondence that followed, Lincoln assured Stephens that the South need not fear interference with slavery in the states where it already existed. "You think slavery is *right* and ought to be extended; while we think it is *wrong* and ought to be restricted. That I suppose is the rub. It certainly is the only substantial difference between us."[51]

Lincoln was right, but the one "difference" was critical. It turned out to be enough to disrupt their country, destroy their party, and drastically transform the political culture that northern and southern Whigs had once shared. Stephens complained to Lincoln that "the leading object" of the Republican party was "to put the institutions of nearly half the States under the ban of public opinion." He asked for some statement that might encourage southern Unionists. Lincoln could not deny the accuracy of Stephens' description of Republicanism and apparently decided there was nothing more to say. We know, however, that he was pondering at this time whether to invite Stephens to join his cabinet.[52]

The meeting of the Georgia convention on January 16, 1861, found the opponents of secession disorganized. Stephens and Hill were still not speaking to each other. It was typical of the confused and demoralized state of Unionists in the Cotton Belt. The Whig party was no longer an effective vehicle for them to use. Stephens already felt defeatist. "Every incident of what is termed *luck* seems to be against the Conservatives. I call it Providence. My reading of it is that a severe chastisement for sins of ingratitude and other crimes is about to be inflicted upon us." (Years later he would identify the crimes as failures to live up to the paternalist ideal in the treatment of slaves.)[53] Most of the Georgia Whigs had been less guilty than Stephens of trying to appease the "fire-eaters." Now they were less firm than he in opposing them. Drift had become a habit. No alternative to the course of the extremists captured the imagination. The southern Whigs remind one of nothing so much as the former United Party in the Republic of South Africa.

Stephens spoke against secession at the convention so forcefully that the Republicans circulated copies of his speech as propaganda during the Civil War.[54] But it was clear how the votes would go. When Stephens finished, Robert Toombs, who had been thwarting him at every opportunity for months, led the audience in cheering him. The gesture reinforced Stephens' feelings of identity with the other delegates. Outvoted on secession, he nevertheless acknowledged Georgia's continued claim to his loyalty. However he might rationalize his decision in later years, what mattered was not so much a belief in the theoretical right of secession as an elemental, visceral impulse: "My destiny is with the South; whatever awaits her people, awaits me."[55] Countless other southern Unionists, some of whom did not even profess secession as a constitutional doctrine,

made the same decision. The fact that this primitive sectional loyalty
generally ran so much deeper than modern national loyalty is an
index of the failure of southern Whiggery.

From this time on, one can speak only of fragmented Whig tendencies, in Stephens and in the South as a whole. Neither the party nor
its political culture remained viable or coherent any longer. The new
Confederacy did not employ party designations, but it was dominated by Democrats. The Mississippi Democrat Jefferson Davis became its president and chose an all-Democratic cabinet. Stephens
was made vice-president through the operation of the usual considerations of ticket-balancing, considerations that, as so often happens,
were to lead to embarrassment later. The Confederate Constitution, which he played a significant part in writing, revealed the
low estate of Whig principles in the South by its prohibition of protective tariffs and internal improvements undertaken by the central
government. One genuinely Whig suggestion was incorporated, the
provision that enhanced the status of members of the cabinet by
authorizing them to sit in Congress. Stephens felt proud of this, but
it required enabling legislation and was never implemented. When
he expounded the basis of the new constitution in March, 1861, he
declared that "its corner-stone rests upon the great truth, that the
negro [sic] is not equal to the white man." He went on to affirm the
old Jacksonian doctrine of *Herrenvolk* democracy: "With us, all of the
white race, however high or low, rich or poor, are equal in the eye of
the law. Not so with the negro. Subordination is his place."[56]

After the bombardment of Fort Sumter, Stephens went on behalf of
the Confederacy to persuade Virginia to secede. As a prominent
opponent of Georgia's secession, he could carry weight with Unionists and Whigs. The Confederate vice-president undertook to as-
sure Virginians what he had until recently denied, that secession
represented a rational and conservative revolution. Stephens was not
being altogether inconsistent, for he now felt that the best hope of
peace lay in strengthening the Confederacy enough to deter the
North from making war to preserve the Union. The addition of the
Upper South might do this.[57] Probably Stephens nurtured the hope
that the Lincoln administration would respond by offering concessions to induce the southern states to return *en bloc* to the Union.
While establishing his official contacts with the Virginia authorities,
he also established some unofficial ones (via a secret envoy named
Rudolf Schleiden) with Secretary Seward in Washington. But though
his mission to bring Virginia into the Confederacy succeeded, that to
avert war failed.[58]

During the war the Confederate Whigs remained fragmented and unable to offer a unified opposition or alternative to the Davis administration. Some ex-Whigs, like Stephens' old rival Benjamin Hill, even supported the administration. However, there was a tendency for ex-Whigs in the Confederate Congress to back the war effort less enthusiastically than ex-Democrats; this is scarcely surprising, considering that 81 percent of them had opposed secession.[59] The Confederate congressional elections of 1861 returned a majority of ex-Democrats. After the initial enthusiasm for the cause had sobered, the elections of 1863 saw a modest resurgence of ex-Whigs. Even then, however, organized political parties failed to reappear until after the demise of the Confederacy.[60]

Insofar as the Confederate opposition to Davis had a leader, it was Stephens. Vice-president Thomas Jefferson had played much the same role during the administration of John Adams. The parallel is significant, for Stephens reactivated a Jeffersonian-Madisonian strain within Whiggery. Because he conceptualized secession as revolution, he was particularly sensitive to the danger of an autocratic reaction, as in France under the Directory. Consequently, he tried to prevent executive and military usurpation of authority. Critical of the quality of Confederate statesmanship even during the early days of the provisional government at Montgomery, he became ever more so after the permanent government was set up at Richmond. Stephens made himself the voice of the "country party" in Confederate politics. "The North has already run into a complete despotism," he warned in the fall of 1863, and "this has been the usual course and fate of republics." To guard against such corruption in the Confederacy became his highest concern.[61]

Historians have dealt harshly with Stephens as leader of the opposition. They have felt he set his face against measures that were essential to centralized direction of the war effort.[62] The real key to Stephens' vice-presidency, however, lies not in mere petulant obstructionism but in his old Whiggery. Stephens differed with Davis on many substantive aspects of policy. He wanted more attention to economic rationalization and less concentration on military affairs, narrowly conceived. He wanted to do more to cultivate the good will of Britain and the other European powers. He believed that the undercutting of civilian law by military authorities was largely unnecessary and often counterproductive. Finally, he felt that the Confederate administration never recognized the importance of encouraging the northern peace movement and seeking an accord with it. All these areas of disagreement between Davis and Stephens reveal conflicting value judgments appropriate to a former Democrat and a former Whig.

"Much the greater part of war [is] business," Stephens insisted. The greatest business asset the South possessed at the outset of war was cotton. Stephens wanted to export as much as possible to Europe before the blockade could take effect, there to be held as collateral for purchases of munitions. Davis adopted, instead, a policy of withholding cotton from the international market, thinking to blackmail the Europeans into intervening in America in order to replenish their supplies. Stephens' was a policy of commercial accommodation; Davis's, one of coercion. Stephens' was also the course that stood the better chance of succeeding.[63]

President Davis wasted much of his time on details of army operations; he had hoped for a military command and was miscast as a civilian official. Stephens put the battlefield into a broader perspective. He always expected the war to be dreadfully destructive and advocated a strategy that would minimize losses of men and material. He endorsed the Fabian tactics of General Joseph E. Johnston and felt Davis attached too much importance to defending fixed positions at great cost. He would have given higher priority to countering the blockade, making better use of internal lines of communication, and keeping the southern economy running while waiting for the enemy to tire.[64] The financial policies of the Davis administration seemed primitive to Stephens; borrowing and printing money could only lead to inflation. Stephens called for taxation, including a tax in kind on farm produce that would have short-cut the need to contract for provisions. Eventually the Confederacy did impose various economic controls and, in 1863 (after inflation had wrought havoc), the taxes Stephens desired. The Civil War provided an impetus to economic modernization of many kinds in the South, as it did even more in the North, but Stephens was quicker to perceive this than Davis.[65]

There was a connection between Stephens' economic objectives and his constitutional stands. He opposed the conscription of white men between the ages of seventeen and fifty because he felt it deprived the civilian sector of manpower needed to keep the economy going. He opposed the suspension of habeas corpus because it put enforcement of the conscription act in the hands of military tribunals. Under color of martial law, generals sometimes impressed both men and materials arbitrarily. This, Stephens complained, discouraged production.[66] Recent research has begun to show how ruthlessly the Confederate conscription laws sacrificed the interests of all white classes in the South save the planters and how widespread was the suffering and consequent disaffection from the Confederate cause.[67] Alexander Stephens was speaking for many businessmen and nonslaveholding farmers in his criticisms of the unjust operation of the laws.

But Stephens also had a sincere devotion to constitutional principles for their own sake. "Without liberty, I would not turn upon my heel for independence," he told a Georgia audience in early 1864, and he meant it. He simply did not feel that winning the war was worth compromising traditional constitutionalism. He had taken the same line against Polk a generation earlier. Like Lincoln, Stephens believed his real cause was that of self-government: "With us now rest the hopes of the world," was how Stephens put it. The South should not betray these hopes even to secure its revolution. In the North, Lincoln was suspending constitutional procedures in the name of military necessity; Stephens was unwilling to follow this example. Unlike Lincoln, Stephens came to feel that the cause of humanity might not necessarily best be served by the victory of his side.[68]

Throughout the war Stephens hoped for a negotiated compromise. He felt that the South ought to pay more attention to the northern political situation and try to promote the chances of McClellan in the presidential election of 1864. Since ties with former Whigs like Seward and Lincoln could not be reestablished, perhaps former Douglas Democrats like Clement Vallandigham might, as in the mid-1850s, prove helpful to the South. The "Peace Resolutions" of the Georgia legislature, introduced by Stephens' brother Linton and passed in March, 1864, called for an armistice followed by mutual evacuation of the border states and plebiscites to determine which areas would join the Union and which the Confederacy. There is some evidence that Stephens would have been willing, during negotiations, to forgo southern independence in return for sufficient guarantees to slavery.[69] Such a settlement would have accorded with the policies of neither Lincoln nor Davis, and this probably explains why the two presidents frustrated Stephens' peace initiatives.

Twice Stephens managed to persuade Davis to name him to negotiating missions. The first was to be sent in July, 1863, but Lincoln, after victories at Vicksburg and Gettysburg, felt able to refuse to receive the emissaries. At the beginning of 1865, Confederate prospects looked so bleak that Davis consented to another mission by Stephens. This time Lincoln reluctantly met with him and two other commissioners at Hampton Roads, Virginia, on February 3. The leaders reminisced for a while about their old days together as Whigs, but the conference came to naught because Lincoln was unwilling to discuss any terms save unconditional surrender. He was especially resolved to continue his support for the Thirteenth Amendment, abolishing slavery, which had just passed Congress and awaited ratification by the states. R. M. T. Hunter, one of the Confederate commissioners and also a former Whig, pointed out that even Charles I had treated with those in arms against his government. "But he lost his head in the end," Lincoln retorted.[70] Had Stephens been able to offer a proposal for a negotiated peace earlier in the war, he could have embarrassed Lincoln very badly. By 1865 the end was in sight anyway.

The president and vice-president of the Confederacy met the demise of their cause characteristically. Davis tried to escape to Texas, where he hoped to rally further desperate resistance. Stephens waited calmly at his home and told Linton, "Almost anything is better than guerilla [sic] warfare."[71] From Stephens' point of view, honor had been satisfied; a restoration of order was preferable to further bloodshed and turmoil.

For the rest of his life Stephens would be obsessed with vindicating his conduct during the war. Out of this obsession came two principal memoirs, his *Recollections*, written during his five months as a prisoner at Fort Warren, and the *Constitutional View of the Late War between the States*, published in 1868–70. Both works reflect the character trait he had confessed to Linton back in 1851, the urge "to enjoy the gratification of seeing [others] feel that they were wrong."[72] The former is the more human and hence more appealing work, though tinged with unbecoming self-pity. The *Recollections* are concerned in large measure with vindicating Stephens' opposition to Davis, the *Constitutional View*, with vindicating his decision to go with his state after secession. The shift of emphasis between the two was influenced by intervening events.

Whiggery temporarily resurfaced in the South after the war, for a political culture is a deep-seated and durable entity even when buffeted and vitiated for decades. The outcome of the war, a triumph for the northern bourgeoisie, apparently suggested a reconstitution of the old Whig party. In the elections of 1865–66, held in the South under the auspices of President Johnson's Reconstruction plan, the former Confederate Whigs scored something like a sweep.[73] Among them was Alexander Stephens, chosen for the U.S. Senate from Georgia immediately after his release from captivity. As senator-elect, Stephens delivered an address to the Georgia legislature on the traditional Whig occasion, Washington's Birthday, thus indicating an intention to revive Whiggery. He praised Daniel Webster and Lyman's son, Henry Ward Beecher, and he called on the whites of the

South to repay the ex-slaves' "fidelity in times past" with a paternalistic concern to remove any obstacles "which can possibly hinder
or retard the improvement of the blacks to the extent of their capacity."[74] When Congress, for reasons quite understandable, refused to
accept the elections and turned away the would-be members from
the former Confederacy, the chances for a revival of southern Whig
political fortunes were dealt their final blow. It was in the wake of
this rebuff that Stephens composed his *Constitutional View of the Late
War.*

The *Constitutional View* is cast as a dialogue, which enabled
Stephens to score one victory after another in fantasy verbal battles.
It is concerned with justifying secession as an implied power reserved to the states by the Constitution, but it has little to say about
the wisdom of the eleven states that exercised this alleged right in
1860–61. Ulrich B. Phillips called it "a tedious rationalization," and
few are likely to dispute his judgment.[75] Stephens' *Constitutional
View* perverts Whig political philosophy into its opposite. Where
prewar Whiggery emphasized experience, this book emphasizes
logic. Prewar Whiggery respected the law as a system of restraints,
but it also conceived of the law as flexible, rather like Lyman
Beecher's theology. Stephens' postwar legalism is a fundamentalist
religion. Gone is the evolutionary approach that had characterized
antebellum Whig thought. Instead we have a literal-minded constitutionalist, analyzing the situation of 1787 as if nothing had
changed since. The epigraph sums up the spirit of the work: "Times
change, and men often change with them, but principles never!" The
irony is that so much *had* changed. Before the war Stephens was a
political ally of Webster, a consistent opponent of Calhoun on the
issues of nullification and the rights of slavery in the territories. Now
he devotes chapters to supporting Calhoun against Webster on the
nature of the Constitution.[76] From an antebellum defender of the
Union, Stephens has transformed himself into the most influential
postbellum apologist for secession. Nowhere does he frankly face up
to this change; instead he is at pains to minimize and obscure his
prewar Whig associations. Stephens' unreliable retrospective accounts contributed to the myth of an antebellum Solid South, devoted from the start to states' rights.[77]

Both sides in the Civil War saw themselves—accurately—as revolutionary. Whichever won, the old Whig-Jacksonian republic would
come to an end. But it was the revolution of Seward and Lincoln,
not the one Stephens half-heartedly supported, that did win. In
the aftermath of defeat, Stephens' prickly defensiveness captured

the dominant mood of white southerners. He served as the ideologist of the Lost Cause, as Robert E. Lee served as its cult hero. Lee had been a Unionist and a Whig like Stephens; that the two had known better and yet shared the fate of their section must have endeared them to its people. Stephens' *Constitutional View* became the bible of a nostalgic and particularistic political culture in the postwar South. In a sequel called *The Reviewers Reviewed*, in a school textbook, and in a general history of the United States, he maintained his interpretation and continued to warn against the corruptions of encroaching federal power.[78] Even in this fossilized form, the country-party paradigm retained some predictive power. Stephens warned that the centralization of national authority that had occurred under the Republicans would lead to a new round of aggressive American imperialism.[79]

After the amnesty of 1872, Stephens was able to reenter Congress and spend nine years in the House of Representatives. He affiliated with Georgia's probusiness "Bourgeois Triumvirate" of Joseph E. Brown, John B. Gordon, and Alfred H. Colquitt. Like them he supported the intersectional Compromise of 1877, restoring home rule to the South in return for acquiescence in the inauguration of Rutherford B. Hayes as president. Stephens was especially interested in that aspect of the Compromise promising a federal subsidy to the Texas & Pacific Railroad.[80] There is a great deal that smacks of old Whiggery in this, but it was a reactionary Whiggery from which any reform impulse had been excised. In 1872 Stephens refused to support Greeley for president, and in 1874 he bitterly opposed the last civil-rights bill of Charles Sumner.[81] Stephens' brand of postwar neo-Whiggery, if it should be so called, fashioned a durable place for itself within the southern Democratic party on the basis of state sovereignty, white supremacy, and probusiness conservatism.

In old age—and he aged early—Stephens represented a perfect example of a familiar type of southern Congressman: a venerated Confederate hero, regularly reelected as a symbol of sectional fidelity, more wizened and sickly than ever, a trusted friend of the corporations. Tainted by scandal in 1870, he felt it necessary to divest himself of his holdings in the Western & Atlantic Railroad, the same line he had supported as a young legislator back in the 1830s. His last significant speech was at a ceremonial on Lincoln's Birthday in 1878, when he paid tribute to the "warm hearted" and "magnanimous" personal qualities of the man whose policies as president he had always condemned as tyrannical.[82] In 1882, pitifully enfeebled in body and mind, he was nominated for governor to lend respectability to a conservative Democratic state regime that had been badly discredited by corruption. He lived long enough to sign the necessary pardons and died in office March 4, 1883.

The record of the Whig party in the South before the Civil War is one of tragic failure in virtually every respect. It failed to moderate enthusiasm for the expansion of slavery, to diversify the economy, to minimize violence, to provide adequate public education, and to prevent secession. Its declining effectiveness is a measure of the declining appeal of its bourgeois value system and the corresponding success of the premodern value system of the southern Democrats. The operation of the cotton-slave-plantation system always remained subordinate to the worldwide capitalist economic system. However, during the years leading up to the war, southerners tended more and more to emphasize "whatever aristocratic and preindustrial traits they could find in their society."[83] The rise of the plantation mystique and the cult of southern chivalry provide a curious example of cultural reaction: the reverse of a process of modernization.

Since the South did not develop a strong bourgeoisie, Whig leaders like Stephens were driven to ally themselves with other groups in society. During the generation after 1850 they experimented with one such alliance after another in an attempt to influence events. Stephens tried allying himself with the slavery-expansionist planters in the Democratic party for a while. Then, having failed to temper their policies, he aligned himself during the life of the Confederacy with the yeomen farmers in criticizing Davis's conduct of the war. After a brief gesture toward moderates among the newly emancipated blacks in his Washington's Birthday address of 1866, he at length found a home in the conservative "Bourbon" wing of the Democratic party. There the rest of the southern former Whigs eventually joined him, although not before some of them had spent time in the Republican party during the years of Reconstruction.[84]

In the long run, of course, capitalism was destined to triumph in the United States. There was even a capitalistic "New South" that emerged after Reconstruction. But by the time this happened, the Whigs were no longer Whigs, and capitalism itself was no longer the same. Moreover, the wisest interpreters of the southern character tell us that bourgeois values have remained weaker, and premodern values stronger, in the South than anywhere else in the nation.[85]

Eleven

Abraham Lincoln and the Transformation of Northern Whiggery

Abraham Lincoln (1809–65) was both a great revolutionary and a successful counterrevolutionary. Like Seward, he endorsed the peaceful revolution of public opinion that would bring about the immediate restriction of slavery and its ultimate extinction. This was a revolution that he hoped could occur within the context of American democratic institutions. It would reaffirm and revitalize the first American revolution, much as the revivalism of the evangelists was intended to reaffirm and revitalize the Protestant Reformation. But when the election of 1860 wrested control of the federal government from the slave power, heralding the success of this revolution, the southern states refused to accept it. They embarked on the course of secession, which Lincoln held to be unconstitutional and which was certainly at least extraconstitutional, however one looked at it. Because the slave power (or "slaveholding interest," as we would say) refused to acquiesce in its own demise, civil war resulted. To fulfill the northern revolution, the southern revolution had to be put down with massive violence. It was a gigantic disappointment for the hopes of peaceful progress that both the Whigs and the early Republicans had nurtured. Yet, when force finally had to be used, Lincoln resorted to

it with far more constancy of purpose and determination than
Stephens was able to muster. In the last analysis, Lincoln deeply
believed in his revolution as Stephens never quite did in his.[1]

Horace Greeley declared that Abraham Lincoln owed his political
rise to "his unhesitating, uncalculating, self-sacrificing devotion to
the principles and aims of his party." The word "uncalculating"
seems unfortunate; the former rail-splitter turned himself into an
extremely shrewd professional politician. It was true, however, that
Lincoln possessed a deserved reputation for party regularity. The
party to which Greeley referred was the Whig, for Lincoln had become a power in Illinois politics long before the birth of the Republican party. An Illinois state legislator from 1834 to 1841, he advanced
to the position of Whig minority leader in the lower house. He
worked hard for Harrison in 1840 and headed the Illinois campaigns
of Clay in '44 and Taylor in '48. In 1852 he still campaigned loyally for
Scott. Like many other Whigs, Lincoln felt that such partisanship had
been forced on him by the other side. "They set us the example of
organization; and we, in self-defence, are driven into it."[2] In 1836
Lincoln had protested against the Democrats' holding a state convention to choose their nominees; it seemed better to him that outstanding local candidates should simply announce for office. Yet
within a few years he was attending Whig state conventions and
performing in them as effectively as any Jacksonian politician. He
played the game of patronage and endeavored to win appointments
for himself and his friends. Nevertheless, both as a Whig and as a
Republican, Lincoln believed that political parties were based "on
grounds of *measures*—policy—where we can unite" and not on the
quest for office as such.[3]

Of all items in the Whig program, internal improvements held the
greatest appeal for the young Lincoln. He shared the typical Whig
aspiration for humanity to triumph over its physical environment.
His first political platform, announcing his unsuccessful candidacy
for the legislature in 1832, stressed the need for internal improvements, aid to education, and easy credit in promoting the development of the West. Lincoln's views had not changed when he won
election two years later. Though the Whigs were but a small minority
in the legislature of predominantly Democratic Illinois, he contrived
to win passage for a number of improvement projects by linking
them, in a grand demonstration of legislative "logrolling," to removal of the state capital from Vandalia to Springfield. Since Lincoln

came from Springfield and supported internal improvements on principle, he was demonstrating the consummate political skill that consists in winning concessions for doing what one has a mind to do anyway.[4]

Lincoln was also an orthodox Whig on the crucial tariff and banking issues. He took his views on the tariff from such staunch protectionists as Greeley, Clay, and Henry C. Carey. His old law partner, William Herndon, said that Lincoln studied Carey's works, and one can believe it because his arguments for the tariff so closely follow those of the Pennsylvanian. While a congressman in 1847–49, Lincoln pressed for higher duties. It is true that, when seeking to recruit former Democrats into the new Republican party during the 1850s, he sometimes played down his protectionism. However, the Pennsylvania delegation to the 1860 Republican convention swung behind his nomination because they were convinced he was sound on the tariff, and they were not disappointed. As president, Lincoln signed every bill for raising import levies that crossed his desk—and there were ten of them.[5]

In the 1830s and '40s Lincoln consistently defended both state and national banking. To him, the assault on the Bank of the United States was part of a general breakdown of respect for property and morality that was also manifesting itself in lynch law. "I am opposed to encouraging that lawless and mobocratic spirit, whether in relation to the bank or anything else, which is already abroad in the land; and is spreading with rapid and fearful impetuosity to the ultimate overthrow of every institution, or even moral principle, in which persons and property have hitherto found security."[6] Lincoln was still arguing for the constitutionality of a national bank as a congressman in 1848 and even raised the issue several times in his great debates with Douglas a decade later.

To discuss Lincoln the politician, however, is only to scratch the surface of his Whiggery, which sprang from the very depths of his being. To understand Lincoln the Whig, we must begin by trying to understand his ambitiousness. Herndon, who knew him well, observed that "his ambition was a little engine that knew no rest." Yet we also know that there was an authentic humility about the man. In him, ambition meant not simply winning political office but transcending his early limitations. The kind of ambition that possessed Lincoln was no cheap desire to lord it over others but a driving urge to develop himself, to fulfill his destiny in ways that life as a farmer like his father never could. Winning elections validated his program of self-improvement by showing that he had made himself "worthy" of others' esteem. And, at least as early as 1848, he had his eye on the presidency.[7]

The pursuit of his ambition led Lincoln beyond the pioneer folk culture of his childhood and introduced him to a new bourgeois culture. He inevitably remained somewhat influenced by his early environment, but most of his efforts were devoted to distancing himself from it—to rising above it, he would have felt.

> In a hard-drinking frontier society, [Lincoln] avoided alcohol and counseled temperance. Surrounded by cigars and spittoons, he did not smoke or chew. In a violent society obsessed with guns, he would not even use them to hunt. Believing that only those who paid taxes should vote, he opposed universal manhood suffrage. In an aggressively male society, he advocated votes for women. Abraham Lincoln was a Whig, one must conclude, because he preferred what Whigs believed to be a more civilized way of life.

Robert Kelley might well have added religion to this enumeration of ways in which Lincoln rejected frontier culture. Though his parents belonged to a southern sect of Baptists, the young Abraham read infidel books and enjoyed arguing against conservative theological tenets. In the congressional campaign of 1846, Lincoln's Democratic opponent was Peter Cartwright, an itinerant Methodist exhorter of renown whose views we would call "fundamentalist" (the term had not then been invented). Cartwright tried to make an issue of his adversary's unorthodoxy, but Lincoln deftly turned the matter aside.[8]

Though Lincoln always retained the common touch, he became a dignified and reserved man, whom no one called "Abe" to his face. Like Henry Clay, he customarily referred to himself as "old" from the time he was barely middle-aged, suggesting that both men wanted to think of themselves as sober elders. In fact, like many people born in humble and obscure circumstances, Lincoln sought to refashion his identity. Such a desire to make oneself over, widespread in nineteenth-century America, would help to explain why the culture of Whiggery appealed to so many people outside the confines of what we would regard as the bourgeoisie proper. It also underlay, I am persuaded, much of the Whig preoccupation with character-building and control.

Everyone knows that Lincoln was born in a log cabin; but when he grew up, he left the farm, first for the village of New Salem and then for the town of Springfield. Of course it was to Lincoln's political advantage that he was a self-made man; yet he dwelt less on his humble origins than Clay did—probably because they were in fact so much humbler. "It is a great piece of folly to attempt to make anything out of my early life," he told a campaign biographer. "It can all be condensed into a single sentence and that sentence you will find in Gray's Elegy—'The short and simple annals of the poor.'" Jeffersonian idealization of the family farm left him cold.[9] Of course, not all ambitious frontier politicians formulated a world view to take account of their ambition in exactly the same way that Lincoln did; some of them endorsed the Jeffersonian ideal. We do not know enough to explain these variations in any straightforward way. The point is not to *reduce* Lincoln's Whiggery to personal striving for "upward social mobility" but to see his political and social views as *expanding* a dedication to human self-development that his own life manifested. When Lincoln declared, "The way for a young man to rise, is to improve himself every way he can," he was not giving lip service to a platitude; he was voicing the faith he lived by.[10]

If we can believe certain anecdotes told of him, Lincoln at least occasionally shared the common Whig impatience to improve others as well as himself. It is said that he once physically chastised a man for swearing in front of ladies. "Another time, in Springfield, Lincoln warned a shoemaker to stop getting drunk and beating his wife. When the brute disregarded the warning, Lincoln with a few friends one night tied him up and had his wife switch his bare back." Though Whigs discountenanced extralegal violence, they sometimes resorted to it themselves as a didactic instrument. More typical, however, was Lincoln's address to the local temperance society, endorsing moral suasion and renouncing a coercive approach.[11]

Lincoln's critical perspective on the frontier culture he grew up in (which seemed to him a nonculture) is epitomized in his emotional distance from his parents. His mother, Nancy Hanks Lincoln, died when he was nine. We know very little about her, largely because Lincoln wanted it that way. She was apparently illegitimate and illiterate. We know that she was legally married to her husband, but Lincoln seems to have feared otherwise and felt ashamed of her.[12] Thomas Lincoln was likewise functionally illiterate; "he never did more in the way of writing than to bunglingly sign his own name" was how his son bluntly expressed it. A carpenter-turned-farmer, Thomas evidently neither experienced nor understood the ambition to excel that burned in his son. There are tales about how badly the two got along, that Thomas would punish the youth for reading when he should have been out doing some of the backbreaking farm work. How many of these stories are true we cannot be sure, but in later years Lincoln complained that his childhood home had offered "absolutely nothing to excite ambition for education."[13] When he married a daughter of the Kentucky patriciate, he invited no one from his own family to the wedding. And when Thomas Lincoln lay dying in 1851, Abraham refused his request to visit him, extended only the most conventional of consolations, and even added: "If we could meet now, it is doubtful whether it would not be more painful than pleasant." Nor did he attend the funeral. Yet, it should be noted, the son was indebted to his father for physical strength and a man-to-man quality that enabled him to wrestle and tell off-color jokes in male company—abilities valuable to an aspiring leader of men.[14]

Lincoln was afflicted with periodic bouts of melancholia. Perhaps he inherited the tendency from Nancy Hanks, who seems to have possessed a dark personality, brooding, religious, and superstitious. The similarity with Lyman Beecher, however, makes one wonder whether the symptoms in both men were not related to their over-conscientious, self-imposed striving. Beecher could at least relax with his family, but, as is well known, Lincoln's domestic life was unhappy. During a bleak mood in 1856, he compared himself with Senator Douglas and mused, "With *me*, the race of ambition has been a failure—a flat failure." In such times he even doubted his own ability to keep his own resolves, the quality on which this modest man prided himself most.[15] Lincoln took an interest in psychological disorders, perhaps because his own experience led to empathy with others. Fluctuations in mood were not the only temperamental inclination he labored to control; he also had to overcome a disposition toward laziness—for so his aversion to farm work was accounted. Here he compensated with an intellectual industriousness that Herndon described as "indefatigable."[16]

The talents and values that led Lincoln away from farming beckoned him toward commercial and professional work. After struggles as a storekeeper, surveyor, and minor postmaster, he found his vocation in legal and political life. In these callings he kept in close contact with the business world. Biographers have written of Lincoln's ties with business sometimes in the spirit of muckraking and sometimes with admiration.[17] Most of the legal fees he earned, even from corporate clients, were modest. A turning point in his career was a five-thousand-dollar payment for winning an important case for the Illinois Central Railroad; he had to sue to collect it. A sensible and diversified investor, Illinois' most prominent Republican had amassed property worth something over fifteen thousand dollars by the time he left for the White House. Material prosperity mattered to

Lincoln as a sign of success; when first elected to the legislature, he spent sixty dollars on a new suit so that he could make a good impression at the state capitol.[18]

Lincoln shared the attitude, well expressed by his contemporary, the lawyer-turned-theologian Horace Bushnell, that a "grand moral struggle centers in the holding and use and transmission of property." He had nothing but contempt for his ne'er-do-well stepbrother, John Johnston, whom he told: "You are destitute because you have *idled* away all your time. Your thousand pretences for not getting along better are all non-sense—they deceive no body but yourself. *Go to work* is the only cure for your case."[19] On the other hand, Lincoln showed compassion toward those who were helpless to avoid their suffering or whose "reformation" he felt it would help. Moral responsibility justified private property; property did not excuse irresponsibility. It is both accurate and appropriate that Lincoln should be identified with the bourgeois virtue par excellence, honesty.[20]

The law was a logical choice of career for a young man with strong verbal aptitudes and an ambition to be a leader. Once chosen, the profession exerted a powerful influence in shaping Lincoln's mind. Stephen Oates calls him "a lawyer's lawyer," one who won his reputation more by arguing legal points in appellate courts than by persuading jurymen with homespun common sense, although he did his share of that. The legal tradition in which Lincoln anchored himself was that of Chancellor Kent and conservative Whig jurisprudence, with its caution, respect for compromise, and faith in strong government. Like Rufus Choate, Lincoln demanded that law become "the *political religion* of the nation." Later, when confronting the crisis he inherited on assuming the presidency, Lincoln could be certain of one thing: "I hold that in contemplation of universal law, and of the Constitution, the Union of these States is perpetual." To have maintained anything less would have betrayed his legal heritage.[21]

Lincoln's practice of law, like all well-chosen vocations, proved temperamentally congenial. A man who had worked to achieve self-control, he channeled his energies toward "the pursuit of clarity and order in objective legal exercises."[22] By now it will be apparent that Lincoln manifested the Whig personality type of bourgeois compulsiveness in many ways. His preoccupations with self-control, order, rationality, industriousness—and with money, too—all fit the pattern. There is even evidence that he suffered from the classic inconvenience of compulsive people, constipation.[23]

Lincoln's public philosophy was of one piece with his personal character. According to Herndon, he not only read, but "ate up, digested, and assimilated" the writings of Francis Wayland, the most prominent American moral philosopher of that generation and an ardent exponent of character-building. (Wayland returned the compliment by supporting Lincoln for president in 1860.)[24] Lincoln identified the law with superintending rationality just as Choate did, and in Lincoln's case there can be no doubting his sincerity. Sickened by the lynching of a free Negro in Saint Louis and the mob murder of Elijah Lovejoy at Alton, Illinois, Lincoln called on every American to "swear by the blood of the Revolution, never to violate in the least particular the laws of his country, and never to tolerate their violation by others." He was addressing the Young Men's Lyceum of Springfield on this occasion; it was one of his first public speeches and remains among the most important. He went on to declare that, although popular passions had once aided the struggle for independence, they would henceforth be dangerous to the nation:

> Passion has helped us; but can do so no more. It will in future be our enemy. Reason, cold, calculating, unimpassioned reason, must furnish all the materials for our future support and defence. Let those materials be moulded into *general intelligence, sound morality*, and in particular, a *reverence for the constitution and laws*.

Not even John Quincy Adams could have made a more austere demand. The Great Emancipator was also a great believer in discipline. Yet, like Henry Clay, Lincoln saw enlightened self-interest as a potential ally for conscience in the struggle to maintain respect for the laws and keep passion under control.[25]

Lincoln warned the Lyceum members against the dangers of demagogy, which, as an orthodox Whig, he interpreted as passion writ large. In order to ensure "the perpetuation of our political institutions," it would be necessary to guard against any self-anointed "genius," thirsting for "distinction," who might seek to overturn their balance. Remarkably, he suggested that the vehicle for such a demagogue might be either "emancipating slaves or enslaving freemen." Several shrewd commentators have alerted us to the possibility that Lincoln was sensitive to the danger of demagogy precisely because he was himself a person of such tremendous ambition. This rings true, for it shows how his political ideas were influenced not only by cultural antecedents but also by personal experience that gave them plausibility.[26] In the same speech Lincoln evoked the Whig spirit of cross-generational responsibility. Our inheritance of constitutional liberty must be transmitted "undecayed" out of "gratitude to our fathers, justice to ourselves, duty to posterity, and love for our species in general." Lincoln's deeply felt awe of the Founding Fathers contrasts sharply with his cold relationship toward his natural father; very likely they served as surrogate father figures for him. "Let every man remember that to violate the law is to trample on the blood of his father," he warned his audience of young men. During the years to come Lincoln's most characteristic rhetoric would liken the Union to a family, bound indissolubly together by the most intimate organic bonds, responsible both to the "iron men" of previous generations and to the unborn of future generations. By preserving the Union and expanding its freedom, he probably felt himself becoming a Founding Father in his own right, thus successfully resolving the oedipal tensions betwen his veneration for the founders and his driving ambition, which hinted, that evening in Springfield, at admiration for demagogic genius.[27]

Before Lincoln let the young men of the Lyceum go for the night, he exhorted them to make respect for the law permeate American society until it had wrought the nation's collective redemption:

Let reverence for the laws be breathed by every American mother to the lisping babe that prattles on her lap—let it be taught in schools, in seminaries, and in colleges—let it be written in primers, spelling books, and in almanacs—let it be preached from the pulpit, proclaimed in legislative halls, and enforced in courts of justice.

As rhetoric, this is already worthy of comparison with Webster, though it falls far short of Lincoln's later speeches. As social philosophy, it shows that, like Whigs in general, he placed a high value on influencing public opinion through a variety of means. He retained this focus throughout his career. "Our government rests in public opinion," he told Republicans in 1856. "Whoever can change public opinion can change the government."[28] Public opinion would be the key to Lincoln's campaign against slavery, a campaign he at first thought would take two generations but which in the event (such is the rapidity with which public opinion can move at times) took something like two years.

Lincoln's approach to influencing public opinion was maturing and deepening when he delivered his address to the Springfield Temperance Society on Washington's Birthday, 1842. While the Lyceum address reveals his relationship to the conservative Whig legal theorists, the temperance address shows how much he had in common with Whig modernizers. Lincoln endorsed voluntary abstinence rather than denunciation or prohibition of alcohol, and he quoted the old maxim that "a drop of honey catches more flies than a gallon of gall." His attitude toward alcoholics and saloon-keepers already indicates some of that compassion and absence of self-righteousness for which he was to become famous. The speech places temperance in the context of uplifting, redeeming moral reform, likens it to antislavery, and interprets both movements as fulfilling the promise of the American Revolution. Lincoln's peroration illustrates that glorification of mind over matter and reason over passion so typical of American moral philosophy and Whig modernization: "Happy day, when, all appetites controled [sic], all passions subdued, all matters subjected, *mind*, all conquering *mind*, shall live and move the monarch of the world."[29]

Born in Kentucky and married to a Kentuckian, Abraham Lincoln not surprisingly came under the spell of the great Kentucky Whig, Henry Clay. Lincoln called Clay "my beau ideal of a statesman." After being elected president, he declared, "During my whole political life, I have loved and revered [Clay] as a teacher and leader." Lincoln took Clay as his model in many ways, in statecraft, rhetoric, and balance of character. (Clay "owed his pre-eminence to no one quality, but to a fortunate combination of several," he observed.)[30] An enthusiastic supporter of the "American System," Lincoln labored strenuously for Clay in 1844 and, like many Clay supporters, evinced resentment afterward toward the Liberty Party for having deprived his candidate of victory. When Clay died in 1852, Lincoln delivered what has been judged the most insightful of the host of eulogies. Afterward he sought to portray himself as carrying on Clay's political tradition and appealed to former Clay voters on this basis. In his debates with Douglas in 1858, he invoked Clay no less than forty-one times.[31] Lincoln was by no means a simple disciple of Clay; he refused to support him for the nomination in 1848, feeling that time had passed him by. Sharing Clay's ambition to become president, Lincoln determined not to repeat Clay's mistakes. His extreme reluctance to issue public statements during the months between his nomination at Chicago in 1860 and his inauguration in 1861 may well have been influenced by a desire to avoid Clay's horrendous error of saying too much in 1844. Yet Lincoln's conduct after his inauguration shows a solicitude for the support of the border states—and Kentucky in particular—altogether worthy of an heir of Henry Clay.

An assessment of the influence of Clay Whiggery on Abraham Lincoln should also reckon with Mary Todd Lincoln. Daughter of a prominent Whig family in Lexington, Mary Todd had known Henry Clay personally from childhood. In 1856 she stayed loyal to the southern Whig candidacy of Millard Fillmore when her husband had already become a Republican. This cannot but have impressed him with the necessity to conciliate former Fillmore supporters during his 1860 campaign. Always fascinated by politics, Mary might have taken a more active role in a later day. Her growing mental instability may have been due in part to the constraint of having to invest all her ambitions vicariously in her husband and children. When first one son died and then another, she could not cope with the emotional devastation. After Abraham's murder in 1865 she lost contact with reality.[32]

It has been remarked that Lincoln "left no monument of constructive legislation" when he was in Congress. Actually, during his brief term, he focused on the war issue above all. Lincoln was in the audience at Lexington when Clay delivered his masterful indictment of the Mexican War and no doubt took encouragement from it. Best remembered of Lincoln's antiwar efforts are his "spot resolutions," sardonically questioning whether the spot where the fighting began was indeed, as Polk alleged, *"our own soil."* Even more forceful, however, was the speech he gave in support of the resolution the Whig majority in the House of Representatives passed, condemning the war as unnecessarily and unconstitutionally begun by the president. Drawing on his knowledge as a surveyor to refute administration assertions about the Mexican–United States boundary, Lincoln dismissed Polk's rationalizations for the war as "like half insane mumbling." His sympathy extended to the American men and boys doing the fighting but not to the man responsible in Washington: "The blood of Abel is crying to Heaven against him."[33]

There is no denying the importance of Lincoln's Whiggery for understanding his career, his outlook, and his policies. Even after he became the first Republican president, the Whig tradition stayed with him. Who can read these words of Clay's without thinking of Lincoln?

> Secession is treason; and if it were not—if it were a legitimate and rightful exercise of power—it would be a virtual dissolution of the Union. For if one State may secede, every State may secede.
> ... There are those who think the Union must be preserved and kept together by an exclusive reliance upon love and reason. That is not my opinion. I have some confidence in this instrumentality; but depend upon it, that no human government can exist without the power of applying force.[34]

Lincoln's Whiggery helps explain not only his own response to the secession crisis but that of the seceders as well; for Lincoln, precisely because he was an ex-Whig, posed an internal as well as an external threat to the slave power. By means of patronage and federal economic assistance he could cultivate the nucleus of a Republican party below the Mason-Dixon Line if the South did not seal itself off from such influences by seceding. Former southern Whigs would provide him with the most obvious potential recruits. Southern Whig congressmen had already united with Republicans to elect Pennington of New Jersey as speaker of the House in 1859. The *Richmond Whig* reflected a significant body of opinion, at least in the Upper South, when it declared in the same year that Virginia Whigs would prefer Seward to any Democrat as president.[35] John Brown's raid dealt a setback to such moderation; yet, even after it, Robert Toombs could warn Alexander Stephens that a Republican president would "rear up a free labour party in [the] whole South in four years." (Stephens himself gave Toombs cause for worry. He had decided that the Republican Nathaniel Banks had made a good speaker, and he was well disposed toward Pennington too.)[36]

David Herbert Donald has shown how Lincoln's conduct in the White House can be understood in terms of Whig political principles. Lincoln treated Congress with appropriate Whig deference, using only two vetoes and two pocket vetoes. He appointed a strong cabinet, consisting of politicians powerful in their own right, to whom he entrusted considerable autonomy. This much shows his respect for the "country-party" aspect of the Whig tradition. But Lincoln also exploited his war powers extensively, particularly in dealing with slavery. Here he was indebted to the constitutional precepts of old John Quincy Adams, whose ideas concerning emancipation in wartime had been preserved in Whig circles. Another distinguished historian, Kenneth M. Stampp, has argued that Lincoln's program for postwar Reconstruction can be comprehended in terms of a desire to build a Republican party in the South out of the remains of Whiggery there. Toombs's estimate of Republican intentions, it would seem, was essentially correct.[37]

The potential for examining persistent Whiggery in Lincoln's administration is by no means exhausted yet. In Lincoln's handling of military appointments it is not too much to see a reaction against Polk's transparent attempts to use the Army for partisan advantage. One can also identify the legacy of Whiggery in Lincoln's Indian policies, despite his having served against Black Hawk as a young man. He extended mercy to warriors captured during the Great Sioux Uprising and hoped to Christianize, civilize, elevate, and assimilate the Indians. Recently, a student of the tariff has gone so far as to conclude that Lincoln's adoption of a new party label "ultimately came to little more than relinquishing the beloved name of Whig."[38] In 1864, when Lincoln ran for reelection on a coalition ticket, using the name "Union" instead of "Republican," he was substituting nationalism for partisanship as Whigs had so often done in the past. Unlike Webster in 1852 or Bell in 1860, however, Lincoln made the tactic work.

Yet, for all the Whiggery one can rightly find in Lincoln, the Whig party as such came to an end during his career and was replaced by the Republican party. Through Lincoln's own development we can view, probably better than in any other single person, the transformation of the Whig tradition. The final years of the Whig party constituted an intermission in Lincoln's political career. In company with Alexander Stephens and others, he had secured the Whig nomination in 1848 for Zachary Taylor. However, just as Stephens was disappointed by Taylor's policies, Lincoln was disappointed by his administration of the patronage. Neither he nor the friends he recommended received an appropriate reward for their efforts, perhaps because they had not succeeded in delivering Illinois' electoral votes to the ticket. Lincoln retained his standing in the Whig party, gave a eulogy when Taylor died, and campaigned on behalf of Scott in 1852. But holding neither elective nor appointive office, he seemed likely to spend the rest of his life in the role of a prominent Illinois attorney. When he reemerged to public view, it would be with a different party label and a political identity that was not so much new as transformed. This transformation can best be understood as developing out of the internal logic of Whig values.

There had always been an inherent instability or conflict within Whig political culture, arising out of its twin values of social harmony and social morality. For Lincoln the duality was represented by Henry Clay and John Quincy Adams, respectively. Despite all the Clay influences on Lincoln, when the chips were down in the "great secession winter" he pursued no comprehensive compromise like the one Clay's close associate, John J. Crittenden, was proposing (and which Clay himself would no doubt have supported had he been alive). By this time Lincoln had reached the conclusion that the historical time for compromise had passed and that the South would have to accept the restriction and ultimate extinction of slavery. Beginning with the Kansas-Nebraska Act of 1854, events continually pushed him in the direction of regarding the Union as a means to the end of freedom and, eventually, toward implementing Adams' prophecy of wartime emancipation. His conduct in the 1860s fulfilled the declaration he had made in 1854: "We shall not only have saved the Union; but we shall have so saved it, as to make and to keep it forever worthy of the saving."[39] The rise of the Republican party reflected the rise of the reforming impulse within Whiggery at the expense of its conservative aspect.

The Kansas-Nebraska bill of 1854 was sponsored by Senator Stephen A. Douglas and supported by the Democratic administration of President Franklin Pierce. It repealed the Missouri Compromise and opened the new territories of Kansas and Nebraska to the possibility of slavery if their territorial legislatures chose to allow it. Passed through Congress thanks to the power of patronage to influence northern Democratic votes, the bill carried to their ultimate logic the Jacksonian spoils system and the proslavery Democratic party it had created. It also proved to be one of those acts of hubris by which dominant regimes overreach themselves and bring on their own destruction. The worst fears of antiexecutive, antiparty, anti-spoils-system, anti-popular-sovereignty, anti-slavery-extension Whigs had come to pass. By repealing the Missouri Compromise in order to secure a route for a transcontinental railroad, Douglas had shown his typically Democratic preference for quantitative extension over qualitative improvement. His act defied everything northern Whiggery stood for: respect for precedent, redemption of the frontier, the development of a diversified social and economic order, the dignity of labor, and the hope of self-improvement. But when northern public opinion mobilized against the bill, the Whig party proved an inadequate vehicle for the resistance.

Why did the angry northern response to the Kansas-Nebraska Act not lead to a revival in the fortunes of the Whig party? Michael Holt has made a major contribution to answering this important question by pointing out that many working-class Protestants had already deserted the Whig party for the Native Americans in reaction to the flood of Irish refugee immigrants. Middle-class northern Whigs, responsive to moral issues and never overly devoted to their party organization, proved willing to cooperate with anti-Nebraska Democrats and form a new party dedicated to the restriction of slavery. Wealthy Whigs, cautious as people with much to save always are, seem to have clung the longest to the shreds of Whiggery.[40]

However, though the ethnic resentments of the 1850s were important in determining the process by which the Whig party disappeared, in the end the nativists rejoined the former Whigs in the Republican party. To understand more fully why it was the Republican and not the Whig party that emerged from the turmoil, we must take account of changes in northern political consciousness. Republicanism expressed a new, or rather a transformed, northern political culture. The new party represented a distillation of certain components already present in the political culture of northern Whiggery. In many ways it was an intensified version of northern middle-class Whiggery, unashamedly sectional and freed from the impurities of compromise. If southern Whigs were to join, they would have to do so on Republican terms. The older generation of Whig compromisers had passed; no one of the stature of Clay or Webster was left to continue their efforts. Even if there had been, it is unlikely that he could have overcome the cultural polarization taking place. While proslavery ideas of the "positive-good" variety gained ground in the South, a corresponding commitment to free labor was emerging in the North, synthesizing moral values and economic interests, as powerful value systems always do.[41] The Republican party widened its appeal beyond the middle class by freeing itself of much of the old Whig elitism and by endorsing homesteads and a protective tariff, measures attractive to many working-class voters in the North. Before long, most of the northern nativists rejoined the former Whigs in the new party, "Jonathans" leading the "Sams." Though not avowedly anti-Catholic, the Republicans remained largely non-Catholic because of their reputation as friends of public education and the black man.

The organization of the Republicans and their rapid rise to the status of a major party left Whig conservatives in the North temporarily as isolated and confused as Whig conservatives in the South. Members of the old business and political Whig elite had always depended on moral and ethnic appeals to reach out for a mass following. Now that these appeals had been preempted by the Republicans and nativists, the conservatives found themselves with little constituency left. Some of them, like Choate, went over to the Democrats, while others, like Josiah Quincy, strung along with the new party. Still others, like Edward Everett, maintained their bonds with southern Whigs to the last by supporting John Bell's presidential campaign in 1860. Not until after secession did the dispirited conservatives rally once again with enthusiasm, this time to support the war for the Union.[42]

The Kansas-Nebraska Act brought Lincoln back to active political involvement. Surveying the American political scene in August, 1855, with the Great Plains opened up to slavery and nativism on the rise, he judged that "our progress in degeneracy appears to me to be pretty rapid." His hero Clay's expectation of voluntary emancipation in the South had proved delusive, and Lincoln ruefully concluded that "there is no peaceful extinction of slavery in prospect for us."[43] Kansas-Nebraska outraged Lincoln's Whig sense of history as progress. He explained repeatedly to Illinois audiences (the text of the Peoria address being the one that survives) the historical background and how the Act betrayed the expectation that slavery was being restricted in preparation for its ultimate extinction. A reversal of history, it was also a reversal of the process of national redemption: "it hath no relish of salvation in it." Only a political reformation that would revive the faith of the Founding Fathers could save the country now. "Our republican robe is soiled and trailed in the dust. Let us re-purify it. Let us turn and wash it white, in the spirit, if not the blood, of the Revolution."[44]

The call for reformation was typically Whig, yet the prospect of reformation within the Whig party as then constituted seemed dim. The mobilization of northern opposition to the extension of slavery could not be contained within the framework of sectional harmony and compromise that the Whig leaders had constructed. These were times, not merely of political, but of cultural strain. Lincoln voiced the widespread confusion: "I think I am a whig; but others say there are no whigs, and that I am an abolitionist." Yet there were some things of which he was certain. "I am not a Know-Nothing. . . . How can anyone who abhors the oppression of negroes, be in favor of degrading classes of white people?" and he abhorred Kansas-Nebraska from the depths of his soul: "I look upon that enactment not as a *law*, but as *violence* from the beginning. It was conceived in violence, passed in violence, is maintained in violence, and is being executed in violence." This was the strongest condemnation his profoundly legal mind could have conceived.[45]

When men like Lincoln and Seward decided that a second American revolution was necessary to prevent the strangulation of freedom, Whiggery was doomed. By early 1856 Lincoln was helping to organize the Republican party in Illinois. The Whigs had been preoccupied with a classical conception of politics that defined the task as the *preservation* of a republic through mixed and balanced government. Now the Republicans were declaring that the republic had already been subverted by a slave-power conspiracy and that only a revolution (a constitutional one, to be sure) could restore the intentions of the founders. The answering Confederate revolution—secession—would kill the southern Whig party in the winter of 1860–61. North or South, the Whig party could not survive the demise of its hopes for continuity and orderly progress, centrally directed.

When Lincoln and the other Republicans spoke of "revolution," they had in mind a transformation of public opinion. Thus, Lincoln could refer to "the temperance revolution." Through public opinion one could, at least in the long run, change anything in a democracy. To make their revolution against slavery succeed, Republicans did not have to convince the northern public that slavery was wrong; most northerners were probably already convinced of this. The trouble was that the evil seemed remote and its solution hardly urgent.[46] The Whig party had been viable as long as northern antislavery feeling had been carefully excluded from the political arena. The Republican party was born in a dedication to freedom for all the territories, a principle that could not be compromised if the party was to survive. The task of the new Republicans was to convince northerners that slavery was an important issue, requiring that political steps be taken promptly to halt its spread. The task was parallel to that of the evangelists, who also tried to get people to take seriously what they were already willing to admit if pressed. Of course Republicans did not limit themselves to moral appeals; they invoked the whole range of human motivations, including self-interest and sentiment, which faculty psychology and the principles of rhetoric had so well prepared them to exploit.

The difference between Republicanism and Whiggery was one of degree rather than direction. Free soil was not a novel position for northern Whigs; Daniel Webster had enunciated it as early as 1837 ("I frankly avow my entire unwillingness to do any thing that shall extend the slavery of the African race on this continent, or add other slaveholding States to the Union").[47] Whigs resisting the annexation of Texas had done so in terms sounding much like those of later Republicans. In fact, Lincoln had been among them. Yet he had also remarked that he "never was much interested in the Texas question," and there one sees the Whig, not the Republican. Once Lincoln had become a Republican, he would never talk that way.[48] Joshua Giddings had been a Whig who felt an irrepressible zeal to halt the expansion of slavery, and he gave up on the Whig party in 1848. When Lincoln reemerged into public life as a Republican in 1854, he remembered Giddings (his messmate during the time both were in Congress) and started catching up with him. Like Giddings, Lincoln reconciled his hatred for slavery with his dedication to legal tradition by concluding that the Founding Fathers had written a freedom-loving Constitution that corrupt successors were perverting into a proslavery instrument. In later years Giddings advised Lincoln to take Adams rather than Clay as his model, and Lincoln assured him, "If I fail, it will be for lack of *ability*, and not of *purpose*." Once the war began, Giddings was among those who recurred to Adams' opinion that the military powers of the presidency could be used to achieve emancipation.[49]

Of course, the very willingness of Whigs to leave their party in response to pressing issues was characteristic Whig behavior. "Party is properly only a means to an end, and is really valuable—nay, is only justifiable—when it is employed on behalf of the country," the *American Review* had affirmed in 1848.[50] It is no accident that the major party to permanently dissolve during the crisis of the 1850s was the one that set less store by its own existence. The disposition of so many Democrats to put party regularity and concern for office ahead of concern with issues explains why their party was slower to be disrupted by slavery and was ultimately able to put its pieces back together. Even in its disintegration, the Whig party demonstrated the antiparty tradition with which it had begun. The Republicans would come to show a stronger sense of organizational loyalty, typified in the nickname "Grand Old Party."

The Republicans became a party unambiguously in support of modernization. The old Whig political culture had been an unstable compound of modernization with paternalism, exemplified in Nathan Appleton. The new party of Abraham Lincoln left paternalism behind. Where the Whigs had supported mixed public-private monopolies, the Republicans endorsed free enterprise aided by subsidies. Where the Whigs had desired to redeem the West out of fear of it, the Republicans desired to redeem it out of hope. Like many other former Whigs, Lincoln reversed his previous opposition to free land for homesteaders. The Republicans wholeheartedly endorsed the settlement of the West, even while opposing the renewed imperialistic designs of the Democrats on more of Latin America. The old hierarchical idea of a harmony of interests between classes was not encouraged by the Republicans. Instead they argued that America ought to become a classless society, in which individual initiative and hard work received their just reward when the laborer became a capitalist in his own right. To some extent the ideal already existed: "The man who labored for another last year, this year labors for himself," Lincoln declared, proud of his own success. "Next year he will hire others to labor for him."[51]

Although the belief in social mobility would become a deceptive rationalization for industrial exploitation, in its inception it was chiefly an intellectual and moral weapon against the slave-labor system. This was not a matter of asserting the dignity of black people so much as asserting the dignity of work and working people. Seward called "the irrepressible conflict" a class rather than a racial conflict.

"There is no negro question about it at all. It is an eternal question between classes—between the few privileged and the many under-privileged."[52] If the Republicans' revolution was capitalistic, it was a progressive, energetic, and even democratic form of capitalism that they asserted.

As a political strategist, Lincoln wanted to keep most of the old Whig voting bloc within the Republican fold while attracting enough former Democrats to give the new party a majority throughout the North. The strategy relied on the peculiarity of the Electoral College: if a presidential candidate could carry a solid North, he would need no support at all in the South. A few votes of northern "cotton Whigs" could be sacrificed to the plan, but not many. "Nine tenths of the Anti-Nebraska votes have to come from old Whigs," he estimated. In 1856 he supported Supreme Court Justice John McLean as the presidential candidate most likely to achieve Republican ends. The nomination went instead to the more "radical" John C. Frémont, and a small but critical number of northerners voted for the "cotton Whig" Fillmore. Thereafter Lincoln continued to identify the Republican party as the inheritor of Whiggery and to explain his objectives in such a way that conservative Whigs would not be alienated. He had had long practice in this art. "We [Whigs] gained our only national victory," that of Harrison, "by falling in company with [abolitionists]," he had reminded a cautious conservative in the campaign of 1848. Progressive in his intentions, Lincoln was in practice a centrist within the context of the Republican party, much as Lyman Beecher had been both a progressive and an ecumenicist within the evangelical movement.[53]

The relationship between Republicanism and earlier Whig culture can be approached through Lincoln's oratory. The greatest of our antebellum political orators, Lincoln has seldom been studied in terms of this tradition. However, Jacques Barzun has correctly identified Lincoln as a man whose power over others derived from his power over words. He truly exemplified the rhetorician as a leader, a mediator between words and actions. Even during his first term in the Illinois legislature, his Whig colleagues would borrow his literary skill to help prepare their speeches and bills. From the beginning, the mastery of words was an important part of his definition of himself. "He didn't like physical labor, [but] he read all the books he could lay his hands on," his stepmother recalled. "When he came across a passage that struck him he would write it down on boards if he had no paper and keep it there until he did get paper, then he would rewrite it, look at it, repeat it."[54]

The foundation of Lincoln's speaking and writing ability was laid, as it is in most cases, by his reading. Growing up in an environment where books were scarce and literacy was a skill difficult to acquire, Lincoln took the act of reading seriously. His mental development was nurtured by the literary staples of that same tradition of English Dissent that produced the "country party" in politics: Bunyan's *Pilgrim's Progress*, Defoe's *Robinson Crusoe*, Franklin's *Autobiography*, Aesop's *Fables*, Watts's *Hymns*, and, of course, the King James Bible. The spartan austerity, strength, and utilitarianism of the Puritan aesthetic remained powerful influences on Lincoln's own rhetoric. In youth he was also captivated by the didactic, quasi-mythological *Life of George Washington* by Mason Weems and the *Life of Patrick Henry* by William Wirt. Later in life, when confronted with James Prior's *Life and Character of Edmund Burke*, he became justifiably suspicious of such hagiography.[55]

For Lincoln, as for so many other Whigs, reading was generally undertaken in a spirit of severe self-discipline; it was an act of education and self-improvement. Just as the elder statesman John Quincy Adams read Cicero to find a rhetorical model, Abraham Lincoln studied Euclid while in Congress, seeking to achieve comparable demonstrative rigor in his own expositions. Since Lincoln's reading usually belonged in the category of work rather than recreation, it partook of the dignity of work. Though most law students read with the guidance of a practicing attorney, Lincoln was proud to have prepared for the bar on his own, mastering Blackstone's *Commentaries* as his foundation. Being a lawyer and politician, he of course kept abreast of current events in the press. He probably shared the indifference to novels so common among serious-minded Americans of his day, although he could relax with humorists like Petroleum V. Nasby. As everyone knows from the tragic circumstances of his death, Lincoln loved to attend the theater, despite the fact that the theater was by no means altogether respectable at the time.[56]

A person who chose his own words with the greatest care, Lincoln not surprisingly admired the poet's art. He was fond of Byron, Burns, Gray, and some of the nineteenth-century sentimentalists, such as Longfellow and Holmes. "Mortality," a rhymed meditation on Ecclesiastes and Job by the minor Scottish poet William Knox, he especially loved and committed to memory. Its theme of fatalistic resignation struck a responsive chord in the often melancholy Lincoln.[57] Shakespeare also appealed to Lincoln's high sense of tragedy and his feeling for noble oratory; often he carried a copy of the plays in his pocket, and in the White House he would frequently read aloud or recite from memory soliloquies from the great tragedies, adding interpretive comments for the benefit of his listeners. On occasion he grappled with his moods and fears by writing poetry himself. After visiting a childhood friend who had become insane, he composed thirteen stanzas beginning: "But here's an object more of dread / Than aught the grave contains, / A human form with reason fled, / While wretched life remains." What indeed could be more horrifying than insanity to one who prized rationality and self-control?[58]

Like his reading, Lincoln's writing and speaking were highly disciplined. Remarkably, his smattering of schooling supplemented by resolute independent study provided a sound basis in rhetorical theory, as the editor of his works, Roy P. Basler, has proved. William Scott's *Lessons in Elocution*, Samuel Kirkham's *English Grammar in Familiar Lectures*, and Hugh Blair's classic *Lectures on Rhetoric and Belles Lettres* were the authorities he made his own. Their structural formalism, which nevertheless recognized the power of the emotions, appealed to his nature. Edmund Wilson has commented that Lincoln's oratorical style was "inseparable from his personality in all of its manifestations." Through controlling words, Lincoln exercised control over himself. His great political oratory, like his mediocre verse, strove for balance, clarity, and calm forcefulness. We know from the fragments of drafts that have survived that Lincoln would write and rewrite many times in order to find just the right words with which to express himself. Often he was at great pains to achieve precision, as in his famous distinctions between slavery itself and the extension of it, or between his public duty as president and his personal wish that all men should be free.[59]

Lincoln was familiar with the published speeches of both Clay and Webster, and the two Whig orators fascinated him in many ways. He modeled himself upon them and measured himself against them; his friends compared him with them, and his adversaries accused him of misusing their ideas.[60] The influence of Clay, a fellow Kentuckian, has been more widely appreciated than that of Webster. In his youth, Lincoln generally followed the example of Clay's oratory, but he occasionally resorted to a florid rhetoric reminiscent of Webster: "The great volcano at Washington, aroused and directed by the evil spirit that reigns there [Democratic President Martin Van Buren], is belching forth the lava of political corruption." As he matured and found his true literary style, he forged what was really a synthesis of Clay's frontier utilitarianism with Webster's genteel cadences. During the campaign of 1856, when he was trying to undercut the appeal

of Fillmore, Lincoln was particularly given to quoting Webster. Once
a hostile newspaper accused him of plagiarizing from the New Englander.[61] Clay always spoke on behalf of a practical objective; but
Lincoln, like Webster, sometimes placed his oratory at the service of
occasions like memorials or dedications. Even in Lincoln's greatest
masterpieces of eloquence the influence of Webster can be found.
Compare this address, delivered by Webster at Valley Forge, with
Lincoln's at Gettysburg:

> By the blood of our fathers, which cries to us from this hallowed
> ground, by the memory of their many virtues and brilliant
> achievements, by the sad story of their intense sufferings, by the
> blessing of that blood-bought inheritance of liberty which they
> suffered and died to obtain for us, we are called upon to perform
> the important duty that lies before us. . . .

If Lincoln did not have Webster's text at hand when he was contemplating his own address, the diction, the rhythms, and the moral
itself must already have been impressed upon his consciousness.[62]

Between the two common modes of Whig oratory we have identified, the "forensic" and the "inoffensive," Lincoln gravitated most
naturally to the former. His legal training led directly into it. The
preliminary review of history to establish precedents and trends, the
call to resist the adversary, the use of interrogatories and summa-
tions, all are typical of Lincoln's forensic oratory. Some of his
speeches, such as the Springfield-Peoria address of 1854 and the
House Divided address of 1858, are classics of the genre. On the
other hand, he was slow to develop an "inoffensive" mode. He
owned the works of William Ellery Channing, its prime clerical
exemplar, but the volumes show no sign of use. Prompted by
secretary-designate Seward, however, Lincoln added to his First Inaugural Address this famous invocation of sentiment on behalf of
harmony: "Though passion may have strained, it must not break our
bonds of affection. The mystic chords of memory, stretching from
every battle-field and patriot grave to every living heart and hearth-
stone, all over this broad land, will yet swell the chorus of the
Union, when again touched, as surely they will be, by the better
angels of our nature." Thereafter, Lincoln used the inoffensive mode
as one of his most powerful rhetorical instruments.[63]

Contemporary accounts indicate that Lincoln lacked the enthrall-
ing stage presence of Webster, Clay, or Lyman Beecher. Particularly
in the early years, he displayed awkwardness when speaking in
public. To hold the attention of his audience, he had to rely, like

Horace Greeley, more on the content of his words than on impressive delivery.[64] He turned this necessity to such advantage that the power of his speeches endures in print. Nevertheless, it is no disparagement of Lincoln to observe that, like other orators and leaders, he was something of a role-player and possessed a sense of the dramatic. His role-playing extended beyond the podium to his whole public career. The self-made man, the re-founding father, the Great Emancipator, even the martyr—these roles were self-consciously originated and profoundly enacted on the stage of history, not simply read into his actions later, by his followers. "He created himself as a poetic figure, and he thus imposed himself on the nation."[65]

Lincoln's dramatic insight that the Kansas-Nebraska Act marked a momentous reversal of federal policy regarding the extension of slavery was confirmed after four years by the Supreme Court's decision in *Dred Scott* v. *Sanford*. Democratic Chief Justice Roger B. Taney, delivering the majority opinion, held that Congress possessed no power to prohibit slavery in the territories because to do so deprived the slave-owner of property without "due process of law," as guaranteed by the Fifth Amendment to the federal Constitution. The opinion contravened a practice as old as the republic, erred in the historical facts it involved, and interpreted "due process" in a way altogether novel. The justices divided on partisan grounds; six Democrats made up the majority, a Whig and a Republican dissented, and an appointee of John Tyler found against Scott on the narrow grounds that his state's supreme court had already ruled against him. Obviously, Republicans could not accept the *Dred Scott* decision as final, for it would deprive their party of its very reason for being. Because Taney and the concurring justices mentioned several reasons for ruling against Scott, many Republicans claimed that the sweeping invalidation of territorial free soil constituted only a legal *dictum* and not a binding precedent. Thus they avoided being placed in a position of defying the law. In the long run, of course, their main hope lay in electing a Republican president who would reconstitute the Supreme Court.[66]

In 1858 Lincoln received the Republican nomination for the U.S. Senate. He wanted very much to be a senator; it was the natural ambition for an aspiring orator. As Stephen Oates has observed, "All of Lincoln's talents seemed to put him in the Senate—his literary gifts, his love of rational debate, of delivering logical and eloquent speeches from a prepared script." Lincoln had narrowly lost a Senate seat in 1855 when the anti-Nebraska Democrats refused to support such a longtime Whig as he. Accordingly, he had given way to one of them. It had not been easy to sacrifice his personal ambition for the sake of the cause, but he did it. Now he had a second chance. Some out-of-state Republicans, however, were questioning the wisdom of running a candidate against the incumbent, Stephen Douglas. Douglas had fallen out with the Democratic administration over the proposed Lecompton Constitution that would turn Kansas into a slave state against what everyone knew were the wishes of a majority of her people. Lincoln had to show that Douglas still could not be trusted, that there was no substitute for moral reprobation of slavery, that the Republicans needed a candidate of their own, and that he was that man.[67] He rose to the occasion at the Republican state convention with his House Divided speech.

"A house divided against itself cannot stand." The quotation is from Christ (Mark 3:25, slightly adapted), but Lincoln could have picked it up through Daniel Webster, who had used it in a speech of 1851. As a Puritan preacher would have done, Lincoln drew out the moral of his biblical text and applied it to the situation of his own distracted people. "This government cannot endure, permanently half *slave* and half *free*. I do not expect the Union to be *dissolved*—I do not expect the house to *fall*—but I *do* expect it will cease to be divided. It will become *all* one thing, or *all* the other."[68] Seward reached a similar conclusion in his Irrepressible Conflict speech the same year. Like the first American Revolution, the second fed upon a fear of encroaching enslavement.

Belief in moral homogeneity as the only utlimate safeguard of social stability had a long tradition among Whigs; in this sense there is a continuity between antislavery, anti-Catholic, and other evangelical or didactic impulses. However, Republicans like Lincoln and Seward were taking a step beyond Whiggery. The antislavery Whigs had typically believed in the "good slaveholder," a white southerner who could be persuaded (if one were persistent and gentle enough) that emancipation would be for the best. Now this hope was gone. Rather than just a few especially wicked slaveholders, the Republicans felt that they faced a hostile solid bloc of slaveholders.[69] As a result, they redefined their objectives, moving from moral suasion to political mobilization. Instead of trying to win over the South, they wrote it off and concentrated on public opinion in the North. The North, not the South, was where they expected their "revolution" to take place.

Republicans still conceptualized the slave power as a form of conspiracy, even though they recognized that it was far stronger and more pervasive than Whigs had previously supposed. Lincoln employed the conspiracy paradigm in his House Divided speech:

When we see a lot of framed timbers, different portions of which we know have been gotten out at different times and places and by different workmen—Stephen, Franklin, Roger, and James, for instance—and when we see these timbers joined together, and see they exactly make the frame of a house or a mill... we find it impossible to not *believe* that Stephen and Franklin and Roger and James all understood one another from the beginning, and all worked upon a common *plan* or *draft*.

This was the same teleological mode of argument that Lyman Beecher had employed when he inferred the existence of a Catholic conspiracy to propagandize America. Lincoln probably acquired this method of reasoning from natural theology, as Beecher had, for he was an interested student of both Christian and deist works on that subject. He realized that the evidence for conspiracy was indirect ("we cannot absolutely *know*"), yet he found it persuasive ("we find it impossible not to *believe*").[70]

How far was Lincoln justified in drawing his inference that Stephen (Douglas), Franklin (Pierce), Roger (Taney), and James (Buchanan) shared a common purpose? Don Fehrenbacher has pointed out that "in the setting of 1858, the charge carried conviction." He goes on to explain how Douglas' doctrine of squatter sovereignty, by leaving the slavery question to the territorial legislatures, fostered indifference to slavery as a national question. Anesthetizing northern morality, Douglas' position might plausibly be seen as dovetailing with the objectives of the slavery expansionists.[71] One can carry Fehrenbacher's line of argument further: not only were the free-soilers worried; they had grounds for worry. It was in fact the case, as Lincoln charged, that popular sovereignty had been exploited by those seeking the expansion of slavery. Douglas had carefully worded the Kansas-Nebraska bill so that it could command support not only from believers in popular sovereignty as such but also from southerners who claimed what Taney would later affirm, that the Constitution carried slavery into the territories. Douglas rejected an amendment that would have embarrassed this coalition by clarifying the meaning of popular sovereignty. He also maintained that the Missouri Compromise had been unconstitutional.[72] We have already seen how Alexander Stephens found Douglas' popular sovereignty a congenial political strategy for advancing the interests of slavery within the Union. Lincoln was doing no more than calling attention to a mutuality of interest between popular sovereignty and the slave power that Douglas and Stephens had long perceived and made the basis of their statecraft.

In a general way, the coalition between popular sovereignty and slavery expansionism had been fundamental to the Democratic party ever since the Lewis Cass campaign of 1848. Yet the coalition had been less than candid with the public. Its policy was termed congressional "nonintervention" in the territories as a way of obscuring the question of whether slavery was to be left to the settlers or to the Constitution as interpreted by the courts. Douglas' arguments on behalf of Kansas-Nebraska had been full of misrepresentations. Franklin Pierce endorsed this ambiguous "nonintervention" and then watched while it led to a guerrilla war in Kansas.[73] The "conspiracy" Lincoln protested, using the word in its broad, old-fashioned sense, had existed on a very large scale for a very long time, though it was finally in the process of breaking down, now that Douglas and Buchanan were at loggerheads. As for *Dred Scott*, behind that decision lay something more like a "conspiracy" in our own restricted sense—a concealed, illegitimate transaction among a few individuals in high places. President-elect James Buchanan had secretly conferred with justices of the Supreme Court on the case, had persuaded the northern Democratic Justice Grier to go along with the majority, and already knew what the forthcoming decision would be when, in his Inaugural Address, he urged the nation to accept it cheerfully, "whatever it might be."[74]

Lincoln warned that the next step in the unraveling of American freedom might well be "another Supreme Court decision, declaring that the Constitution of the United States does not permit a *state* to exclude slavery from its limits." Historians have customarily dismissed this possibility as imaginary, though only one more step in Taney's constitutional interpretation could have effected it: a ruling that the Fifth Amendment was binding on the states. Chief Justice Marshall had held otherwise in *Barron* v. *Baltimore* (1833), but a court that had produced so startling an opinion as *Dred Scott* could hardly be trusted not to overturn *Barron*. Indeed, in the *Scott* case itself, it had been held that residence in the free state of Illinois no more freed the plaintiff than had his residence in the Louisiana Purchase.[75] For his part, Lincoln desired the closing of the territories to slavery as a cautious first step toward the ultimate extinction of the institution. He was alert to the danger of the nationalization of slavery for the same reason that Lyman Beecher could recognize the Catholic ambition to propagandize America: because it was the converse of his own intentions. Since he knew that his program for the territories implied a judgment on slavery in general, it would have been only natural for Lincoln to conclude that his adversaries' policies for the territories also indicated their long-range plans for the nation.

The logic of Lincoln's and Douglas' positions on slavery in the territories unfolded in their great debates of 1858. Douglas' fame and Lincoln's insistence on challenging him focused nationwide attention on the debates. During the campaign, journalists followed the two candidates about, reporting their speeches to the newspapers. The whole situation was virtually unprecedented; for in that day state legislatures chose U.S. senators, party conventions did not usually nominate senatorial candidates, as Lincoln had been nominated, and the candidates themselves did not usually campaign openly for the election of legislators pledged to support them. Douglas considered the important issue confronting the American people to be westward expansion; slavery was a mere distraction. He occasionally acknowledged slavery to be an evil, but he seemed willing to wait indefinitely for some undefined providential deliverance from it, rather like an Old School Calvinist contemplating the millennium. Lincoln's policy, on the other hand, was (in Harry Jaffa's words) "a denial that things would take care of themselves, that progress would result from anything but man's foresight, judgment, and courage." He believed as a Republican, just as he had believed when a Whig, that social progress must be guided and controlled.[76] The styles of the debaters provided as much contrast as the substance of their policies: Lincoln, the more reflective of the two, exploiting humor to underscore his logic as Webster had once used sentiment; Douglas, the more combative, shamelessly inflaming racial hatred. The campaign marked another stage in Lincoln's learning to put his political ambition to constructive use in the service of his cause. He lost the Senate race but mastered his disappointment and remained politically active. The debates established Lincoln as a political figure of national stature while isolating Douglas from the possibility of coalition with either Republicans or southern Democrats. Thus they laid the foundation for Lincoln's election as president over Douglas two years later—the election that provoked secession. Truly, "it would be difficult to find in all history a precise instance in which rhetoric played a more important role in human destiny."[77]

The issues between Lincoln and Douglas were not identical with those that had separated Whigs from Jacksonians. The new party system revealed a recombination of the cultural elements that had made up the old one. Douglas Democrats had come to endorse economic development, while Republicans now endorsed the westward movement and had lost interest in the old Whig "mixed" corporations. On strictly economic issues there was little difference between them, save for the tariff.[78] It was in the politicomoral realm that Lincoln and Douglas fought out their differences. During the course of the campaign, Lincoln developed a distinctive Republican political philosophy, which he continued to elaborate in the year and a half that followed. This philosophy transcended old Whiggery by synthesizing it with elements from Jacksonian political thought. Alexander Stephens had also synthesized Whiggery with Democratic beliefs, but he took over the worst side of Jacksonianism, the commitment to white supremacy. Lincoln took over what was best in Jacksonian Democracy: the commitment to the rights of the common man.

The Republicans consciously revived the memory of the first American Revolution and selected a name for themselves that laid claim to the heritage of Thomas Jefferson. By demanding a new birth of freedom, they strongly implied that one of those rare moments of constituent power had arrived—a cultural crossroads where the nation's destiny would be reshaped. The Declaration of Independence became a focus of concern not only for "radicals" like Giddings but also for Lincoln. Through the debates with Douglas and his other speeches, Lincoln sought to restore the Declaration to a central place in the public mind. He called the ideals of the Declaration "apples of gold" in "pictures of silver," a reference to Proverbs 25:11 he had picked up from Alexander Stephens. He felt those ideals defined the ends of national existence, toward which the Constitution and the Union were means. John Quincy Adams had reached the same conclusion.[79]

In Chicago, at the beginning of his campaign against Douglas, Lincoln traced the Whig interpretation of history and found that it led back to the expectation of the Founding Fathers that slavery was destined for ultimate extinction. "Let us then turn this government back into the channel in which the framers of the Constitution originally placed it," he urged. Many free-soilers had long been calling for just such a "cultural purge" of corruption (Giddings among them), but no one had expressed it so effectively as Lincoln. It was a line of argument he repeated time and again, most notably in his address at the Cooper Institute in New York, where he boldly challenged Seward on his home ground for the Republican presidential nomination in 1860.[80] The Republicans' Whiggish use of Burkean methods was leading them back to the Lockean principles of the Declaration. Through their examination of history, ironically, they were rediscovering the antehistorical state of nature Locke had described. Lincoln explained that the new territories of the West were still in a "state of nature" and that it would therefore be criminal to introduce slavery into them as the British had once introduced it into the colonies. With their new emphasis on Locke and natural rights, the Republicans were moving away from the adulation of Burke that had characterized the Whigs. Seward, for example, declared in 1856 (contrary to both Burke and Choate): "The maxim that a sacred veil must be drawn over the beginning of all governments does not hold under our system."[81]

The Republicans' use of the Declaration of Independence looked forward in time as well as backward. In Lincoln's reinterpretation of Jefferson, "the proposition that all men are created equal" became a positive goal for political action, not simply a prepolitical state that government should preserve by inaction. The principles of the Declaration were to be "constantly looked to, constantly labored for, and even though never perfectly attained, constantly approximated." Lincoln explained equality, John P. Diggins has pointed out, "as a moral imperative rather than as a scientific postulate." Lincoln could exhort his followers to the application of natural rights by using biblical rhetoric: "As your Father in Heaven is perfect, be ye also perfect." Truly, he had synthesized Whiggery and Democracy in his concept of an equality that was as much a *duty* of the community as a *right* of the individual and as much the end product of historical striving as a condition preceding history.[82]

Lincoln's idea of equality was closely connected with property and work. Equality meant, in the first instance, an equal opportunity to work for a living and an equal right to retain the fruits of one's labor. This was clearly incompatible with slavery. Lincoln avoided both the Jacksonian zero-sum game (seeing one person's gain as another's loss) and Whiggish condescension. In place of these alternatives, he glorified upward social mobility and made himself its greatest archetype. "Improvement in condition is the order of things in a society of equals." The statement sounds paradoxical to us, but to Lincoln it seemed logical enough. It also had the advantage of appealing to both the native-born and the immigrant worker. "Whatever is calculated to advance the condition of the honest, struggling laboring man," he told a group of immigrants, "I am for that thing."[83]

Arguments such as these, emphasizing the dignity of labor and the rights of the common workingman, seem to have been important in expanding the attractiveness of the new Republican party during the 1850s. The last Whig presidential campaign, Winfield Scott's in 1852, anticipated some later Republican appeals because of the influence of Seward. The new party made these appeals more effective in 1856, when the Frémont campaign wrote off the South and improved on

Scott's showing in the Electoral College. The emphasis on the workingman recovered most of the antiimmigrant labor vote the Whig party had lost to the nativists, while also winning over certain immigrant voters (notably Germans) from the Democrats. During the following years the Republicans picked up enough strength beyond their natural base in antislavery Whiggery to make the Electoral College work for them. One of the crucial states was Pennsylvania, where the tariff was important; another was Illinois—to the advantage of the rising orator who made that state his home. Historians have argued over how much of the Republicans' strength came from old Whigs and how much from Democratic converts. The truth is that the Republicans needed most northern ex-Whigs plus a critical minority of ex-Democrats—which is just what they got.[84]

Lincoln's policies on race illustrate concretely that process of groping and striving by which he believed equal rights were gradually implemented. His point of departure was the colonization program of Henry Clay's American System. During the 1840s Lincoln had been active in the Illinois State Colonization Society. He felt, as Clay did, that slavery was evil but that amicable cooperation between the races was unlikely. It followed that peaceful separation was the ideal solution. In the meantime, he frankly acknowledged, it would be just as well if his own race occupied the "superior position" in society. When Clay died, Lincoln singled out the fallen leader's contributions to the colonization movement for the climax of his eulogy.[85]

By the 1850s the practicality of colonization as an acceptable resolution of the American race problem seemed increasingly doubtful, yet Lincoln endorsed it at Springfield in 1858 and, after becoming president, made a serious effort to implement Clay's old program of gradual, compensated emancipation, to be followed by deportation of the freedpeople. He considered trying the program out in Delaware first, on an experimental basis. But the border-state politicians with whom he tried to work were paralyzed, unable to face the crisis, and threw away what proved to be their last chance of compensation for emancipation. When a conference between Lincoln and black leaders in 1862 failed to elicit much support for colonization in the black community, the idea was doomed. Two small colonization projects, one in Panama and one in Haiti, received serious consideration; but only the latter was attempted, and it ended in failure.[86]

Immediate political and military realities conditioned Lincoln's racial policies even more directly than his respect for Clay's teachings. Early in his presidency Lincoln was motivated primarily by the need to contain the secession movement. Having lost the Upper South after the clash at Sumter, he was determined not to lose the remaining loyal border states. Bold actions against slavery were incompatible with this strategy. Hence he countermanded the local emancipation proclamations of Generals Frémont and Hunter. Once the strategic situation permitted it, however, Lincoln moved to issue an emancipation proclamation of his own. He based it on the war powers of the commander-in-chief to which Adams had called attention so long before. After the proclamation had been planned but before it was made public, Lincoln dispatched an open letter to Greeley, insisting that his racial policies were entirely dictated by a desire to save the Union. No doubt the president felt this would cast his coming proclamation in terms as noncontroversial as possible for so momentous an action. Greeley had been urging emancipation, and Lincoln probably relished the opportunity to slap at a gadfly who had often annoyed him, beginning with the time Greeley had suggested that the Republicans not oppose Douglas in 1858. But the military aspect of the proclamation was not merely northern public relations, nor was it a constitutional ruse. Lincoln's action served a genuine military objective by encouraging large-scale slave desertion of plantations, a process we now know was seriously weakening the Confederacy from within.[87] By exempting areas already occupied by Union forces, Lincoln avoided antagonizing loyal whites there or creating disruptions behind his armies' lines. Despite his caution, however, heavy Republican losses in the 1862 midterm elections showed how unpopular the Emancipation Proclamation was with many northern voters.

Apart from the strong influence of Clay and the constraints of politicomilitary strategy, what purposes lay behind Lincoln's racial policies? We may be sure that he really hated slavery and welcomed the opportunity to end it, but the extent to which he would have been willing to accept black-white equality is unclear. Probably his views changed over time, and this compounds the difficulty of analyzing them. In the campaign against Douglas he insisted on equal rights to the fruits of one's labor but drew the line at political or social equality. Before his death, his evolving consciousness had been raised to the point where he advocated voting for some, though not all, black men.[88] Another interpretive difficulty arises from the fact that most of Lincoln's statements on race were defensive disclaimers, in which he stated "the *maximum* that he was willing to deny the Negro and the *minimum* that he claimed for the Negro." Lincoln lived among a people deeply prejudiced, and it would be quite unhistorical to imagine that he could altogether escape this influence. On the other hand, his acute self-awareness and desire to subordinate the aspects of his personality he did not approve may well have "made it possible for him to control his prejudices precisely because he acknowledged their existence and recognized their irrational character."[89] It seems reasonable to conclude that Lincoln's racial views were, by the standards of his time, enlightened, that he definitely included black men and black women among the "all men" of the Declaration, and—most importantly—that he was committed in both principle and practice to the progressively wider implementation of the promise of equality. Mere formal emancipation would not be enough for the freedpeople, Lincoln recognized. As an old Whig, he knew well the importance of education and other forms of "moral and physical elevation" if, in the years to come, the black population were to achieve meaningful redemption from the degradation of slavery. As a Republican, he placed, at least theoretically, more responsibility on black self-help and less on white paternalism.[90]

White America needed its own form of redemption, as Lincoln more and more realized while the war went on. Lincoln was a peace-loving man who had opposed war with Mexico and who grieved over casualty reports. For decades, Whigs and Republicans had considered themselves opposed to violence and had criticized the Democrats for encouraging it. In Kansas the free-state men had prided themselves on representing peace (if not always law) and order against the "border ruffians," as Greeley named them. But after the coming of the war itself, Republicans could no longer escape sharing responsibility for the resort to violence. Indeed, Lincoln personally bore much of this burden because of his firm rejection of the Crittenden Compromise and his insistence on provisioning Fort Sumter. A recognition of guilt, individual and collective, seems to have saddened the president even as the tide of war turned slowly in his favor. Edmund Wilson has reminded us that, although we remember the cases in which Lincoln pardoned soldiers condemned to death, in 267 cases he authorized the executions and probably experienced guilt over this.[91] The president may also have been bothered by the horrible suffering in prisoner-of-war camps brought on by the Union refusal to exchange prisoners. No doubt he worried over the concentration of executive power brought about by the war, typified in the suspension of habeas corpus, so contrary to traditions of the "country party." And he experienced personal tragedy in the death of his young son, Willie.

Wrestling with these agonies, Lincoln found religion taking on deeper meaning for him. In youth he had rejected the orthodox Protestant literalism of the frontier, not only on intellectual grounds but also because he had no taste for its emotionality and sectarian bickering. Some of those who knew him best considered him a secularist.[92] But during his White House years Lincoln's sense of spiritual things deepened, and he transcended the polarities of dogmatism and skepticism. From his Whig past he retained an awesome sense of moral responsibility to future generations. "Fellow citizens, *we* cannot escape history," he declared in his Annual Message to Congress of 1862. "The fiery trial through which we pass will light us down, in honor or dishonor, to the latest generation." Now he infused this sense of responsibility with a reverent agnosticism before unfathomable Divinity. "The will of God prevails," he meditated during the time when the Emancipation Proclamation was much on his mind.

> In great contests each party claims to act in accordance with the will of God. Both *may* be, and one *must* be wrong. . . . In the present civil war it is quite possible that God's purpose is something different from the purpose of either party—and yet the human instrumentalities, working just as they do, are of the best adaptation to effect His purpose.[93]

As Lincoln grew spiritually, he developed qualities of humility and compassion that carried him far beyond the bourgeois-compulsive virtues of financial honesty and ambition for advancement. He coped with his guilt feelings by recognizing the ancient Judeo-Christian doctrine that suffering can be morally redemptive, both for the individual and the group. Lincoln was far from alone in seeing the war as a process of atonement for sin, out of which the nation would emerge strengthened and purged. Among the countless other northerners who conceived events in this way, Julia Ward Howe is the best-remembered (for her "Battle Hymn of the Republic"); Horace Bushnell, the most theologically sophisticated. The organic conception of national community and the religious sense of history, which had characterized the old Whigs, made such a view of the war plausible. A modern scholar has interpreted these feelings in psychoanalytic terms: with their blood, the Americans of the mid-nineteenth century atoned for the sin of the fathers in permitting slavery; by acquitting themselves of their debt to the fathers, they attained their own national adulthood.[94] Lincoln's own concept of the war as redemptive was singularly devoid of self-righteousness. In his Second Inaugural Address he achieved matchless expression of the idea:

> Fondly do we hope—fervently do we pray—that this mighty scourge of war may speedily pass away. Yet, if God wills that it

continue, until all the wealth piled by the bond-man's two hundred and fifty years of unrequited toil shall be sunk, and until every drop of blood drawn with the lash, shall be paid by another drawn with the sword, as was said three thousand years ago, so still it must be said "the judgments of the Lord, are true and righteous altogether."[95]

Lincoln's martyrdom, coming soon after these words were spoken, enhanced the compelling power of the atonement analogy for the American people. Like a suffering servant, their leader had died for their sins.

Alexander Stephens, while condemning Lincoln's "Caesarism," nevertheless acknowledged after the war that "the Union with him in sentiment, rose to the sublimity of a religious mysticism." A more recent commentator has observed that Lincoln "incorporated the truths of the Declaration of Independence into a sacred and ritual canon, making them objects of faith as well as of cognition." Thus Lincoln fulfilled the hopes of Whig conservatives like Webster and Choate, who had wanted to endow American nationality with a sacrosanct aura—though Webster did not live to see it, and Choate rejected Republicanism before his death in 1859. Lincoln enlisted religious sentiment on behalf of Enlightenment reason in a body of unmatched political rhetoric. He succeeded, as perhaps no one else ever has, in creating a "tradition of modernity," a Burkean justification for the rights of man.[96]

As Lincoln transcended the limitations of his ambition, his Whiggery, and his youthful religious skepticism, so too he transcended the limitations of American nationalism. The American Union was precious to him because it was "the last, best hope of earth," because its success or failure tested "whether any nation so conceived and so dedicated can long endure." When Lincoln gave his eulogy for Henry Clay, he declared: "[Mr. Clay] loved his country partly because it was his own country, but mostly because it was a free country."[97] David Potter, commenting on the eulogy, has remarked that this attitude was even more characteristic of Lincoln himself than of Clay, adding, "The most distinctively American figure in the national history, and the major leader in the consolidation of American national power, bore a significance least narrowly American." In the midst of the Civil War, Lincoln could write to a workingmen's association in New York City: "The strongest bond of human sympathy, outside of the family relation, should be one uniting all working people, of all nations, and tongues, and kindreds."[98]

The final estimate of Lincoln's second American revolution must take into account the unintended nature of its consequences. The triumph of the northern bourgeoisie ushered in an era very different from anything Lincoln could have expected or wanted. His objective, in the broadest sense, was to defend and extend the kind of free society he had known in Springfield. This was a society of small entrepreneurs, market-oriented farmers, young men working for others until they could save enough to set up for themselves, and striving professionals like himself. It was the same "mixed" society that Henry C. Carey had celebrated. In one of his great prewar speeches, delivered in Milwaukee in 1859, Lincoln described this society and showed how it provided each individual with the proper opportunities to grow and develop according to his capabilities. "Let us hope," he concluded, "that by the best cultivation of the physical world beneath and around us, and the intellectual and moral world within us," that this society and the aspirations it embodies "shall not pass away." Even as he voiced this hope, however, he felt forebodings, for history had taught him that nothing was ever permanent. It was the fear rather than the hope that events bore out.[99]

With the railroads, fully "modern," impersonal, bureaucratic corporations came into being and began their rapid rise to power in the United States. They, rather than the paternalistic Whig merchants, mill-owners, or planter-capitalists, brought in "big business" as we know it. The railroads were privately owned rather than mixed public-private enterprises and were hence less subject to public control, though no less eager for public subsidies. Before the war they were of great benefit to midwestern commerce and agriculture and were accordingly welcomed and encouraged by both Lincoln and Douglas. Eventually Lincoln's son Robert would enter the railroad business and become president of the Pullman Company. But economic change could not be contained within the limits of Abraham Lincoln's outlook. Within a generation after his death, the kind of society Lincoln loved was already being superseded by urban-industrial capitalism, and nowhere faster than in his own state of Illinois. Henry C. Carey was horrified when he saw the new economy, and we may believe that Lincoln, too, would have been grieved by its oppression and sordid materialism. Richard Hofstadter has observed that Booth's bullet spared Lincoln a painful recognition: "It confined his life to the happier age that Lincoln understood—which unwittingly he helped to destroy—the age that gave sanction to the honest compromises of his thought."[100]

The Whigs had always emphasized the importance of self-determination, and idealized the man who shaped himself and transcended the constraints of his time and place. Inevitably, however, most of them were extremely time-bound and culture-bound in outlook. Lincoln stands out as a Whig who really did transcend his situation and made himself a man for all seasons. Yet, with typical humility, he recognized that even he had not been able to master the course of history. "I claim not to have controlled events, but confess plainly that events have controlled me."[101] He spoke more truly than he knew.

Conclusion

The political culture of the Whig party in America was a remarkable amalgam of old and new components. It preserved the distrust of executive power and the fear of moral corruption that had characterized the country-party tradition for at least two centuries. However, unlike the older exponents of those ideals, the Whigs came to accept prosperity and wholeheartedly endorsed economic development. This change identifies them as supporters of one phase of "modernization" in American history. During their lifetime, economic development tended to foster inequality; indeed, it had already been doing so for a century or more.[1] This did not deter the Whigs, for they approved the patterns of social deference against which the Jacksonians protested. When the Whigs became Republicans, a significant weakening occurred in this old-fashioned elitism and in the patriarchal sense of responsibility toward inferiors that went with it. The United States was a country in which modernization was led by the bourgeoisie, and, in Marxian terms, Whig political culture expressed the class interests of the bourgeoisie. The party's strength in different parts of the nation reflected variations in bourgeois cultural hegemony, complicated by ethnoreligious loyalties.[2]

I have sought in this book to show that a cultural interpretation of politics need not preclude a recognition of the economic differences between the parties or the rationality of their programs, given their different constituencies. Some aspects of Whiggery, such as the tariff, were primarily beneficial to the industrialists; other aspects had much wider appeal, such as suspicion of party, sense of redemptive mission, concern with self-improvement, or loyalty to a particular religious tradition. The political culture of the American Whigs was an elaborate set of interrelated strategies serving the purposes of many different people, all of whom, for complicated and various reasons, were willing to accord leadership to a modernizing bourgeoisie. One of the marvels of Whiggery is that so many appeals could be so coherently synthesized.

As we observed at the outset, the Whigs were optimistic about economic progress and consolidation but were apprehensive regarding social and moral development. Their economic ideal was the "mixed" or "middle" landscape that included industry and trading as well as agriculture. They took their social ideal from the New England town, approving both its formal democracy and its informal habits of respect. They frequently applied their conservative social values in imaginative, constructive ways. The classic example would be the desire of John Quincy Adams and Abraham Lincoln to place slavery on the road to ultimate extinction as a means of preserving the Founding Fathers' original intentions. The institutional creativity of the Whigs likewise illustrates their way of combining progressive measures with conservative objectives. The reformed penitentiaries of Seward and the phalanxes of Greeley, like the public schools of Horace Mann and the insane asylums of Dorothea Dix, all synthesized innovation with the maintenance of control—as, indeed, did Nathan Appleton's town of Lowell. It was precisely this emphasis on controlling others that the Jacksonians objected to in Whig reforms. The Democrats, faithful in many ways to premodern folk traditions, resented the imposition of the novel Whig order.

Historians have long recognized that not only Whig conservatives but also Whig reformers were deeply concerned with social control. Here I have tried to show that this concern mirrored a concern with self-control. In their quest for means of control, individual as well as collective, the Whigs tried many mechanisms. Their ancient country-party heritage suggested to them that one appropriate device consisted of the institutional structures of "mixed government." Their newfound enthusiasm for economic development suggested that prosperity could act as another means of social control by keeping the public contented. Moral philosophy suggested to them that the various faculties of human nature could also be made to reinforce social imperatives. Accordingly, different Whigs appealed to different faculties in the interest of order. John Quincy Adams relied on conscience; Henry Clay, on enlightened self-interest; Daniel Webster, on the gentle sentiments. Other means of control were not lacking: the evangelicals invoked the aid of Providence; modernizers like Horace Greeley, the beneficial effects of hard work. Rufus Choate even resorted to deception. By the end of our period, Abraham Lincoln had attained a deep wisdom regarding the evolution of public opinion and a fine sophistication at influencing it. Though the Whig party had ceased to exist as such by the time of the Civil War, the war itself could be interpreted as making a contribution, if a tragic one, to this long-term Whig effort at imposing order. A writer in the *Atlantic Monthly* declared, as the war drew to a close: "We have proved that we are a nation equal to the task of self-discipline and self-control."[3]

Behind Whig economic and social values (or beneath them, to adopt the Freudian preposition), lay the distinctive psychological value of self-control. The Whig personality ideal emphasized self-development but not self-indulgence, and it encouraged striving to shape the self according to an approved plan. Although self-mastery, especially mastery of the "passions," was important, the ideal was not exclusively repressive. Indeed, it was broadly humanistic in a structured way. The Whig personality ideal corresponded generally with what Wilhelm Reich has identified as the compulsive character type. The Whig social and political programs can be viewed as compulsiveness writ large, emphasizing, as they did, order, balance, formal logic, advance planning, and control of others.[4] In this book, the Whig personality has been explored through a number of prominent individuals in order to observe the variations within it. Henry Carey, for example, displayed humorlessness and hyperintensity. In William H. Seward, on the other hand, there was a cheerful confidence that harmony and good order would be successfully imposed. As a psychological ideal, the personality type here termed "Whig" has been far more widespread than the Whig political party of the United States. Different versions of this personality seem to have played an important role in many phases of modernization throughout Western civilization.[5]

The Whig party as a political entity was far more evanescent than the cultural or personal values it embodied. Around the middle of the nineteenth century, the Whig program for promoting American economic development through mixed public-private enterprise lost its hold on the imagination of its constituency. As American capitalism grew stronger, the attractions of an entrepreneurship unfettered by government regulation increased. Railway promoters found ways of raising capital without resorting to the mixed corporation; financiers decided that "free banking" (that is, free-enterprise banking) was the policy best suited to their self-interest. Thus, the principal economic appeal of Whiggery was disappearing at the same time that the political issues of nativism and antislavery were acquiring new urgency. Those who had been Whig voters felt this urgency and found their party an ineffective vehicle for expressing it. By the 1850s a widespread feeling existed that the issues the second party system addressed had become irrelevant and that other issues had arisen to replace them.[6] It is a measure of how closely the politics of the era was keyed to issues that such a change in issues created a whole new party system.

The Whigs had been selective in the forms of modernization they espoused. They had supported industrialization, technological innovation, education, nationalism, and the work ethic; yet they remained hostile to certain other aspects of modernity, such as socioeconomic equality, toleration of diversity, and acceptance of political conflict. The Republican party that came after them was more unambiguously modern. Without rejecting any of the Whigs' devotion to self-improvement or purposeful control of the environment, the Republicans moved away from paternalism toward a more impersonal, secular society. The Democrats retained more of their Jacksonian ethos during and after the Civil War, along with their continuity of organization and name.[7] Their distinctive version of country-party political culture remained and, with it, their dedication to popular virtue, white supremacy, strict construction of the Constitution, and suspicion of the money power. The fear of conspiracy became more typical of Democrats than of Republicans in this period, for Republicans were moving toward an acceptance of competing interest groups. Because of such cultural conservatism, the postwar Democratic party bore certain similarities to prewar Whiggery, as in the evangelical oratory of William Jennings Bryan or the respect which some Democratic leaders avowed for Edmund Burke. However, investigations of the social bases of the Republican-Democratic division within the electorate reveal much continuity with the antebellum Whig-Democratic division.[8] Republicans usually commanded the allegiance of the affluent and culturally dominant, as the Whigs had done; Democrats, that of Catholics and (more than ever) southerners. The southern bourgeoisie, still torn between its economic affinities with northern interests and its sectional loyalties, found ways to cooperate with the Republicans even after joining the Democratic party.[9]

Apart from such economic and political developments, the culture of Whiggery in the form we have studied it was eventually doomed by transformations of a more subtle kind. Oratory as a means of influence declined, oral-aural communication being extensively superseded by the printed media. Horace Greeley's successful pioneering of modern journalism represented the future; Lincoln would remain the last of Whig orators as well as the first of Republican presidents. Classical learning, which had contributed so much of the rationale for heroic oratory, lost its central place in the educational system as new forms of technical and vocational training arose. Moral philosophy fragmented when its various subdivisions attained the rank of independent social sciences: economics, anthropology, sociology, and the rest. The old faculty psychology, which had linked moral philosophy with rhetoric, was gradually left behind by postwar academicians like G. Stanley Hall. Germany with its research replaced Scotland with its moralism as the principal source of intellectual inspiration for Americans. The New School Calvinist theology that had formed an important systematic expression of Whig culture also crumbled in the later years of the Victorian era.[10]

Even so, neo-Whig values were not without defenders after the Civil War. The postbellum group bearing the closest resemblance to antebellum Whiggery were the Liberal Republicans of 1872. They rebelled against the regular Republicans' emphasis on party organization, renewed the old Whig cause of opposition to the spoils system, and nominated Greeley for president. The Liberals also became disillusioned with the tariff and other government subsidies to business now that American industries were no longer "infant." Although defeated in 1872, the Republican independents allied with the Democrats again in 1884, and this time they were successful. "Mugwumps" the party regulars called them, and the derisive name has stuck. In the 1890s, when the Republican party pursued overseas colonialism with avidity, heirs of the Mugwump tradition appeared prominently along with Democrats in resisting this new form of imperial expansion. The Liberal Republicans had hoped to build a coalition with respectable white southerners through a policy of sectional conciliation. They proved unable to break out of the confines of the Protestant upper-middle class and establish themselves as a major political party. Nevertheless, it is too facile to write off the Liberal-Mugwumps as ineffectual decadents.[11]

The late-nineteenth-century American urban gentry, of which

Mugwumpery constituted the political expression, had not lost the dynamic and innovative spirit of the prewar Whigs. They institutionalized their cultural values in important, if often nonpolitical, ways—a significant parallel with Whiggery.[12] The great American universities were created by them, either out of preexisting Protestant colleges or *de nihilo;* major museums and libraries were founded; influential boarding schools perpetuated their ideals. Another institutional precipitation of the Whig-Mugwump tradition was the American public-school system. Its organization shaped by Horace Mann and its instruction by Noah Webster and William Holmes McGuffey, the public school long continued to inculcate Whig values of self-discipline, ambition, time-thrift, and (sometimes) humanitarianism.[13] The American Victorian gentry provided considerable leadership to the cause of women's rights, as their prewar counterparts had to antislavery, and the United States led the world in establishing higher education for women. Even the federal civil service came into being, after all.[14]

In the early twentieth century, the progressive movement carried on some of the spirit of old Whiggery. The didacticism and crusading zeal of certain progressives remind one of the Whig reformers. So do the progressives' distrust of political party organizations and their warnings of dangerous conspiracies against the public interest (warnings which, like those of the Antimasons and Conscience Whigs, were by no means without foundation). The progressives, too, were modernizers and institution-builders who sought to forge a working alliance between government and a morally reinvigorated capitalism.

Actually, something like a Whig point of view has not been without defenders even in more recent times, if one considers social thinkers like Walter Lippmann and Robert Nisbet as standing within a Whig tradition. Although the language of the nineteenth-century Whigs often seems old-fashioned, their values are less so, and the problems they confronted least of all. Psychoanalysts no longer use the terminology of faculty psycholgy, but they still address problems of reconciling nonrational impulses with civilization. Marxists still address the imperatives of economic development and occasionally even recognize the contribution made by the bourgeoisie to historical evolution. Many of us living in the developed countries during the late twentieth century have become disenchanted with the benefits of the modernity that the Whigs and early Republicans worked so conscientiously to achieve. Yet is is hard to see how we can resolve the problems of our day without at least a measure of the self-discipline the Whigs would remind us to maintain. To the extent that we continue to face issues like the conservation or exploitation of resources, the integration or separatism of ethnicity, morality in the media, responsibility in the use of alcohol and drugs, and the reaction to unjust wars, the Whigs and their times will never seem totally alien.

Notes

Introduction

1 Marvin Meyers, *The Jacksonian Persuasion: Politics and Belief,* rev. ed. (New York: Vintage Books, 1960); Eric Foner, *Free Soil, Free Labor, Free Men: The Ideology of the Republican Party before the Civil War* (New York: Oxford University Press, 1970).

2 Various ideas of Claude Lévi-Strauss, Clyde Kluckhohn, and Clifford Geertz have contributed in their different ways. The historian who has explored the application of the concept of "culture" most thoroughly is Robert F. Berkhofer, Jr., in *A Behavioral Approach to Historical Analysis* (New York: Free Press, 1969).

3 Among the works I have found most suggestive are Kenneth Burke, *The Philosophy of Literary Form: Studies in Symbolic Action* (Baton Rouge: Louisiana State University Press, 1941); Harold Lasswell et al., *The Language of Politics* (New York: George Stewart, 1949); Karl Deutsch, *Nationalism and Social Communication* (Cambridge: MIT Press, 1953); James T. Boulton, *The Language of Politics in the Age of Wilkes and Burke* (London: Routledge & Kegan Paul, 1963); and J. G. A. Pocock, *Politics, Language, and Time* (New York: Athenaeum, 1973).

4 "A Declaration of Principles and Purposes, Adopted by a General Convention of the Whigs of New England," published in *Writings and Speeches of Daniel Webster* (Boston: Little, Brown, 1903), 3:42.

5 Clifford Geertz, "Ideology as a Cultural System," in *Ideology and Discontent,* ed. David Apter (New York: Free Press, 1964), pp. 47–76.

6 Robert Kelley, *The Cultural Pattern in American Politics: The First Century* (New York: Knopf, 1979), became available just as I was finishing this book. Kelley ties "culture" closely to ethnoreligious identity,

307

leaving it with less of the relationship to ideology and purposeful action that I wish to retain. Nevertheless, his is a welcome and impressive synthesis in the field of cultural history.

7   See Daniel Walker Howe, "Victorian Culture in America," in *Victorian America*, ed. D. W. Howe (Philadelphia: University of Pennsylvania Press, 1975), pp. 3–28.

8   D. H. Meyer, "American Intellectuals and the Victorian Crisis of Faith," ibid., p. 75; John Dunn, "The Identity of the History of Ideas," *Philosophy* 43 (April, 1968): 92.

9   Philip Greven, Jr., *The Protestant Temperament* (New York: Knopf, 1977), p. 17; David B. Davis, "Some Recent Directions in Cultural History," *American Historical Review* 73 (Feb., 1968): 705. Recently, personality psychology has been applied in collective biographical studies of the American Revolutionaries; see Kenneth S. Lynn, *A Divided People* (Westport, Conn.: Greenwood Press, 1977); N. E. H. Hull, Peter C. Hoffer, and Steven L. Allen, "Choosing Sides: A Quantitative Study of the Personality Determinants of Loyalist and Revolutionary Political Affiliation in New York," *Journal of American History* 65 (Sept., 1978): 344–66.

10 Arthur M. Schlesinger, Jr., *The Age of Jackson* (Boston: Little, Brown, 1945), p. 144 and passim; this view finds recent confirmation in William G. Shade, *Banks or No Banks: The Money Issue in Western Politics, 1832–1865* (Detroit: Wayne State University Press, 1972), esp. pp. 84–86.

11 Thomas B. Alexander, *Sectional Stress and Party Strength: A Study of Roll-Call Voting Patterns in the United States House of Representatives, 1836–1860* (Nashville: Vanderbilt University Press, 1967), passim.

12 Bruce Kuklick, "Myth and Symbol in American Studies," *American Quarterly* 24 (Oct., 1972): 440; cf. Gilbert Ryle, *The Concept of Mind* (London: Hutchinson, 1949), chap. 1.

13 See Quentin Skinner et al., "Political Thought and Political Action: A Symposium on Quentin Skinner," *Political Theory* 2 (Aug., 1974): 251–303. I am also indebted to a talk of Skinner's, "Explaining Political Action: The Namierite Fallacy," presented at Yale University on April 6, 1972.

14 "Highbrow" and "lowbrow" were invented by Van Wyck Brooks in *America's Coming of Age* (New York: B. W. Huebsch, 1915); see esp. pp. 9–19.

15 Cf. Meyers, *The Jacksonian Persuasion*, p. 104. See also Robert J. Pranger, *Action, Symbolism, and Order* (Nashville: Vanderbilt University Press, 1968), esp. pp. 168–95.

16 Henry Clay, "The State of the Country under Mr. Van Buren" (Hanover County Address), *Works* (New York: G. P. Putnam's Sons, 1904), 8:195–214; Daniel Webster, "Speech at a Mass Meeting in Saratoga," *Writings and Speeches* (Boston: Little, Brown, 1903), 3:5–36.

17 See also William N. Chambers, "The Election of 1840," in *History of American Presidential Elections*, ed. Arthur M. Schlesinger, Jr. (New York: Chelsea House, 1971), esp. pp. 683 f., and V. O. Key, *The Responsible Electorate: Rationality in Presidential Voting* (Cambridge: Harvard University Press, 1966).

18 Quoted in Robert Gray Gunderson, *The Log Cabin Campaign* (Lexington: University of Kentucky Press, 1957), p. 273.
19 I have commented on the Weber thesis in "The Decline of Calvinism: An Approach to Its Study," *Comparative Studies in Society and History* 14 (June, 1972): 306–27. On modernization theory, see two essays by Samuel P. Huntington, "The Change to Change: Modernization, Development and Politics," *Comparative Politics* 3 (April, 1971): 283–322, and "Political Modernization: America vs. Europe," *World Politics* 18 (1966): 378–414. The second discusses the combination of a "modern" economy with antique political ideas and institutions in the United States.
20 G. M. Young, *Victorian England: Portrait of an Age*, 2d. ed. (London: Oxford University Press, 1953), p. vi.

Chapter One

1 Henry Adams, *The Life of Albert Gallatin* (Philadelphia, 1879), p. 635; George W. Julian, *The Life of Joshua R. Giddings* (Chicago, 1892), pp. 192–94; Joshua R. Giddings, *A History of the Rebellion: Its Authors and Causes* (New York, 1864), pp. 225 and 356.
2 Henry R. Mueller, *The Whig Party in Pennsylvania* (New York: Columbia University Press, 1922), p. 236. For the progressive and consensus perspectives, see Vernon Parrington, *Main Currents in American Thought* (New York: Harcourt, Brace, 1927), p. 310, and Eric McKitrick, "Is There an American Political Philosophy?" *New Republic* 132 (April 11, 1955): 22–25.
3 "The Responsibility of the Ballot Box," *American Review* 4 (Nov., 1846): 445; see also, e.g., John Pendleton Kennedy, "The Twenty-Ninth Congress," ibid. (Dec., 1846): 545–50.
4 Ralph Waldo Emerson, journal entry, March, 1845, in *Journals and Miscellaneous Notebooks* (Cambridge: Harvard University Press, 1970), 9:160.
5 Quoted in Bertram Wyatt-Brown, *Lewis Tappan and the Evangelical War against Slavery* (Cleveland: Case Western Reserve University Press, 1969), p. 63.
6 Voting statistics are provided and discussed in Richard P. McCormick, "New Perspectives on Jacksonian Politics," *American Historical Review* 65 (Jan., 1960): 288–301; idem, *The Second American Party System* (Chapel Hill: University of North Carolina Press, 1966); and Walter Dean Burnham, "The Changing Shape of the American Political Universe," *American Political Science Review* 59 (March, 1965): 7–21.
7 See, e.g., Roy F. Nichols, *The Disruption of American Democracy* (New York: Macmillan, 1948), p. 20.
8 John William Ward, *Andrew Jackson, Symbol for an Age* (New York: Oxford University Press, 1953), pp. 114 f.; Glyndon G. Van Deusen, *William Henry Seward* (New York: Oxford University Press, 1967), p. 44.
9 See Richard Edwards, "Economic Sophistication in Nineteenth-Century Congressional Debates," *Journal of Economic History* 30 (Dec., 1970): 802–38; Bennett D. Baak and Edward J. Ray, "Tariff Policy and

Income Distribution," *Explorations in Economic History* 11 (Winter, 1973–74): 103–22.

10 Phillip S. Paludan, "The American Civil War Considered as a Crisis in Law and Order," *American Historical Review* 77 (Oct., 1972): 1027 n.

11 Joel H. Silbey, *The Shrine of Party: Congressional Voting Behavior, 1841–1852* (Pittsburgh: University of Pittsburgh Press, 1967); Thomas B. Alexander, *Sectional Stress and Party Strength: A Study of Roll-Call Voting Patterns in the United States House of Representatives, 1836–1860* (Nashville: Vanderbilt University Press, 1967); David J. Russo, "The Major Political Issues of the Jacksonian Period and the Development of Party Loyalty in Congress, 1830–1840," in American Philosophical Society, *Transactions* n.s. 62 (1972); Herbert Ershkowitz and William G. Shade, "Consensus or Conflict? Political Behavior in the State Legislatures during the Jacksonian Era," *Journal of American History* 58 (Dec., 1971): 591–621.

12 See Michael Holt, *The Political Crisis of the 1850's* (New York: John Wiley & Sons, 1978); Robert E. Shalhope, "Jacksonian Politics in Missouri," *Civil War History* 15 (Sept., 1969): 210–25; Donald J. Ratcliffe, "The Role of Voters and Issues in Party Formation: Ohio, 1824," *Journal of American History* 59 (March, 1973): 847–70. A high degree of party unity is now admitted even by historians reluctant to attribute it to ideological differences between the parties; see Rodney O. Davis, "Partisanship in Jacksonian State Politics: Party Divisions in the Illinois State Legislature, 1834–1841," in Robert P. Swierenga, ed., *Quantification in American History* (New York: Athenaeum, 1970), pp. 149–62, and Peter Levine, "State Legislative Parties in the Jacksonian Era: New Jersey, 1829–1844," *Journal of American History* 62 (Dec., 1975): 591–608.

13 Arthur M. Schlesinger, Jr., *The Age of Jackson* (Boston: Little, Brown, 1945), has been confirmed by a number of recent studies; see Frank Otto Gatell, "Sober Second Thoughts on Van Buren, the Albany Regency, and the Wall Street Conspiracy," *Journal of American History* 53 (June, 1966): 19–40; Robert V. Remini, *Andrew Jackson and the Bank War* (New York: W. W. Norton, 1967); John M. McFaul, *The Politics of Jacksonian Finance* (Ithaca: Cornell University Press, 1972); David Martin, "Metallism, Small Notes, and Jackson's War with the B.U.S.," *Explorations in Economic History* 2 (Spring, 1974): 227–47.

14 See William Carleton, "Political Aspects of the Van Buren Era," *South Atlantic Quarterly* 50 (April, 1951): 167–85; James R. Sharp, *The Jacksonians versus the Banks* (New York: Columbia University Press, 1970); and Richard B. Latner, "A New Look at Jacksonian Politics," *Journal of American History* 61 (March, 1975): 943–69. A good contemporary exposition of the broadening of the issues is Henry Clay's "The Plan of the Sub-Treasury" (1838), *Works* (New York: G. P. Putnam's Sons, 1904), 8:103–20.

15 An excellent survey of the historical literature on this subject may be found in Richard McCormick, "Ethno-Cultural Interpretations of Nineteenth-Century American Voting Behavior," *Political Science Quarterly* 89 (June, 1974): 351–77.

16 See Michael Holt, *Forging a Majority: The Formation of the Republican*

Party in Pittsburgh, 1848–1860 (New Haven: Yale University Press, 1969), chap. 2.

17 Ronald P. Formisano, "Toward a Reorientation of Jacksonian Politics," *Journal of American History* 63 (June, 1976): 62; see also Arthur S. Goldberg, "Social Determinism and Rationality as Bases of Party Identification," *American Political Science Review* 63 (March, 1969): 5–25.

18 See Leon Litwack, *North of Slavery: The Negro in the Free States* (Chicago: University of Chicago Press, 1961), pp. 74–93; Eric Foner, "Politics and Prejudice: The Free Soil Party and the Negro," *Journal of Negro History* 50 (Oct., 1965): 239–56; John L. Stanley, "Majority Tyranny in Tocqueville's America: The Failure of Negro Suffrage in 1846," *Political Science Quarterly* 84 (Sept., 1969): 412–35.

19 See, e.g., Herbert H. Hyman (who invented the term), "Reflections on Reference Groups," *Public Opinion Quarterly* 24 (Fall, 1960): 383–96, and Robert Doherty, "Status Anxiety and American Reform: Some Alternatives," *American Quarterly* 19 (Summer, 1967): 329–37.

20 Anon., "The Result of the Election," *American Review* 1 (Feb., 1845): 120.

21 George Marsden, *The Evangelical Mind and the New School Presbyterian Experience* (New Haven: Yale University Press, 1970), p. 3. I follow the example of Perry Miller in using the term "Second Great Awakening" broadly to include evangelical Protestant crusades throughout the first half of the nineteenth century.

22 Charles G. Finney, *Lectures on Systematic Theology* (Oberlin, Ohio, 1846), p. 431; Henry Clay, in U.S. Congress, *Register of Debates*, 22d Cong., 1st sess., 8 (June 27, 1832): 1127 f. Webster's argument in "The Girard Will Case" (1844) (in Daniel Webster, *Writings and Speeches* [Boston: Little, Brown, 1903], 11:135–77) was reprinted as a religious tract. Girard also excluded nonwhites from his foundation, but in the twentieth century this stipulation was set aside by the courts.

23 See, e.g., "The Debts of the States," *North American Review* 58 (Jan., 1844): 109–57.

24 William G. Shade, *Banks or No Banks: The Money Issue in Western Politics* (Detroit: Wayne State University Press, 1972).

25 Richard McCormick's finding that the Whigs got their best voter turnout in presidential elections, while the Democrats did relatively better in races for local office, lends itself to this interpretation; see his *Second American Party System*, p. 326.

26 For further information, see Carlton Jackson, *Presidential Vetoes* (Athens, Ga.: University of Georgia Press, 1967).

27 Van Buren and Clay are quoted in E. Malcolm Carroll, *Origins of the Whig Party* (Durham, N.C.: Duke University Press, 1925), p. 214; Ralph Waldo Emerson, journal entry, Feb.–March, 1843, *Journals*, 8:314.

28 Schlesinger, *Age of Jackson*, p. 282; Marvin Meyers, *The Jacksonian Persuasion: Politics and Belief* (Stanford: Stanford University Press, 1957), esp. p. 13. See also Glyndon G. Van Deusen, "Some Aspects of Whig Thought and Theory in the Jacksonian Period," *American Historical Review* 63 (Jan., 1958): 305–22; Rush Welter, *The Mind of America, 1820–1860* (New York: Columbia University Press, 1975), p. 190; and, because political cartoons are often among the most revealing arti-

facts of an age, see Peter Walsh, "Henry R. Robinson: Printmaker to the Whig Party," *New York History* 53 (Jan., 1972): 25–53.

29 Lee Benson, *The Concept of Jacksonian Democracy: New York as a Test Case* (Princeton: Princeton University Press, 1961), quotation from p. 103.

30 Major L. Wilson, *Space, Time, and Freedom: The Quest for Nationality and the Irrepressible Conflict* (Westport, Conn.: Greenwood Press, 1974).

31 Horace Greeley, *Why I Am a Whig* (New York, 1851), p. 6. Cf. John Higham: "While Jacksonian Democrats sought to diffuse power and to push outward the spatial limits of freedom, Whig reformers sought to cleanse and purify men's relations with one another" (*From Boundlessness to Consolidation: The Transformation of American Culture, 1848–1860* [Ann Arbor: William L. Clements Library, 1969], p. 12).

32 Portions of this chapter were originally published in the introduction to Daniel Walker Howe, ed., *The American Whigs: An Anthology* (New York: John Wiley, 1973).

Chapter Two

1 Jonathan Bingham, quoted in Eric Foner, *Free Soil, Free Labor, Free Men* (New York: Oxford University Press, 1970), p. 85.

2 See Quentin Skinner et al., "Political Thought and Political Action," *Political Theory* 2 (Aug., 1974): 251–303. See also Arthur Bestor, "The American Civil War as a Constitutional Crisis," *American Historical Review* 69 (Jan., 1964): 327–52.

3 The expression "oral literature" has been rejected as an etymological contradiction, since "literature" is derived from Latin *litera*, "letter of the alphabet"; see Walter J. Ong, *The Presence of the Word* (New Haven: Yale University Press, 1967), pp. 19–22. I still feel the term is too valuable to surrender.

4 See Lawrence I. Buell, *Literary Transcendentalism: Style and Vision in the American Renaissance* (Ithaca: Cornell University Press, 1973).

5 See, e.g., Charles W. March, *Reminiscences of Congress* (New York, 1850), p. 142.

6 Daniel Boorstin, *The Americans: The National Experience* (New York: Random House, 1965), p. 307.

7 "Memoir of Daniel Webster," in Daniel Webster, *Writings and Speeches* (Boston: Little, Brown, 1903), 1:89; "The Warnings of History," *National Intelligencer*, Sept. 3, 1844; "Everett's Orations and Speeches," *North American Review* 71 (Oct., 1850): 454. See also Edwin A. Miles, "The Young American Nation and the Classical World," *Journal of the History of Ideas* 35 (April–June, 1974): 259–74.

8 See Jerrold Seigel, *Rhetoric and Philosophy in Renaissance Humanism* (Princeton: Princeton University Press, 1968), and Wilbur Howell, *Eighteenth-Century British Logic and Rhetoric* (Princeton: Princeton University Press, 1971).

9 George Santayana, *Character and Opinion in the United States* (London: Constable, 1920), p. 3.

10 See, e.g., "On Moral Science as a Branch of Academic Education," *Quarterly Christian Spectator* 6 (Dec., 1834): 561–80.

11 See Donald H. Meyer, *The Instructed Conscience: The Shaping of the American National Ethic* (Philadelphia: University of Pennsylvania Press, 1972), and, for background, Norman S. Fiering, "Samuel Johnson and the Circle of Knowledge," *William and Mary Quarterly* 3d ser. 28 (April, 1971): 199–236.

12 "The Last Chief Executive," *American Review* 1 (April, 1845): 339.

13 Wilson Smith, in his *Professors and Public Ethics: Studies of Northern Moral Philosophers before the Civil War* (Ithaca: Cornell University Press, 1956), first connected moral philosophy with Whiggery.

14 Seward's and Webster's stands were defended by their supporters in terms of moral philosophy; see William Hosmer, *The Higher Law and Its Relation to Civil Government* (Auburn, N.Y., 1852), and Rufus Choate, "Discourse Commemorative of Daniel Webster" (1853), in Choate, *Works* (Boston, 1862), 1:552–57.

15 See Daniel Walker Howe, *The Unitarian Conscience: Harvard Moral Philosophy, 1805–1861* (Cambridge: Harvard University Press, 1970), pp. 56–64.

16 The quotations are from Alexander H. Stephens' "Address at Emory College" (1852), published in Henry Cleveland, *Alexander H. Stephens* (Philadelphia, 1866), p. 368, and from Lyman Beecher, *Instructions for Young Christians* (Cincinnati, 1833), p. 16.

17 See Daniel Webster, "Speech at a Mass Meeting in Saratoga" (1840), *Writings and Speeches*, 3:7; Horace Greeley, introduction to William Atkinson, *Principles of Political Economy; or The Laws of the Formation of National Wealth Developed by Means of the Christian Law of Government* (New York, 1843).

18 Henry C. Carey, *Principles of Social Science* (Philadelphia, 1877), 2:241; Henry Clay, "On Giving Lands for Railroads" (1850), *Works* (New York: G. P. Putnam's Sons, 1904), 9:422.

19 Thomas Reid, *Works*, ed. Sir William Hamilton (Edinburgh, 1863), 2:535 f.

20 *New York Tribune*, May 12, 1841; cf. Daniel Webster, "Festival of New Hampshire Sons" (1849), *Writings and Speeches*, 4:211.

21 On Locke, see C. B. MacPherson, *The Political Theory of Possessive Individualism* (Oxford: Clarendon Press, 1962), pp. 222–27; on Bolingbroke, see Kurt Kluxen, *Das Problem der politischen Opposition: Entwicklung und Wesen der englischen Zweiparteienpolitik im 18. Jahrhundert* (Freiburg: Karl Alber, 1956), pp. 126–36.

22 R. McKinley Ormsby, *History of the Whig Party* (Boston, 1859), p. 190.

23 "Griswold's *Poets and Poetry of America*," *North American Review* 58 (Jan., 1844): 38; Daniel Webster, "The Removal of the Deposits" (1834), *Writings and Speeches*, 6:266.

24 See Ronald G. Walters, "The Erotic South: Civilization and Sexuality in American Abolitionism," *American Quarterly* 25 (May, 1973): 177–210.

25 "Calhoun's Speech against the Conquest of Mexico," *American Review* 7 (March, 1848): 225.

26 See J. R. Pole, "Historians and the Problem of Early American Democracy," *American Historical Review* 67 (April, 1962): 626–46; Ronald P. Formisano, "Deferential-Participant Politics: The Early Republic's Political Culture," *American Political Science Review* 68 (June, 1974):

473–87. Elite leadership had not gone unchallenged, however; see Bernard Friedman, "The Shaping of the Radical Consciousness in Provincial New York," *Journal of American History* 56 (March, 1970): 781–801.

27   Sidney Aronson, in *Status and Kinship in the Higher Civil Service* (Cambridge: Harvard University Press, 1964), argues that Jackson's appointive policies were only moderately innovative in practice. However, until the middle to lower levels of the Jacksonian bureaucracy have been examined, we shall not know the full extent of the changes instituted.

28   For background on competing social ideals amid growing economic inequality in the period 1725–1825, see Roland Berthoff and John M. Murrin, "Feudalism, Communalism, and the Yeoman Farmer," in Stephen Kurtz and James H. Hutson, eds., *Essays in the American Revolution* (New York: Norton, 1973).

29   John Bell, May 23, 1835, quoted in Perry Goldman, "Political Virtue in the Age of Jackson," *Political Science Quarterly* 87 (March, 1972): 50.

30   Robert F. Dalzell, Jr., *Daniel Webster and the Trial of American Nationalism* (Boston: Houghton Mifflin, 1973), p. 33. On the party affiliation of the rich, see Edward Pessen, *Riches, Class, and Power before the Civil War* (Lexington, Mass.: D. C. Heath, 1973), pp. 294 f., and Frank Otto Gatell, "Money and Party in Jacksonian America," *Political Science Quarterly* 82 (June, 1967): 235–52.

31   See the *New York Tribune*, Oct. 19, 1847, cited by Michael Holt, *Forging a Majority: The Formation of the Republican Party in Pittsburgh, 1848–1860* (New Haven: Yale University Press, 1969), pp. 81 f.; see also Stephen C. Fox, "The Group Bases of Ohio Political Behavior, 1803–1848" (Ph.D. diss., University of Cincinnati, 1973).

32   Cf. Robert E. Lane, *Political Life: Why People Get Involved in Politics* (Glencoe, Ill.: Free Press, 1959), p. 131.

33   See Jackson Turner Main, *Political Parties before the Constitution* (Chapel Hill: University of North Carolina Press, 1973).

34   On political sentiment in Ohio, Mississippi, and Virginia, see James R. Sharp, *The Jacksonians versus the Banks* (New York: Columbia University Press, 1970); for Pennsylvania, see Roger D. Peterson, "The Reaction to a Heterogeneous Society, 1845–1870" (Ph.D. diss., University of Pittsburgh, 1970).

35   See Alan Heimert, *Religion and the American Mind from the Great Awakening to the Revolution* (Cambridge: Harvard University Press, 1966).

36   E. P. Thompson, *The Making of the English Working Class* (New York: Pantheon Books, 1963), p. 403. See also Herbert Gutman, "Work, Culture, and Society in Industrializing America," *American Historical Review* 78 (June, 1973): 531–88.

37   Quoted in Gertrude Himmelfarb, *Victorian Minds* (New York: Knopf, 1968), p. 120.

38   Lyman Beecher, "The Perils of Atheism," *Works* (Cleveland, 1852–53), 1:95.

39   Isaac M. Wise, *Reminiscences*, ed. David Philipson (Cincinnati: Leo Wise, 1901), p. 83.

40   R. Wheaton, "The Revolution of 1848 in Sicily," *North American Review* 69 (Oct., 1849): 506; *New York Tribune*, March 20, April 4, and July 13,

1848. See also Francis Bowen, "The Revolutions in Europe," *North American Review* 67 (July, 1848): 194–240.

41 *The Autobiography of Lyman Beecher*, ed. Barbara M. Cross (Cambridge: Harvard University Press, 1961; first published, 1884), 2:170.

42 The dominant group in Schlesinger's scheme is "the business community"; see his *The Age of Jackson* (Boston: Little, Brown, 1945), p. 514. See also Robert Kelley, "Ideology and Political Culture from Jefferson to Nixon," *American Historical Review* 82 (June, 1977): 531–62.

43 Beecher, *Autobiography*, 1:251; Horace Greeley, *Why I Am a Whig* (New York, 1851), p. 13.

44 Robert E. Lane, *Political Thinking and Consciousness* (Chicago: Markham Co., 1969), p. 212.

45 Horace Greeley, in Henry James [Sr.] et al., *Love, Marriage, and Divorce* (New York, 1853), [p. 71].

46 U.S. Congress, *Register of Debates*, 22d Cong., 1st sess., 8:3 (May 23, 1832), appendix, 85.

47 Michael Katz, *The Irony of Early School Reform* (Cambridge: Harvard University Press, 1968), is an incisive—if extremely hostile—account of the educators' objectives, but it does not link the public-school controversies of the day to partisan politics.

48 See Jonathan Messerli, *Horace Mann* (New York: Knopf, 1972); Horace Mann, "The Necessity of Education in a Republican Government" (1838), in *Life and Works of Horace Mann*, ed. Mary Mann (Cambridge, Mass., 1867), 2:143–88; Rush Welter, *The Mind of America, 1820–1860* (New York: Columbia University Press, 1975), chap. 11.

49 Guido de Ruggiero, *The History of European Liberalism*, trans. R. G. Collingwood (London: Oxford University Press, 1927), p. 351.

50 For sophisticated presentations of the Democratic and Whig philosophies, respectively, see George Sidney Camp, *Democracy* (New York, 1841), and Anon., "Civilization: American and European," *American Review* 3 (June, 1846): 611–24.

51 See W. David Lewis, *From Newgate to Dannemora: The Rise of the Penitentiary in New York, 1796–1848* (Ithaca: Cornell University Press, 1965).

52 See William H. Seward, "Discipline in the Navy" (1849), *Works* (New York, 1853), 1:285 f. For general statements of Whig uplift, see "Whig Principle and Its Development," *American Review* 15 (Feb., 1852): 124–35, or the party's platform for New York State (1844), quoted in Jabez Hammond, *The Life of Silas Wright* (Syracuse, 1848), p. 436.

53 Ralph Waldo Emerson, *Journals and Miscellaneous Notebooks*, ed. W. H. Gilman and J. E. Parsons (Cambridge: Harvard University Press, 1960–75), 8:87.

54 The divisions within the Whig party over slavery and the indifference of northern Democrats are well substantiated in Thomas B. Alexander, *Sectional Stress and Party Strength* (Nashville: Vanderbilt University Press, 1967). See also Gerald S. Henig, "The Jacksonian Attitude toward Abolitionism in the 1830s," *Tennessee Historical Quarterly* 28 (Spring, 1969): 42–56, and Richard H. Brown, "The Missouri Crisis, Slavery, and the Politics of Jacksonianism," *South Atlantic Quarterly* 65 (Winter, 1966): 55–72. John M. McFaul, in "Expediency vs. Morality:

Jacksonian Politics and Slavery," *Journal of American History* 62 (June, 1975): 24–39, seeks to minimize Democratic support for slavery.

55 See, e.g., Joel Silbey, *The Shrine of Party* (Pittsburgh: University of Pittsburgh Press, 1967), p. 59. On the varying attitudes of whites, see George M. Fredrickson, *The Black Image in the White Mind: The Debate on Afro-American Character and Destiny, 1817–1914* (New York: Harper & Row, 1971).

56 Lyman Beecher to William Beecher, June 5, 1830, *Autobiography*, 2:165.

57 Here I am indebted to Frederick Cooper, "Elevating the Race: The Social Thought of Black Leaders, 1827–1850," *American Quarterly* 24 (Dec., 1972): 604–25. Cooper, however, does not make a connection between the views of these leaders and black support for the Whig party.

58 See, e.g., *The New Yorker* 1 (May 21, 1836): 132.

59 See Webster, "Remarks on Sunday Schools" (1831), *Writings and Speeches*, 13:39; Everett, "Education and Civilization" (1852), *Orations and Speeches* (Boston, 1883), 3:128 f.; J. H. Perkins, "Grimke on Free Institutions," *North American Review* 69 (Oct., 1849): 440–69.

60 D. R. Goodwin, "The Unity of Language and of Mankind," *North American Review* 73 (July, 1851): 172; cf. Anon., "The Unity of the Human Race," *American Review* 12 (Dec., 1850): 567–86. See also the *National Intelligencer*, Jan. 15, 1848.

61 "Calhoun's Speech against the Conquest of Mexico," *American Review* 7 (March, 1848): 223.

62 Francis Bowen, *Principles of Political Economy* (Boston, 1856), p. 77; Webster, "The Landing at Plymouth Rock" (1843), *Writings and Speeches*, 3:214 f.

63 Henry W. Bellows, "The Destiny of the Country," *American Whig Review* 5 (March, 1847): 231–39; Horace Bushnell, *Barbarism the First Danger* (New York, 1847), p. 23.

64 See David J. Russo, "The Major Political Issues of the Jacksonian Period and the Development of Party Loyalty in Congress, 1830–1840," *American Philosophical Society, Transactions* n.s. 62 (1972): 13 ff., and Robert F. Berkhofer, Jr., *The White Man's Indian* (New York: Knopf, 1978), pp. 157–66.

65 Everett, in U.S. Congress, *Register of Debates*, 21st Cong., 1st sess., 6 (May 19, 1830), 1069, and 21st Cong., 2d sess., 7 (Feb. 14, 1831): 689; John Quincy Adams, *The New England Confederacy* (Boston, 1843), pp. 13–15. See also Robert F. Berkhofer, Jr., *Salvation and the Savage: An Analysis of Protestant Missions and American Indian Response* (New York: Athenaeum, 1972; first published, 1965).

66 *The Spirit of the Pilgrims* 3 (March, 1830): 160; 5 (Jan., 1832): 41. See also Beecher, *Autobiography*, 1:125 f., and 2:163, 168.

67 The psychological sources of Jackson's conduct are explored in James C. Curtis, *Andrew Jackson and the Search for Vindication* (Boston: Little, Brown, 1976); and in Michael Rogin, *Fathers and Children: Andrew Jackson and the Subjugation of the American Indian* (New York: Knopf, 1975). Rogin takes Jackson as representing white society in general and emphasizes both the paternalism and the violence in his attitude toward the Indians. I seek here to distinguish between the two impulses, showing paternalism was more favored by the Whigs, while violence was more common among Jackson and his supporters.

68 See Carl Resek, *Lewis Henry Morgan* (Chicago: University of Chicago Press, 1960), pp. 31 and passim; Reginald Horsman, "Scientific Racism and the American Indian in the Mid-Nineteenth Century," *American Quarterly* 27 (May, 1975): 152–68. Horsman himself does not call attention to the difference between the parties, but much of his evidence indicates it. For examples of Whig opinion, see the *American Review* 1 (May, 1845): 502–10; 5 (June, 1847): 614–29; 9 (April, 1849): 385–98, and the *North American Review* 64 (April, 1847).

69 *Worcester v. Georgia,* 6 Peters 515 (1832); Charles Warren, *The Supreme Court in United States History* (Boston: Little, Brown, 1922), 1:768–73; Joseph C. Burke, "The Cherokee Cases: A Study in Law, Politics, and Morality," *Stanford Law Review* 21 (Feb., 1969): 500–531.

70 Edwin A. Miles, "After John Marshall's Decision," *Journal of Southern History* 39 (Nov., 1973): 519–44. Secondary literature on Cherokee removal is extensive, and interpretations differ sharply. See especially the writings of Grant Foreman, Francis Paul Prucha, and Ronald Satz.

71 Calvin Colton, *A Tour of the American Lakes, and among the Indians of the North-West Territory, Disclosing the Character and Prospects of the Indian Race,* 2 vols. (London, 1833).

72 Linda Kerber, "The Abolitionist Perception of the Indian," *Journal of American History* 62 (Sept., 1975): 271–95; Marvin Winitsky, "The Jurisprudence of Roger B. Taney" (Ph.D. diss., UCLA, 1973), pp. 80–85.

73 Horace Greeley, in *The Jeffersonian* 1 (Oct. 20, 1838): 281; David Crockett, *Sketch of Remarks on the Bill for the Removal of the Indians, Made May 19, 1830* (Washington, 1830). (Crockett's speech does not appear in the congressional *Register of Debates;* it may have been suppressed by a hostile reporter, as sometimes happened.)

74 Humanitarianism among Democrats is described (and overemphasized, in my opinion) in Francis Paul Prucha, S.J., "Andrew Jackson's Indian Policy: A Reassessment," *Journal of American History* 56 (Dec., 1969): 527–39, and in Bernard W. Sheehan, *Seeds of Extinction: Jeffersonian Philanthropy and the American Indian* (Chapel Hill: University of North Carolina Press, 1973).

75 William Henry Harrison, *A Discourse on the Aborigines of the Valley of the Ohio* (Cincinnati, 1838); *The Log Cabin,* May 16, 1840; Richard Hildreth, *The Contrast: William Henry Harrison versus Martin Van Buren* (Boston, 1840), pp. 40 f.

76 The first volume of Robert Remini's new biography of the great Democratic leader, *Andrew Jackson and the Course of American Empire* (New York: Harper & Row, 1977), though it reaches only the year 1821, establishes more firmly than ever the centrality of Indian expropriation in Jackson's statecraft.

Chapter Three

1 Diary entry for Nov. 6, 1830, in *Memoirs of John Quincy Adams, Comprising Portions of His Diary from 1795 to 1848,* ed. Charles Francis Adams (Philadelphia, 1874–77), 8:247.

2 JQA, *Lectures on Rhetoric and Oratory* (Cambridge, Mass., 1810), esp. 1:11–34, 65–72, and 117–38; "John Quincy Adams on Cicero," *National Intelligencer,* Dec. 3, 1839; JQA, diary, Oct. 24, 1830, *Memoirs,* 8:243 f.

3   See JQA, *Poems of Religion and Society* (Auburn and Buffalo, 1854); and JQA, *Dermot MacMorrough, or The Conquest of Ireland . . . In Four Cantos* (Boston, 1832). For his own modest assessment of his poetic abilities, see JQA, diary, March 10, 1831, *Memoirs*, 8:340 f.

4   JQA, diary, July 11, 1836, *Memoirs*, 9:302 f. An interesting, sympathetic interview with Adams appeared in *Niles' Register*, Oct. 11, 1834.

5   See, for example, *Congressional Globe*, 25th Cong., 3d sess., 7 (March 2, 1839), appendix, 284.

6   Harriet Martineau, *A Retrospect of Western Travel* (New York, 1838), 1:137; JQA to George Washington Adams, Nov. 28, 1827, Adams Family Papers. The Adams Papers, which include the complete ms. of JQA's diary, are at the Massachusetts Historical Society. I used the microfilm copy at UCLA.

7   A provocative general treatment of the strong family relationships within the nineteenth-century European bourgeoisie may be found in Edward Shorter, *The Making of the Modern Family* (New York: Basic Books, 1975).

8   JQA, diary, Jan. 9, 1825, Adams Papers. The significance of this blank space is discussed in Samuel Flagg Bemis, *John Quincy Adams and the Union* (New York: Alfred A. Knopf, 1956), pp. 40 f. Bemis' biography is a magnificent model of scholarship, to which everyone interested in Adams will always be much indebted.

9   For example, see his protesting letter to the editor, *National Intelligencer*, Jan. 31, 1837, and the subsequent publication, *Letters from John Quincy Adams to His Constituents . . . to which is Added His Speech in Congress* (Boston, 1837).

10 See Walter LaFeber, ed., *John Quincy Adams and American Continental Empire* (Chicago: Quadrangle Books, 1965).

11 Marie Hecht, *John Quincy Adams: A Personal History* (New York: Macmillan, 1972), p. 405; Ernest R. May, *The Making of the Monroe Doctrine* (Cambridge: Harvard University Press, 1975).

12 The debates among historians concerning the nature of this understanding are surveyed in William G. Morgan, "John Quincy Adams versus Andrew Jackson: Their Biographers and the 'Corrupt Bargain' Charge," *Tennessee Historical Quarterly* 26 (Spring, 1967): 43–58.

13 Richard Hofstadter, *The Idea of a Party System: The Rise of Legitimate Opposition in the United States, 1780–1840* (Berkeley and Los Angeles: University of California Press, 1970), p. 232.

14 David F. Musto, "The Youth of John Quincy Adams," *Proceedings of the American Philosophical Society* 113 (June, 1969): 269–82.

15 Carl Schurz, *The Life of Henry Clay* (Boston, 1899), 1:226 f.

16 JQA, diary, Aug. 30, 1831, *Memoirs*, 8:405.

17 See T. H. Breen, *The Character of the Good Ruler: Puritan Political Ideas in New England, 1630–1730* (New Haven: Yale University Press, 1970). There was, of course, a particular continuity between John Quincy Adams' ideas and those of his father; on this, see John R. Howe, *The Changing Political Thought of John Adams* (Princeton: Princeton University Press, 1965).

18 *Niles' Register*, July 8 and Aug. 5, 1837. Cf. J. G. A. Pocock, "Virtue and Commerce in the Eighteenth Century," *Journal of Interdisciplinary History* 3 (Summer, 1972): 119–34.

19 E.g., JQA, diary, Aug. 4, 1842, *Memoirs*, 11:227 f.

20 JQA, "Report on Manufactures," in U.S. Congress, *Register of Debates*, 22d Cong., 1st sess., 8:3 (May 23, 1832), appendix, 85–87; JQA to Charles W. Upham, Feb. 2, 1837, in Edward H. Tatum, ed., "Ten Unpublished Letters of John Quincy Adams," *Huntington Library Quarterly* 4 (April, 1941): 383.

21 William H. Seward, "John Quincy Adams" (1848), *Works* (New York, 1853), 3:85. Recent scholarship reaches a similar conclusion; see Harry Ammon, *James Monroe: The Quest for National Identity* (New York: McGraw-Hill, 1971), esp. pp. 543 f.

22 JQA, *The Lives of James Madison and James Monroe* (Buffalo, 1850); the quotation is from pp. 288 f. The eulogies were originally delivered in 1836 and 1831, respectively.

23 JQA, "Society and Civilization," *American Review* 2 (July, 1845): 80–89. His debt to Ferguson was noticed by Yehoshua Arieli, *Individualism and Nationalism in American Ideology* (Cambridge: Harvard University Press, 1964), p. 113.

24 For Adams' own assessment of his presidency, see JQA to Charles W. Upham, Feb. 2, 1837, in Edward H. Tatum, ed., "Ten Unpublished Letters of John Quincy Adams," pp. 381–84.

25 Henry Clay, "Tyler's Vetoes" (Aug. 19, 1841), *Works* (New York: G. P. Putnam's Sons, 1904), 8:277; [John Pendleton Kennedy], *Defence of the Whigs* (New York, 1844), pp. 12–24. For an example of Whig invocation of Jefferson, see the *American Review* 8 (Oct., 1848): 333. On Jefferson's views, see William D. Grampp, "A Re-examination of Jeffersonian Economics," *Southern Economic Journal* 12 (Jan., 1946): 263–82.

26 See Kim Phillips, "Democrats of the Old School in the Era of Good Feelings," *Pennsylvania Magazine of History and Biography* 95 (July, 1971): 363–82.

27 On the rapprochement between Adams and the Federalists, see Shaw Livermore, *The Twilight of Federalism* (Princeton: Princeton University Press, 1962), pp. 172–96. On the place of former Federalists in the Whig party, see also Frank Otto Gatell, "Beyond Jacksonian Consensus," in *The State of American History*, ed. Herbert J. Bass (Chicago: Quadrangle Books, 1970), pp. 349–61.

28 JQA, "Inaugural Address" (March 4, 1825), *Messages and Papers of the Presidents*, ed. James D. Richardson (Washington, D.C., 1900), 2:296.

29 Schurz, *Life of Henry Clay*, 1:261.

30 There is a substantial literature on the development of parties. See Roy F. Nichols, *The Invention of the American Political Parties* (New York: Macmillan, 1967); Michael Wallace, "Changing Concepts of Party in the United States," *American Historical Review* 74 (Dec., 1968): 453–91; Stephen Patterson, *Political Parties in Revolutionary Massachusetts* (Madison: University of Wisconsin Press, 1973); Daniel Sisson, *The American Revolution of 1800* (New York: Knopf, 1974); and Hofstadter's work cited in n. 13.

31 See George Dangerfield, *The Era of Good Feelings* (New York: Harcourt, Brace, 1952), esp. p. 95; Isaac Kramnick, *Bolingbroke and His Circle* (Cambridge: Harvard University Press, 1968), esp. pp. 26–28.

32 Ronald P. Formisano, *The Birth of Mass Political Parties: Michigan, 1827–1861* (Princeton: Princeton University Press, 1971), p. 77. See also

his "Political Character, Antipartyism and the Second Party System," *American Quarterly* 21 (Winter, 1969): 683–709.

33 *Congressional Globe*, 25th Cong., 1st sess., 5 (Oct. 14, 1837), appendix, 268; William H. Seward, *The Life and Public Services of John Quincy Adams* (Auburn, N.Y., 1849), p. 86; JQA, diary, Aug. 29, 1840, *Memoirs*, 10:352.

34 JQA, diary, July 25, 1840, *Memoirs*, 10:342; Anon., "Will There Be War with Mexico?" *American Review* 2 (Sept., 1845): 221–29. For a succinct definition of "faction," see "Party Discontents," ibid. 8 (Oct., 1848): 332 n.

35 There is an interesting discussion of the differences between Democratic and Whig views of party in Lynn Marshall, "The Strange Stillbirth of the Whig Party," *American Historical Review* 72 (Jan., 1967): 445–68. Van Buren's writings are discussed in Hofstadter, *Idea of a Party System*, pp. 221–26.

36 Sydney Nathans, *Daniel Webster and Jacksonian Democracy* (Baltimore: Johns Hopkins University Press, 1973), p. 6.

37 E.g., Horace Bushnell, *Politics under the Law of God* (Hartford, 1844), p. 13; James Walker, "Public Opinion" (1856), published in his collected sermons, *Reason, Faith, and Duty* (Boston, 1876), p. 235.

38 JQA, diary, Aug. 23, 1840, *Memoirs*, 10:350. On the moral philosophers, see D. H. Meyer, *The Instructed Conscience* (Philadelphia: University of Pennsylvania Press, 1972), pp. 114 f.

39 Richard Hildreth, *The Contrast: William Henry Harrison versus Martin Van Buren* (Boston, 1840), p. 61; *New York Herald*, Nov. 10, 1840.

40 Washington, D.C., *National Intelligencer*, June 9, 1849; Horace Greeley, *Why I Am a Whig* (New York, [1851]), p. 3. Cf. Daniel Webster, "Speech at Pepperell" (1844), *Works* (Boston: Little, Brown, 1903), 13:278; Henry Clay, "The Compromise Resolutions" (1850), *Works* (New York: G. P. Putnam's Sons, 1904), 3:304.

41 See John M. McFaul, "Expediency or Morality: Jacksonian Politics and Slavery," *Journal of American History* 62 (June, 1975): 24–40; Ronald P. Formisano, works cited in n. 32.

42 The *OED* lists the political usage of "campaign" as originating in nineteenth-century America. See also Perry Goldman, "Political Virtue in the Age of Jackson," *Political Science Quarterly* 87 (March, 1972): 46–62.

43 See Daniel Walker Howe, *The Unitarian Conscience* (Cambridge: Harvard University Press, 1970), pp. 211–26.

44 "The Result of the Election," *American Review* 1 (Feb., 1845): 113–20.

45 See Lynn Marshall, "Stillbirth of the Whig Party" (n. 35, above), and John McFaul, "Expediency or Morality" (n. 41, above).

46 Henry Clay anticipated both the Tenure of Office Act of 1867 and the Pendleton Act of 1883 in his address "On the Appointing and Removing Power" (U.S. Senate, Feb. 18, 1835), *Works*, 8:11–26. See also Geoffrey Blodgett, "A New Look at the American Gilded Age," *Historical Reflections* 1 (Winter, 1974): 231–44.

47 See Jabez Hammond, *History of the Political Parties in the State of New York* (Syracuse, 1852), 2:369–403; Charles McCarthy, "The Antimasonic Party," in American Historical Association, *Annual Report* 1 (1902):

365–574; Whitney Cross, *The Burned-Over District* (Ithaca: Cornell University Press, 1950), pp. 113–25.

48 His statements were later collected by his son; see JQA, *Letters on the Masonic Institution*, ed. Charles Francis Adams (Boston, 1847).

49 Henry Adams, *The Education of Henry Adams* (Boston: Houghton Mifflin, 1961; first published 1918), chaps. 1 and 2.

50 Besides the works of Formisano cited earlier, see Lee Benson, *The Concept of Jacksonian Democracy: New York as a Test Case* (Princeton: Princeton University Press, 1961), pp. 11–46.

51 For an example of early hostile criticism, see James K. Paulding [Democratic politician], "A Narrative of the Anti-Masonic Excitement," *American Quarterly Review* 7 (March, 1830): 162–88. Recent critics include David B. Davis, "Some Themes of Counter-Subversion: An Analysis of Anti-Masonic, Anti-Catholic, and Anti-Mormon Literature," *Mississippi Valley Historical Review* 47 (Sept., 1960): 205–24; Richard Hofstadter, *The Paranoid Style in American Politics* (New York: Alfred A. Knopf, 1965), pp. 14–18; Seymour Lipset and Earl Raab, *The Politics of Unreason* (London: Heinemann, 1971), pp. 39–47.

52 See George Blakeslee, "The History of the Antimasonic Party" (Ph.D. diss., Harvard University, 1903); or Bemis, *John Quincy Adams and the Union*, chap. 15. The Masons' defense, such as it is, may be found in Stanley Mock, *The Morgan Episode in American Free Masonry* (East Aurora, N.Y.: Roycrofters, 1930), or in the more temperate John C. Palmer, *The Morgan Affair and Anti-Masonry* (Washington, Masonic Service Association, 1924). The best recent account is in Ronald P. Formisano and Kathleen S. Kutolowski, "Antimasonry and Masonry," *American Quarterly* 29 (Summer, 1977): 139–65.

53 See Michael F. Holt, "The Antimasonic and Know Nothing Parties," in *History of U.S. Political Parties*, ed. Arthur M. Schlesinger, Jr. (New York: Chelsea House, 1973), 1:575–620, and William Gribbin, "Antimasonry, Religious Radicalism, and the Paranoid Style," *History Teacher* 7 (Feb., 1974): 239–54. Both authors characterize the outlook of Antimasonry without denying the reality of the Masonic provocation.

54 JQA, *Letters and Addresses on Freemasonry* (Dayton, Ohio, 1875). David Davis applies the term "nativists" to the Antimasons and links them with the Know-Nothings in "Some Themes of Counter-Subversion" (cited in n. 51). However, it has since been shown that former Antimasons more often stayed out of the Know-Nothing organization because of their ingrained hostility to secret societies. See Michael F. Holt, *Forging a Majority: The Formation of the Republican Party in Pittsburgh* (New Haven: Yale University Press, 1969), p. 150.

55 JQA, *Letters on the Masonic Institution*, p. 271. See also his diary, Nov. 16 and Dec. 22, 1833; Jan. 7, 1834, *Memoirs*, 9:34, 58, 71.

56 Michael Holt has found that the Antimasons remained a distinctive component of the Whig party in the 1850s at the grassroots level; see his *Forging a Majority*, pp. 40, 54, and passim.

57 Robert J. Rayback, *Millard Fillmore* (Buffalo: Henry Stewart, 1959), p. 33.

58 JQA, *Letters on the Entered Apprentice's Oath* . . . (Boston, 1833), p. 2. Rhys Isaac, "Evangelical Revolt: The Nature of the Baptists' Challenge

to the Traditional Order in Virginia," *William and Mary Quarterly* 3d ser. 31 (July, 1974): 345–68.

59 Roy Cheeseboro, "The Preaching of Charles G. Finney" (Ph.D. diss., Yale University, 1948), p. 5; David Ludlum, *Social Ferment in Vermont, 1791–1850* (New York: Columbia University Press, 1939), pp. 96, 104 f.; Cross, *Burned-Over District*, pp. 121 f.

60 JQA, *Letters to His Son on the Bible and Its Teachings* (New York, 1848); *Congressional Globe*, 25th Cong., 1st sess., 5 (Oct. 4, 1837), appendix, 269; *Niles' Register*, June 22, 1838; JQA to John Adams, Jan. 3, 1817, *Writings*, 6:134–36; JQA, diary, Dec. 23, 1838, *Memoirs*, 10:76.

61 JQA, diary, Nov. 16, 1842; July 2, 1831; Jan. 1, 1837, *Memoirs*, 11:269 f.; 8:375; 9:340.

62 Ibid., March 19, 1843; Jan. 23, 1842; Dec. 29, 1839; June 2, 1838, *Memoirs*, 11:340 f.; 11:69 f.; 10:178 f.; 10:7 f.

63 JQA, *Address to the Norfolk County Temperance Society* (Boston, 1842); on sabbatarianism, see *Niles' Register*, April 2, 1836, and JQA, diary, Dec. 1, 1838, *Memoirs*, 10:48.

64 JQA, *Remarks on the Letter from a Gentleman in Boston to a Unitarian Clergyman of That City* (Boston, 1828). The doctrine Adams there espouses is known as "restorationism." JQA, diary, Jan. 11, 1831; April 22, 1844; Aug. 2 and 23, 1840; Dec. 3, 1837, *Memoirs*, 8:270 f.; 12:14; 10:345 and 350; 9:437.

65 James Knox Polk, *Address to the People of Tennessee* (1839), quoted in Rush Welter, *The Mind of America, 1820–1860* (New York: Columbia University Press, 1975), p. 170. Reared as an Old School Presbyterian, Polk later became a Methodist.

66 Quotations are from JQA, *An Oration Delivered at Newburyport . . .* (Newburyport, Mass., 1837), p. 54; *Niles' Register*, Aug. 13, 1831, and Aug. 2, 1834. Cf. James D. Richardson, ed., *Messages and Papers of the Presidents*, 2:316 f.

67 JQA, *Report on Weights and Measures* (Philadelphia, 1821), p. 48.

68 U.S. Congress, H.R., *Reports of the Minority of the Committee Appointed to Examine the Books and Proceedings of the Bank of the United States* (Washington, D.C., 1832); JQA, *Speech (Suppressed by the Previous Question) on the Removal of the Public Deposits* (Washington, D.C., 1834); *Washington Globe*, Aug. 1, 1837.

69 See John D. Macoll, "Representative John Quincy Adams' Compromise Tariff of 1832," *Capitol Studies* 2 (Fall, 1972): 40–58; JQA, "Report on Manufactures," in U.S. Congress, *Register of Debates*, 22d Cong., 1st sess., 8:3 (May 23, 1832), appendix, 79–92; U.S. Congress, H.R., *Report of the Minority of the Committee on Manufactures* (Washington, D.C., 1833).

70 For examples of good relations between Adams and southern Whigs at this time, see George W. Julian, *The Life of Joshua Giddings* (Chicago, 1892), pp. 51, 54; John T. Morse, *John Quincy Adams* (Boston, 1898), pp. 290–95.

71 Marshall's reaction is noted in Julian, *Joshua Giddings*, p. 109.

72 There are accounts of the censure debate in Benjamin Thomas, *Theodore Weld* (New Brunswick: Rutgers University Press, 1950), chap. 14; and Bemis, *John Quincy Adams and the Union*, chap. 20. However, neither supplements the unreliable *Congressional Globe* with the *National Intelligencer*; for the full devastation of Marshall, see the *Intelli-*

gencer, Feb. 15, 1842. The editorial policy of this Whig organ attempted conciliation, opposing censure while regretting Adams' decision to present the petition (see the issue of Feb. 8.)

73 JQA, diary, Feb. 24, 1820, and June 1, 1830, *Memoirs*, 4:530 f.; 8:229.

74 JQA, "To the Inhabitants of the Twelfth Congressional District of Massachusetts," *Niles' Register*, Sept. 22, 1838; JQA, diary, Oct. 13, 1833, and Dec. 13, 1838, *Memoirs*, 9:23; 10:63; JQA, *Oration Delivered before the Cincinnati Astronomical Society* (Cincinnati, 1843), p. 62.

75 My interpretation has been influenced by Richard H. Brown, "The Missouri Crisis, Slavery, and the Politics of Jacksonianism," *South Atlantic Quarterly* 65 (Winter, 1966): 55–72, and William W. Freehling, *Prelude to Civil War* (New York: Harper & Row, 1965). For JQA on class conflict, see *Niles' Register*, Sept. 22, 1838.

76 U.S. Congress, *Register of Debates*, 22d Cong., 2d sess., 9 (Feb. 7, 1833): 1647 f.; JQA to Isaac Hedge et al., *Niles' Register*, Nov. 17, 1838; JQA to "The Citizens whose Petitions have been Entrusted to Me," *National Intelligencer*, April 23, 1839; JQA, diary, Jan. 31, 1842, *Memoirs*, 9:80.

77 The influence of the English "country party" on American political thought, traced by such eminent historians as Caroline Robbins, Bernard Bailyn, and J. G. A. Pocock, will be explored further in the next chapter.

78 Henry A. Wise in the *Congressional Globe*, 27th Cong., 2d sess., 11 (Jan. 26, 1842): 175; Frederick Merk, *Fruits of Propaganda in the Tyler Administration* (Cambridge: Harvard University Press, 1971); Bemis, *John Quincy Adams and the Union*, pp. 423–25.

79 JQA, diary, Feb. 24, 1820, *Memoirs*, 4:531. Page Smith made an analogous point about Isaac Barré and the American Revolution in a bicentennial lecture at UCLA, April 14, 1976.

80 See, e.g., JQA, *Speech on Distributing Rations to the Distressed Fugitives from Indian Hostilities* (Washington, D.C., 1836); JQA, "Speech on War with Great Britain and Mexico," *Congressional Globe*, 27th Cong., 2d sess., 11 (April 15, 1842): 429; JQA, diary, March 3 and Dec. 23, 1842, *Memoirs*, 11:103, 282.

81 JQA, *Oration at Newburyport* (cited in n. 66), p. 64; JQA, introduction to Joseph and Owen Lovejoy, *Memoir of the Rev. Elijah Lovejoy* (New York, 1838); JQA, diary, Oct. 23–Nov. 13, 1837, *Memoirs*, 9:417–29.

82 JQA, *Argument before the Supreme Court of the United States in the Case of U.S. v. Cinqué et al.* (New York, 1841); JQA, speech in the House of Representatives reported in *National Intelligencer*, June 4, 1842; Lynn . H. Parsons, "'A Perpetual Harrow Upon My Feelings': John Quincy Adams and the American Indian," *New England Quarterly* 46 (Sept., 1973): 339–79; JQA, "Misconceptions of Shakespeare," *New England Magazine* 9 (Dec., 1835): 435–40.

83 JQA to "The Citizens whose Petitions have been Entrusted to Me," *National Intelligencer*, May 28, 1839; *Congressional Globe*, 25th Cong., 3d sess., 7 (Feb. 25, 1839): 218; JQA to Solomon Lincoln (April 4, 1836), quoted in John T. Morse, *John Quincy Adams*, p. 265.

84 See JQA to Henry Williams, *Niles' Register*, Aug. 31, 1839; *Congressional Globe*, 25th Cong., 3d sess., 7 (Jan. 21, 1839): 137.

85 See Robert P. Ludlum, "Anti-Slavery 'Gag Rule,'" *Journal of Negro History* 26 (April, 1941): 203–43; David J. Russo, "Major Political Issues of the Jacksonian Period," American Philosophical Society, *Trans-*

actions, n.s. 62 (1972): 14–23; JQA to "The Inhabitants of the Twelfth Congressional District of Mass.," *Boston Courier,* June 6, 1839; *Congressional Globe,* 25th Cong., 3d sess., 7 (Jan. 21, 1839): 137.

86 On women: *Congressional Globe,* 24th Cong., 2d sess., 4 (Jan. 9, 1837): 79; *National Intelligencer,* July 10–12, 1838. On slaves: *Congressional Globe,* 24th Cong., 2d sess., 4 (Feb. 7, 1837): 168, and appendix, 262; also JQA, *Letters to His Constituents* (cited in n. 9). See also JQA, *The Right of the People, Men and Women, to Petition* . . . (Washington, D.C., 1838).

87 Examples of the hate mail preserved in the Adams Papers are printed in Bemis, *John Quincy Adams and the Union,* pp. 348, 375 f., 435. Isaac Watts' hymn is quoted in JQA, diary, May 29, 1836, *Memoirs,* 9:289; the comment for Dec. 3, 1844 is ibid., 12:116.

88 *National Intelligencer,* Aug. 9, 10, 17, 1842. The *Intelligencer* was printing more speeches by Adams than by anyone else in this period. See also U.S. Congress, H.R., *Report of the Committee on the President's Veto of the Tariff Bill* (Washington, D.C., 1842).

89 JQA, *Address to His Constituents of the Twelfth Congressional District at Braintree, Sept. 17, 1842* (Boston, 1842). The speech was also carried in the *National Intelligencer,* Oct. 22, Nov. 5, and Nov. 9.

90 See Bemis, *John Quincy Adams and the Union,* pp. 436 and 520.

91 JQA, *The Right of the People to Petition,* esp. p. 65; *Niles' Register,* Sept. 18, 1837; *Congressional Globe,* 28th Cong., 2d sess., 14 (Jan. 23–25, 1845): 188–90.

92 *Congressional Globe,* 29th Cong., 1st sess., 15 (Feb. 9, 1846): 341 f.

93 JQA, *Address* (cited in n. 89); JQA, "Address at the Meeting of the Boston Whig Young Men's Club," *National Intelligencer,* Oct. 12, 1844; JQA, "Speech Delivered at North Bridgewater, Nov. 6th," *Niles' Register,* Nov. 23, 1844.

94 JQA, diary, Feb. 28, 1845, *Memoirs,* 12:174.

95 JQA, "Report on Manufactures" (cited in n. 69), p. 89; JQA, *The Jubilee of the Constitution* (New York, 1839), p. 69; JQA to Thomas Boylston Adams (his brother), Feb. 14, 1801, and JQA to John Adams (his father), Aug. 1, 1816, both in *Writings of John Quincy Adams,* ed. W. C. Ford (New York: Macmillan, 1913–17), 2:495; 6:60–62.

96 JQA, diary, May 27, 1843, *Memoirs,* 11:377; JQA, *The New England Confederacy of 1643: A Discourse Delivered before the Massachusetts Historical Society* (Boston, 1843), esp. pp. 44 f.

97 JQA, diary, June 16, 1844, *Memoirs,* 12:57. Adams' late pessimism is also discussed in Major Wilson, "'Liberty and Union': An Analysis of Three Concepts Involved in the Nullification Controversy," *Journal of Southern History* 33 (Aug., 1967): 345–48.

98 JQA, diary, Feb. 19, 1845, *Memoirs,* 12:171; Thomas Hart Benton, in *Congressional Globe,* 30th Cong., 1st sess., 17 (Feb. 24, 1848): 389.

Chapter Four

1 Horace Bushnell, *Reverses Needed: A Discourse Delivered on the Sunday after the Disaster of Bull Run* (Hartford, 1861), pp. 10–13.

2 Lord Acton, quoted in Gertrude Himmelfarb, *Victorian Minds* (New

York: Knopf, 1968), p. 197; *Democratic Review* 8 (Sept., 1840): 227; 11 (Sept., 1842): 225; Thomas Paine, *The Rights of Man, Part First* (London, 1795; first published 1791), p. 1.

3 *Moniteur universel,* May 15, 1793, quoted in George Sabine, *A History of Political Theory,* 3d ed. (London: George Harrap, 1951), p. 463. George Bancroft, *History of the United States* (Boston, 1845), 2:377–80.

4 Daniel Webster, "The Rhode Island Government" (1848), *Writings and Speeches* (Boston: Little, Brown, 1903), 11:220; Edward Everett, "The Seven Years' War the School of the Revolution" (1833), *Orations and Speeches* (Boston, 1883), 1:395.

5 [Edward Everett], "Guizot's Washington," *North American Review* 51 (July, 1840): 74 f.; Anon., "California," *American Review* 9 (April, 1849): 337.

6 Jean Mathews, "'Whig History': The New England Whigs and a Usable Past," *New England Quarterly* 51 (June, 1978): 193–208; quotation from p. 196. For the censure debate, see the *Congressional Globe,* 24th Cong., 1st and 2d sess., 3 and 4 (1836–37), passim; also the *National Intelligencer,* Jan. 17, 1837.

7 Horace Bushnell, *A Speech for Connecticut: Being an Historical Estimate of the State* (Hartford, 1851), p. 6; cf. Rufus Choate, "The Colonial Age of New England" (1834), *Works* (Boston, 1862), 1:347–70, esp. pp. 349 f.

8 See Andrew C. McLaughlin, "Social Compact and Constitutional Construction," *American Historical Review* 5 (April, 1900): 467–90—an excellent statement of the late-nineteenth-century perspective.

9 Edward Everett, "Stability and Progress" (1853), *Orations and Speeches,* 3:226; Rufus Choate, "The Importance of Illustrating New England History" (1833), *Works,* 1:344.

10 Lyman Beecher, "Political Atheism" (1835), *Works* (Cleveland, 1853), 1:328 f. See also [George Tucker], "Dangers to Be Guarded Against in the Progress of the United States," *American Review* 5 (June, 1847): 614–29.

11 Data are provided in George H. Callcott, *History in the United States, 1800–1860* (Baltimore: Johns Hopkins University Press, 1970). To try to correlate the consumption of historical materials with Whig voting patterns would make an interesting research project.

12 William Henry Seward, "Annual Message" (1840), *Works* (New York, 1853), 4:240–42. This theme in Whig thought is discussed very ably in Major L. Wilson, *Space, Time, and Freedom: The Quest for Nationality and the Irrepressible Conflict* (Westport, Conn.: Greenwood Press, 1974), where it is made the basis of a major distinction between Whigs and Democrats.

13 Daniel Webster, "The Sub-Treasury" (1838), *Writings and Speeches,* 8:237; John Quincy Adams, diary entry, April 22, 1844, in *Memoirs* (Philadelphia, 1877), 12:13 f.

14 E.g., Horace Greeley, introduction to *Principles of Political Economy,* by William Atkinson (New York, 1843), pp. iii–iv; Daniel Webster, "Reply to Mr. Calhoun" (1838) and "The Sub-Treasury" (1838), *Writings and Speeches,* 8:254 and 196.

15 John Quincy Adams, "Report on Manufactures" (1832), U.S. Congress, *Register of Debates,* 22d Cong., 1st sess., 8:3 (May 23, 1832), appendix,

83. The meaning of the word "experiment" in the political language of the day is discussed in Rush Welter, *The Mind of America, 1820–1860* (New York: Columbia University Press, 1975), p. 23.

16   For a few examples, see Horace Bushnell, *A Discourse on the Moral Tendencies and Results of Human History* (New Haven, 1843); Samuel Lorenzo Knapp, "Address to the New England Society of New York City" (1829), in *New England Society Orations*, ed. Cephas and Eveline Brainerd (New York: Century Co., 1901), 1:143–64; and George Weber, *Outlines of Universal History*, trans. M. Behr, rev. by Francis Bowen (Boston, 1853), esp. the chapters on United States history, which were written by Bowen.

17   Adam Ferguson, *Essay on the History of Civil Society*, 8th ed. (Philadelphia, 1819), part i, secs. i–ii; Gladys Bryson, *Man and Society: The Scottish Inquiry of the Eighteenth Century* (Princeton: Princeton University Press, 1945), chap. 2. There is a recent edition of Ferguson's *Essay*, with an introduction by Duncan Forbes (Edinburgh: University of Edinburgh Press, 1966).

18   Henry Clay, "The Public Lands" (1832), *Works* (New York: G. P. Putnam's Sons, 1904), 7:493 f. On the American reception of Ferguson, see Herbert Schneider, "The Intellectual Background of William Ellery Channing," *Church History* 7 (March, 1938): 11. Also see Rush Welter, "The Idea of Progress in America," *Journal of the History of Ideas* 16 (June, 1955): 401–15 (though I disagree with some of Welter's judgments, particularly those minimizing the differences between Democrats and Whigs).

19   Octavius B. Frothingham, *Boston Unitarianism, 1820–1850* (New York, 1890), p. 52. An excellent example of the Whig conception of progress is provided in Millard Fillmore's "Third Annual Message" (1852), in *Messages and Papers of the Presidents*, ed. James D. Richardson (Washington, D.C., 1900), 5:163–82.

20   Daniel Webster to Edward S. Rand, May 15, 1850, *Writings and Speeches*, 12:235. The role of an enlightened elite in furthering progress is well explained in James Walker, *Address before the Alumni of Harvard College* (Cambridge, 1863); the balance between change and order is described in Anon., "The Inductive Theory of Civilization: The Social System and Its Modern Reformers," *American Review* 6 (Oct., 1847): 381–98.

21   William Hickling Prescott, *A History of the Reign of Ferdinand and Isabella* (New York, 1851); George Ticknor, *A History of Spanish Literature* (New York, 1849); John Lothrop Motley, *The Rise of the Dutch Republic* (New York, 1856).

22   Ferguson, *Essay*, pt. v, sec. i. Two impressive studies providing background on this subject are Robert Nisbet, *Social Change and History: Aspects of the Western Theory of Development* (New York: Oxford University Press, 1969); and J. G. A. Pocock, *The Machiavellian Moment: Florentine Political Thought and the Atlantic Republican Tradition* (Princeton: Princeton University Press, 1975).

23   William Henry Seward, "The Physical, Moral, and Intellectual Development of the American People" (1854), and "Patriotism" (1831), *Works*, 4:160 and 3:204 f. See also Stow Persons, "The Cyclical Theory of History in 18th-Century America" in *The American Culture*, ed.

Hennig Cohen (Boston: Houghton Mifflin, 1968), pp. 112–28, and Douglass Adair, "Experience Must Be Our Only Guide," in his *Fame and the Founding Fathers*, ed. Trevor Colbourn (New York: W. W. Norton, 1974), pp. 107–23.

24 Alexis de Tocqueville, *Democracy in America*, trans. Phillips Bradley (New York: Knopf, 1945), 2:352; Rufus Choate, "The Colonial Age of New England" (1834), *Works*, 1:360.

25 William H. Seward, "The Destiny of America" (1853), *Works*, 4:136; Lyman Beecher, "Political Atheism," pp. 15 and 102; Beecher, *A Plea for Colleges* (Cincinnati, 1836), p. 89.

26 Even in a panic year, a Whig writer could emphasize political rather than economic problems; see "Our Political Errors," *American Quarterly Review* 22 (Sept., 1837): 530–76. Cf. "Political Symptoms and Popular Rights," ibid. 10 (June, 1836): 363–81.

27 Marvin Meyers, *The Jacksonian Persuasion: Politics and Belief*, rev. ed. (New York: Vintage Books, 1960), pp. 13–15 and passim.

28 Samuel P. Huntington's essay, "Political Modernization: America vs. Europe," *World Politics* 18 (April, 1966): 378–414, deserves to be better known. Also see W. B. Gwyn, *The Meaning of the Separation of Powers* (New Orleans: Tulane University Press, 1965).

29 John Witherspoon, "Lectures on Moral Philosophy," *Works* (Philadelphia, 1802), 3:435; *American Review* 10 (Sept., 1849): 278; *National Intelligencer*, June 16, 1842.

30 Daniel Webster, "The Revolution in Greece" (1824), *Writings and Speeches*, 5:65; [Alfred Langdon Elwyn,] "The British Revolution of 1688," *American Quarterly Review* 12 (Sept., 1832): 154.

31 Quotations from William H. Seward, "Daniel O'Connell" (1847), *Works*, 3:74, and Francis Bowen, ed., *Documents of the Constitution of England and America, from Magna Carta to the Constitution of 1789* (Cambridge, Mass., 1854), p. v. For a good example of the affinity American Whigs felt for British Whigs see Calvin Colton, *Four Years in Great Britain* (New York, 1836), pp. 281–305.

32 Caroline Robbins, *The Eighteenth-Century Commonwealthman* (Cambridge: Harvard University Press, 1959), has proved one of the most fruitful works of intellectual history of the past generation. Its implications for America have been developed in Bernard Bailyn, *Ideological Origins of the American Revolution* (Cambridge: Harvard University Press, 1967), and in many other works.

33 Webster, "The First Settlement of New England" (Plymouth, 1820), "The Basis of the Senate" (the Massachusetts Constitutional Convention of 1820), *Writings and Speeches*, 1:210–16; 5:14–16. Cf. J. Q. Adams, *Memoirs*, 9:228; Lyman Beecher, *Works*, 1:180 f.

34 The anomaly of a Tory who contributed so much to Whig ideology is well explained in Isaac Kramnick, *Bolingbroke and His Circle* (Cambridge: Harvard University Press, 1968). (The situation is not without parallel; Edmund Burke, who contributed so much to Tory ideology, was a Whig.)

35 William Henry Seward, "Speech at a Whig Mass Meeting in Yates County, N. Y., Oct. 29, 1844," *Works*, 3:260. John Quincy Adams inherited a handsome eleven-volume set of Bolingbroke's works from his father; the marginal annotations made by both of them are still visible.

See *A Catalogue of the Books of J. Q. Adams*, ed. W. C. Ford (Boston: The Boston Athenaeum, 1938), p. 4.

36 See Pocock, *The Machiavellian Moment* and others of his works; Choate, "Eulogy on Webster" (1852), *Works*, 1:538; cf. ibid., 378–91, or Bushnell, *Speech for Connecticut*, p. 4.

37 Webster, *Writings and Speeches*, 1:216 f.; Choate, *Works*, 1:423–38; Adams, *Memoirs*, 8:116 f. and passim; Joseph Story, *Commentaries on the Constitution of the United States* (Boston, 1833), title page.

38 Robert P. Hay picked up a number of classic country-party themes in the rhetoric of early Jacksonianism (before the second party system), but he did not recognize them as such. See "The Case for Andrew Jackson in 1824," *Tennessee Historical Quarterly* 29 (Summer, 1970): 139–50.

39 Gordon S. Wood, *The Creation of the American Republic* (Chapel Hill: University of North Carolina Press, 1967), p. 606. The relevance of classical republican concepts to the first party system of the new nation is displayed in Lance G. Banning, "The Quarrel with Federalism: A Study in the Origins and Character of Republican Thought" (Ph.D. diss., Washington University, 1971). See also Linda K. Kerber, *Federalists in Dissent* (Ithaca: Cornell University Press, 1970), pp. 95–134.

40 See Edwin A. Miles, "The Whig Party and the Menace of Caesar," *Tennessee Historical Quarterly* 27 (Winter, 1968): 361–79.

41 Richard Hofstadter originated it; see his *The Paranoid Style in American Politics* (New York: Knopf, 1965). More cautious in using the term is David Brion Davis, *The Slave Power Conspiracy and the Paranoid Style* (Baton Rouge: Louisiana State University Press, 1969), which explores its implications in some detail.

42 On the concept of "paradigm," see J. G. A. Pocock, "Languages and Their Implications," in his *Politics, Language, and Time* (New York: Athenaeum, 1973), and Thomas Kuhn, *The Structure of Scientific Revolutions*, 2d ed. (Chicago: University of Chicago Press, 1970), p. viii.

43 Lyman Beecher, *A Plea for the West* (Cincinnati, 1835), pp. 129 f.; Walter Ong, *The Presence of the Word* (New Haven: Yale University Press, 1967), pp. 195–204, 255–62.

44 Timothy J. Sehr, in a lucid article, shows how assumptions like these led northern moderates to believe that most slaveholders were good men, potentially responsive to moral suasion. See his "Leonard Bacon and the Myth of the Good Slaveholder," *New England Quarterly* 49 (June, 1976): 194–213.

45 Hofstadter, *The Paranoid Style*, p. 5. Though I here dispute him, my respect for his achievements is attested in "Richard Hofstadter: The Ironies of an American Historian," *Pacific Historical Review* 43 (Feb., 1974): 1–23.

46 *OED*, 2:2, definition 3 of "conspiracy." The compilers found this usage obsolete in 1893 but recorded it as being current in the United States as late as 1847.

47 J. Wendell Knox, *Conspiracy in American Politics, 1787–1815* (New York: Arno Press, 1972), p. 316.

48 Joshua Giddings, "The Mexican War" (1848), *Speeches in Congress* (Boston, 1852), pp. 252 f.

49 Madison's justly famous Tenth Federalist Paper, which both deplores "factions" and accepts "interests," looks both backward to classical political thought and forward to a new pluralism. See Douglas Adair, "That Politics May Be Reduced to a Science" (1957), in his *Fame and the Founding Fathers* (New York: W. W. Norton, 1974), pp. 73–106.

50 With the coming of liberal pluralism, the conspiracy paradigm was displaced from its prominent position in American thought. It became the property of angry minorities who did not accept the dominant liberalism. By generalizing backward from these groups, Hofstadter derived his notion of a "paranoid style" (see *The Paranoid Style*, pp. 7–9).

51 See Story, *Commentaries on the Constitution*, vol. 1, bk. 3, chap. 3 (see n. 37, above); Daniel Webster, *Writings and Speeches*, 2:157–65; Rufus Choate, "The Position and Functions of the American Bar" (1845), *Works*, 1:414–38; "The Future Policy of the Whigs," *American Review* 7 (April, 1848): 229–340. The quotations in the text are from Webster, pp. 162 f., and from the *American Review*, p. 330.

52 Descriptions of society in these terms abound in Whig writings. See, e.g., Story, *Commentaries*, loc. cit.; Everett, *Orations and Speeches*, 1:120–22; "Civilization: American and European," *American Review* 3 (June, 1846): 611–24; "The Resolutions and Manifesto of the Southern Caucus," ibid. 9 (March, 1849): 221–34.

53 [Charles Francis Adams,] "The Madison Papers," *North American Review* 53 (July, 1841): 43; Webster, *Writings and Speeches*, 1:273–76.

54 Second *Treatise of Civil Government*, chap. 7, par. 77.

55 John Quincy Adams, *The Social Compact, Exemplified in the Constitution of the Commonwealth of Massachusetts . . . A Lecture Delivered before the Franklin Lyceum at Providence, R.I.* (Providence, 1842); the quotations are from pp. 31 f. and from Adams, diary entry for Oct. 6, 1842 (*Memoirs*, 11:258).

56 The loci classici of Whig doctrine on the nature of the Union are Webster's great addresses: "Second Speech on Foot's Resolution" (1830) and "The Constitution Not a Compact between Sovereign States" (1833), *Writings and Speeches*, 6:3–75 and 181–238; the latter is superior, though less well known. See also Story's *Commentaries*, vol. 1, bk. 3, chap. 4; John Quincy Adams, *The Jubilee of the Constitution . . .* (New York, 1839); or, e.g., [Henry W. Warner,] "The Republic—the Primary Platform," *American Review* 10 (July, 1849): 39–56.

57 See, e.g., Wood, *Creation of the American Republic* (n. 39, above), esp. pp. 532–36.

58 James Madison, quoted by John Quincy Adams, in U.S. Congress, *Register of Debates*, 22d Cong., 2d sess., 9 (Feb. 7, 1833): 1646.

59 Sir Edward Coke, "On the Lords' Amendment to the Petition of Right" (1628), in John Rushworth, ed., *Historical Collections* (London, 1659), 1:568.

60 John Quincy Adams, *An Oration Delivered at Newburyport . . .* (Newburyport, Mass., 1837), esp. p. 24; see also *Niles' Register*, July 13, 1831.

61 Everett, "Principle of the American Constitutions" (July 4, 1826), *Orations and Speeches*, 1:111–17.

62 "Second Speech on Foot's Resolution," p. 54; "The Constitution Not a

Compact," p. 201. See also Webster's neglected third reply to Hayne (1830), *Writings and Speeches*, 6:76–80.

63 William H. Seward, "Freedom in the New Territories" (1850), *Works*, 1:90 f.; see also *Works*, 3:447 f. The subject can be pursued in Paul Nagel, *One Nation Indivisible: The Union in American Thought* (New York: Oxford University Press, 1964).

64 After a long period of historical neglect, important new work on the Dorrite uprising has suddenly appeared. See George M. Dennison, *The Dorr War* (Lexington: University of Kentucky Press, 1976); Marvin Gettleman, *The Dorr Rebellion* (New York: Random House, 1973); William Wiecek, "Popular Sovereignty in the Dorr War," *Rhode Island History* 32 (Spring, 1973): 35–51; and Patrick T. Conley, *Democracy in Decline: Rhode Island Constitutional Development, 1776–1841* (Providence: Rhode Island Historical Society, 1977).

65 Henry Clay, "Address at Lexington" (1842), *Works*, 9:359–84; Horace Greeley, "The Law of Organic Changes in Popular Government," *New York Tribune*, May 24, 1842. See also Seward, "Speech at Whig Mass Meeting" (1844), *Works*, 3:261, and Francis Bowen, *The Recent Contest in Rhode Island* (Boston, 1844).

66 Webster's argument appears in *Writings and Speeches*, 11:217–42; the quotations are from pp. 225 f. Hallett's argument, also very interesting, was published as *The Right of the People to Establish Forms of Government* (Boston, 1848).

67 48 U.S. (7 Howard) 1–88 (1849).

68 Daniel D. Barnard, *Man and the State: An Address Delivered before the Connecticut Alpha of the Phi Beta Kappa at Yale College* (New Haven, 1846). See also his *The Social System: An Address Pronounced before the House of Convocation of Trinity College* (Hartford, 1848). There is a biography of Barnard, though it does not treat his philosophy; see Sherry Penney, *Patrician in Politics: Daniel Dewey Barnard of New York* (Port Washington, N.Y.: Kennikat Press, 1974).

69 Francis Lieber, *The Manual of Political Ethics* (Philadelphia, 1890), 1:352; *Boston Quarterly Review* 2 (Jan., 1839): 113–23; 3 (April, 1840): 181–93. The standard biography of Lieber, Frank Freidel, *Francis Lieber: Nineteenth Century Liberal* (Baton Rouge: Louisiana State University Press, 1947), must now be supplemented by Mark E. Neely, Jr., "The Organic Theory of the State, 1838–1918" (Ph.D. diss., Yale University, 1973). Neely correctly perceives Lieber as a pioneer of the German organicism that became predominant in American political thought after the Civil War. He is not concerned, however, with Lieber's influence on antebellum Whig political culture.

70 See Gerald Stourzh, *Alexander Hamilton and the Idea of Republican Government* (Stanford: Stanford University Press, 1970), and J. G. A. Pocock, "Virtue and Commerce in the Eighteenth Century," *Journal of Interdisciplinary History* 3 (Summer, 1972): 119–34.

71 Horace Greeley, *Why I Am a Whig* (New York, 1851), p. 2; cf. William Ellery Channing, "Life and Character of Napoleon" (1828), *Works* (Boston, 1848), 1:155.

72 Henry Clay, "The Seminole War" (1818) and "On the Removal of the Deposits" (1833), *Works*, 6:204; 7:576 f. Cf. Daniel Webster, *Writings and Speeches*, 6:180; 7:130–34.

73 Clay's first public appropriation of the name came in the Senate, March 14, 1834 (*Works*, 7:628–30); he may have picked it up from either the *New York Courier and Enquirer* or the *Salem* (Mass.) *Gazette*. By summer it was common currency.
74 John Sullivan, "Jackson Caricatured," *Tennessee Historical Quarterly* 31 (Spring, 1972): 39–44; "Executive Power," *American Quarterly Review* 16 (Sept., 1834): 249; Henry Clay, *Works*, 8:191 and 60.
75 "Speech of Mr. John P. Kennedy," *National Intelligencer*, Oct. 19, 1848.
76 "Politics of the Puritans," *New York Review* 6 (Jan., 1840): 71; "Politics of the Puritans," *North American Review* 50 (April, 1840): 433–61.
77 See Pershing Vartanian, "The Puritan as a Symbol in American Thought: A Study of the New England Societies" (Ph.D. diss., University of Michigan, 1971); and Cephas and Eveline Brainerd, eds., *New England Society Orations* (New York: Century Co., 1901).
78 Lee Benson, *The Concept of Jacksonian Democracy* (Princeton: Princeton University Press, 1961), pp. 198–207; "Memoirs of the Court of Charles I," *American Quarterly Review* 15 (March, 1834): 1–30 (one of many essays by American Whigs on Cromwell); Seward, "The Advent of the Republican Party," *Works*, 4:238.
79 Arthur M. Schlesinger, Jr., *The Age of Jackson* (Boston: Little, Brown, 1945), esp. pp. 38, 275 f.; Daniel Webster, *Writings and Speeches*, 11:242.
80 Ralph Waldo Emerson, journal entry for June [?], 1840, in *Journals*, ed. A. W. Plumstead and Harrison Hayford (Cambridge: Harvard University Press, 1969), 7:376; Daniel Webster, "Speech at Trenton, N.J." (1844), *Writings and Speeches*, 13:233; [Charles Francis Adams,] "The Madison Papers," *North American Review* 53 (July, 1841): 77.
81 Harrison was both the Whig and the Antimasonic candidate in 1840. He ran his two campaigns on the same set of pledges (*National Intelligencer*, Feb. 14, 1839, Jan. 16, 1840). See also Henry Clay, "Address in Hanover County, Va." (1840), *Works*, 8:197–213.
82 See William G. Shade, *Banks or No Banks: The Money Issue in Western Politics* (Detroit: Wayne State University Press, 1972), p. 121.
83 This still seems to be the conventional view, employed as recently as Rush Welter's *The Mind of America* (cited in note 15), p. 190.
84 Daniel Webster, "Speech at Concord, N.H." (1834), *Writings and Speeches*, 13:54; cf. Henry Clay, "Hanover County Address" (1840), *Works*, 8:206, or "Origin of the Two Parties," *American Review* 9 (Jan., 1849): 7–9. Merrill Peterson gives a fine analysis of the uses both Jacksonians and Whigs made of Jefferson's memory in *The Jefferson Image in the American Mind* (New York: Oxford University Press, 1960), pp. 99–111; he leans slightly toward thinking the Whig version more accurate.
85 The best sense of the Republican "moderates" and their differences from the "radicals" can be derived from Richard Ellis, *The Jeffersonian Crisis: Courts and Politics in the Young Republic* (New York: Oxford University Press, 1971). The Jeffersonian antecedents of Whiggery are also implicit in Richard D. Buel, *Securing the Revolution: Ideology in American Politics, 1789–1815* (Ithaca: Cornell University Press, 1973).
86 William Henry Harrison, "Inaugural Address" (1841), *Messages and Papers of the Presidents*, 4:5–21.
87 See two works by Frederick Merk, *Slavery and the Annexation of Texas*

(New York: Knopf, 1972); and *Fruits of Propaganda in the Tyler Administration* (Cambridge: Harvard University Press, 1971). See also Merk's *Manifest Destiny and Mission in American History* (New York: Knopf, 1963); and David M. Pletcher, *The Diplomacy of Annexation: Texas, Oregon, and the Mexican War* (Columbia: University of Missouri Press, 1973).

88   William H. Seward, addressing a Whig ralley at Auburn, New York; see *Works*, 3:242; [Calvin Colton,] *The Junius Tracts* (New York, 1843–44).

89   [John Pendleton Kennedy,] *Defence of the Whigs, by a Member of the Twenty-Seventh Congress* (New York, 1844), has been reprinted in part in *The American Whigs: An Anthology*, ed. Daniel Walker Howe (New York: John Wiley & Sons, 1973), pp. 79–88.

90   Joshua Giddings, "The Annexation of Texas" (1844), *Speeches in Congress* (Boston, 1852), p. 113. Cf. Rufus Choate—who was no radical— "Speech before the Young Men's Whig Club of Boston, on the Annexation of Texas" (1844), *Works*, 2:267–83.

91   The best account of the impact of the Mexican War on U.S. domestic politics is John H. Schroeder, *Mr. Polk's War* (Madison: University of Wisconsin Press, 1973), and I am much indebted to it. See also Frederick Merk, "Dissent in the Mexican War," in Samuel Eliot Morison et al., *Dissent in Three American Wars* (Cambridge: Harvard University Press, 1970), pp. 33–64.

92   For an example of southern antiwar literature, see Philip Berry, *A Review of the Mexican War on Christian Principles* (Charleston, S.C., 1849). Besides the southern Whigs, the followers of John C. Calhoun also opposed the war.

93   For tabulations of votes on war-related issues, see Joel Silbey, *The Shrine of Party: Congressional Voting Behavior, 1841–1852* (Pittsburgh: University of Pittsburgh Press, 1967), p. 86 and passim; Thomas P. Alexander, *Sectional Stress and Party Strength: A Study of Roll-Call Voting Patterns in the United States House of Representatives, 1836–1860* (Nashville: Vanderbilt University Press, 1967), pp. 57–60. Even in a state like Missouri, where war enthusiasm might be expected, the Whigs opposed the declaration; see John V. Mering, *The Whig Party in Missouri* (Columbia: University of Missouri Press, 1967), p. 142.

94   *Congressional Globe*, 29th Cong., 1st sess., 15 (1846), appendix, 946–50.

95   Thomas Corwin, "The Mexican War" (1847), *Life and Speeches of Thomas Corwin*, ed. Josiah Morrow (Cincinnati, 1896), pp. 277–314.

96   [Daniel D. Barnard,] "The War with Mexico," *American Review* 3 (June, 1846): 571–80; "Our Relations with Mexico," ibid. 4 (July, 1846): 1–15; "The President's Message," ibid. 5 (Jan., 1847): 1–15; "Mr. Slidel's Mission to Mexico," ibid. 5 (April, 1847): 325–38; "The Constitution: Written and Unwritten," ibid. 6 (July, 1847): 1–17; "The Whigs and the War," ibid. 6 (Oct., 1847): 331–46; "The War: The New Issue," ibid 7 (Feb., 1848): 105–17; "The President and His Administration," ibid. 7 (May, 1848): 437–52.

97   *New York Tribune*, March 18–19, 1847; Anon., "Executive Usurpations," *American Review* 5 (March, 1847): 217–30.

98   [J. T. Headley,] "Our Army of Occupation," *American Review* 4 (Aug., 1846): 179.

99 *National Intelligencer,* March 14, 1848. (The phrase was borrowed from a comment by Sir Philip Francis on the Treaty of Amiens). See also ibid., Feb. 29, 1848.
100 *American Review* 7 (Feb., 1848): 207–9.

Chapter Five

1 "New England Capitalist" was first published, with an introduction by Carl Strauch, in the *Harvard Library Bulletin* 10 (Spring, 1956): 245–53.
2 See, e.g., Kenneth Porter, *The Jacksons and the Lees* (Cambridge: Harvard University Press, 1937); W. T. Baxter, *The House of Hancock* (Cambridge: Harvard University Press, 1945); or Jacques Downs, "The Merchant as Gambler," *Rhode Island History* 28 (Fall, 1969): 99–110.
3 Robert C. Winthrop, "Memoir of the Hon. N. Appleton," *Proceedings of the Massachusetts Historical Society* 5 (1861): 249–306; Frances W. Gregory, *Nathan Appleton: Merchant and Entrepreneur* (Charlottesville: University of Virginia Press, 1975), pp. 1–12.
4 The kinship networks of New England entrepreneurs are analyzed in Robert K. Lamb, "The Entrepreneur and the Community," *Men in Business,* ed. William Miller, 2d ed. (New York: Harper & Row, 1962), pp. 91–119, and in Sally Griffen and Clyde Griffen, "Family and Business in a Small City: Poughkeepsie, 1850–1880," *Journal of Urban History* 1 (May, 1975): 316–38.
5 Daniel J. Boorstin, *The Americans: The National Experience* (New York: Random House, 1965), p. 26.
6 For an interesting discussion of the meaning of this word, see Rush Welter, *The Mind of America, 1820–1860* (New York: Columbia University Press, 1975), pp. 156–58.
7 Henry Clay, *Works* (New York: G. P. Putnam's Sons, 1904), 9:425.
8 Among many works on mixed corporations, see Carter Goodrich, "American Development Policy," *Journal of Economic History* 16 (Dec., 1956): 449–60; Nathan Miller, *The Enterprise of a Free People: Aspects of Economic Development in New York State* (Ithaca: Cornell University Press, 1962); and Oscar Handlin and Mary Handlin, *Commonwealth: Massachusetts, 1774–1861,* rev. ed. (Cambridge: Harvard University Press, 1969).
9 Appleton's shift from commerce to industry illustrates in microcosm the thesis of Douglass C. North, *The Economic Growth of the United States, 1790–1860* (Englewood Cliffs, N.J.: Prentice-Hall, 1961), although the book does not mention him.
10 Nathan Appleton, *The Introduction of the Power Loom and the Origin of Lowell* (Lowell, Mass., 1858), pp. 8–9.
11 Edward Everett, "The First Settlement of New England" (1824), *Orations and Speeches* (Boston, 1883), 1:54; William Ellery Channing, "The Present Age" (1841), *Complete Works* (London, 1872), p. 133; Daniel Webster, "Lecture before the Society for the Diffusion of Useful Knowledge" (1836), *Writings and Speeches* (Boston: Little, Brown, 1903), 13:69; see also 2:27–40.
12 Edward Everett, "Address before the Mechanics' Association" (1837), *Orations and Speeches,* 2:248; cf. Timothy Walker, "Defence of

Mechanical Philosophy," *North American Review* 33 (July, 1831): 122–36.

13 Working-class and other opinion critical of mechanization is sampled in Thomas H. Bender, *Toward a Urban Vision: Ideas and Institutions in Nineteenth-Century America* (Lexington: University of Kentucky Press, 1975), chap. 3, and John F. Kasson, *Civilizing the Machine: Technology and Republican Values in America* (New York: Viking Press, 1976), pp. 86–98.

14 Marvin Meyers, *The Jacksonian Persuasion*, rev. ed. (New York: Vintage Books, 1960), esp. pp. 13–15; Daniel Webster, *Writings and Speeches*, 4:117.

15 Rufus Choate, *Works* (Boston, 1862), 1:125; Horace Bushnell, *Prosperity Our Duty* (Hartford, Conn., 1847), p. 6.

16 Daniel Webster, "Address at Pittsburgh" (1833), *Writings and Speeches*, 2:150. See also Andrew P. Peabody, "The Progress of Society," *North American Review* 63 (Oct., 1846): 334–57, and an essay by a businessman named Roland G. Hazard, *The Philosophical Character of Channing* (Boston, 1845).

17 See Samuel Reznick, "Industrial Consciousness in the United States, 1760–1830," *Economic and Business History* 4 (1931–32): 784–811.

18 William Henry Seward, quoted in Eric Foner, *Free Soil, Free Labor, Free Men* (New York: Oxford University Press, 1970), p. 39; Horace Bushnell, *Barbarism the First Danger* (New York, 1847), p. 27. "The General Improvement of Society," *Quarterly Christian Spectator* 6 (Dec., 1834): 647, expresses a typical Whig view.

19 Appleton, quoted in Frances Gregory, *Nathan Appleton*, p. 277; Edward Everett, "Address at Lowell, Mass." (1830), *Orations and Speeches*, 2:64 f.; "The Progress of Nations," *American Review* 4 (Dec., 1846): 649.

20 Thomas Corwin to William Greene, June 16, 1846, quoted in William G. Shade, *Banks or No Banks* (Detroit: Wayne State University Press, 1972), p. 144. For samples of Webster's public pronouncements, see *Niles' National Register* 64 (June 3, 1843): 219–22, or Webster's *Writings and Speeches*, 3:121. For his private views (which were the same), see Peter Harvey, *Reminiscences and Anecdotes of Daniel Webster* (Boston, 1877), pp. 390–92.

21 Edward Everett, "American Manufactures" (1831), *Orations and Speeches*, 2:69–71. Cf. "The Importance of the Mechanic Arts" (1837), ibid., pp. 238–55.

22 F. B. Crowninshield to Nathan Appleton, June 21, 1858, in Appleton, *Introduction of the Power Loom*, p. iii.

23 Everett, *Orations and Speeches*, 2:65. Cf. the fascinating and detailed account of a Pennsylvania mill town by A. F. C. Wallace, *Rockdale: The Growth of an American Village in the Early Industrial Revolution* (New York: Knopf, 1978).

24 Henry Clay to William Schouler, Nov. 10, 1843, quoted in Bender, *Toward an Urban Vision*, p. 39. See also Charles L. Sanford, "The Intellectual Origins and New-Worldliness of American Industry," *Journal of Economic History* 18 (1958): 1–16.

25 Erving Goffman has developed the concept of a "total institution" as

one that controls all aspects of life; John Kasson applies it to Lowell in *Civilizing the Machine*, p. 64.

26 Gregory, *Nathan Appleton*, p. 190.

27 Robert F. Dalzell, Jr., "The Rise of the Waltham-Lowell System and Some Thoughts on the Political Economy of Modernization in Ante-Bellum Massachusetts," *Perspectives in American History* 9 (1975): 229–68.

28 Kasson, *Civilizing the Machine*, p. 73.

29 There are a number of accounts of Lowell, written from varying perspectives. In addition to works already cited, see Caroline Ware, *Early New England Cotton Manufacture* (Boston: Houghton Mifflin, 1931). Lucy Larcom, *A New England Girlhood Outlined from Memory* (Boston, 1889), is a minor American classic by a former "mill girl" who shared Appleton's value system.

30 See James Willard Hurst, *The Legitimacy of the Business Corporation in the Law of the United States* (Charlottesville: University of Virginia Press, 1970), pp. 13–57.

31 John Quincy Adams, "Report on Manufactures" in U.S. Congress, *Register of Debates*, 22d Cong., 1st sess., 8:3 (May 23, 1832), appendix, 84. A similar Whig defense of corporations is in [Henry Lee et al.], *Exposition of Facts and Arguments in Support of . . . a Bank of Ten Millions* (Boston, 1836). Webster and Everett took this line many times.

32 On the modest size and old-fashioned organization of business enterprises at this time, see North, *Economic Growth*, pp. 159–63; George Rogers Taylor, *The Transportation Revolution* (New York: Rinehart, 1951), p. 247; and Lynn Marshall, "The Strange Stillbirth of the Whig Party," *American Historical Review* 72 (Jan., 1967): 445–68.

33 William Ellery Channing, "Lectures on the Elevation of the Laboring Classes" (1840), *Complete Works*, p. 38. The members of the Boston Associates and the Friday Evening Club are listed in Gregory, *Nathan Appleton*, p. 195.

34 Robert F. Dalzell, Jr., *Daniel Webster and the Trial of American Nationalism* (Boston: Houghton Mifflin, 1973), p. 59; see also Robert Rich, "'A Wilderness of Whigs': The Wealthy Men of Boston," *Journal of Social History* 4 (Spring, 1971): 263–76, and William Appleton (son of Nathan), "The Whigs of Massachusetts," *Proceedings of the Massachusetts Historical Society*, 2d ser. 11 (1897): 278–82.

35 Nathan Appleton, *An Examination of the Banking System of Massachusetts* (Boston, 1831); Nathan Appleton, *Remarks on Currency and Banking* (Boston, 1841), quotation from p. 20. See also Fritz Redlich, *The Molding of American Banking: Men and Ideas*, 2d ed. (New York: Johnson, 1968), pp. 67–87.

36 How valuable it was to prevent "wildcat" banking is still controversial. See the debate between Richard Sylla and Fritz Redlich, *Explorations in Economic History* 9 (Winter, 1971–72): 197–227, and 10 (Spring, 1973): 305–18. On the relations between Appleton's group and Biddle, see Arthur M. Schlesinger, Jr., *The Age of Jackson* (Boston: Little, Brown, 1945), pp. 74, 111, 395.

37 For a contemporary application of the term "aristocratic" to the Boston businessmen, see [Thomas L. Wilson], *The Aristocracy of Boston: Who*

They Are and What They Were (Boston, 1848). For a brief description of their value system, see Paul Goodman, "Ethics and Enterprise: The Values of a Boston Elite," *American Quarterly* 18 (Fall, 1966): 437–51.

38   *The Doctrines of Original Sin & the Trinity: Discussed in a Correspondence between a Clergyman of the Episcopal Church in England and a Layman of Boston, U.S*. (Boston, 1859).

39   "Proofs That General and Powerful Currents Have Swept and Worn the Surface of the Earth," *American Journal of Science and Art* 11 (Oct., 1826): 100–104.

40   Francis Bowen, *Principles of Political Economy* (Boston, 1856), p. i; George McDuffie, "The Tariff," in U.S. Congress, *Register of Debates*, 22d Cong., 1st sess., 8:3 (May 28, 1832): 3119–70.

41   Quoted by Robert C. Winthrop, to whom Appleton said it, "Memoir," pp. 304 f. (see n. 3 above).

42   [Washington, D.C.], *Banner of the Constitution*, Aug. 31, 1831.

43   U.S. Congress, *Register of Debates*, 22d Cong., 1st sess., 8:3 (May 30, 1832): 3203; Nathan Appleton, *Speech of Mr. Appleton of Massachusetts on the Bill to Reduce & Otherwise Alter the Duties on Imports . . . Jan. 23, 1833* (Washington, D.C., 1833), p. 12.

44   See *Correspondence between Nathan Appleton and John G. Palfrey* (Boston, 1846); Nathan Appleton, *Letter to the Hon. Wm. C. Rives of Virginia, on Slavery and the Union* (Boston, 1860); Thomas H. O'Connor, *Lords of the Loom: The Cotton Whigs and the Coming of the Civil War* (New York: Charles Scribner's Sons, 1968).

45   *Testimonials to Henry C. Carey, Esq.* (Philadelphia, 1859).

46   Rufus Griswold, "Henry C. Carey: The Apostle of the American School of Political Economy," *American Whig Review* 13 (Jan., 1851): 80. Cf. "Political Economists: Henry Carey," ibid. 12 (Oct., 1850): 376–89.

47   Frédéric Bastiat, *Harmonies économiques* (Paris, 1851); cf. Henry C. Carey, *The Past, the Present, and the Future* (Philadelphia, 1848).

48   See Friedrich List, *Das nationale System der politischen Ökonomie* (Jena: G. Fischer, 1922; first published 1841); and Eugen Karl Dühring, *Careys Umwälzung der Volkswirthschaftslehre und Sozialwissenschaft* (Munich, 1865).

49   Ugo Rabbeno, in his *The American Commercial Policy: Three Historical Essays*, trans. from the Italian (London, 1895), called Carey's earlier reputation inflated; Charles H. Levermore ("Henry C. Carey and His Social System," *Political Science Quarterly* 5 [1890]: 553–82), while less overtly critical, still regarded Carey with detachment.

50   Daniel M. Fox, *The Discovery of Abundance: Simon Patten and the Transformation of Social Theory* (Ithaca: Cornell University Press, 1967), p. 184.

51   For biographies of the Careys, see Kenneth W. Rowe, *Mathew Carey: A Study in American Economic Development* (Baltimore: Johns Hopkins University Press, 1933), and Arnold W. Green, *Henry Charles Carey, Nineteenth-Century Sociologist* (Philadelphia: University of Pennsylvania Press, 1951).

52   See William W. Elder, *Memoir of Henry C. Carey, Read before the Historical Society of Pennsylvania* (Philadelphia, 1880).

53   See Carey's *Letters on International Copyright* (Philadelphia, 1853) and *The International Copyright Question Considered* (Philadelphia, 1872).

54	Isaiah Berlin, *The Hedgehog and the Fox* (New York: New American Library, 1957), pp. 7 f.
55	Stuart Bruchey, for example, points out that industrialization is almost always necessary for economic development, though he admits of exceptions like Argentina and New Zealand. See his *The Roots of American Economic Growth, 1607–1861*, 2d ed. (New York: Harper & Row, 1968), pp. 12–15.
56	Henry C. Carey, *Principles of Social Science*, 3 vols. (Philadelphia, London, etc., 1858–59), 1:9–40. (This was a cumulative work, bringing together ideas that had been expressed piecemeal since the 1830s and '40s. Though Carey had become a Republican by the time of its publication, it still reflects his thinking as a Whig.)
57	Henry C. Carey, *The Unity of Law: Exhibited in the Relations of Physical, Social, Mental, and Moral Science* (Philadelphia, 1873).
58	Henry C. Carey, *Essay on the Rate of Wages: With an Examination of the Causes of the Differences in the Condition of the Laboring Population throughout the World* (Philadelphia, 1835), pp. 246–55; *Principles of Social Science*, 3:265.
59	*Principles of Social Science*, 2:308–34; cf. Daniel Webster, "Speech at Pepperell, Mass." (1844), *Writings and Speeches*, 13:290.
60	*Principles of Social Science*, 3:131–70.
61	Ibid., pp. 233–62.
62	See Carey's *The Credit System in France, Gt. Britain, and the U.S.* (Philadelphia, 1838), *Money: A Lecture* (New York, 1857), and *Essay on the Rate of Wages*, esp. p. 80.
63	Henry C. Carey, *Answers to the Questions: What Constitutes Currency? . . .* (Philadelphia, 1840); *Principles of Social Science*, 1:147–76.
64	For an evaluation of Carey's monetary views, see Abraham Kaplan, *Henry Charles Carey: A Study in American Economic Thought* (Baltimore: Johns Hopkins University Press, 1931), pp. 59 and 81. On the importance of cheap money to economic development, see T. S. Ashton, *The Industrial Revolution*, rev. ed. (London: Oxford University Press, 1962), pp. 8–10, and John Kenneth Galbraith, *Money* (Boston: Houghton Mifflin Co., 1975), pp. 84–86.
65	See Carey, *Essay on the Rate of Wages*, p. 56; contrast Nassau Senior, *Three Lectures on the Rate of Wages* (London, 1831).
66	Carey's most thorough attack on Malthus is in *Principles of Social Science*, 3:263–367. Cf. Nathan Appleton in *Register of Debates in Congress*, 8:3 (May 30, 1832): 3207; Calvin Colton, *Public Economy for the United States* (New York, 1848), p. 159; Francis Bowen, "The Social Condition of England," *North American Review* 65 (Oct., 1847): 461–504.
67	See Kaplan, *Carey*, p. 77. For background, see Kenneth Smith, *The Malthusian Controversy* (London: Routledge & Kegan Paul, 1951), and Gertrude Himmelfarb, *Victorian Minds* (New York: Knopf, 1968), pp. 82–110.
68	Carey, *The Past, the Present, and the Future*, passim; *Principles of Social Science*, 2:410–18.
69	Carey's Comteanism is discussed in Ernest Teilhac, *Histoire de la pensée économique aux États-Unis au dix-neuvième siècle* (Paris: Recueil Sirey, 1928), chap. 2.
70	*Principles of Social Science*, 1:463. Such arguments endeared Carey to

religious magazines like the *Christian Examiner*—see volume 29 (Sept., 1840), pp. 127 f.

71 Quoted in Levermore (cited in n. 49 above), p. 568.

72 Emile Durkheim, *De la division du travail social* (Paris: Presses Universitaires de France, 1960), p. 389; for Carey's rejection of Spencer, see *The Unity of Law*, p. 299.

73 *The Unity of Law*, pp. 374 f. Henry C. Carey, *The Harmony of Interests* (New York, 1851), collects essays of his that had appeared earlier in a magazine he published, *The Plough, the Loom, and the Anvil*. See also his *The Prospect: Agricultural, Manufacturing, Commercial, Financial* (Philadelphia, 1851), pp. 77 f.

74 See Leo Marx, *The Machine in the Garden: Technology and the Pastoral Ideal in America* (New York: Oxford University Press, 1964), passim, and Ruth Miller Elson, *Guardians of Tradition: American Schoolbooks in the Nineteenth Century* (Lincoln: University of Nebraska Press, 1964), p. 25. Elson, but not Marx, notes the Whiggish aspect of this motif.

75 See Edward Everett, "American Manufactures" (1831), *Orations and Speeches*, 2:72; Rufus Choate, "Protecting American Labor" (1844), *Works* (Boston, 1862), 2:216. On the meaning of the "log cabin," see Congressman Joseph Underwood of Kentucky, quoted in Welter, *The Mind of America*, p. 116.

76 John Quincy Adams, diary entry, June 29, 1840, in *Memoirs* (Philadelphia, 1877), 10:324; Lyman Beecher, "Lectures on Political Atheism" (1829), *Works* (Cleveland, 1853), 1:80–82.

77 Kenneth Lockridge, *A New England Town: The First Hundred Years* (New York: W. W. Norton, 1970), p. 180; Henry Carey, *Principles of Social Science*, chap. 22; George W. Smith, "Ante-Bellum Attempts of Northern Business Interest to 'Redeem' the Upper South," *Journal of Southern History* 11 (May, 1945): 177–213.

78 Henry Clay, "American Industry" (1824), *Works*, 6:263 (cf. Henry Carey, *The Harmony of Interests*); "The Influence of the Trading Spirit upon the Social and Moral Life of America," *American Review* 1 (Jan., 1845): 97.

79 Marvin Meyers, *The Jacksonian Persuasion*, esp. pp. 24–32; Daniel Webster, "Remarks in the State House" (1840), *Writings and Speeches*, 6:293–307; Horace Greeley, *Recollections* (New York, 1868), pp. 295 ff.

80 Henry Clay in 1839, quoted in Clement Eaton, *Henry Clay and the Art of American Politics* (Boston: Little, Brown, 1957), p. 114. On urbanization, see George Rogers Taylor, "The National Economy before and after the Civil War," in *Economic Change in the Civil War Era*, ed. David T. Gilchrist and W. David Lewis (Greenville, Del.: Eleutherian Mills–Hagley Foundation, 1965), pp. 1–22.

81 Rufus Choate, "Protecting American Labor" (1844), *Works*, 2:215. For another interesting celebration of the city by a Whig philanthropist, see Joseph Tuckerman, *Principles and Results of the Ministry-at-Large in Boston* (Boston, 1838), pp. 159 ff. and 247 ff.

82 Edward Everett, "The Importance of Agriculture" (1857), *Orations and Speeches*, 3:555.

83 How the Whig social ideal translated itself into landscape architecture may be seen in Stanley French, "The Cemetery as Cultural Institu-

tion," in *Death in America,* ed. David Stannard (Philadelphia: University of Pennsylvania Press, 1975), pp. 69–91, and Thomas Bender, *Toward an Urban Vision,* pp. 159–88.

84   *Principles of Social Science,* 1:198–233; *Unity of Law,* pp. 395–403.

85   *Principles of Social Science,* 1:234–62. See also Carey's *Ireland's Miseries* (New York, 1852).

86   *Principles of Social Science,* 1:285–307. See also Carey's *The Slave Trade, Domestic and Foreign* (Philadelphia, 1853), pp. 35–73, 95–106.

87   *Principles of Social Science,* 1:308–32; *Unity of Law,* pp. 258, 273.

88   *Principles of Social Science,* 1:394–411 (cf. Horace Greeley, *The Tariff as It Is* [New York, 1844]); John Stuart Mill, *Principles of Political Economy,* ed. W. A. Ashley (London: Longmans, Green, 1929), p. 925.

89   Carey, *Unity of Law,* 174–99; Henry Clay, "Domestic Manufactures" (1810), *Works,* 6:9.

90   See Levermore, "Henry C. Carey," p. 570; List, quoted in Margaret Hirst, *Life of Friedrich List* (London: Smith, Elder, 1909), p. 279.

91   Henry Clay, "The Public Lands" (1832), *Works,* 7:490; Carl Schurz, *Life of Henry Clay* (Boston, 1887), 2:151. Cf. Edward Everett, "American Manufactures" (1831), *Orations and Speeches,* 2:77–79; Junius [pseud. for Calvin Colton], *The Tariff Triumphant* (New York, 1844), p. 4; Horace Greeley, *Why I Am a Whig* (New York, 1851), p. 8. In emphasizing the "infant-industries" argument, I dissent from Frank W. Taussig, *The Tariff History of the United States* (New York: G. P. Putnam's Sons, 1931), pp. 7 and 65.

92   Rodney J. Morrison, "Henry C. Carey and American Economic Development," *Explorations in Entrepreneurial History,* 2d ser. 5 (Winter, 1968): 132–44.

93   George W. Smith, *Henry C. Carey and American Sectional Conflict* (Albuquerque: University of New Mexico Press, 1951), pp. 47, 50–53, 75; Henry C. Carey, *Letters to the President on the Foreign and Domestic Policy of the Union* (Philadelphia, 1858); Joseph H. Parke, *John Bell of Tennessee* (Baton Rouge: Louisiana State University Press, 1950), p. 345.

94   See Carey's *The North and the South* (New York, 1854); "The Slave Question," *The Plough, the Loom, and the Anvil* 1 (Jan., 1849): 401–11; and *The Slave Trade,* passim.

95   Henry C. Carey, *Reconstruction: Industrial, Financial, and Political* (Philadelphia, 1867), and *The Resources of the Union* (Philadelphia, 1866).

96   See the following, all by Carey: *Beauties of the Monopoly System of New Jersey* (Philadelphia, 1848); *Review of an Address of the Joint Board of Directors of the Delaware & Raritan Canal and Camden & Amboy Railroad* (Philadelphia, 1848); *Can the Monopoly Lawfully Be Abolished?* (Philadelphia, 1849); *Correspondence between the Commissioners for Investigating the Affairs of the Joint Companies and a Citizen of Burlington* (Philadelphia, 1850).

97   Robert P. Sharkey, "Commercial Banking," in *Economic Change in the Civil War Era* (cited in n. 80), p. 27. See also Walter T. K. Nugent, *Money and American Society, 1865–1880* (New York: Free Press, 1968), pp. 33–43.

98 Henry C. Carey, *Our Future* (Philadelphia, 1869), p. 6. See also Henry
    C. Carey, *The Finance Minister, the Currency, and the Public Debt*
    (Philadelphia, 1868).
99 Henry C. Carey, *Resumption: When and How Will It End?* (Philadelphia,
    1877), pp. 5 f.; Henry C. Carey, *Reconstruction: Letters to Henry Wilson*
    (Philadelphia, 1867); *Unity of Law*, pp. 209–34. See also Smith, *Carey
    and Sectional Conflict*, pp. 110–13.
100 E. R. A. Seligman, "Early Teaching of Economics in the United States,"
    in *Economic Essays in Honor of John Bates Clark*, ed. J. H. Hollander
    (New York: Macmillan, 1927), pp. 283–320; *North American Review* 103
    (Oct., 1866): 573–80.

Chapter Six

1 Abraham Lincoln, "Eulogy on Henry Clay" (1852), *Collected Works*, ed.
   Roy P. Basler (New Brunswick: Rutgers University Press, 1953), 2:121;
   National Intelligencer, Aug. 8, 1844.
2 Horace Greeley, *Recollections of a Busy Life* (New York, 1868), p. 166;
   Charles Dickens to Charles Sumner, March 13, 1842, *Letters of Charles
   Dickens*, ed. Madeline House et al. (Oxford: Clarendon Press, 1974),
   3:127; Holman Hamilton, "Henry Clay," *Encyclopedia of American Biography*, ed. John Garraty (New York: Harper & Row, 1974), p. 200.
3 Diary entry for April 6, 1820, in *Memoirs of John Quincy Adams, Comprising Portions of His Diary from 1795 to 1848*, ed. Charles Francis
   Adams (Philadelphia, 1874), 5:59.
4 Christopher Dawson, introduction to *Ideas and Beliefs of the Victorians*,
   ed. Harmon Grisewood et al. (London: Sylvan Press, 1949), p. 28.
5 Henry Clay, "The Beginning of Jackson's Administration" (1829), *The
   Works of Henry Clay, Comprising His Life, Correspondence, and Speeches*,
   ed. Calvin Colton . . . (New York: G. P. Putnam's Sons, 1904), 7:373.
   Unfortunately, *The Papers of Henry Clay*, edited by James F. Hopkins
   and Mary Hargreaves (Lexington: University of Kentucky Press,
   1959——) have reached only the year 1826 in the five volumes published so far.
6 E. L. Magoon, *Living Orators in America* (New York, 1851), p. 154.
   There is a brilliant sketch of the young Henry Clay in George Dangerfield, *The Era of Good Feelings* (London: Methuen & Co., 1953), pp.
   10–13.
7 See Henry Clay to Alexander Plummer et al., Aug. 1, 1844, *Works*, 3:
   415 f.
8 Harriet Martineau, *A Retrospect of Western Travel* (New York, 1838),
   1:130; Clay, *Works*, 6:295; 7:371, 417.
9 U.S. Congress, *Register of Debates*, 19th Cong., 1st sess., 2 (March 30,
   1826): 401.
10 Back in 1806, after Aaron Burr killed Alexander Hamilton in a duel,
   Lyman Beecher had published a sermon calling on men not to vote for
   any duelist. In 1844 the Democrats unearthed this and gleefully reprinted forty thousand copies to use against Clay.
11 See Bernard Bailyn, *The Origins of American Politics* (New York: Knopf,
   1968), chap. 2.

12   Erik Erikson, *Young Man Luther: A Study in Psychoanalysis and History* (New York: W. W. Norton, 1958); idem, *Gandhi's Truth* (New York: W. W. Norton, 1969); William H. Seward, "Remarks on the Death of Henry Clay," reprinted in Clay, *Works*, 3:248.

13   On general problems of violence, see David Grimsted, "Rioting in Its Jacksonian Setting," *American Historical Review* 77 (April, 1972): 361–97; Richard Maxwell Brown, *Strain of Violence* (New York: Oxford University Press, 1975); and Richard Slotkin, *Regeneration through Violence* (Middletown, Conn.: Wesleyan University Press, 1973).

14   William Ellery Channing to Henry Clay, Aug. 1, 1837, in Channing, *Works* (Boston, 1848), 2:245; Horace Bushnell, *Barbarism the First Danger* (New York, 1847), p. 20; Henry Ware, Jr., "The Law of Honor," *Works* (Boston, 1847), 3:153.

15   Maurice Quinlan, *Victorian Prelude: A History of English Manners, 1700–1830* (New York: Columbia University Press, 1941), pp. 176 f.; Henry Clay, "On Mr. Foote's Motion" (1850) *Works*, 9:418.

16   *National Intelligencer*, July 17, 1855; Daniel Webster, "The Revolution in Greece" (1824), *Writings and Speeches* (Boston: Little, Brown, 1903), 5:77; Clement Eaton, *The Freedom-of-Thought Struggle in the Old South* (New York: Harper Torchbooks, 1964), passim.

17   Henry Clay, "Address at Lexington" (1842), "On the Pre-Emption Bill" (1838), *Works*, 9:359–84; 8:87–93.

18   Contrast Clay's opinions in the cabinet meeting recorded in Adams' diary, Dec. 22, 1825 (*Memoirs*, 7:89–91), with his speech on "Our Relations with the Cherokees" (1835), *Works*, 7:637–56.

19   "Uses and Abuses of Lynch Law," *American Whig Review* 13 (March, 1851): 213–20. Leonard Richards found members of antiabolition mobs predominantly affluent but not predominantly Whig. They included a disproportionate number of men from nonevangelical religious denominations and avowed party-line voters, two characteristics negatively associated with Whiggery (Leonard Richards, *"Gentlemen of Property and Standing": Anti-Abolition Mobs in Jacksonian America* [New York: Oxford University Press, 1970]).

20   On southern acceptance of violence, see John Hope Franklin, *The Militant South, 1800–1861* (Cambridge: Harvard University Press, 1956). Franklin, however, does not draw any Whig-Democratic distinction.

21   See Chilton Williamson, *American Suffrage from Property to Democracy* (Princeton: Princeton University Press, 1960), p. 275, and Glyndon G. Van Deusen, "The Whig Party," in *History of U.S. Political Parties*, ed. Arthur M. Schlesinger, Jr. (New York: Chelsea House, 1973), p. 353.

22   William Craigie and James Hurlburt, eds., *A Dictionary of American English on Historical Principles* (Chicago: University of Chicago Press, 1938–44), 4:2065.

23   Carl Schurz, *The Life of Henry Clay* (Boston, 1887; rev. ed., 1899), is a classic; other biographies include Bernard Mayo, *Henry Clay* (Boston: Houghton Mifflin, 1937), Glyndon G. Van Deusen, *The Life of Henry Clay* (Boston: Little, Brown, 1937), and Clement Eaton, *Henry Clay and the Art of American Politics* (Boston: Little, Brown, 1957).

24   "The American System" (1832), *Works*, 7:464.

25   Eaton, *Henry Clay*, pp. 78–81; Richard B. Latner, "A New Look at

Jacksonian Politics," *Journal of American History* 61 (March, 1975): 944–46.

26 Eaton, *Henry Clay*, p. 61.

27 E. P. Thompson, "Patrician Society, Plebeian Culture," *Journal of Social History* 7 (Summer, 1974): 390. Cf. C. B. MacPherson, *The Political Theory of Possessive Individualism* (Oxford: Clarendon Press, 1962), chap. 4. Like the term "oral literature" used in chapter 2, "agrarian bourgeois" is etymologically contradictory but conveys a useful idea.

28 Robert F. Dalzell, Jr., "The Rise of the Waltham-Lowell System and Some Thoughts on the Political Economy of Modernization in Ante-Bellum Massachusetts," *Perspectives in American History* 9 (1975): 263.

29 Prominent examples of the one are Kenneth Stampp, *The Peculiar Institution* (New York: Knopf, 1956), and Robert Fogel and Stanley Engerman, *Time on the Cross* (Boston: Little, Brown, 1974); of the other, Ulrich B. Phillips, *American Negro Slavery* (New York: D. Appleton, 1918), and Eugene Genovese, *The World the Slaveholders Made* (New York: Pantheon, 1969).

30 See William R. Taylor, *Cavalier and Yankee: The Old South and American National Character* (New York: George Braziller, 1961), pp. 95–141.

31 The overview provided in Charles Grier Sellers, Jr., "Who Were the Southern Whigs?" *American Historical Review* 59 (Jan., 1954): 335–46, should now be supplemented with Robert Kelley, *The Cultural Pattern in American Politics* (New York: Knopf, 1979), pp. 176–81. See also John V. Mering, *The Whig Party in Missouri* (Columbia: University of Missouri Press, 1967), and William H. Adams, *The Whig Party in Louisiana* (Lafayette: University of Southwestern Louisiana Press, 1973).

32 See, e.g., James R. Sharp, *The Jacksonians versus the Banks* (New York: Columbia University Press, 1970); Thomas B. Alexander et al., "The Basis of Alabama's Antebellum Two-Party System," *Alabama Review* 19 (Oct., 1966): 243–76; or Edwin A. Miles, *Jacksonian Democracy in Mississippi* (Chapel Hill: University of North Carolina Press, 1960).

33 See, e.g., Max R. Williams, "The Foundations of the Whig Party in North Carolina," *North Carolina Historical Review* 47 (April, 1970): 115–29.

34 Clay, quoted in Eaton, *Henry Clay*, pp. 90 f. and 103.

35 Henry Clay, "The American System" (1832), *Works*, 7:463; Robert S. Starobin, *Industrial Slavery in the Old South* (New York: Oxford University Press, 1970); R. Keith Aufhauser, "Slavery and Technological Change," *Journal of Economic History* 34 (March, 1974): 36–50.

36 Henry Clay, "American Industry" (1824), *Works*, 6:272.

37 Henry Clay to Richard Pindall, Feb. 17, 1849, *Works*, 3:346–52; "Will," *Works*, 3:153.

38 Schurz, *Life of Clay*, 2:255; George Rawlings Poage, *Henry Clay and the Whig Party* (Chapel Hill: University of North Carolina Press, 1936), p. 149.

39 Henry Clay, "Reply to Mr. Mendenhall" (1842), and "On Abolition" (1839), *Works*, 9:385–90 and 7:158. See also Clay's address to the Kentucky Colonization Society, *African Repository* 6 (March, 1830): 11.

40 Henry Clay to Peter B. Porter, Dec. 24, 1837, quoted in Van Deusen, *Henry Clay*, p. 314; Clay in the Senate, Dec. 20, 1849, *Works*, 9:392. See

also William Van Deburg, "Henry Clay, the Right of Petition, and Slavery in the Nation's Capital," *Register of the Kentucky Historical Society* 68 (1970): 132–46.

41 See, e.g., Patricia Hickin, "Gentle Agitator: Samuel M. Janney and the Anti-Slavery Movement in Virginia, 1842–1851," *Journal of Southern History* 37 (May, 1971): 159–90. A northern Whig moderate could claim, "North and South, it is a common sentiment with Whigs that slavery is a great evil" (Daniel D. Barnard, "The Whigs and Their Candidate," *American Review* 8 [Sept., 1848]: 234).

42 For Clay's objection that the "positive-good" proslavery argument could justify enslaving whites, see his letter to Pindall, *Works*, 3:347.

43 The goals of the American Colonization Society were often stated in its organ, the *African Repository*; see also Edward Everett, "Colonization and Civilization of Africa" (1832), *Orations and Speeches* (Boston, 1883), 1:329–43, and Calvin Colton, *Colonization and Abolition Contrasted* (Philadelphia, 1839). Colonizationist racial attitudes are well discussed in George M. Fredrickson, *The Black Image in the White Mind: The Debate on Afro-American Character and Destiny, 1817–1914* (New York: Harper & Row, 1971), chap. 1.

44 Cf. David Brion Davis, *The Problem of Slavery in the Age of Revolution* (Ithaca: Cornell University Press, 1975), p. 304.

45 Henry Clay, "African Colonization" (1827), *Works*, 6:332.

46 See P. J. Staudenraus, *The African Colonization Movement, 1816–1865* (New York: Columbia University Press, 1961).

47 U.S. Congress, *Register of Debates*, 22d Congress, vols. 8 and 9 (1831–33), passim; James D. Richardson, ed., *Messages and Papers of the Presidents* (Washington, D.C., 1900), 3:1275–88.

48 Webster, "The Colony of Liberia" (1852), *Writings and Speeches*, 13:505 f.; Edward Everett, "The Colonization of Africa" (1853), *Orations and Speeches*, 3:167–85; Abraham Lincoln, "Speech at Springfield" (1857), *Collected Works*, 2:409; Robert Rayback, *Millard Fillmore* (Buffalo: Henry Stuart, 1959), pp. 367–69.

49 Clifford Geertz, "Ideology as a Cultural System," in *Ideology and Discontent*, ed. David Apter (New York: Free Press, 1964), pp. 47–76.

50 Henry Clay, "The American System" (1832), *Works*, 7:477, 450.

51 Henry Clay, "Internal Improvement" (1818), *Works*, 6:115–35; "On American Industry" (1824), ibid., pp. 254–94. Mathew Carey is cited on p. 284.

52 Henry Clay, "The Public Lands" (1832), *Works*, 7:495.

53 Clay in the Senate, May 21, 1850, *Works*, 9:467; "The Public Lands" (1832), *Works*, 7:515; Paul Nagel, *This Sacred Trust: American Nationality, 1798–1898* (New York: Oxford University Press, 1971), pp. 90–93.

54 U.S. Congress, *Register of Debates*, 22d Cong., 1st sess., 8:3 (May 23, 1832), appendix, 89; cf. "Our Position," *American Review* 2 (July, 1845): 1–2.

55 Daniel Webster, "The Removal of the Deposits" (1834), *Writings and Speeches*, 6:267; cf. Lyman Beecher, "Political Atheism" (1829; rev. ed., 1835), *Works* (Cleveland, 1852), 1:111, and James T. Austin, "Manufactures of Massachusetts," *North American Review* 50 (Jan., 1840): 230 f.

56   Herbert Ershkowitz and William G. Shade, "Consensus or Conflict? Political Behavior in the State Legislatures during the Jacksonian Era," *Journal of American History* 58 (Dec., 1971): 618; Edward Pessen, *Riches, Class, and Power Before the Civil War* (Lexington, Mass.: D. C. Heath, 1973); Lee Soltow, *Men and Wealth in the United States, 1850–1870* (New Haven: Yale University Press, 1975).

57   The historiography of the Bank War is large, technical, and highly controversial. Some interesting recent works are: Jean Wilburn, *Biddle's Bank: The Crucial Years* (New York: Columbia University Press, 1967); Robert V. Remini, *Andrew Jackson and the Bank War* (New York: W. W. Norton, 1967); Peter Temin, *The Jacksonian Economy* (New York: W. W. Norton, 1969); John M. McFaul, *The Politics of Jacksonian Finance* (Ithaca: Cornell University Press, 1972); Marie Sushka, "The Antebellum Money Market and the Economic Impact of the Bank War," *Journal of Economic History* 36 (Dec., 1976): 809–35.

58   See William Freehling, *Prelude to Civil War: The Nullification Controversy in South Carolina* (New York: Harper Torchbooks, 1968).

59   Henry Clay, "Our Relations with France" (1835), *Works*, 7:632–36; the quotation is from Clay, "The Mexican War" (1847), *Works*, 3:61.

60   Joel Silbey confirms the greater belligerence of the Democrats in his counts of congressional votes; see his *The Shrine of Party* (Pittsburgh: University of Pittsburgh Press, 1967), pp. 58 and 86. Whig ideals in international relations are stated in Daniel Webster, "Speech at New York" (1842), *Writings and Speeches*, 13:146 f., and Rufus Choate, "Speech in the Case of Alexander McLeod" (1841), *Works* (Boston, 1862), 2:7–11.

61   See Daniel Webster, "Speech at the National Republican Convention" (1832), *Writings and Speeches*, 2:96 f.

62   Alexis de Tocqueville, *Democracy in America*, ed. Phillips Bradley (New York: Knopf, 1945), 2:254. See also "The Oregon Question: War and Peace," *American Review* 3 (Feb., 1846): 113–28; "The Oregon Treaty," ibid. 4 (Aug., 1846): 105–14; and Frederick Merk, *Manifest Destiny and Mission* (New York: Knopf, 1963).

63   Schurz, *Henry Clay*, 2:394–96; Silbey, *Shrine of Party*, pp. 133–35. See also Rush Welter, *The Mind of America, 1820–1860* (New York: Columbia University Press, 1975), pp. 48–61; Kenneth Shewmaker, "Daniel Webster and the Politics of Foreign Policy, 1850–52," *Journal of American History* 63 (Sept., 1976): 303–15; Donald Spencer, *Louis Kossuth and Young America* (Columbia: University of Missouri Press, 1977).

64   Henry Clay, "On Abolition" (1839), *Works*, 8:141–59.

65   Henry Stanton to James G. Birney, March 21, 1840, *Letters of James Gillespie Birney*, ed. Dwight Dumond (New York: Appleton-Century, 1938), 1:541 f.; R. Carlyle Buley, *The Old Northwest* (Indianapolis: Indiana Historical Society, 1950), 2:211; Richard H. Sewall, *Ballots for Freedom: Antislavery Politics in the United States* (New York: Oxford University Press, 1976), pp. 62–65, 76–77.

66   See James B. Lambert, *Presidential Politics in the United States, 1841–1844* (Durham, N.C.: Duke University Press, 1936), and Sylvan H. Kesilman, "John Tyler and the Presidency" (Ph.D. diss., Ohio State University, 1973).

67 George R. Poage's book, cited in note 38, is rather critical of Clay. See also Sydney Nathans, *Daniel Webster and Jacksonian Democracy* (Baltimore: Johns Hopkins University Press, 1973), pp. 164–78.

68 On the regal aspirations of Julia Gardiner Tyler, see Robert Seager, *And Tyler Too* (New York: McGraw-Hill, 1963), pp. xvi–xvii.

69 Cf. Edmund Burke, *Thoughts on the Cause of the Present Discontents* (London, 1770).

70 E.g., William Ellery Channing, "The Duty of the Free States" (1842), *Works*, 6:349.

71 Partisan and sectional votes on Texas are analyzed in Thomas B. Alexander, *Sectional Stress and Party Strength: A Study of Roll-Call Voting Patterns in the United States House of Representatives, 1836–1860* (Nashville: Vanderbilt University Press, 1967), pp. 51–60.

72 Daniel Webster, "The Revolution in Greece" (1824), *Writings and Speeches*, 5:64. This aspect of Whig thought is well examined in Major L. Wilson, *Space, Time, and Freedom: The Quest for Nationality and the Irrepressible Conflict* (Westport, Conn.: Greenwood Press, 1974).

73 See Schurz, *Life of Clay*, 2:260–63; also Charles Sellers, "The Election of 1844," *History of American Presidential Elections*, ed. Arthur M. Schlesinger, Jr. (cited in n. 21, above), 1:747–98.

74 Henry Clay, "The Mexican War" (1847), *Works*, 3:62. See also [Charles King], "Mr. Clay's Resolutions," *American Review* 6 (Dec., 1847): 554–60.

75 See Margaret Ruth Morley, "The Edge of Empire: Henry Clay's American System and the Formation of American Foreign Policy" (Ph.D. diss., University of Wisconsin, 1972); also Clay, *Works*, 6:100–102, 135–47; 8:42 and passim.

76 Henry Clay to John M. Clayton, April 16, 1847, quoted in Van Deusen, *Henry Clay*, p. 382.

77 Webster, "Pilgrim Festival in New York" (1850), *Writings and Speeches*, 4:224.

78 "California," *American Review* 9 (April, 1849): 331–38; quotation from p. 334.

79 See Rush Welter, "The Frontier West as Image of American Society: Conservative Attitudes before the Civil War," *Mississippi Valley Historical Review* 46 (March, 1960): 593–614.

80 See Norman A. Graebner, "1848: Southern Politics at the Crossroads," *The Historian* 25 (Nov., 1962): 14–34.

81 See Holman Hamilton, *Zachary Taylor* (Indianapolis: Bobbs-Merrill, 1951), 2:178–85.

82 On the split between Taylor and Clay, see Michael Holt, *The Political Crisis of the 1850's* (New York: John Wiley & Sons, 1978), chap. 4.

83 Clay, "The Compromise Resolutions" (1850), *Works*, 3:309 and 9:418.

84 Ibid., 3:304 and 9:563 f.

85 See Major Wilson, "Ideological Fruits of Manifest Destiny," *Journal of the Illinois State Historical Society* 63 (Summer, 1970): 132–57, and Holman Hamilton, *Prologue to Conflict: The Crisis and Compromise of 1850* (Lexington: University of Kentucky Press, 1964).

86 Henry Clay, "The Compromise Bills" (1850), *Works*, 9:551–61; contrast Clay, "The American System" (1832), *Works*, 7:463.

87 Henry Clay, "Last Parliamentary Effort" (1852), *Works*, 9:629–32.
88 R. McKinley Ormsby, *History of the Whig Party* (Boston, 1859), pp. 372 f.

Chapter Seven

1 See *Victorian America*, ed. Daniel Walker Howe (Philadelphia: University of Pennsylvania Press, 1976). Marie Yoshiko Caskey, in *Chariot of Fire: Religion and the Beecher Family* (New Haven: Yale University Press, 1978), approaches her subject with sensitivity and fresh insight. Stuart C. Henry, *Unvanquished Puritan: A Portrait of Lyman Beecher* (Grand Rapids, Mich.: William B. Eerdmans, 1973), is the closest thing to a biography that has yet been written.

2 As the eldest of thirteen, Catharine occupied a special place in the family; the powerful love between her and her father is beautifully portrayed in Kathryn Kish Sklar, *Catharine Beecher: A Study in American Domesticity* (New Haven: Yale University Press, 1973).

3 *The Autobiography of Lyman Beecher*, ed. Barbara M. Cross (Cambridge: Harvard University Press, 1961; first published 1884), 1:394–96; 2:84, 399. The parallel with Johnson was suggested by my research assistant, Geraldine Moyle.

4 Jonathan Edwards, "Thoughts on the Revival of Religion," *Works* (New York, 1849), vol. 3, esp. pp. 313–34; Lyman Beecher, *A Plea for the West* (Cincinnati, 1835), pp. 9 f.

5 Compare Jonathan Edwards, "History of the Work of Redemption," *Works*, 1:462–64, with (for example), "The General Improvement of Society," *Quarterly Christian Spectator* 6 (Dec., 1834): 632–54, or "The Destiny of the Country," *American Review* 5 (March, 1847): 231–39.

6 Lyman Beecher, "A Reformation of Morals Practicable and Indispensable" (1812), *Works* (Cleveland, 1852–53), 2:81; *Autobiography*, 2:3, 432. For background, see C. C. Goen, "Edwards' New Departure in Eschatology," *Church History* 28 (March, 1959): 25–40, and Robert K. Whalen, "Millenarianism and Millennialism in America, 1790–1880" (Ph.D. diss., State University of New York at Stony Brook, 1971).

7 Lyman Beecher, *A Sermon Addressed to the Legislature of Connecticut* (New Haven, 1826), p. 6. On the contribution of postmillennialism to modern ideas of progress, see Ernest L. Tuveson, *Millennium and Utopia* (Berkeley and Los Angeles: University of California Press, 1949).

8 Lyman Beecher, *Instructions for Young Christians* (Cincinnati, 1833), p. 16; idem, *A Sermon Delivered at the Funeral of Henry Obookish, a Native of Owhynee and a Member of the Foreign Mission School* (New Haven, 1818), p. 32.

9 Cf. Page Smith, "Anxiety and Despair in American History," *William and Mary Quarterly* 3d ser. 26 (July, 1969): 416–24, and Phyllis Della Vecchia, "Rhetoric, Religion, Politics: The Sermons of Lyman Beecher" (Ph.D. diss., University of Pennsylvania, 1973), p. 216.

10 See Gary B. Nash, "The American Clergy and the French Revolution," *William and Mary Quarterly* 3d ser. 22 (July, 1965): 392–412. I am taking the term "Revolutionary Enlightenment" from Henry F. May, *The En-*

lightenment in America (New York: Oxford University Press, 1976), pt. 3.

11 David Brion Davis, *The Slave Power Conspiracy and the Paranoid Style* (Baton Rouge: Louisiana State University Press, 1969), pp. 75 f.; Edward Everett, "Education Favorable to Liberty, Knowledge, and Morals," *Orations and Speeches* (Boston, 1883), 1:604.

12 Lyman Beecher, "A Remedy for Duelling" (1806), *Works*, 2:33–74; Anon., *The Ballot Box a Remedy for National Crime: A Sermon Entitled 'A Remedy for Duelling,' by Lyman Beecher Applied to the Crime of Slaveholding; By One of his Former Parishioners* (Boston, 1838). For the context of Beecher's efforts, see Charles I. Foster, *An Errand of Mercy: The Evangelical United Front* (Chapel Hill: University of North Carolina Press, 1960).

13 Lyman Beecher, *A Plea for Colleges* (Cincinnati, 1836), pp. 11 f. On the role of prosperous lay men (and women) in the evangelical movement, see Lois W. Banner, "The Protestant Crusade: Religious Missions, Benevolence, and Reform in the United States, 1790–1840" (Ph.D. diss., Columbia University, 1970), pp. 247–60 and 291–300; Edward Pessen, *Riches, Class, and Power before the Civil War* (Lexington, Mass.: D. C. Heath, 1973), pp. 251–80; and A. F. C. Wallace, *Rockdale: The Growth of an American Village in the Early Industrial Revolution* (New York: Knopf, 1978).

14 William Ellery Channing to Jean Charles de Sismondi, July 1, 1833, Waterson Papers, Massachusetts Historical Society; Anon., "The Progress of Society," *North American Review* 63 (Oct., 1846): 334–57.

15 Richard Hofstadter and Walter P. Metzger use this term in *The Development of Academic Freedom in the United States* (New York: Columbia University Press, 1955), 1:209.

16 Horace Bushnell, "The Evangelical Alliance," *New Englander* 5 (Jan., 1847): 104.

17 *Correspondence of William Ellery Channing and Lucy Aikin* (Boston, 1874), p. 396. My interpretation of the importance of evangelicalism for Victorian society has been influenced by Elie Halévy, *England in 1815*, trans. E. I. Watkin and D. A. Barker (London: Ernest Benn, 1964; first pub. in French in 1913); Maurice J. Quinlan, *Victorian Prelude: A History of English Manners, 1700–1830* (New York: Columbia University Press, 1941); Gertrude Himmelfarb, *Victorian Minds* (New York: Knopf, 1968), chap. 10.

18 Barbara M. Cross, introduction to the *Autobiography of Lyman Beecher*, p. xxiv. See also Timothy Dwight, *Travels in New England and New York* (London, 1823), 2:443; Jedidiah Morse, *American Universal Geography* (Charlestown, 1819), 1:213; and Richard D. Birdsall, "The Second Great Awakening and the New England Social Order," *Church History* 39 (Sept., 1970): 345–64.

19 Lyman Beecher, "Lectures on Political Atheism," *Works*, 1:13, 20, 103, 109, 130, 136.

20 Ibid., pp. 15, 59, 116, 132, 315–21, 326–42.

21 Alexis de Tocqueville, *Democracy in America*, trans. Phillips Bradley (New York: Vintage, 1945), 2:114–18. Marvin Zetterbaum, *Tocqueville and the Problem of Democracy* (Stanford: Stanford University Press,

1967), pp. 97 f., notes this but does not connect it with Tocqueville's Whig contacts.

22 Beecher, *Autobiography*, 1:179; Joseph R. Gusfield, *Symbolic Crusade: Status Politics and the American Temperance Movement* (Urbana: University of Illinois Press, 1963), p. 48.

23 Beecher, *Works*, 1:370–72, 386–89, 390–94, 400–405.

24 Ibid., p. 370. Unfortunately, there is no study of American temperance comparable to Brian Harrison's exemplary examination of its English counterpart, *Drink and the Victorians* (London: Faber & Faber, 1971).

25 Bertram Wyatt-Brown, *Lewis Tappan and the Evangelical War against Slavery* (Cleveland: Case Western Reserve University Press, 1969), p. 60. Scott Miyakawa, *Protestants and Pioneers: Individualism and Conformity on the American Frontier* (Chicago: University of Chicago Press, 1964), also addresses this problem.

26 James D. Hart, *The Popular Book* (New York: Oxford University Press, 1950), p. 108.

27 See Gregory Singleton, "Protestant Voluntary Organizations and the Shaping of Victorian America," in *Victorian America* (cited in n. 1).

28 John V. Mering, *The Whig Party in Missouri* (Columbia: University of Missouri Press, 1967), p. 82; Michael F. Holt, *Forging a Majority: The Formation of the Republican Party in Pittsburgh* (New Haven: Yale University Press, 1969), p. 115; Ronald P. Formisano, *The Birth of Mass Political Parties: Michigan, 1827–1861* (Princeton: Princeton University Press, 1971), p. 116; Norman Jacobson, "The Concept of Equality in the Assumptions and Propaganda of Massachusetts Conservatives, 1790–1840" (Ph.D. diss., University of Wisconsin, 1951), pp. 437–42.

29 See Sidney Mead, *Nathaniel William Taylor* (Chicago: University of Chicago Press, 1942); George M. Marsden, *The Evangelical Mind and the New School Presbyterian Experience* (New Haven: Yale University Press, 1970); and Wayne C. Tyner, "The Theology of Timothy Dwight in Historical Perspective" (Ph.D. diss., University of North Carolina, 1971).

30 See, e.g., Nathaniel William Taylor, *Concio ad Clerum* (New Haven, 1828); Lyman Beecher, "Dependence and Free Agency" (1832), *Works*, 3:13–52.

31 There is a good brief statement of their self-image in "Moral Characteristics of the Nineteenth Century," *Quarterly Christian Spectator* 5 (June, 1833): 193–207.

32 See Lyman Beecher, "The Faith Once Delivered to the Saints" (1823), *Works*, 2:243–300, and Beecher's articles in *The Spirit of the Pilgrims*, beginning in volume 1 (Jan., 1828), pp. 42–52, and ending in volume 3 (April, 1830), pp. 181–95. I have commented on the Unitarian side of this debate in *The Unitarian Conscience* (Cambridge: Harvard University Press, 1970), pp. 100–106.

33 The standard assessment of the New Lebanon Conference is that of William G. McLoughlin, *Modern Revivalism: Charles G. Finney to Billy Graham* (New York: Ronald Press, 1959), p. 37. However, the most thorough account is to be found in Vincent Harding, "Lyman Beecher and the Transformation of American Protestantism" (Ph.D. diss., University of Chicago, 1965), chap. 14.

34 See McLoughlin, *Modern Revivalism*, p. 100. Privately, Beecher sympathized with Antimasonry, but he was not active in the movement; see his *Autobiography*, 2:169.
35 See Perry Miller, *The Life of the Mind in America* (New York: Harcourt, Brace & World, 1965), p. 8, and Sydney Ahlstrom, *Religious History of the American People* (New Haven: Yale University Press, 1975), p. 459.
36 Lyman Beecher, *A Plea for the West* (Cincinnati, 1835), pp. 15, 35, 42, 47, 50. See also idem, *A Plea for Colleges* (Cincinnati, 1835), "The Claims of the West," *Quarterly Christian Spectator* 6 (Dec., 1834): 513–24, and "The Relative Importance of New England," *The Spirit of Pilgrims* 1 (July, 1828): 338.
37 *Home Missionary* 36 (Aug., 1863): 91; *The Country Gentleman* (Albany, N.Y.), June 15, 1854, quoted in Richard L. Power, *Planting Corn-Belt Culture* (Indianapolis: Indiana Historical Society, 1953), p. 5. See also Raymond D. Gastil, *Cultural Regions of the United States* (Seattle: University of Washington Press, 1975).
38 Gerhard Lenski, *The Religious Factor: A Sociological Study*, rev. ed. (Garden City: Doubleday, 1963), quotation from p. 207; Richard Jensen, "The Religious and Occupational Roots of Party Identification: Illinois and Indiana in the 1870s," *Civil War History* 16 (Dec., 1970): 325–43; Paul Kleppner, *The Cross of Culture: A Social Analysis of Midwestern Politics, 1850–1900* (New York: Free Press, 1970). See also Benton Johnson, "Ascetic Protestantism and Political Preference," *Public Opinion Quarterly* 26 (Spring, 1962): 35–46, and Martin Marty, "Ethnicity: The Skeleton of Religion in America," *Church History* 41 (March, 1972): 5–22.
39 Bertram Wyatt-Brown, "The Antimission Movement in the Jacksonian South: A Study in Regional Folk Culture," *Journal of Southern History* 36 (Nov., 1970): 501–29.
40 David Brion Davis, *The Fear of Conspiracy: Images of Un-American Subversion* (Ithaca: Cornell University Press, 1971), p. 86.
41 See [Archbishop] John Hughes, *The Decline of Protestantism and Its Causes* (New York, 1850); Ray Billington, *The Protestant Crusade* (New York: Macmillan, 1938), pp. 289–303; Ronald P. Formisano, *The Birth of Mass Political Parties* (Princeton: Princeton University Press, 1971), p. 223. The Irish Catholic laity, it has been observed, frequently used "disruption, destruction, and intimidation to compensate for their political or economic weakness" (Michael Feldberg, *The Philadelphia Riots of 1844* [Westport, Conn.: Greenwood Press, 1975], p. 34).
42 Total immigration in the decade 1845–54 was just under three million. That was 14.5 percent of the U.S. population in 1845, making this proportionately "the heaviest influx of immigrants in American history" (David M. Potter, *The Impending Crisis, 1848–1861* [New York: Harper & Row, 1976], p. 244).
43 Francis Bowen, "Pius the Ninth and the Revolutions at Rome," *North American Review* 74 (Jan., 1852): 23–71; Benjamin Blied, *Austrian Aid to American Catholics, 1830–1860* (Milwaukee: [Marquette University Press,] 1944). Horace Bushnell's indictment of the government of the Papal States was translated into Italian: *Lettera al Romano Pontefice . . .* (Lugano, Switzerland, 1846). Margaret Fuller, correspondent

for the Whig *New York Tribune*, married the Italian revolutionary Ossoli.

44 Clayton Ellsworth, "American Churches and the Mexican War," *American Historical Review* 45 (Jan., 1940): 301–26.

45 "Mob Law," *American Quarterly Review* 17 (March, 1835): 209–31; Theodore M. Hammet, "Two Mobs of Jacksonian Boston: Ideology and Interest," *Journal of American History* 62 (March, 1976): 845–68; Alexander Saxton, *The Indispensable Enemy: Labor and the Anti-Chinese Movement in California* (Berkeley and Los Angeles: University of California Press, 1971).

46 William Shade, *Banks or No Banks: The Money Issue in Western Politics* (Detroit: Wayne State University Press, 1972), p. 181; Eric Foner, *Free Soil, Free Labor, Free Men* (New York: Oxford University Press, 1970), pp. 240–48.

47 Beecher, *Autobiography*, 2:432; "Lectures on Political Atheism," *Works*, 1:242–45; *A Plea for the West*, pp. 64, 91; italics in original. On the Jews and nativism, see Rudolf Glanz, *Jew and Irish: Historic Group Relations and Immigration* (New York: Alexander Kohut Foundation, 1966).

48 Beecher, *Autobiography*, 2:242–49; Vincent Harding, "Lyman Beecher," pp. 480–509; J. Earl Thompson, "Lyman Beecher's Long Road to Conservative Abolitionism," *Church History* 42 (March, 1973): 89–109. For attempts to mediate between colonization and abolition, see *Quarterly Christian Spectator* 5 (Dec., 1833): 631 f. and 6 (June, 1834): 332 f.

49 Wendell P. Garrison and Francis J. Garrison, *William Lloyd Garrison* (New York, 1855), 1:212 f.

50 "Dr. Beecher's Trial for Heresy before the Presbytery of Cincinnati, June, 1835," in Beecher's *Works*, 3:63–413; Beecher, "Remarks," *Works*, 3:455; James Walker, "The Trial of Dr. Lyman Beecher," *Christian Examiner* 19 (Sept., 1835): 116–33; Marsden, *The Evangelical Mind*, pp. 53–58.

51 Elwyn A. Smith, "The Role of the South in the Presbyterian Schism of 1837," *Church History* 29 (March, 1960): 44–63; Robert Doherty, "Social Bases for the Presbyterian Schism of 1837–38: The Philadelphia Case," *Journal of Social History* 2 (Fall, 1968): 69–79.

52 Ezra Stiles Ely, *The Duty of Christian Freemen to Elect Christian Rulers* (Philadelphia, 1828); Robert Kelley, "Presbyterianism, Jacksonianism, and Grover Cleveland," *American Quarterly* 18 (Winter, 1966): 615–36.

53 Richard Jensen, "The Religious and Occupational Roots of Party Identification: Illinois and Indiana in the 1870s," *Civil War History* 16 (Dec., 1970): 325–43. For an exploration of broader implications, see Daniel Walker Howe, "The Decline of Calvinism: An Approach to Its Study," *Comparative Studies in Society and History* 14 (June, 1972): 306–27.

54 See Bertram Wyatt-Brown, "Prelude to Abolitionism: Sabbatarian Politics and the Rise of the Second Party System," *Journal of American History* 58 (Sept., 1971): 316–41; Ronald P. Formisano, *The Birth of Mass Political Parties* (Princeton: Princeton University Press, 1971), pp. 137–64; Roger D. Peterson, "The Reaction to a Heterogeneous Society: Northern Voting Behavior, 1845–1870" (Ph.D. diss., University of Pittsburgh, 1970).

55 *Spirit of the Pilgrims* 3 (July, 1830): 392; Daniel Webster, *Writings and Speeches* (Boston: Little, Brown, 1903), 3:158; [Moses Stuart,] *Mr. Webster's Andover Address and His Political Course* (Essex County, Mass., 1844). The Stuart-Webster correspondence is in the Daniel Webster Papers, Dartmouth College.
56 *Autobiography*, 2:414.
57 Allan G. Bogue et al., "Members of the House of Representatives and the Process of Modernization," *Journal of American History* 63 (Sept., 1976): 293; Joshua R. Giddings, *Speeches in Congress* (Boston, 1852), p. 248.
58 Joshua R. Giddings, *Speech on the Duty of This Government in Maintaining the Law of Nations* (Washington, D.C., 1852). The best description of the evangelical vision of history, within which both Beecher and Giddings should be located, is in Sydney Ahlstrom, "Religion, Revolution, and the Rise of Modern Nationalism: Reflections on the American Experience," *Church History* 44 (Dec., 1975): 492–504.
59 James Brewer Stewart, *Joshua R. Giddings and the Tactics of Radical Politics* (Cleveland: Case Western Reserve University Press, 1970) is an excellent biography; see also Richard W. Solberg, "Joshua Giddings: Politician and Idealist" (Ph.D. diss., University of Chicago, 1952). The Joshua R. Giddings–George W. Julian Papers are in the Library of Congress; I used them on microfilm.
60 Robert P. Ludlum, "Joshua R. Giddings, Radical," *Mississippi Valley Historical Review* 23 (June, 1936): 52.
61 See Stephen C. Fox, "The Group Bases of Ohio Political Behavior, 1803–1848" (Ph.D. diss., University of Cincinnati, 1973).
62 Joshua R. Giddings to Laura Waters Giddings, July 20, 1837, quoted in Stewart, *Giddings*, pp. 24 f.
63 George W. Julian, *The Life of Joshua R. Giddings* (Chicago, 1892) pp. 145 f., 174 f., 241–44. Giddings' comments when Preston Brooks assaulted Charles Sumner on the Senate floor are illuminating; see *Congressional Globe*, 34th Cong., 1st sess. (July 11, 1856), appendix, 1117–21.
64 Robert C. Winthrop to Charles Dean, Aug. 27, 1872, printed in *Mississippi Valley Historical Review* 38 (Sept., 1951): 291–94. Insight into Giddings' feelings can be obtained from correspondence; see, e.g., Joshua Giddings to his daughter Laura, Feb. 5, 1846; or George W. Julian (who boarded with the Giddings in Washington) to Isaac Julian, Jan. 25, 1850, both in the Giddings-Julian Collection (original in the Library of Congress). Also see Martin Duberman, "The Abolitionists and Psychology," *Journal of Negro History* 47 (July, 1962): 183–91.
65 Giddings, *Speeches*, p. 242; John Gorham Palfrey to Mary Ann Palfrey (his wife), July 2, 1848, quoted in Frank Otto Gatell, *John Gorham Palfrey and the New England Conscience* (Cambridge: Harvard University Press, 1963), p. 165.
66 Giddings, *Speeches*, p. iii, 98, 251, 266, and passim.
67 Rhys Isaac, "Dramatizing the Ideology of Revolution: Popular Mobilization in Virginia," *William and Mary Quarterly* 3d ser. 33 (July, 1976): 360.
68 Solberg, "Giddings," p. 36; Stewart, *Giddings*, p. 6; Giddings, *Speeches*, pp. 106, 114 f.

69 Giddings, *Speeches*, pp. 66, 286–88; *Congressional Globe*, 29th Cong., 1st sess., 15 (May 12, 1846), appendix, 644; Joshua Giddings, *Executive Influence* (Washington, D.C., 1854).
70 Joshua Giddings, diary, Feb. 7, 1839 (original in Ohio Historical Society); *Niles' Register*, Feb. 23, 1839; *National Intelligencer*, June 6, 1840.
71 See Walter Merrill, *Against Wind and Tide: A Biography of William Lloyd Garrison* (Cambridge: Harvard University Press, 1963), p. 122; Julian, *Giddings*, pp. 54, 89, 100.
72 Quoted in Stewart, *Giddings*, p. 85. Cf. Giddings, *Speeches*, pp. 128 and 133.
73 Giddings, *Speeches*, pp. 206 f. and 136.
74 The poem Adams wrote in honor of his friend may be found in Stewart, *Joshua Giddings*, p. 57, n. 9. My sense of the contrasting personalities of Adams and Giddings benefited much from discussion with Patricia Wilson. The tenderness of their relationship can be seen in letters Giddings wrote his wife, June 7 and Dec. 13, 1846 (Giddings-Julian Collection, Library of Congress).
75 *Congressional Globe*, 27th Cong., 2d sess., 11 (March 22, 1842): 346. Party affiliations are taken from U.S. Congress, *Biographical Directory of the American Congress* (Washington, D.C.: U.S. Government Printing Office, 1971).
76 Carl Schurz, *The Life of Henry Clay* (Boston, 1887), 2:234. See also Julian, *Giddings*, pp. 114–25; and Stewart, *Giddings*, pp. 73 f.
77 See [Joshua Giddings,] *The Rights of the Free States Subverted...* (Washington, D.C., 1845), and Giddings in the *National Intelligencer*, Oct. 15, 1842. On the Seminole War, see Giddings, "The Florida War" (Feb. 9, 1841), *Speeches*, pp. 1–20, and Julian, *Giddings*, pp. 175–78; Giddings recurred to this episode in later years when he wrote *The Exiles of Florida; or, The Crimes Committed by Our Government against the Maroons* (Columbus, Ohio, 1858).
78 The Pacificus Letters were reprinted in [Joshua R. Giddings,] *The Rights and Privileges of the Several States in Regard to Slavery* (Warren, Ohio, 1843). See also his *Speech, Delivered in... Concord, New Hampshire* (n.p., 1847), and Giddings, *Speeches*, pp. 56, 107–11, 223.
79 W. W. Warner, "The Republic, No. IV," *American Review* 10 (Sept., 1849): 286; John L. Thomas, *Theodore Dwight Weld* (New Brunswick: Rutgers University Press, 1950), p. 210; Charles Sumner, "Address to the People of Massachusetts" (1849), *Works* (Boston, 1874), 2:287. See also William M. Wiecek, *The Sources of Antislavery Constitutionalism in America* (Ithaca: Cornell University Press, 1977), and Eric Foner, *Free Soil, Free Labor, Free Men* (New York: Oxford University Press), chap. 3.
80 Giddings, "Speaker of the House of Representatives" (1849), *Speeches*, p. 384; see also Stewart, *Giddings*, p. 87, and *Congressional Globe*, 29th Cong., 1st sess., 15 (July 14, 1846), appendix, 826–29.
81 Merrill, *Against Wind and Tide*, p. 234; Joshua R. Giddings to Oran Follett, May 12, 1844, *Quarterly Publications of the Historical and Philosophical Society of Ohio* 10 (Jan., 1915): 15 f.; Stewart, *Giddings*, pp. 46–49.
82 Giddings, quoted in Solberg, "Giddings," p. 132. For the notion of

"cultural purge," see Major L. Wilson, "The Free Soil Concept of Progress and the Irrepressible Conflict," *American Quarterly* 22 (Winter, 1970): 773.

83 Joshua R. Giddings, *A Letter upon the Duty of Anti-Slavery Men in the Present Crisis* (Ravenna, Ohio, 1844), quotation from p. 8; Joshua R. Giddings to Laura Waters Giddings, April 28, 1844, Giddings-Julian Collection; Theodore C. Smith, *The Liberty and Free Soil Parties in the Northwest* (New York, 1897), pp. 112 f.

84 Giddings, "Joint Occupation of Oregon" (1846), *Speeches*, pp. 160–62; "The Annexation of Texas" (1845), ibid., p. 105. See also Byron Long, "Joshua Reed Giddings, Champion of Political Freedom," *Ohio Archaeological and Historical Publications* 27 (Jan., 1919): 36.

85 Giddings, "The Wilmot Proviso" (1847), *Speeches*, p. 203. Data relating to Giddings' political context may be found in Norman Tutorow, *Texas Annexation and the Mexican War: A Political Study of the Old Northwest* (Palo Alto: Chadwick House, 1978).

86 Besides the selections contained in Giddings' *Speeches*, see also the *Congressional Globe*, 29th Cong., 2d sess., 16 (December 15, 1846), appendix, 47–52.

87 *Boston Daily Whig*, July 3, 1848, quoted in Solberg, "Giddings," p. 304; Giddings, "The Mexican War" (1848), *Speeches*, p. 332.

88 Smith, *Liberty and Free Soil Parties*, pp. 169–72; Stewart, *Giddings*, pp. 175–79.

89 *Congressional Globe*, 32d Cong., 1st sess., 21 (June 23, 1852), appendix, 738–42; Giddings, "Relation of the Federal Government to Slavery" (Feb. 17, 1849), *Speeches*, p. 357.

90 Giddings, "New Mexico" (Aug. 13, 1850), *Speeches*, p. 410; Joshua R. Giddings, *The Amistad Claim* (Washington, D.C., 1853); *Congressional Globe*, 35th Cong., 1st sess., 27 (Feb. 26, 1858), appendix, 65.

91 Joshua Giddings, "To the People of Cuyahoga, Lake, and Geauga Counties" (March 8, 1853), quoted in Solberg, "Giddings," pp. 383 f. See also George W. Julian, "The First Republican National Convention," *American Historical Review* 4 (Jan., 1899): 313–22.

92 "The Appeal of the Independent Democrats" (so called because the Free-Soil party had by that time changed its name to the Free Democracy) is reprinted in J. W. Schuckers, *The Life and Public Services of Salmon P. Chase* (New York, 1874), pp. 140–47. Giddings' *The Moral Responsibility of Statesmen* (Washington, D.C., 1854) is perhaps his greatest speech; the quotation is from p. 6.

93 *Congressional Globe*, 34th Cong., 3d sess., 26 (Dec. 10, 1856): 78–81; ibid., 36th Cong., 1st sess., 4 (April 23, 1860), appendix, 250; Stewart, *Giddings*, pp. 225 f. The final quotation is from *Congressional Globe*, 32d Cong., 1st sess., 21 (July 16, 1852): 1815; italics in original.

94 Joshua R. Giddings, "To the People of the Twentieth Congressional District of Ohio," *National Era*, Feb. 14, 1856.

95 Foner's *Free Soil, Free Labor, Free Men* (cited in n. 79) is an excellent discussion of the ideology of the Republican party; on Giddings, see esp. pp. 130, 133, 283.

96 See Stewart, *Giddings*, pp. 275, 277; Joshua R. Giddings, *A History of the Rebellion* (Cleveland, 1864).

97 Solberg, "Giddings," p. 544. Actually, Giddings lived for about a year after uttering this benediction—as Adams had done also.

98 For Beecher's views on economic issues—including the tariff, banking, and internal improvements—see his *The Means of National Prosperity* (Hartford, 1820). On Giddings, see Stewart, *Giddings*, pp. 38, 45, 68, and passim. For comparison with the movement in Britain, see Geoffrey Best, "Evangelicalism and the Victorians," in *The Victorian Crisis of Faith*, ed. A. Symondson (London: Society for Promoting Christian Knowledge, 1970), pp. 37–56.

Chapter Eight

1 Alexis de Tocqueville to Eugene Stoffels, July, 24, 1836, *Oeuvres et correspondance* (Paris, 1861), 1:432; my translation. Edward Everett in the Senate, *Congressional Globe*, 32d Cong., 2d sess., 27 (1853), appendix, 285.

2 "The Permanency and Power of Whig Principles," *American Review* 15 (March, 1852): 271. For "ordered liberty," see *Palko v. Connecticut*, 302 U.S. 319 (1937).

3 In F. J. C. Hearnshaw, ed., *The Social and Political Ideas of Some Representative Thinkers of the Victorian Age* (London: George Harrap, 1933), p. 11.

4 Francis Bowen, "The Spirit of Reform," Commencement Oration, Aug. 28, 1833 (MS in Harvard University Archives); "Reorganization of the Judiciary," *American Review* 2 (Nov., 1845): 474.

5 The extensive literature on modernization is surveyed in John Brode, ed., *The Process of Modernization—An Annotated Bibliography* (Cambridge: Harvard University Press, 1969). The concept is applied to the United States in Richard D. Brown, *Modernization: The Transformation of American Life* (New York: Hill & Wang, 1976).

6 E.g., Dean Tips, "Modernization Theory and the Comparative Study of Societies: A Critical Perspective," *Comparative Studies in Society and History* 15 (March, 1973): 199–226.

7 See Lynn Marshall, "The Strange Stillbirth of the Whig Party," *American Historical Review* 62 (Jan., 1967): 445–68.

8 See Michael Lebowitz, "The Jacksonians: Paradox Lost?" in *Towards a New Past: Dissenting Essays in American History*, ed. Barton J. Bernstein (New York: Random House, 1968), pp. 65–89.

9 Glyndon G. Van Deusen, *Horace Greeley: Nineteenth-Century Crusader* (Philadelphia: University of Pennsylvania Press, 1953); Constance Rourke, *Trumpets of Jubilee: Henry Ward Beecher, Harriet Beecher Stowe, Lyman Beecher, Horace Greeley, P. T. Barnum* (New York: Harcourt Brace & World, 1963; first published in 1927), pp. 180–275.

10 Horace Greeley, "Reforms and Reformers" (c. 1853), in *Recollections of a Busy Life, To Which Are Added Miscellanies* (New York: J. B. Ford, 1868), pp. 514 f.

11 Horace Greeley, *Recollections*, p. 67.

12 Quoted in Don Seitz, *Horace Greeley: Founder of the New York Tribune* (Indianapolis: Bobbs-Merrill, 1926), p. 28.

13 The figures come from Van Deusen, *Horace Greeley*, pp. 35 and 45, and

Jeter Isely, *Horace Greeley and the Republican Party* (Princeton: Princeton University Press, 1947), p. 4.

14 The *Tribune's* reporting of a lawsuit between James Fenimore Cooper and Thurlow Weed led Cooper (a prominent Democrat) to sue Greeley for libel. Greeley was forced to pay damages when the court refused to accept truth as a defense. Though Greeley lost this battle, he won the war by mobilizing public opinion to force the New York courts to change their interpretation of the law soon after. See Ethel R. Outland, *The "Effingham" Libels on Cooper* (Madison: University of Wisconsin Press, 1929).

15 Horace Greeley, *Hints toward Reforms* (New York: Fowler & Wells, 1858; first published in 1850), pp. 5 f.

16 *Recollections and Miscellanies*, p. 433; *Hints toward Reforms*, pp. 112 and 385.

17 *The Rose of Sharon: A Religious Souvenir*, ed. Miss Sarah C. Edgarton (Boston, 1842), pp. 246 f.; Edgar Allan Poe, *A Chapter on Autography* (New York: Dial Press, 1926), p. 68.

18 *Hints toward Reforms*, p. 8; *Recollections and Miscellanies*, p. 525.

19 Horace Greeley, *Why I Am a Whig: Reply to an Inquiring Friend* (New York: Greeley & McElrath, [1851]), 16 pp.

20 E.g., Norman Ware, *The Industrial Worker, 1840–60* (Boston: Houghton Mifflin, 1924), pp. 21 f.; and Arthur M. Schlesinger, Jr., *The Age of Jackson* (Boston: Little, Brown, 1946), pp. 294–96.

21 *Log Cabin*, May 9, 16, 23, and 30, 1840; "The Emancipation of Labor," *Hints toward Reforms*, pp. 13–50; *New York Tribune*, March 20, 1843. Many other issues of the *Tribune* could also be cited.

22 Lyman Beecher, *A Plea for Colleges* (Cincinnati, 1836), p. 11; *New York Tribune*, July 24, 1841; *Hints toward Reforms*, pp. 342–47.

23 *Hints toward Reforms* includes an essay on "The Formation of Character" (pp. 85–111).

24 "Reforms and Reformers" (c. 1853), *Recollections and Miscellanies*, p. 498.

25 Ibid., pp. 497–527; "Human Life," *Hints toward Reforms*, pp. 149–78. Greeley's classic description of the early West, *An Overland Journey from New York to San Francisco* (New York, 1860), was written to publicize the need for a transcontinental railroad.

26 *Recollections*, pp. 68–74; *Hints toward Reforms*, 385–92. On March 2, 1842, the *New York Tribune* reassured its readers with an "extra" containing elaborate refutations of Miller based on an examination of the Books of Daniel and Revelation by a Baptist clergyman.

27 *Hints toward Reforms*, pp. 82 and 118.

28 See, e.g., "The Duty to Labor," lead editorial in the *New York Tribune*, May 11, 1841. For general discussions of the dignity of work and its role in self-discipline, see Eric Foner, *Free Soil, Free Labor, Free Men* (New York: Oxford University Press, 1970), chap. 1; D. H. Meyer, *The Instructed Conscience: The Shaping of the American National Ethic* (Philadelphia: University of Pennsylvania Press, 1972), chap. 7; and Marie Ahearn, "The Rhetoric of Work and Vocation in Some Popular Northern Writings before 1860" (Ph.D. diss., Brown University, 1965).

29 *Recollections and Miscellanies*, p. 509; Roy M. Robbins, "Horace

Greeley: Land Reform and Unemployment," *Agricultural History* 7 (Jan., 1933): 18–41.

30 *Hints toward Reforms*, p. 223.

31 Ibid., pp. 131 f.

32 See Edmund S. Morgan, "The Puritan Ethic and the American Revolution," *William and Mary Quarterly* 3d ser. 24 (Jan., 1967): 3–43.

33 See Horace Greeley, "The Grounds of Protection" (speech delivered Feb. 10, 1843), *Recollections and Miscellanies*, pp. 528–53; *Protection and Free Trade* (New York, [1844]), pp. 9–13; introduction to William Atkinson, *Principles of Political Economy* (New York, 1843), p. iii.

34 [Horace Greeley,] "The Tariff Question," *American Review* 2 (Aug., 1845): 114.

35 Horace Greeley, *The Crystal Palace and Its Lessons* (New York, 1851), pp. 2, 21 f.; Horace Greeley, ed., *Art and Industry as Represented in the Exhibition at the Crystal Palace, New York* (New York, 1853).

36 *An Overland Journey from New York to San Francisco*, pp. 151–55.

37 Horace Bushnell, *Prosperity Our Duty* (Hartford, 1847), p. 6. A few other examples of homage to work are Henry C. Carey, *Essay on the Rate of Wages* (Philadelphia, 1835), pp. 145–59; Daniel Webster, "Speech in Faneuil Hall" (Oct. 24, 1848), *Writings and Speeches* (Boston, 1903), 4:165; James Walker, "Difficulty, Struggle, Progress," *Sermons* (Boston, 1861), 206–8.

38 Greeley, *Hints toward Reforms*, pp. 118 f.; David C. McClelland, *The Achieving Society* (Princeton: D. Van Nostrand, 1961), esp. p. 391.

39 Rufus Choate, "The Importance of Illustrating New England History," *Works* (Boston, 1862), 1:333, 335; italics in original.

40 As quoted in George Pierson, *Tocqueville and Beaumont in America* (New York: Oxford University Press, 1938), p. 418; the conversation took place in French.

41 Max Weber, *The Protestant Ethic and the Spirit of Capitalism*, trans. Talcott Parsons (New York, 1930; first published in German in 1904). I have discussed the relationship between the "Protestant ethic" and the "spirit of capitalism" in "The Decline of Calvinism: An Approach to Its Study," *Comparative Studies in Society and History* 14 (June, 1972): 306–27. See also David Little, "Max Weber Revisited," *Harvard Theological Review* 59 (Oct., 1966): 415–28.

42 Van Deusen, *Horace Greeley*, chap. 25 and passim.

43 Albert Brisbane, *The Social Destiny of Man* (Philadelphia, 1840); idem, *A Concise Exposition of the Doctrine of Association* (New York, 1843).

44 *New Yorker*, Oct. 17, 1840; *New York Tribune*, Jan. 16 and June 21, 1841; *New York Courier & Enquirer*, Nov. 23, 1846. The Greeley-Raymond debate was carried in both the *Tribune* and the *Courier* and lasted from November 20, 1846, until the following May 22. See also Cecelia Koretsky Michael, "Horace Greeley and Fourierism in the United States" (M.A. thesis, University of Rochester, 1949).

45 J. F. C. Harrison, *Robert Owen and the Owenites in Britain and America* (London: Routledge & Kegan Paul, 1969); *New York Tribune*, Aug. 3, 1842, and Dec. 28, 1846.

46 Greeley, *Recollections*, pp. 145–58; "The Social Architects—Fourier" (a lecture), *Hints toward Reforms*, pp. 272–99. On the virtues of Lowell, see

the *New York Tribune*, April 22, 1844. The *Lowell Offering* advertised for subscribers in the *Tribune*.

47 Schlesinger, *The Age of Jackson*, p. 367; Greeley, *Hamilton College Address* (Clinton, N.Y., 1844), pp. 24–30.

48 Ralph Waldo Emerson, "Historic Notes of Life and Letters in New England," *Complete Works* (Boston: Houghton Mifflin, 1911), 10: 357 f.

49 *New York Tribune*, Nov. 25, Dec. 1, and Dec. 8, 1846; Horace Greeley, "The Unfulfilled Mission of Christianity," *Rose of Sharon* (Boston, 1843), 50–59; *New York Tribune*, Jan. 29, 1847.

50 Parke Godwin, *Democracy: Constructive and Pacific* (New York: J. Winchester, 1844); Stephen Pearl Andrews, "Introductory Chapter," in Henry James [Sr.] et al., *Love, Marriage, and Divorce* (New York: Source Book Press, 1972; first published in 1853), p. 23.

51 *New York Tribune*, Jan. 3, 1842, Sept. 1, 1849, Dec. 31, 1849; "Death by Human Law" and "Alcoholic Liquors," in *Hints toward Reforms*, 301–10 and 257–71.

52 Arthur W. Brown, *Margaret Fuller* (New Haven: College & University Press, 1964), p. 75; Greeley, *Recollections*, pp. 169–91. Though Greeley found things to admire in the Transcendentalists—such as Emerson's maxims—their glorification of spontaneity was quite alien to him. When Brook Farm was converted from a Transcendental utopia into a Fourierist phalanx, Greeley rejoiced (*Tribune*, Feb. 1, 1844).

53 One debate is contained in *Love, Marriage, and Divorce*, cited above, another (against the prominent Democrat Robert Dale Owen) is in the *New York Tribune*, March 1, 1860. See also the *New Yorker* 1 (April 23, 1836): 73, and the *Tribune*, March 14, 1843.

54 The best description of Mary Cheney Greeley is contained in Constance Rourke, *Trumpets*, p. 189.

55 *Hints toward Reforms*, pp. 18–37; Horace Greeley, *What the Sister Arts Teach as to Farming: An Address before the Indiana State Agricultural Society* (New York, 1853). Roland Van Zandt, "Horace Greeley: Agrarian Exponent of American Idealism," *Rural Sociology* 13 (Dec., 1948): 411–19, correctly identifies Greeley's interest in agriculture but mistakenly interprets it as antiindustrial.

56 Quoted in Van Deusen, *Horace Greeley*, p. 90. See also Greeley, *Recollections*, p. 285; *The Jeffersonian* 1 (May 26, 1838): 113; *New York Tribune*, Feb. 1, 1844.

57 The quotation is from the *New York Tribune*, July 3, 1848. Greeley's position on secession, which has sometimes been misunderstood and even ridiculed by those who would make him out to be an inconsistent buffoon, is beautifully explained by David Potter in "Horace Greeley and Peaceable Secession," first published in 1941 and reprinted in *The South and Sectional Conflict* (Baton Rouge: Louisiana State University Press, 1968), pp. 219–42.

58 The maneuverings described in this paragraph are recounted in Van Deusen, *Horace Greeley*, pp. 120–41, 159–98, 242–47.

59 The best description of the Liberal Republicans is that by Richard Allen Gerber, in "The Liberal Republicans of 1872," *Journal of American History* 62 (June, 1975): 40–73: "Liberals sought above all a sense of civilized social order in America" (p. 72).

60 Kenneth S. Lynn, introduction to Constance Rourke, *Trumpets of Jubilee*, p. xvii.

61 Wendell Phillips, *Speeches, Lectures, and Letters* (Boston, 1864), pp. 352 f.

62 William Henry Seward, *Autobiography, With a Memoir of His Life and Selections from His Letters*, ed. Frederick W. Seward (New York: D. Appleton, 1877), pp. 1–32; Glyndon Van Deusen, *William Henry Seward* (New York: Oxford University Press, 1967), pp. 3–17.

63 Seward, *Autobiography*, 89–91; Van Deusen, *Seward*, pp. 19, 106 f.; William H. Seward, *The Life and Public Services of John Quincy Adams* (Auburn, N.Y.: Derby, Miller & Co., 1849); William H. Seward, *Works* ed. George E. Baker (New York, 1853), 3:75–103, 605–18; 4:305.

64 Seward, "The True Greatness of Our Country" (1848) *Works*, 3:11–24.

65 William H. Seward, *Speech on the Resolution against Renewing the Charter of the U.S. Bank, in the Senate of New York* (Albany, 1832); Anon., *An Address to the Electors of the State of New York* (New York, 1838).

66 Seward, *Works*, 2:183–255; Van Deusen, *Seward*, pp. 63 f.

67 Seward's denunciation of Franklin Pierce's veto of the Dix bill may be found in the *Congressional Globe*, 33d Cong., 1st sess., 31 (June 19, 1854), appendix, 959–61. Dorothea Dix was also a friend of Millard Fillmore, and the Fillmore-Dix correspondence has recently been published; see Charles M. Snyder, ed., *The Lady and the President* (Lexington: University of Kentucky Press, 1975).

68 The best treatment of the Anti-Rent War so far is in David Maldwyn Ellis, *Landlords and Farmers in the Hudson-Mohawk Region* (Ithaca: Cornell University Press, 1946).

69 Seward, "Notes on New York," *Works*, 2:9–182.

70 Annual messages to the New York state legislature (1839 and 1840), *Works*, 2:197 and 215.

71 See Glyndon Van Deusen, "Seward and the School Question Reconsidered," *Journal. of American History* 52 (Sept., 1965): 313–19; and Vincent P. Lannie, *Public Money and Parochial Education: Bishop Hughes, Governor Seward, and the New York School Controversy* (Cleveland: Case Western Reserve University Press, 1968).

72 Seward, *Works*, 3:44 ff., 153 ff., etc.; Seward to [Benjamin Squire?], Nov. 12, 1840, *Works*, 2:387; *New York Tribune*, Nov. 20, 1854.

73 See Henry Clay, *Works* (New York: G. P. Putnam's Sons, 1904), 7:451 and 9:391; Daniel Webster, *Writings and Speeches* (Boston: Little, Brown, 1903), 4:239, 288; Edward Everett, *Orations and Speeches* (Boston, 1883), 2:191, 533; 3:103, 152.

74 Seward, letter from Ireland (June 24, 1833), *Works*, 3:520; "The Western Railroad" (1842), ibid., pp. 330 f. See also Foner, *Free Soil, Free Labor, Free Men*, pp. 234–36.

75 Seward, "The Pilgrims and Liberty" (1855), *Works*, 4:205.

76 Daniel Webster, "Address at Buffalo" (1851), *Writings and Speeches*, 4:236. There is an interesting presentation of Whig ethnocultural attitudes in "The Anglo-Saxons and the Americans: European Races in the United States," *American Review* 14 (Sept., 1851): 187–93.

77 Seward to James Maher (March 15, 1844), *Works*, 3:495 f. Cf. his speech

in the Senate, April 9, 1856, ibid., 4:485.
78 Speech in the U.S. Senate (1850), ibid., 1:295.
79 Ibid., 3:148, 4:138, 1:323–26.
80 *Autobiography*, pp. 27 f. See also *Works*, 4:357.
81 See Seward, *Works*, 2:449–518; Frederic Bancroft, *Life of William H. Seward* (New York: Harper & Bros., 1899), 2:34; Lee Benson, *The Concept of Jacksonian Democracy: New York as a Test Case* (Princeton: Princeton University Press, 1961), pp. 179 f.
82 "The True Greatness of Our Country" (1848), *Works*, 3:14. Cf. "The National Divergence" (1860), ibid., 4:317.
83 "Freedom in the New Territories" (1850), ibid., 1:60–93.
84 Van Deusen, *Seward*, p. 127.
85 Seward in the *Congressional Globe*, 31st Cong., 1st sess., 22 (July 25, 1850), appendix, 1444; William Hosmer, *The Higher Law in Its Relations to Civil Government* (Auburn, N.Y., 1852). Giddings cited the "higher law" in avowing his determination to refuse obedience to the Fugitive Slave Act in a speech on December 9, 1850 (Joshua R. Giddings, *Speeches in Congress* [Boston, 1852], p. 433). The subject may be pursued in Edward H. Madden, *Civil Disobedience and Moral Law in Nineteenth-Century American Philosophy* (Seattle: University of Washington Press, 1968).
86 Seward, *Works*, 1:119–31, 314, 319, 99 f.
87 Henry Clay, *Works*, 9:472, 537; Daniel Webster, *Writings and Speeches*, 4:225.
88 Quoted in Eric Foner, *Free Soil, Free Labor, Free Men*, p. 39.
89 Seward, *Works*, 1:154. This interpretation of Seward's imperialism is indebted to the fine recent study by Ernest N. Paolino, *The Foundations of the American Empire: William H. Seward and U.S. Foreign Policy* (Ithaca, N.Y.: Cornell University Press, 1973).
90 Seward, "American Steam Navigation" (1852) *Works*, 1:222–35; "Survey of the Arctic and Pacific Oceans" (1852), ibid., pp. 236–53 (published separately under the title *Commerce in the Pacific Ocean* [Washington, D.C., 1852]); *Congressional Globe*, 32d Cong., 2d sess., 27 (Jan. 26, 1852), appendix, 126.
91 "J. Q. Adams on the Opium War" (1841), printed in Massachusetts Historical Society, *Proceedings* 43 (Feb., 1910): 295–325. *Niles' Weekly Register*, July 23, 1836.
92 Seward, *Works*, 1:56 f.
93 The Fillmore Whigs have not attracted much interest from historians, but one may consult Robert Rayback, *Millard Fillmore* (Buffalo: Henry Stuart, 1959), and Lee Warner, "The Silver Grays" (Ph.D. diss., University of Wisconsin, 1971).
94 Seward, "The Advent of the Republican Party" (Albany, Oct. 12, 1855), *Works*, 4:225–40, esp. 227 and 239. Henry C. Carey to Josiah Quincy, Sept. 28, 1856, quoted in George W. Smith, *Henry Carey and American Sectional Conflict* (Albuquerque: University of New Mexico Press, 1951), p. 46.
95 Charles and Mary Beard, *The Rise of American Civilization*, 2d ed. (New York: Macmillan, 1934), 2:52–121. Some more recent suggestions regarding the Civil War as a crisis in modernization may be found in Eric

Foner, "The Causes of the Civil War: Recent Interpretations and New Directions," *Civil War History* 20 (Sept., 1974): 197–214.

96 Seward, "The Contest and the Crisis" (Buffalo, Oct. 19, 1855), *Works*, 4:241–52. See also idem, *The Aims and Purposes of Modern Parties* (Detroit, 1860).

97 Seward, "Immediate Admission of Kansas" (1856), ibid., p. 485; "The Irrepressible Conflict," (1858), ibid., pp. 289–302; cf. "The Higher Law," ibid., 1:87.

98 Ibid., 4:505 and 202.

99 Major L. Wilson, *Space, Time and Freedom* (Westport, Conn.: Greenwood Press, 1974), p. 231. On Seward's receptivity to some form of compromise to avert the Civil War, see David Potter, *Lincoln and His Party in the Secession Crisis* (New Haven: Yale University Press, 1942), pp. 166–70, 184.

100 On Seward's motives, see Kinley Brauer, "Seward's 'Foreign War Panacea': An Interpretation," *New York History* 55 (April, 1974): 133–57.

Chapter Nine

1 The quotations are from "Responsibility of the Ballot Box," *American Review* 4 (Nov., 1846): 445, and from Millard Fillmore, quoted in Paul Nagel, *This Sacred Trust* (New York: Oxford University Press, 1971), p. 154.

2 J. W. McIntyre, preface to *The Writings and Speeches of Daniel Webster* (Boston: Little, Brown, 1903), 1:vii. (In my own researches I supplemented this edition with *The Papers of Daniel Webster on Microfilm*, ed. Charles M. Wiltse [Ann Arbor: University Microfilms, 1971].) Leroy Pope, *A Eulogy upon the Life and Public Services of Daniel Webster* (Memphis, Tenn., 1853), p. 22.

3 See, e.g., Charles Lanman, *The Private Life of Daniel Webster* (New York, 1852); George Ticknor Curtis, *Life and Letters of Daniel Webster* (New York, 1869); Peter Harvey, *Reminiscences and Anecdotes of Daniel Webster* (Boston, 1877); Horatio Alger, *From Farm Boy to Senator: The History of Daniel Webster* (New York, 1882).

4 John William Ward, *Andrew Jackson, Symbol for an Age* (New York: Oxford University Press, 1962). For Webster and civilization, see B. J. Lefft, *Life of Webster* (Philadelphia, 1854), p. 21, and Daniel Webster, "The First Settlement of New England" (1820), *Writings and Speeches*, 1:198; for Webster and history, see "Daniel Webster as an Author," *North American Review* 59 (July, 1844): 50; for Webster and peace, see "Daniel Webster," *American Review* 4 (July, 1846): 81–86.

5 Mary Douglas, *Natural Symbols* (London: Cresset Press, 1970), p. 14. There is also an article by Irving H. Bartlett, "Daniel Webster as a Symbolic Hero," *New England Quarterly* 45 (Dec., 1972): 484–507. Bartlett's excellent biography, *Daniel Webster* (New York: W. W. Norton, 1978), which came into my hands after this chapter was written, pursues the subject further.

6 See, e.g., Arthur M. Schlesinger, Jr., *The Age of Jackson* (Boston: Little,

Brown, 1945), pp. 385 f.; Frank Otto Gatell, "Reflections on a Former Deity," *Reviews in American History* 2 (March, 1974): 80–84.

7 Edward Everett, "Memoir of Daniel Webster" (1851), reprinted in Webster, *Writings and Speeches*, 1:68 f.; "American Letters," *American Review* 1 (June, 1845): 575 (italics in original); "Daniel Webster as an Author" (cited in n. 4).

8 Compare the spoken version of the famous "Liberty and Union" peroration, taken down at the time and printed in *Proceedings of the Webster Centennial* (Hanover, N.H.: Dartmouth College, 1902), p. 135, with the usual published version. For literary influences on Webster, see Rufus Choate, "Remarks before the Circuit Court on the Death of Mr. Webster," *Works* (Boston, 1862), 1:488 f., and Herbert D. Foster, "Webster and Choate in College," *Collected Papers* (n.p., 1929), pp. 213–49.

9 John Quincy Adams, diary, Sept. 3, 1838, in Adams' *Memoirs* (Philadelphia, 1874–77), 10:35; Lanman, *Private Life of Webster*, p. 130.

10 Webster, "The Bunker Hill Monument" (1825), *Writings and Speeches*, 1:238.

11 Lewis G. Clark, *The Life, Eulogy, and Great Orations of Daniel Webster* (Rochester, 1854), p. 56.

12 Henry Cabot Lodge, *Daniel Webster* (Boston: Houghton Mifflin, 1883), p. 354; William A. Stearns, *The Great Lamentation: A Sermon in Commemoration of Daniel Webster* (Cambridge, 1852), p. 14.

13 Clark, *Life, Eulogy, and Great Orations*, p. 70; [Cornelius C. Fenton,] "Daniel Webster," *American Review* 16 (Dec., 1852): 503.

14 William Ellery Channing, "Likeness to God" (1828), *Works* (Boston, 1841), 3:229–58; Pope, *Eulogy* (cited in n. 2), p. 25.

15 Richard N. Current, *Daniel Webster and the Rise of National Conservatism* (Boston: Little, Brown, 1955), p. 5; Norman D. Brown, *Daniel Webster and the Politics of Availability* (Athens: University of Georgia Press, 1969), p. 5; R. K. Webb, *Harriet Martineau* (London: William Heinemann, 1960), p. 160. Sydney Smith is quoted in Gilbert Highet, *A Clerk of Oxonford* (New York: Oxford University Press, 1954), p. 119.

16 John Quincy Adams, diary, Sept. 17, 1841, *Memoirs*, 11:20; Lodge, *Webster*, p. 360. The best discussion of Webster's private vices is in Bartlett, *Daniel Webster*, chap. 15.

17 Daniel Webster to Charles March, June 14, 1813, *Writings and Speeches*, 16:21; Magdalen Eichert, "Daniel Webster's Western Land Investments," *Historical New Hampshire* 26 (Fall, 1971): 29–35; Thomas P. Govan, *Nicholas Biddle* (Chicago: University of Chicago Press, 1959), pp. 260–64, 389. Evidence of Webster's venality is presented in Norman Jacobson, "The Concept of Equality in the Assumptions and Propaganda of Massachusetts Conservatives, 1790–1840" (Ph.D. diss., University of Wisconsin, 1951), pp. 292–301.

18 Robert F. Dalzell, Jr., *Daniel Webster and the Trial of American Nationalism* (Boston: Houghton Mifflin, 1973).

19 Current, *Daniel Webster and the Rise of National Conservatism*, pp. 182 f., 192 f., and passim; *Letters of Charles Dickens*, ed. Madeline House et al. (Oxford: Clarendon Press, 1974), 3:133 f. See also Bartlett, *Daniel Webster*, esp. chap. 1.

20 Edward Tyrell Channing, *Lectures Read to Seniors in Harvard College* (Boston, 1856), p. 24; William Wirt, *Sketches of the Life and Character of Patrick Henry* (Philadelphia, 1817).

21 The term "genteel tradition" was invented by George Santayana, who intended it to be derogatory. By now, perhaps, it can be used neutrally, like "carpetbagger" or "mugwump."

22 On the antebellum concern with "national character," see also Stuart Joel Horn, "Edward Everett and American Nationalism" (Ph.D. diss., City University of New York, 1973), and George B. Forgie, *Patricide in the House Divided: A Psychological Interpretation of Lincoln and His Age* (New York: W. W. Norton, 1979).

23 See David Hackett Fischer, *The Revolution of American Conservatism* (New York: Harper & Row, 1965), and James M. Banner, Jr., *To the Hartford Convention* (New York: Knopf, 1969).

24 On Webster's role in 1825, see Shaw Livermore, *The Twilight of Federalism* (Princeton: Princeton University Press, 1962), pp. 172–96; on his constitutional cases, see Maurice Baxter, *Daniel Webster and the Supreme Court* (Amherst: University of Massachusetts Press, 1966).

25 Webster, "The Basis of the Senate" (1820), *Writings and Speeches*, 5:14; Vernon Louis Parrington, *Main Currents in American Thought* (New York: Harcourt, Brace, 1927), 2:305–8.

26 Webster, "The Basis of the Senate" (1820), *Writings and Speeches*, 5:15 f.; "The Sub-Treasury" (1838), ibid., 8:170. Cf. "The First Settlement of New England" (1820), ibid., 1:211–14.

27 Webster, "Reply to Mr. Calhoun" (1838), ibid., 8:247 f.

28 On Webster and the "broker state," see Major Wilson, "'Liberty and Union': An Analysis of Three Concepts Involved in the Nullification Controversy," *Journal of Southern History* 33 (Aug., 1967): 331–55; on Webster's economic ideas, see Melvin Dubofsky, "Daniel Webster and the Whig Theory of Economic Growth," *New England Quarterly* 42 (Dec., 1969): 551–72.

29 Webster, "The Right of Preemption to Actual Settlers on the Public Lands" (1838), *Writings and Speeches*, 8:129–39; Peter J. Parish, "Daniel Webster, New England, and the West," *Journal of American History* 54 (Dec., 1967): 524–49.

30 Dalzell has pointed out the importance of "character" in Webster's thought but not its origins in moral philosophy; see his *Daniel Webster and the Trial of American Nationalism*, pp. xiii–xiv. See also Foster, "Webster and Choate in College" (cited in n. 8, above) and the surviving student essays and orations in the microfilm edition of the Webster Papers.

31 Webster, *Writings and Speeches*, 10:238 ff.; 12:261; Anon., "Washington," *North American Review* 51 (July, 1840): 69–91; Marcus Cunliffe, *George Washington, Man and Monument* (London: Collins, 1959), pp. 15–18; E. L. Magoon, "Daniel Webster," *Living Orators in America* (New York, 1851), pp. 22 f.

32 The Webster quotation is from "Reception at Madison, Indiana" (1837), *Writings and Speeches*, 2:254. See also Edward Everett, "The Importance of Education in a Republic" (1838), *Orations and Speeches* (Boston, 1883), 2:313–24.

33 Michael Katz, in *The Irony of Early School Reform* (Cambridge: Harvard University Press, 1968), does not recognize the partisan aspect of the public schools, but the summary of the Whig educators' philosophy on pp. 122–31 is excellent. The quotation in the text is from the *Common School Journal* 2 (Dec., 1840): 373 f. See also Webster's own "Remarks on Education" (n.d.), *Writings and Speeches*, 3:106 f.

34 Linda Kerber, *Federalists in Dissent: Imagery and Ideology in Jeffersonian America* (Ithaca: Cornell University Press, 1970); Hugh Blair, *Lectures on Rhetoric and Belles Lettres* (1783), ed. Harold Harding (Carbondale: Southern Illinois University Press, 1965).

35 Webster, "Adams and Jefferson" (1826), *Writings and Speeches*, 1:290. For examples of emotional Unionism, see his speeches at Valley Forge (1844) or Westchester (1851), ibid., 3:279 and 12:260.

36 See *OED*, 9:470, definition 9b of "sentiment," and Daniel Walker Howe, *The Unitarian Conscience: Harvard Moral Philosophy, 1805–1861* (Cambridge: Harvard University Press, 1970), pp. 62 f. The second Reply to Hayne (1830) is printed under the title "Second Speech on Foot's Resolution" in Webster's *Writings and Speeches*, 6:3–75.

37 Webster, "The Character of Washington" (1832), *Writings and Speeches*, 2:70; Charles W. March, *Reminiscences of Congress* (New York, 1850), p. 145.

38 Webster, "Second Speech on Foot's Resolution," cited in n. 36; "Speech at a Mass Meeting in Saratoga" (1840), *Writings and Speeches*, 3:5–36; John C. Sterling, *Daniel Webster and a Small College* (Hanover, N.H.: Dartmouth Publications, 1965).

39 *The Federalist Papers*, number 49.

40 Webster, "The First Settlement of New England" (1820), *Writings and Speeches*, 1:181; James Rees, *The Beauties of Daniel Webster* (New York, 1839), p. 11.

41 See William Charvat, *Origins of American Critical Thought* (Philadelphia: University of Pennsylvania Press, 1936; reprinted in 1961); Terence Martin, *The Instructed Vision* (Bloomington: Indiana University Press, 1961); James Mulquees, "Literary Standards of American Whigs," *American Literature* 41 (Nov., 1969): 355–72.

42 Alexander Saxton, "Blackface Minstrelsy and Jacksonian Ideology," *American Quarterly* 27 (May, 1975): 3–28. On literature and the Democratic party, see also John Stafford, *The Literary Criticism of "Young America"* (Berkeley: University of California Press, 1952).

43 On the historical background of disputatious oratory, see Walter J. Ong, *Rhetoric, Romance, and Technology* (Ithaca: Cornell University Press, 1971), esp. pp. 14–18 and 113–41.

44 William R. Taylor, *Cavalier and Yankee* (New York: George Braziller, 1961), p. 110.

45 See, e.g., the speeches of Webster's "Southern Tour" (1847), *Writings and Speeches*, 4:69–103. The religious influences on Webster's rhetoric are suggested in Elizabeth Palmer Peabody, *Reminiscences of William Ellery Channing* (Boston, 1880), p. 153. Cf. Hoxie N. Fairchild, *Religious Trends in English Poetry* (New York: Columbia University Press, 1939), 1:535–76.

46 Claude M. Fuess, *Daniel Webster* (Boston: Little, Brown, 1930), 2:407 f.;

Lanman, *Private Life*, pp. 101–7; Harvey, *Reminiscences*, pp. 395 and 406. (Fuess's biography, while laudatory, is thorough and still valuable.)

47 Samuel Mosheim Schmucker, *Life, Speeches, and Memorials of Daniel Webster* (Philadelphia, 1859), p. 126; Anon., "Daniel Webster as an Author," p. 48 (cited in n. 4, above); *Proceedings of the Webster Centennial* (Hanover, N.H.: Dartmouth College, 1902), p. 223; March, *Reminiscences of Congress*, p. 142 (italics in original).

48 See Taylor, *Cavalier and Yankee*, chap. 3. Though it does not mention the Whig party, Ann Douglas, *The Feminization of American Culture* (New York: Knopf, 1977) is also relevant.

49 Specialists will notice that this interpretation is slightly different from Norman D. Brown's in *Daniel Webster and the Politics of Availability* (cited in n. 15).

50 Sydney Nathans, *Daniel Webster and Jacksonian Democracy* (Baltimore: Johns Hopkins University Press, 1973); Dalzell, *Daniel Webster and the Trial of American Nationalism*, pp. 39–58.

51 Frederick Merk, *The Oregon Question* (Cambridge: Harvard University Press, 1967), pp. 287–93; John O. Geiger, "A Scholar Meets John Bull," *New England Quarterly* 49 (Dec., 1976): 577–95.

52 Ralph W. Hidy, *The House of Baring in American Trade and Finance* (Cambridge: Harvard University Press, 1949); William Brock, "The Image of England and American Nationalism," *Journal of American Studies* 5 (Dec., 1971): 225–45; Charles M. Wiltse, "Daniel Webster and the British Experience," Massachusetts Historical Society, *Proceedings* 85 (1973): 58–77.

53 Quotation from Webster, "Completion of the Bunker Hill Monument" (1843), *Writings and Speeches*, 1:278.

54 Webster, "Speech at Marshfield" (1848), ibid., 4:131–37.

55 See Philip Foner, *Business and Slavery* (Chapel Hill: University of North Carolina Press, 1941; reprinted in 1968).

56 Webster, "The Constitution and the Union" (1850), *Writings and Speeches*, 10:56–99. There is an excellent discussion of the speech and its background in Dalzell, *Daniel Webster and the Trial of American Nationalism*, pp. 178–95.

57 Edward Everett to Daniel Webster, March 8, 1852, quoted in Dalzell, *Daniel Webster and the Trial of American Nationalism*, p. 250; Webster, quoted in Fuess, *Daniel Webster*, 2:289.

58 Edward Everett, "Memoir of Daniel Webster" (1851), reprinted in Webster's *Writings and Speeches*, 1:171.

59 See Claude M. Fuess, *Rufus Choate, Wizard of the Law* (New York: 1928); John W. Black, "Rufus Choate," in *History and Criticism of American Public Address*, ed. William Brigance (New York: McGraw-Hill, 1943), 1:434–58; David B. Walker, "Rufus Choate: A Case Study in Old Whiggery," *Essex Institute Historical Collections* 94 (Oct., 1958): 334–55; and R. Kent Newmyer, "Justice Joseph Story on Circuit," *American Journal of Legal History* 14 (April, 1970): 112–35.

60 Joseph Story, quoted in Perry Miller, *The Life of the Mind in America* (New York: Harcourt, Brace, 1965), p. 147; Richard Henry Dana, Jr.,

quoted in Samuel G. Brown, *Memoir of Rufus Choate* (Boston, 1862), p. 254.

61 See Nehemiah Adams, *A Sabbath Discourse on the Death of Hon. Rufus Choate* (Boston, 1859), pp. 54–56, and Edwin Whipple, *Some Recollections of Rufus Choate* (New York, 1879), pp. 8–11, 25.

62 See Whipple, *Some Recollections*, pp. 60–65, 75, 83; Theophilus Parsons, *Address Commemorative of R. Choate* (Boston, 1859), p. 23; Edward G. Parker, *Reminiscences of Rufus Choate* (Boston, 1860), pp. 15, 25, 41, 80, 190; and Fuess, *Rufus Choate*, p. 272.

63 Rufus Choate, "Discourse Commemorative of Daniel Webster" (1853), *Works* (Boston, 1862), 1:495.

64 *Davidson* v *Boston & Maine Railroad*, 57 Mass. (3 Cushing) 91 (1849); *Commonwealth* v. *Nashua & Lowell Railroad*, 68 Mass. (2 Gray) 54 (1854).

65 Choate pleads for the establishment of a railroad competing with an existing monopoly in *Abstract of the Arguments for a Railroad from Danvers to Malden* (Boston, 1847). He pleads against such an establishment in *Application of Salem & Lawrence Railroad Co. for a Parallel Railroad from Salem to Danvers* (Boston, 1851).

66 Quoted in Fuess, *Rufus Choate*, p. 171. In his greatest patent case, Choate vindicated Charles Goodyear's right to the patent on vulcanized rubber; see *Horace H. Day ads. Charles Goodyear: The Points for Defendant, Argued by Hon. Rufus Choate* (Trenton, 1852).

67 The quotations are from Rufus Choate, "American Nationality: An Oration Delivered July 5 [sic], 1858," *Works*, 2:416, and "Address to the Story Association" (1851), ibid., 1:172.

68 Rufus Choate to Charles Sumner, Jan., 1845, MS in Sumner Papers, Houghton Library, Harvard University.

69 Choate, "The Position and Functions of the American Bar, as an Element of Conservatism in the State," *Works*, 1:423.

70 Choate, "The Colonial Age of New England: An Address Delivered at Ipswich, Mass." (1834), ibid., pp. 351, 355.

71 Louis Hartz, in *The Liberal Tradition in America* (New York, 1955), argues that the institutions American conservatives defend are in actuality "Lockean." I agree with Marvin Meyers, however, that when Hartz speaks of "Lockeanism" he evidently has in mind the whole of bourgeois capitalism as a way of life—not simply the philosophy of one man. See Meyers, "Louis Hartz, *The Liberal Tradition in America*: An Appraisal," *Comparative Studies in Society and History* 5 (April, 1963): 251–68.

72 Choate, "Position and Functions of the American Bar," *Works*, 1:432–33.

73 Edmund Burke, "Speech in Opening the Impeachment of Warren Hastings" (1788), *Works* (Boston, 1871), 9:401.

74 Choate, "Speech on the Judicial Tenure" (1853), *Works*, 2:286. Cf. his argument in *Commonwealth* v. *Thomas Aves*, 34 Mass. (18 Pickering) 205 (1836).

75 Choate, "Position and Functions of the American Bar," *Works*, 1:424. On the relationship between Burkean political thought and common law, see J. G. A. Pocock, "Burke and the Ancient Constitution," in his *Politics, Language, and Time* (New York, 1971), pp. 202–32.

76 Choate, "Position and Functions of the American Bar," *Works,*.1:417, 426. Choate was exposed to the influence of Coleridge through his acquaintance with James Marsh; see Lewis S. Feuer, "James Marsh and the Conservative Transcendentalist Philosophy: A Political Interpretation," *New England Quarterly* 21 (March, 1958): 3–31.

77 Parker, *Reminiscences,* pp. 394–411; Choate, "Argument on the Removal of Judge Davis" (1856), *Works,* 2:342–86. On the codification controversy, see Perry Miller, *The Life of the Mind,* pp. 239–65, and Maxwell Bloomfield, *American Lawyers in a Changing Society* (Cambridge: Harvard University Press, 1976), pp. 59–90.

78 Choate, "Position and Functions of the American Bar," *Works,* 1:417; 12 *Coke's Reports* 65.

79 Choate, "Position and Functions of the American Bar," *Works,* 1:430. Because of the context, it might seem that Choate is referring only to common law; elsewhere, however, he tries to ground even statutory law in "reason" rather than "will." See his "Protecting American Labor by Duties on Imports" (1844), ibid., 2:173–247. Cf. Daniel Boorstin, *The Mysterious Science of the Law: An Essay on Blackstone's Commentaries* (Cambridge: Harvard University Press, 1941), esp. pp. 20–31.

80 Morton Horwitz, *The Transformation of American Law, 1780–1860* (Cambridge: Harvard University Press, 1977), chap. 8; Choate, "American Nationality," *Works,* 2:427.

81 Choate, "American Nationality," *Works,* 2:430.

82 For examples of Choate's classical scholarship, see ibid., pp. 451–515.

83 Brown, *Memoir of Rufus Choate* (cited in n. 60), p. 73.

84 Choate, "The Age of the Pilgrims the Heroic Period of Our History" (1843), *Works,* 1:371–93; quotation from p. 378.

85 Choate, "The Colonial Age of New England," ibid., p. 370; "Position and Functions of the American Bar," ibid., p. 422.

86 Choate, journal entry for Aug. 2, 1850, ibid., p. 153.

87 Rufus Choate in conversation, quoted in Parker, *Reminiscences,* p. 269 (Parker's italics). The *Catalogue of the Valuable Private Library of the Late Hon. Rufus Choate* (Boston, 1859) reveals his tastes.

88 Choate, "The Importance of Illustrating New-England History by a Series of Romances like the Waverly Novels" (1833), *Works,* 1:319–46; idem, *Letter, Resigning the Office of Regent of the Smithsonian Institution* (Boston, 1855).

89 Choate, "Address to the Story Association," *Works,* 1:172; "Speech Delivered at the Constitutional Meeting," ibid., 2:324. Burke's famous passage that begins, "Society is indeed a contract, but...," occurs in *Reflections on the Revolution in France* (1790). For Jefferson the essence of the "contract" was that the people retained the right to revoke their grant of authority to the government; this was the very point that Burke and Choate were seeking to refute by their reference to a social contract.

90 This ambiguity has created controversy over whether Burke was a believer in natural law or a positivist. For the two sides, see Francis P. Canarvan, S.J., *The Political Reason of Edmund Burke* (Durham, N.C.: Duke University Press, 1960), and Paul Lucas, "On Edmund Burke's

Doctrine of Prescription," *Historical Journal* 11 (Jan., 1968): 35–63. Gertrude Himmelfarb, in *Victorian Minds* (New York, 1968), chap. 1, argues the case both ways and leaves it "for the reader to decide which is the real Burke" (p. 4). Finally, see Frank O'Gorman, *Edmund Burke* (Bloomington: Indiana University Press, 1973).

91 *Ela* v. *Smith et al.*, 71 Mass. (5 Gray) 121–43 (1855). There is an amusing sidelight to Choate's stern defense of law and order: while an undergraduate at Dartmouth, he himself had been arrested for engaging in a student riot. He was represented in court by Daniel Webster, who succeeded in getting the charges dropped.

92 Rufus Choate to E. W. Farley, Aug. 9, 1856, *Works*, 1:215. Ralph Waldo Emerson was outraged when Choate's letter was made public: "Glittering generalities! He means blazing ubiquities!"

93 Choate, *Argument for the Division of Worcester County* (Boston, 1854), p. 39, and "The Political Topics Now Prominent before the Country" (1856), *Works*, 2:403–6.

94 Alfred Cobban, *Edmund Burke and the Revolt against the Eighteenth Century*, 2d ed. (London: Allen & Unwin, 1960), esp. pp. 97–130.

95 Alexis de Tocqueville, *Democracy in America*, trans. Phillips Bradley (New York: Vintage, 1945), 2:230 f.

96 Rajni Kothari, "Tradition and Modernity Revisited," *Government and Opposition* 3 (Summer, 1968): 273–93; the quotations are from pp. 289 and 291 (his italics).

97 See Webster, "The Compromise Measures" (1850), *Writings and Speeches*, 10:144; Everett, "The Importance of Agriculture" (1857), *Orations and Speeches*, 3:560; Joseph Story, *Commentaries on the Constitution* (Boston, 1833), vol. 1, epigraphs on the title page; Leroy Pope, *Eulogy* (cited in n. 2, above), p. 21; Alexander Stephens, "Farewell Speech" (1859), in *Alexander Stephens in Public and Private*, ed. Henry Cleveland (Philadelphia, 1866), p. 643.

98 Horace Greeley, *Hints toward Reforms* (New York, 1853), p. 78; James B. Stewart, *Joshua R. Giddings* (Cleveland: Case Western Reserve University Press, 1970), p. 125; David H. Donald, *Charles Sumner and the Coming of the Civil War* (New York: Knopf, 1960), pp. 228 f.; Major L. Wilson, *Space, Time, and Freedom* (Westport, Conn.: Greenwood, 1974), p. 222; John Quincy Adams, "Letters of Publicola" (1791), *Writings of John Quincy Adams*, ed. W. C. Ford, (New York: Macmillan, 1913), 1:65–135.

99 Rush Welter, in *The Mind of America, 1820–1860* (New York: Columbia University Press, 1975), p. 205, denies that the Whigs invoked Burke; Allen Guttmann, in *The Conservative Tradition in America* (New York: Oxford University Press, 1967), has much that is valuable to say about Burkeanism in American literature but ignores the Whigs; Robert Kelley, in *The Transatlantic Persuasion: The Liberal-Democratic Mind in the Age of Gladstone* (New York: Knopf, 1969), shows how Burke could appeal to reformers, but he is concerned with the later nineteenth century; the connection he seeks to establish between Burke and postbellum American Democrats seems to me much less direct than the connection between Burke and antebellum American Whigs.

100 See, e.g., the following anonymous essays: "Thoughts on the Causes of the Present Discontents," *New England Magazine* 8 (Nov., 1834):

345–51; "Reform of the Judiciary," *American Review* 2 (Nov., 1845): 493; "The War—Conquest Its Object and Aim," *National Intelligencer*, Nov. 20, 1847. The quotation in the text is from "Edmund Burke," *American Review* 16 (Oct., 1852): 323.

101 Edmund Burke, "Letters on a Regicide Peace" (1796), *Works*, 5:208.

102 "The Character and Writings of Edmund Burke," *Quarterly Christian Spectator* 6 (June, 1834): 226–50; "The Inductive Theory of Civilization," *American Review* 6 (Oct., 1847): 381–98; George Hillard, *The Dangers and Duties of the Mercantile Profession* (Boston, 1850), pp. 10 f.; *Proceedings of the Webster Centennial* (cited in n. 8), p. 141. On the relationship of aesthetics to social control, see also Neil Harris, *The Artist in American Society* (New York: George Braziller, 1966), pp. 158–68.

Chapter Ten

1 My indebtedness to the work of Eugene D. Genovese on planter culture will be obvious; for the culture of the smaller landholders, see the older writings of Wilbur Cash and Frank Owsley. On the weakening of bourgeois self-confidence, Genovese's essay, "The Industrialists under the Slave Regime," in his *The Political Economy of Slavery* (New York: Pantheon, 1966), pp. 180–220, is excellent.

2 Rudolph Von Abele, *Alexander H. Stephens* (New York: Knopf, 1946), p. 325. Von Abele is especially good on Stephens' psychology. Less sophisticated accounts are by Louis Pendleton, *Alexander H. Stephens* (Philadelphia: George Jacobs, 1907), and E. Ramsay Richardson, *Little Aleck: A Life of Alexander H. Stephens* (New York: Grosset & Dunlap, 1938).

3 AHS, "Address before the Few and Phi Gamma Societies of Emory College" (1852); "Address to the Sophomore Class at the State University" (1859); "Farewell Speech Delivered in Augusta, Ga." (1859), all published in *Alexander Stephens in Public and Private*, ed. Henry Cleveland (Philadelphia, 1866), pp. 365, 368, 655, 643. Stephens' Papers are owned by Manhattanville College; microfilm copies are available at other libraries. Whenever possible, I cite either Cleveland's or other published collections of Stephens' writings for ease of reference.

4 Much of Alexander Stephens' journal and correspondence with Linton Stephens was published in Richard Johnston and William Browne, *Life of Alexander H. Stephens* (Philadelphia, 1878; rev. ed., 1884). All the biographers suggest impotency, with varying degrees of confidence; see Von Abele, p. 136; Richardson, p. 57; Pendleton, p. 33.

5 AHS to Linton Stephens, Feb. 3, 1851, in Johnston and Browne, *Life*, p. 263.

6 See Charles G. Sellers, Jr., "Who Were the Southern Whigs?" *American Historical Review* 59 (Jan., 1954): 335–46.

7 Stephens' brother wrote to him: "If I know you, one of your leading virtues is a resolute, determined, almost dogged kindness and devotion of service to mankind, who have in your judgment, no claim on your affection, and whom your impulses lead you to despise. This is a great battle that often rages, the conflict between your resolution to be kind and your impulse to be almost revengeful" (Linton Stephens to AHS, c. Jan. 1, 1859, in Johnston and Browne, *Life*, p. 340).

8   Ulrich B. Phillips, "Georgia and State Rights," in American Historical Association, *Annual Report* 2 (1901): 3–224; Charles S. Sydnor, *The Development of Southern Sectionalism* (Baton Rouge: Louisiana State University Press, 1948), pp. 182–84; Ronald W. Faircloth, "The Impact of Andrew Jackson in Georgia Politics" (Ph.D. diss., University of Georgia, 1971); Richardson, *Little Aleck*, p. 66.

9   *National Intelligencer*, May 9, 1844; *Congressional Globe*, 28th Cong., 1st sess., 13:2 (Feb. 9, 1844), appendix, 196–201. Adams' verses are in Richardson, *Little Aleck*, p. 87. On southern Whiggery, see also Joel Silbey, "John C. Calhoun and the Limits of Southern Congressional Unity," *The Historian* 30 (Nov., 1967): 58–71.

10 AHS to James Thomas, March 7, 1844, quoted in Richardson, *Little Aleck*, p. 90.

11 *Congressional Globe*, 28th Cong., 2d sess., 14 (Jan. 25, 1845): 190, and appendix, 309–14; John Quincy Adams, diary entry for Jan. 25, 1845, in *Memoirs* (Philadelphia, 1877), 12:153.

12 *Congressional Globe*, 29th Cong., 1st sess., 15 (June 16, 1846), appendix, 948 (italics in original); ibid., 2d sess., 16 (Feb. 12, 1847), appendix, 351. For Stephens' reading, see Von Abele, *Alexander H. Stephens*, p. 93.

13 *Congressional Globe*, 30th Cong., 1st sess., 17 (Feb. 2, 1848), appendix, 162; Abraham Lincoln to W. L. Herndon, February 2, 1848, *Collected Works of Abraham Lincoln*, ed. Roy Basler (New Brunswick: Rutgers University Press, 1953), 1:448.

14 *Congressional Globe*, 29th Cong., 2d sess., 16 (Jan. 22, 1847): 240; ibid. 16 (Feb. 12, 1847), appendix, 354; ibid., 30th Cong., 2d sess., 18 (Feb. 17, 1849), appendix, 145–50.

15 Ibid., 30th Cong., 1st sess., 17 (Aug. 7, 1848), appendix, 1103–9.

16 Johnston and Browne, *Life of Alexander H. Stephens*, pp. 232–34; Richardson, *Little Aleck*, pp. 119 f.

17 AHS to Linton Stephens, April 15, 1850, in Johnston and Browne, *Life*, p. 252; Alan Nevins, *Ordeal of the Union* (New York: Charles Scribner's Sons, 1947), 1:195–97; Holman Hamilton, *Zachary Taylor* (Indianapolis: Bobbs-Merrill, 1951), 2:285 and passim.

18 *Congressional Globe*, 31st Cong., 1st sess., 22 (June 12, 1850), appendix, 1188 f.; Von Abele, *Alexander H. Stephens*, p. 125.

19 On colonization, see AHS to Linton Stephens, Jan. 18, 1845, quoted in Richardson, *Little Aleck*, p. 95. On slavery, etc., see Stephens' manuscripts for 1849–50, quoted in Von Abele, *Alexander H. Stephens*, pp. 122, 128, 134.

20 AHS to James Thomas, Feb. 13, 1850; AHS to the *National Intelligencer*, July 3, 1850 (both in Ulrich B. Phillips, ed., *Correspondence of Robert Toombs, Alexander H. Stephens, and Howell Cobb* [Washington, D.C.: American Historical Association, 1911], 2:184, 192 f.).

21 AHS to Linton Stephens, Dec. 4, 1849, quoted in Von Abele, *Alexander H. Stephens*, p. 122.

22 "Letter from Mr. Stephens," *National Intelligencer*, Feb. 28, 1852; *Congressional Globe*, 32d Cong., 1st sess., 24 (Jan. 27, 1852): 405; ibid. 25 (April 27, 1852), appendix, 462 f.

23 AHS to the Augusta, Georgia, *Chronicle and Sentinel*, June 28, 1852, in Phillips, ed., *Correspondence*, 2:304–6.

24 *Congressional Globe*, 31st Cong., 1st sess., 21 (May 1, 1850): 875; ibid.,

32d Cong., 1st sess., 24 (Dec. 30, 1851): 166; AHS to Linton Stephens, June 14, 1843, in Johnston and Browne, *Life*, p. 171. The exhortation to suppress "passion" is repeated in Stephens' Emory College Address of 1852, cited in note 3, above.

25 AHS to Howell Cobb, June 23, 1851, in Phillips, ed., *Correspondence*, 2:238; *Congressional Globe*, 32d Cong., 1st sess., 25 (April 27, 1852), appendix, 460; "Address on the Birthday of Washington" (1852), in Cleveland, ed., *Alexander Stephens in Public and Private* (cited in n. 3), pp. 352–64.

26 *Congressional Globe*, 32d Cong., 1st sess., 24 (Dec. 30, 1851): 165 f.; ibid. (Jan. 2, 1852): 189 f.; ibid., 32d Cong., 2d sess., 26 (Jan. 3, 1853): 192 f.

27 Alan Nevins presents a sample of southern Whig reactions in *Ordeal of the Union*, 2:132–38.

28 Epitaphs were appearing within a month of the passage of the Kansas-Nebraska Act; see the *National Intelligencer* of June 29 and July 1, 1854. See also Eric Foner, *Free Soil, Free Labor, Free Men* (New York: Oxford University Press, 1970), p. 194.

29 *Congressional Globe*, 33d Cong., 1st sess., 29 (Feb. 17, 1854), appendix, 193–97; 33d Cong., 2d sess., 31 (Dec. 14, 1854), appendix, 420–45; AHS to J. W. Duncan, in Phillips, ed., *Correspondence*, 2:345.

30 Cleveland, ed., *Stephens in Public and Private*, p. 416.

31 For background, see Eugene Genovese, "The Significance of the Slave Plantation for Southern Economic Development," in his *Political Economy of Slavery*, pp. 157–79, and Norris W. Preyer, "Why Did Industrialization Lag in the Old South?" *Georgia Historical Quarterly* 55 (Fall, 1971): 378–96.

32 Cleveland, ed., *Stephens in Public and Private*, pp. 416–58.

33 AHS to W. W. Burwell, June 26, 1854, in Phillips, ed., *Correspondence*, 2:346.

34 See Cleveland, ed., *Stephens in Public and Private*, pp. 459–71; *Congressional Globe*, 34th Cong., 1st sess. (Jan. 5, 1856): 151 f.

35 Cleveland, ed., *Stephens in Public and Private*, pp. 472–89; Von Abele, *Alexander H. Stephens*, pp. 147–50.

36 Robert Rayback, *Millard Fillmore* (Buffalo: Henry Stuart, 1959), p. 413; Carl Degler, *The Other South* (New York: Harper & Row, 1974), pp. 158–63.

37 AHS to Thomas W. Thomas, Dec. 29, 1856, in Phillips, ed., 2:386–89; Richardson, *Little Aleck*, p. 162; Pendleton, *Alexander H. Stephens*, pp. 86 f.; Von Abele, *Alexander H. Stephens*, p. 158.

38 Quoted in Richard Mentor Johnson (to whom Stephens said it), *Autobiography* (Washington, D.C., Neale, 1901), p. 151. See also Phillips, ed., *Correspondence*, 2:367–72, 389–93, 409–20; Cleveland, ed., *Stephens in Public and Private*, pp. 489–515; and Stephens' numerous speeches in the *Congressional Globe*, 34th and 35th Congresses.

39 AHS, "Farewell Speech" (1859), in Cleveland, ed., *Stephens in Public and Private*, pp. 637–51.

40 Ibid., p. 647; *Congressional Globe*, 35th Cong., 2d sess., 2 (Feb. 12, 1859), appendix, 124.

41 Johnston and Browne, *Life*, pp. 347 f., 353. Curiously, Von Abele finds it impossible to explain Stephens' resignation (*Alexander H. Stephens*, p. 172).

42 A majority of southern Whigs in Congress, under the leadership of

Crittenden, opposed the Lecompton Constitution; see Arthur C. Cole, *The Whig Party in the South* (Washington, D.C.: American Historical Association, 1913), p. 331.

43 Von Abele, *Alexander H. Stephens*, p. 56; AHS, *Recollections of Alexander H. Stephens: His Diary Kept While a Prisoner at Fort Warren*, ed. Myrta Lockett Avary (New York: Doubleday, 1910), pp. 427 f.

44 AHS to J. Henley Smith, Jan. 22, 1860, in Phillips, ed., *Correspondence*, 2:458; AHS to "Thirteen Gentlemen of Macon," May 9, 1860, in Cleveland, ed., *Stephens in Public and Private*, p. 661.

45 See William Barney, *The Road to Secession* (New York: Praeger, 1972), pp. 137–50, and Ollinger Crenshaw, *The Slave States in the Election of 1860* (Baltimore: Johns Hopkins University Press, 1945), pp. 29–35 and passim.

46 AHS, in conversation, May, 1860, in Johnston and Browne, *Life*, p. 356. Cf. Johnson, *Autobiography*, pp. 147–49.

47 See Barney, *Road to Secession*, pp. 145, 202, and passim, and Michael Holt, *The Political Crisis of the 1850's* (New York: John Wiley & Sons, 1978), chap. 8. Barney emphasizes the Whigs' lack of interest in slavery expansion; Holt, more general conservative attitudes.

48 See Phillips, ed., *Correspondence*, 2:504 f., 498. Stephens had talked exactly the same way in warning against secession in 1850–51; see ibid., p. 238.

49 AHS to J. Henley Smith, July 10, 1860, ibid., p. 487.

50 "Speech against Secession" (1860), in Cleveland, ed., *Stephens in Public and Private*, 694–713. Cf. David Donald, "An Excess of Democracy: The American Civil War and the Social Process," in his *Lincoln Reconsidered* (New York: Knopf, 1956), pp. 209–35.

51 Abraham Lincoln to AHS, Nov. 30 and Dec. 22, 1860, in *Collected Works of Abraham Lincoln*, ed. Basler, 4:146, 160.

52 AHS to Lincoln, Dec. 30, 1860, in Johnston and Browne, *Life*, pp. 371–73; Lincoln to John Defrees, Dec. 18, 1860, in Lincoln, *Collected Works*, 4:155.

53 AHS to Linton Stephens, Jan. 3, 1861, in Johnston and Browne, *Life*, p. 379; AHS, journal entries for June 5 and June 22, 1865, in *Recollections*, ed. Avary, pp. 174, 250.

54 AHS, *The Rebellion Inexcusable: A Warning and Protest against It* (Boston, 1864).

55 AHS to Z. P. Landrum, July 1, 1860, in Cleveland, ed., *Stephens in Public and Private*, p. 672.

56 AHS, "The Corner-Stone Speech" (1861), ibid., pp. 717–29.

57 AHS, "Speech before the Virginia Secession Convention" (1861), ibid., pp. 729–45.

58 Glyndon G. Van Deusen, *William Henry Seward* (New York: Oxford University Press, 1967), pp. 286 f. See also AHS to Alexander Marshall, Nov. 4, 1864, in Cleveland, ed., *Stephens in Public and Private*, p. 798.

59 Conversely, 81 percent of former Democratic congressmen had supported secession; see Thomas B. Alexander and Richard E. Beringer, *Anatomy of the Confederate Congress* (Nashville: Vanderbilt University Press, 1972), p. 35. See also Ezra Warner and W. B. Yearns, *Biographical Register of the Confederate Congress* (Baton Rouge: Louisiana State University Press, 1975).

60 Thomas B. Alexander's valuable study, "Persistent Whiggery in the

Confederate South," *Journal of Southern History* 27 (Aug., 1961): 305–29, may exaggerate the effectiveness of Whig organization; see John V. Mering, "Persistent Whiggery in the Confederate South: A Reconsideration," *South Atlantic Quarterly* 69 (Winter, 1970): 124–43.

61 AHS to R. M. Johnston, Sept. 1, 1862, in Johnston and Browne, *Life*, p. 419; Cleveland, ed., *Stephens in Public and Private*, pp. 177, 747–49, 794.

62 Typical is James Z. Rabun, "Alexander Stephens and Jefferson Davis," *American Historical Review* 58 (Jan., 1953): 290–321. On the general lack of centralized direction in the Confederacy, see David Donald, "Died of Democracy" in his *Why the North Won the Civil War* (n.p.: Louisiana State University Press, 1960), pp. 77–90.

63 AHS, "Address at Crawfordville, Ga." (1862), in Cleveland, ed., *Stephens in Public and Private*, pp. 749–60; Johnston and Browne, *Life*, pp. 415, 424.

64 There is a good overview of Stephens' strategy in his address to the Confederate Senate, published in his *Constitutional View of the Late War between the States* (Philadelphia, 1868–70), 2:587–89. See also Richardson, *Little Aleck*, pp. 201, 218, 253. On Davis' shortcomings, see David M. Potter, "Jefferson Davis and the Political Factors in Confederate Defeat," in Donald, ed., *Why the North Won the Civil War*, pp. 91–114.

65 See AHS to James R. Seddon (Confederate secretary of war), April 29, 1864, in Cleveland, ed., *Stephens in Public and Private*, pp. 786–90. A good account of the modernizing effect of war on the Confederate States, more favorable to Davis than mine, is Emory M. Thomas, *The Confederacy as a Revolutionary Experience* (Englewood Cliffs, N.J.: Prentice-Hall, 1971), esp. pp. 66–77, 133–37. The superior ability of the North to modernize its war effort is analyzed in George Fredrickson, "Blue Over Gray: Sources of Success and Failure in the Civil War," in his *A Nation Divided* (Minneapolis: Burgess, 1975), pp. 57–80. See also Raimondo Luraghi, "The Civil War and the Modernization of America," *Civil War History* 18 (Sept., 1972), esp. pp. 244–45.

66 AHS, "Speech on the State of the Confederacy, Milledgeville, Ga." (1864), in Cleveland, ed., *Stephens in Public and Private*, pp. 761–86; Letter to Seddon, ibid., p. 789. See also Charles Ramsdell, *Behind the Lines in the Southern Confederacy* (Baton Rouge: Louisiana State University Press, 1944).

67 See David P. Escott, "Jefferson Davis and the Failure of Confederate Nationalism" (Ph.D. diss., Duke University, 1974), and Armstead Robinson, "Day of Jubilo: Civil War and the Demise of Slavery" (Ph.D. diss., University of Rochester, 1976).

68 AHS, Milledgeville speech and Crawfordville speech, in Cleveland, ed. *Stephens in Public and Private*, pp. 785, 760.

69 Johnston and Browne, *Life*, pp. 457–59; AHS, journal entry for July 13, 1865, in *Recollections* (cited in n. 43), pp. 326–35.

70 Richardson, *Little Aleck*, pp. 263–65; Von Abele, *Alexander H. Stephens*, pp. 216–18, 236–44; Lincoln to Samuel Lee, July 4, 1863, and Lincoln to W. H. Seward, Jan. 31, 1865, in Lincoln, *Collected Works*, ed. Basler, 6:314 f., 8:250.

71 AHS to Linton Stephens, April 20, 1865, in Johnston and Browne, *Life*, p. 487.

72 AHS to Linton Stephens, Feb. 3, 1851, ibid., p. 263.
   Alexander, "Persistent Whiggery" (cited in n. 60), pp. 311–15.

74 AHS, "Address ¡before the General Assembly" (1866), in Cleveland,
   ed., *Stephens in Public and Private*, pp. 804–18 (the quotations are from
   pp. 812, 813).

75 Ulrich B. Phillips, "Alexander Hamilton Stephens," in the *Dictionary of
   American Biography*, 9:574. The best discussion of the work is in Edmund Wilson, *Patriotic Gore* (London: André Deutsch, 1962), pp. 395–
   437.

76 AHS, *Constitutional View* (cited in n. 64), 1:298–388.

77 Henry Cleveland, editor of *Stephens in Public and Private*, and the compilers of the Johnston-Browne *Life* also fell under the spell of this
   spurious consistency.

78 AHS, *The Reviewers Reviewed* (Philadelphia, 1872); *A Compendium of
   the History of the United States* (New York, 1877); *A Comprehensive and
   Popular History of the United States* (Philadelphia, 1882).

79 AHS, *Constitutional View*, 2:667–70.

80 C. Vann Woodward, *Origins of the New South* (Baton Rouge: Louisiana
   State University Press, 1951), p. 21; idem, *Reunion and Reaction: The
   Compromise of 1877*, rev. ed. (Garden City, N.Y.: Doubleday, 1956), pp.
   86, 245, 256.

81 *Congressional Record*, 43d Cong., 1st sess., 2:1 (Jan. 5, 1874): 152–54.

82 Ibid., 45th Cong., 2d sess., 7:1 (Feb. 12, 1878): 970 f.; cf. AHS, *Constitutional View*, 2:448, 551–56.

83 Barrington Moore, *Social Origins of Dictatorship and Democracy: Lord
   and Peasant in the Making of the Modern World* (Boston: Beacon Press,
   1966), p. 122. Moore's treatment of the American Civil War as "the last
   capitalist revolution" is extremely interesting; see pp. 111–52.

84 The rapidly growing historiography of Reconstruction describes a
   shifting political kaleidoscope of local alliances among black and white
   elements in southern society during these turbulent years. Relevant to
   Stephens' Georgia are Elizabeth Nathans, *Losing the Peace* (Baton
   Rouge: Louisiana State University Press, 1968), and Derrell Roberts,
   Joseph E. Brown and the Politics of Reconstruction (University, Ala.: University of Alabama Press, 1973).

85 See David Potter, "The Enigma of the South," *Yale Review* 51 (Autumn,
   1961): 142–51, and C. Vann Woodward, "The Southern Ethic in a Puritan World," in his *American Counterpoint* (Boston: Little, Brown, 1971),
   pp. 13–46.

Chapter Eleven

1 Because the secondary literature dealing with Lincoln is so vast, cita-
  tions in this chapter will necessarily be selective. The latest, and in my
  opinion the best, biography is Stephen B. Oates, *With Malice toward
  None* (New York: Harper & Row, 1977). Also recommended are
  Reinhard Luthin, *The Real Abraham Lincoln* (Englewood Cliffs, N.J.:
  Prentice-Hall, 1960); Benjamin P. Thomas, *Abraham Lincoln* (New York:
  Random House, 1952); and Godfrey Benson, Lord Charnwood, *Abra-
  ham Lincoln* (New York: Henry Holt, 1917).

2 Horace Greeley, "An Estimate of Abraham Lincoln," *Greeley on Lin-

coln, ed. Joel Benton (New York, 1893), pp. 19 f.; AL, "Communication to the Readers of *The Old Soldier*," Feb. 28, 1840, *Collected Works of Abraham Lincoln*, ed. Roy P. Basler (New Brunswick: Rutgers University Press, 1953), 1:205. Hereafter cited as *CWAL*.

3   AL to Josiah M. Lucas, Nov. 17, 1849, *CWAL*, 2:67; see also 1:506.

4   AL to "The People of Sangamo [sic] County," March 9, 1832, *CWAL*, 1:5–9; see also ibid., pp. 73, 126, 144, 196, 200, and passim.

5   William Herndon, MS letter to Jesse Weik, Jan. 1, 1866, quoted in Gabor S. Borit, "Old Wine into New Bottles: Abraham Lincoln and the Tariff Reconsidered," *Historian* 28 (Feb., 1966): 289–317. Borit revises the views of earlier historians, such as James G. Randall, who had minimized Lincoln's protectionism. See also "Tariff Discussion" (1847), *CWAL*, 1:407–16, and AL to Edward Wallace, Oct. 11, 1859, *CWAL*, 3:486 f.

6   AL, "Speech in the Illinois Legislature Concerning the State Bank" (1837), *CWAL*, 1:69. Cf. his "Speech on the Sub-Treasury" (1839), ibid., pp. 159–79.

7   William H. Herndon and Jesse Weik, *Abraham Lincoln* (Chicago, 1889; reprinted in 1921), p. 375; *CWAL*, 1:8 and 454. See also Richard Hofstadter, "Abraham Lincoln and the Self-Made Myth," in his *The American Political Tradition* (New York: Knopf, 1948), pp. 93–136.

8   Robert Kelley, "Ideology and Political Culture from Jefferson to Nixon," *American Historical Review* 82 (June, 1977): 545; AL, "Handbill Replying to Charges of Infidelity" (1846), *CWAL*, 1:382.

9   Herndon and Weik, *Abraham Lincoln*, p. 2. It was Herndon who first called attention to Lincoln's rejection of his early environment. Some of what he said went too far, but the most recent biographers, Luthin and Oates, vindicate Herndon's sense of the matter.

10   AL to William Herndon, July 10, 1848, *CWAL*, 1:497.

11   The quotation is from Richard N. Current, *The Lincoln Nobody Knows* (New York: McGraw-Hill, 1958), p. 33. AL, "Temperance Address" (1842), *CWAL*, 1:277.

12   William E. Barton, *The Lineage of Lincoln* (Indianapolis: Bobbs-Merrill, 1929), established that Lincoln's parents were in fact legally married.

13   "Autobiography" (1860), *CWAL*, 4:61; Current, *The Lincoln Nobody Knows*, pp. 22–25, 30; AL to Jesse Fell, Dec. 20, 1859, *CWAL*, 3:511.

14   AL to John D. Johnston, Jan. 12, 1851, *CWAL*, 2:96 f.

15   For the quotation, see ibid., p. 383; see also 1:229, 289. It has been suggested that Lincoln's melancholia originated in the traumatic loss of his mother during childhood, which is psychologically plausible. See Charles B. Strozier, "Abraham Lincoln," *Psychobiography* 1 (May, 1978): 3–15.

16   Ibid., 1:47, 265, 369; Herndon and Weik, *Abraham Lincoln*, p. 325.

17   Contrasting value judgments are passed by Albert J. Beveridge, *Abraham Lincoln* (Boston: Houghton Mifflin, 1928), and James G. Randall, *Lincoln the President* (New York: Dodd, Mead, 1945).

18   Oates, *With Malice toward None*, p. 98; Luthin, *The Real Abraham Lincoln*, pp. 39, 122 f.

19   Horace Bushnell, *The Moral Uses of Dark Things* (New York: Scribner's, 1898), p. 42; AL to John D. Johnston, Nov. 4, 1858, *CWAL*, 2:111. Cf. AL to Thomas Lincoln and John D. Johnston, Dec. 24, 1848, ibid., pp. 15 f.

20   See, e.g., *CWAL*, 2:160, 161, 332, 426.

21 Oates, *With Malice toward None,* p. 104; *CWAL,* 1:112, 450, 480–90; "First Inaugural Address" (1861), first and final drafts, *CWAL,* 4:252, 264.
22 David Anderson, *Abraham Lincoln* (New York: Twayne, 1970), p. 57.
23 W. H. Herndon to Truman Bartlett, Aug. 16, 1887, quoted in David Donald, *Lincoln's Herndon* (New York: Knopf, 1948), p. 360; Herndon and Weik, *Abraham Lincoln,* p. 588n.
24 W. H. Herndon to Jesse K. Weik, Jan. 1, 1866, quoted in Borit, "Old Wine into New Bottles," p. 300; Joseph L. Blau, introduction to Francis Wayland, *Elements of Moral Science* (Cambridge: Harvard University Press, 1963), p. xlvii.
25 "Address before the Young Men's Lyceum" (1838), *CWAL,* 1:108–15. Lincoln's endorsement of self-interest is discussed in Alan Heimert, "The Politics and Political Theory of Abraham Lincoln" (Harvard College senior honors essay, 1949).
26 Edmund Wilson, *Patriotic Gore* (London: André Deutsch, 1962), pp. 106 f.; Perry Miller, *The Life of the Mind in America* (New York: Harcourt, Brace & World, 1965), pp. 148 f.; Norman Jacobson, "Lincoln's Abraham," *Helderberg Review* 1 (Spring, 1971): 16.
27 A group of citations from the months of July through November, 1858, suggest something of Lincoln's admiration for the fathers and related ambition for himself; see *CWAL,* 2:482, 499, 546, and 3:339. For a fascinating exploration of the meaning of Lincoln's Lyceum speech, see George B. Forgie, *Patricide in the House Divided: A Psychological Interpretation of Lincoln and His Age* (New York: W. W. Norton, 1979), chap. 2.
28 "Speech at a Republican Banquet" (1856), *CWAL,* 2:385.
29 "Temperance Address" (1842), *CWAL,* 1:271–79. I disagree with Harry Jaffa, who has argued that the temperance movement and the prescriptive psychology implicit in it were so intolerant that Lincoln could not possibly have sincerely believed in them. He interprets this passage as a satire; see his *Crisis of the House Divided* (Garden City, N.Y.: Doubleday, 1959), pp. 250, 269–72.
30 *CWAL,* 3:29; 4:184; 2:125.
31 Counted by Edgar DeWitt Jones in his *The Influence of Henry Clay on Abraham Lincoln* (Lexington, Ky.: Henry Clay Memorial Foundation, 1952), p. 21. Mark Neely discusses "Abraham Lincoln's Eulogy on Henry Clay" in *Register of the Kentucky Historical Society* 73 (Jan., 1975): 31–61. Lincoln reproached Liberty voters in a letter to Williamson Durley, Oct. 3, 1845, *CWAL,* 1:347 f.
32 My interpretation of Mary Todd Lincoln is indebted to Oates, *With Malice toward None,* esp. pp. 66–72, and to Kathryn Kish Sklar, "Female Strategies in Victorian Families," a paper presented to the Conference on Lincoln's Thought and the Present, Springfield, Ill., June, 1976.
33 Current, *The Lincoln Nobody Knows,* p. 189; AL, "'Spot' Resolutions in the House of Representatives" (1847) and "The War with Mexico" (1848), *CWAL,* 1:420–22, 431–42. The quotations are from pp. 440 and 439.
34 Henry Clay to Thomas B. Stevenson, May 17, 1851, *Works,* ed. Calvin Colton (New York: G. P. Putnam's Sons, 1904), 3:499 f.
35 Arthur C. Cole, *The Whig Party in the South* (Washington, D.C.: Ameri-

can Historical Association, 1913), pp. 332–37, quotes the *Richmond Whig* of Sept. 30, 1859, and discusses the extent of such opinions; see also Thomas B. Alexander, *Sectional Stress and Party Strength* (Nashville: Vanderbilt University Press, 1967), pp. 98–104.

36 Robert Toombs to Alexander Stephens, Feb. 10, 1860, in Ulrich B. Phillips, ed., *Correspondence of Toombs, Stephens, and Cobb* (Washington, D.C.: American Historical Association, 1911), 2:462. See also Stephens to J. Henley Smith, Feb. 4, 1860, ibid., p. 460.

37 David Donald, "Whig in the White House," in his *Lincoln Reconsidered* (New York: Knopf, 1956), pp. 187–208; Kenneth Stampp, "The Politics of a Practical Whig," in his *The Era of Reconstruction* (New York: Knopf, 1965), pp. 24–49.

38 David A. Nichols, "Lincoln and the Indians," *Minnesota History* 44 (Spring, 1974): 3–15; AL, "Annual Message" (1863), *CWAL*, 7:47 f.; Borit, "Old Wine into New Bottles," p. 305.

39 "Speech at Peoria" (1854), *CWAL*, 2:276. Cf. Paul Nagel, *One Nation Indivisible* (New York: Oxford University Press, 1964), p. 84.

40 Michael Holt, "The Politics of Impatience: The Origins of Know Nothingism," *Journal of American History* 60 (Sept., 1973): 309–31; see also idem, *Forging a Majority* (New Haven: Yale University Press, 1969). Holt expands his analysis in *The Political Crisis of the 1850's* (New York: John Wiley & Sons, 1978).

41 Here, of course, I am following Eric Foner, *Free Soil, Free Labor, Free Men* (New York: Oxford University Press, 1970).

42 The pathetic editorials in the *National Intelligencer* are a good source for conservative Whig opinion in the late 1850s.

43 AL to Joshua F. Speed, Aug. 24, 1855, *CWAL*, 2:323; AL to George Robertson, Aug. 15, 1855, ibid., p. 318.

44 "Speech at Peoria" (1854), ibid., 2:247–83; the quotations are from pp. 270 and 276.

45 AL to Joshua F. Speed, Aug. 24, 1855, ibid., 2:320–23.

46 See, for example, Alexander's work, *Sectional Stress and Party Strength*, pp. 111 f.

47 Daniel Webster, "Speech at a Reception in New York" (1837), *Writings and Speeches* (Boston: Little, Brown, 1903), 2:206.

48 "Speech on Annexation of Texas" (1844), *CWAL*, 1:337; AL to Williamson Durley, Oct. 3, 1845, ibid., p. 347.

49 AL to Joshua R. Giddings, June 26, 1860, *CWAL*, 4:81; James B. Stewart, *Joshua R. Giddings and the Tactics of Radical Politics* (Cleveland: Case Western Reserve University Press, 1970), pp. 273–75. For Giddings' formulation of the theory of wartime emancipation, see the *National Intelligencer*, Feb. 2, 1844.

50 Daniel D. Barnard, "The Whigs and Their Candidate," *American Review* 8 (Sept., 1848): 221.

51 "Speech at Kalamazoo" (1856), *CWAL*, 2:364. On modernization, see Eric Foner, "The Causes of the American Civil War," *Civil War History* 20 (Sept., 1974): 197–214; on the development of proto-Republican economic ideas during the later years of the Whig party, see Rush Welter, *The Mind of America, 1820–1860* (New York: Columbia University Press, 1975), pp. 117–28.

52 William H. Seward, "The Republican Party and One Idea" (1860), *Works*, ed. George E. Baker (New York, 1884), 4:372.

53 AL to Lyman Trumbull, June 7, 1856, *CWAL*, 2:342 f.; AL to Usher F.
   Linder, March 22, 1848, ibid., 1:458; "Speech at Tremont, Ill." (1858),
   ibid., pp. 76 f. William G. Shade bears out Lincoln's estimate of the
   connection between Whig and Republican voting in *Banks or No Banks*
   (Detroit: Wayne State University Press, 1972), p. 196.
54 See Jacques Barzun, *Lincoln the Literary Genius* (Evanston, Ill.: Schori
   Press, 1960); Sarah Lincoln is quoted on p. 16.
55 See David C. Mearns, "Mr. Lincoln and the Books He Read," in *Three
   Presidents and Their Books*, by Arthur Bestor et al. (Urbana: University
   of Illinois Press, 1955), pp. 45–88, and M. L. Houser, *The Books That
   Lincoln Read* (Peoria, Ill.: Edward Jacob, 1929).
56 Charnwood's biography (p. 12) first called attention to the self-discipline in Lincoln's reading (see n. 1, above). See also AL to "The
   People of Sangamo County," March 9, 1832, *CWAL*, 1:8; AL, "Autobiography" (1860), ibid., 4:62.
57 For Lincoln's regard for the poem and his use of it in his eulogy for
   Taylor, see *CWAL*, 1:367, 378, and 2:90.
58 Francis P. Carpenter, *The Inner Life of Abraham Lincoln* (New York,
   1868), pp. 49–58; Charnwood, *Abraham Lincoln*, p. 459; Herndon and
   Weik, *Abraham Lincoln*, pp. 320 f.; AL, *CWAL*, 1:385.
59 Roy P. Basler, "Lincoln's Development as a Writer," in Basler, ed.,
   Abraham Lincoln: His Speeches and Writings (Cleveland: World, 1946),
   pp. 1–49; Edmund Wilson, *Patriotic Gore* (cited in n. 26), p. 120. See
   also Barzun, *Lincoln the Literary Genius*, p. 20, and the newspaper account of a Lincoln speech in *CWAL*, 2:348 f.
60 See, e.g., *CWAL*, 2:282, 370, 380, 545; 4:230.
61 "Speech on the Sub-Treasury" (1839), ibid., 1:178; for 1856 see ibid.,
   2:341 f., 367 (the hostile newspaper account), or 383–85.
62 Daniel Webster, "Speech Delivered at Valley Forge" (1844), *Writings
   and Speeches* (Boston: Little, Brown, 1903), 3:279. On Webster-Lincoln
   parallels, see also Richard N. Current, *Daniel Webster and the Rise of
   National Conservatism* (Boston: Little, Brown, 1955), pp. 186 f.
63 On Lincoln's set of Channing, see Mearns, "Mr. Lincoln and the Books
   He Read," p. 73. Seward's editorial suggestions for the First Inaugural
   Address are indicated in *CWAL*, 4:249–62.
64 *CWAL*, 1:49; 2:7; eyewitness account of Second Inaugural, quoted in
   Russel B. Nye, *Society and Culture in America, 1830–1860* (New York:
   Harper & Row, 1974), p. 145.
65 Wilson, *Patriotic Gore*, p. 123. See also Richard Hofstadter, "Abraham
   Lincoln and the Self-Made Myth," in his *The American Political Tradition* (New York: Knopf, 1948), esp. p. 94.
66 19 Howard (60 U.S.) 393–633 (1857); David M. Potter, *The Impending
   Crisis* (New York: Harper & Row, 1976), pp. 272–93; *CWAL*, 3:401, 543.
67 Oates, *With Malice toward None*, p. 162; Don E. Fehrenbacher, *Prelude
   to Greatness: Lincoln in the 1850s* (Stanford: Stanford University Press,
   1962), pp. 70–95.
68 Webster, *Writings and Speeches*, 4:244; AL, *CWAL*, 2:461. Like most
   orators preparing a script, Lincoln punctuated and italicized on
   rhetorical rather than grammatical grounds.
69 Cf. pp. 80–81, above. See Timothy J. Sehr, "Leonard Bacon and the
   Myth of the Good Slaveholder," *New England Quarterly* 49 (June, 1976):
   194–213. For the changing mood of the 1850s, see also David Brion

Davis, *The Slave Power Conspiracy and the Paranoid Style* (Baton Rouge: Louisiana State University Press, 1969), pp. 18–20.

70 *CWAL*, 2:465 f. Among the writers on natural theology with whom Lincoln was familiar were Chambers, Volney, Paine, Paley, James Smith, and possibly Joseph Butler.

71 Fehrenbacher, *Prelude to Greatness*, pp. 80–82.

72 George Fort Milton, *The Eve of Conflict* (Boston: Houghton Mifflin, 1934), pp. 108–31; Robert W. Johannsen, *Stephen A. Douglas* (New York: Oxford University Press, 1973), pp. 401–34.

73 The Democratic principle of congressional "nonintervention" has been called "dissimulation" by Fehrenbacher (*Prelude to Greatness*, pp. 129–33). On the "shiftiness and subterfuge" of Douglas, see Alan Nevins, *Ordeal of the Union* (New York: Scribner's, 1947), 2:100–115.

74 For a thorough analysis, see Don E. Fehrenbacher, *The Dred Scott Case* (New York: Oxford University Press, 1978), esp. pp. 307–14, 394, 451–55.

75 *CWAL*, 2:467; cf. ibid., p. 453 and 3:100–101. See also Jaffa, *Crisis of the House Divided* (cited in n. 29), pp. 275–93.

76 Jaffa, *Crisis of the House Divided*, p. 409; see also idem, "Expediency and Morality in the Lincoln-Douglas Debates," *Anchor Review* 2 (1957): 179–204. A worldly man who took little interest in spiritual things, Stephen Douglas was nevertheless of Scottish Calvinist ancestry. He married a Roman Catholic, replicating the religious coalition so important to the Democratic party.

77 Basler, "Lincoln's Development as a Writer," p. 28 (see n. 59, above). My discussion of the Lincoln-Douglas debates follows Fehrenbacher, *Prelude to Greatness*, pp. 49, 104, and passim. On Lincoln's ambition, see *CWAL*, 3:334.

78 See Welter, *The Mind of America*, pp. 134 f. and 438 f. (see n. 51, above).

79 AL, "On the Constitution and the Union" (c. 1861), *CWAL*, 4:169; cf. JQA, "Letter to the Twelfth Congressional District," *Boston Courier*, June 6, 1839, or JQA, *Oration before the Astronomical Society* (Cincinnati, 1843).

80 AL, "Speech at Chicago" (1858), *CWAL*, 2:501; Major L. Wilson, "The Free Soil Concept of Progress," *American Quarterly* 22 (Winter, 1970): 769–90 (the term "cultural purge" is from p. 773); AL, "Address at Cooper Institute" (1860), *CWAL*, 3:522–50.

81 AL to James Brown, Oct. 18, 1858, *CWAL*, 3:327 f.; William H. Seward, "Immediate Admission of Kansas" (1856), *Works*, 4:481.

82 Jaffa, *Crisis of the House Divided*, pp. 320–24; AL, "Speech at Springfield" (1857), *CWAL*, 2:406; John P. Diggins, "Slavery, Race, and Equality: Jefferson and the Pathos of the Enlightenment," *American Quarterly* 28 (Summer, 1976): 206–28 (quotation from p. 217); AL, "Speech at Chicago" (1858), *CWAL*, 2:501.

83 "On Free Labor" (1859), *CWAL*, 3:462; "Speech at Cincinnati" (1861), ibid., 4:202. Cf. ibid., 3:469.

84 The best works on this critical transition, in addition to those of Foner and Shade, are Michael F. Holt, *Forging a Majority* (New Haven: Yale University Press, 1969), esp. pp. 196–206, and Ronald P. Formisano, *The Birth of Mass Political Parties* (Princeton: Princeton University Press, 1971), esp. pp. 325–31.

85 Gary R. Planck, "Abraham Lincoln and Black Colonization," *Lincoln Herald* 72 (Summer, 1970): 61–77; AL, "Outline for Speech to Colonization Society" (1855?), *CWAL*, 2:298 f.; "Debate at Ottawa" (1858), ibid., 3:16; "Eulogy on Henry Clay" (1852), ibid., 2:131 f.

86 AL, "Speech at Springfield" (1858), *CWAL*, 2:521; Oates, *With Malice toward None*, pp. 268 f., 298 f., 307, 312 f.

87 AL to Horace Greeley, Aug. 22, 1862, *CWAL*, 5:388 f.; Armstead Robinson, "Day of Jubilo: Civil War and the Demise of Slavery" (Ph.D. diss., University of Rochester, 1976), passim.

88 "Speech at Springfield" (1857), *CWAL*, 2:405; AL to Michael Hahn, March 13, 1864, ibid., 7:243.

89 The quotations are from Don Fehrenbacher, "Only His Stepchildren: Lincoln and the Negro," *Civil War History* 22 (Dec., 1974): 293–310, and George M. Fredrickson, "A Man But Not a Brother: Abraham Lincoln and Racial Equality," *Journal of Southern History* 41 (Feb., 1975): 39–58.

90 AL to Thomas Conway, March 1, 1865, *CWAL*, 8:325; "Speech at Springfield" (1858), ibid., 2:520. On Lincoln's gradualist and organicist approach to implementing the ideals of the Declaration, see Garry Wills, *Inventing America: Jefferson's Declaration of Independence* (Garden City: Doubleday, 1978), pp. xiv–xxiv.

91 Wilson, *Patriotic Gore*, p. 130.

92 Herndon and Weik, *Abraham Lincoln*, pp. 149–56.

93 Carpenter, *The Inner Life of Abraham Lincoln* (cited in n. 58), pp. 185–96; AL, "Annual Message to Congress" (1862); "Meditation on the Divine Will" (1862), *CWAL*, 5:537, 403 f.

94 Forgie, *Patricide in the House Divided* (cited in n. 27), pp. 291–93. See also Paul Nagel, *This Sacred Trust* (New York: Oxford University Press, 1971), chap. 3; William Clebsch and Sydney Ahlstrom, "Christian Interpretations of the Civil War," *Church History* 30 (June, 1961): 1–19; and Elton Trueblood, *Abraham Lincoln: Theologian of American Anguish* (New York: Harper & Row, 1973), chap. 6.

95 "Second Inaugural Address" (1865), *CWAL*, 8:333. Lincoln quotes Psalm 19:19. See also AL to Thurlow Weed, March 15, 1865, *CWAL*, 8:356, in which he comments on the address.

96 Alexander Stephens, *Constitutional View of the Late War between the States* (Philadelphia, 1868–70), 2:448; Jaffa, *Crisis of the House Divided*, p. 229; Rajni Kothari, "Tradition and Modernity Revisited," *Government and Opposition* 3 (Summer, 1968): 289. See also Glen E. Thurow, *Abraham Lincoln and American Political Religion* (Albany: State University of New York Press, 1976).

97 "Message to Congress" (1862), *CWAL*, 5:537; "Gettysburg Address" (1863), ibid., 7:21; "Eulogy on Henry Clay" (1852), ibid., 2:126. See also James A. Rawley, "The Nationalism of Abraham Lincoln," *Civil War History* 9 (Sept., 1963): 283–98.

98 David Potter, "The Lincoln Theme and American National Historiography," in his *The South and the Sectional Conflict* (Baton Rouge: Louisiana State University Press, 1968), p. 176; AL to Democratic-Republican Workingmen's Association, March 21, 1864, *CWAL*, 7:259.

99 AL, "Address before the Wisconsin State Agricultural Society" (1859), *CWAL*, 3:482. Cf. "Annual Message to Congress" (1861), ibid., 5:51–53.

100 Albert Fishlow, *American Railroads and the Transformation of the Ante-*

Bellum Economy (Cambridge: Harvard University Press, 1965); AL, "Open Letter on Springfield and Alton Railroad" (1847), *CWAL*, 1:395–405; Hofstadter, *The American Political Tradition* (cited in n. 65), p. 107.

101 AL to Albert G. Hodges, April 4, 1864, *CWAL*, 7:282.

Conclusion

1 An excellent overview of this process, showing how it led up to the Whig-Jacksonian confrontation, can be found in Rowland Berthoff and John M. Murrin, "Feudalism, Communalism, and the Yeoman Farmer," in *Essays on the American Revolution*, ed. Stephen Kurtz and James H. Hutson (New York: Norton, 1973), pp. 256–88.

2 My use of the concept "cultural hegemony" follows Eugene Genovese, *In Red and Black: Marxian Explorations on Southern and Afro-American History* (New York: Pantheon Books, 1971), pp. 406–10.

3 T. J. Trowbridge, "We Are a Nation," *Atlantic Monthly* 14 (Dec., 1864): 771.

4 Wilhelm Reich, *Character-Analysis*, 3d ed., trans. Theodore P. Wolfe (New York: Orgone Press, 1949), pp. 193–200.

5 Michael Walzer, *The Revolution of the Saints* (Cambridge: Harvard University Press, 1965), examines the Calvinist personality as "an agent of modernization" (p. 300). Walzer's early European Calvinists generally evinced a harsher and more anxious form of compulsive personality than "my" Whigs. See also the classic work of David Riesman et al., *The Lonely Crowd*, rev. ed. (New Haven: Yale University Press, 1969), which relates changing character types to phases of industrial development in the Western world.

6 On the decline of mixed public-private enterprise, see Louis Hartz, *Economic Policy and Democratic Thought: Pennsylvania, 1776–1860* (Cambridge: Harvard University Press, 1948); on the declining appeal of the Whig program in general, see Michael Holt, *The Political Crisis of the 1850's* (New York: John Wiley & Sons, 1978), esp. pp. 102–13.

7 On the continuity of Democratic political ideas, see Richard O. Curry, "The Union as It Was: A Critique of Recent Interpretations of the 'Copperheads,'" *Civil War History* 13 (March, 1967): 25–39; see also Frank Klement, *The Limits of Dissent: Clement L. Vallandigham and the Civil War* (Lexington: University of Kentucky Press, 1970).

8 See Paul Kleppner, *The Third Electoral System: Parties, Voters, and Political Cultures* (Chapel Hill: University of North Carolina Press, 1979), esp. chap. 3, and Robert Kelley, *The Transatlantic Persuasion: The Liberal-Democratic Mind in the Age of Gladstone* (New York: Knopf, 1969), esp. chap. 1.

9 See C. Vann Woodward, *Origins of the New South* (Baton Rouge: Louisiana State University Press, 1951).

10 On the rise and fall of Victorian culture in its various aspects, see Daniel W. Howe, ed., *Victorian America* (Philadelphia: University of Pennsylvania Press, 1976). On the transition between moral philosophy and social science, see Dorothy Ross, *G. Stanley Hall* (Chicago: University of Chicago Press, 1972).

11   Diverging interpretations of the Mugwumps may be found in John G. Sproat, *"The Best Men": Liberal Reformers in the Gilded Age* (New York: Oxford University Press, 1968), and Geoffrey Blodgett, "A New Look at the Gilded Age," in Howe, ed., *Victorian America*, pp. 95–108. I follow Blodgett.

12   John Tomsich, *A Genteel Endeavor: American Culture and Politics in the Gilded Age* (Stanford: Stanford University Press, 1971), and Stow Persons, *The Decline of American Gentility* (New York: Columbia University Press, 1973), are both valuable studies, but neither captures the innovative spirit of its subjects. On Mugwump antiimperialism, see Robert Beisner, *Twelve against Empire* (New York: McGraw-Hill, 1968).

13   See Richard D. Mosier, *Making the American Mind: Social and Moral Ideas in the McGuffey Readers* (New York: Columbia University Press, 1947), and Ruth Miller Elson, *Guardians of Tradition: American Schoolbooks in the 19th Century* (Lincoln: University of Nebraska Press, 1964).

14   The civil-service reformers looked back on the prewar Whigs as precursors; see Thomas F. Bayard, *Daniel Webster and the Spoils System* (New York, 1882).

Index